GET THE MOST FROM YOUR BOOK

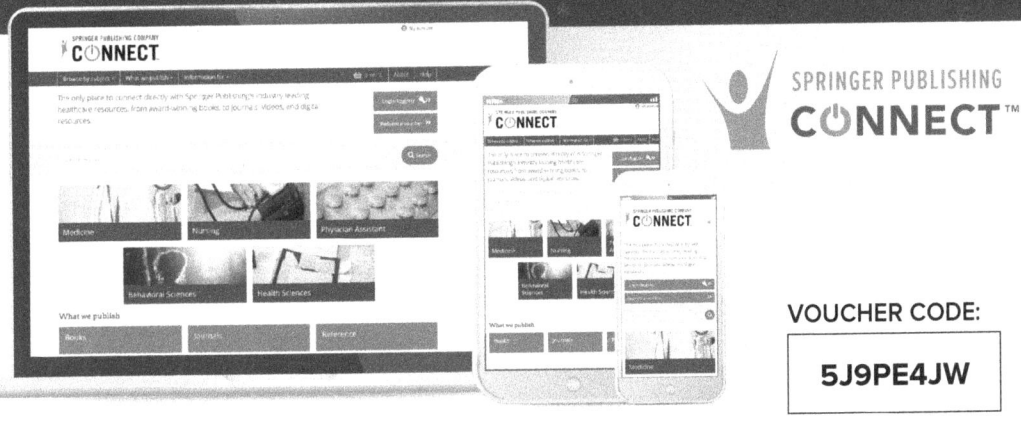

VOUCHER CODE:

5J9PE4JW

Online Access

Your print purchase of *Social Work Skills for Community Practice, Second Edition*, includes **online access via Springer Publishing Connect**™ to increase accessibility, portability, and searchability.

Insert the code at https://connect.springerpub.com/content/book/978-0-8261-5835-2 today!

Having trouble? Contact our customer service department at cs@springerpub.com

Instructor Resource Access for Adopters

Let us do some of the heavy lifting to create an engaging classroom experience with a variety of instructor resources included in most textbooks SUCH AS:

Visit **https://connect.springerpub.com/** and look for the **"Show Supplementary"** button on your **book homepage** to see what is available to instructors! First time using Springer Publishing Connect?

Email **textbook@springerpub.com** to create an account and start unlocking valuable resources.

SOCIAL WORK SKILLS FOR COMMUNITY PRACTICE

Mary-Ellen Brown, PhD, MSW, MPA, LCSW, is an associate professor in the School of Social Work and the founder/director of the Office of Community Health, Engagement, and Resiliency at Arizona State University (ASU). Dr. Brown is also the founder/director of the national Center for Community Health and Resilience, a training and research center for community health workers that is affiliated with the Substance Abuse and Mental Health Services Administration's National Child Traumatic Stress Network. She is the chair of the Policy, Administration, and Community Practice Concentration Committee at ASU, and has over a decade of experience teaching macro social work courses, including introductory macro practice, advanced community practice, program planning and evaluation, grant writing, administration, and leadership. Dr. Brown has been a community organizer, program manager, evaluator, and researcher for nearly 20 years. She has a robust background in community health; positive youth development; nonprofit administration; and equitable, holistic place-based community development. Dr. Brown uses participatory action research to engage, mobilize, and strengthen or activate resilience in partnership with communities. Her scholarship has earned her recognition through several awards, including Social Worker of the Year (National Association of Social Workers, Arizona [NASW-AZ], Branch II), the Association for Community Organization and Social Action (ACOSA) Emerging Scholar Award, the Watts College Community Solutions Research Team Award, and the ASU President's Medal for Social Embeddedness.

With Contributions by

Katie Stalker, PhD, MSW, is an associate professor and the director of Field Education at the University at Buffalo School of Social Work. Dr. Stalker is passionate about macro social work practice and education. Her research focuses on youth violence prevention across the adolescent social ecology (i.e., juvenile justice, school, family settings) and implementation science for community-centered prevention. In her line of research, Dr. Stalker uses a community-based participatory research approach in which she examines social problems and codevelops solutions in local contexts through partnerships with communities. In her role as director of field education, she continues her community-based work by collaborating with agencies and organizations to develop rich field-placement opportunities that provide students with the chance to apply their classroom learning to social work settings.

SOCIAL WORK SKILLS FOR COMMUNITY PRACTICE

Applied Macro Social Work

Second Edition

Mary-Ellen Brown, PhD, MSW, MPA, LCSW

With Contributions by
Katie Stalker, PhD, MSW

Copyright © 2023 Springer Publishing Company, LLC
All rights reserved.

First Springer Publishing edition 2012 (978-0-8261-0811-1).

No part of this publication may be reproduced, stored in a retrieval system, or transmitted in any form or by any means, electronic, mechanical, photocopying, recording, or otherwise, without the prior permission of Springer Publishing Company, LLC, or authorization through payment of the appropriate fees to the Copyright Clearance Center, Inc., 222 Rosewood Drive, Danvers, MA 01923, 978-750-8400, fax 978-646-8600, info@copyright.com or at www.copyright.com.

Springer Publishing Company, LLC
11 West 42nd Street, New York, NY 10036
www.springerpub.com
connect.springerpub.com

Acquisitions Editor: Rhonda Dearborn
Compositor: S4Carlisle Publishing Services

ISBN: 978-0-8261-5834-5
ebook ISBN: 978-0-8261-5835-2
DOI: 10.1891/9780826158352

SUPPLEMENTS:

 A robust set of instructor resources designed to supplement this text is located at http://connect.springerpub.com/content/book/978-0-8261-5835-2. Qualifying instructors may request access by emailing textbook@springerpub.com.

Instructor's Manual: 978-0-8261-5836-9
Instructor's Test Bank: 978-0-8261-5837-6
Instructor's PowerPoints: 978-0-8261-5838-3

Printed by LSI

The author and the publisher of this Work have made every effort to use sources believed to be reliable to provide information that is accurate and compatible with the standards generally accepted at the time of publication. The author and publisher shall not be liable for any special, consequential, or exemplary damages resulting, in whole or in part, from the readers' use of, or reliance on, the information contained in this book. The publisher has no responsibility for the persistence or accuracy of URLs for external or third-party Internet websites referred to in this publication and does not guarantee that any content on such websites is, or will remain, accurate or appropriate.

Library of Congress Control Number: 2022918947

Contact sales@springerpub.com to receive discount rates on bulk purchases.

Publisher's Note: New and used products purchased from third-party sellers are not guaranteed for quality, authenticity, or access to any included digital components.

Printed in the United States of America.

This book is dedicated to the residents and other community partners of the Thrive in the 05 community in Tucson, Arizona; the BR Choice community in Baton Rouge, Louisiana; the Allendale, Ledbetter Heights, and West Edge communities in Shreveport, Louisiana; and the Pascua Yaqui Tribe. It is the unwavering strength, resilience, expertise, and passion for positive community and social change from community champions like these that continues to move the needle forward in community practice toward achieving a more just, equitable society. They are our not only our partners, but also our most important teachers. In Lak'ech Ala K'in (You are my other me).

CONTENTS

Preface xiii
Acknowledgments xix
Available Resources xxi

1. **Introduction: The Application of Community Practice Skills in Macro Social Work** 1
   Introduction 1
   Social Work and Community Practice: The Merging of Micro, Mezzo, and Macro Social Work Skills 1
   Community Practice and Organizing Models 2
   Integrating Ethics, Values, and a Human Rights Perspective Into Macro Social Work Skills Development 6
   Integrating Social Work Grand Challenges Into Macro Social Work Skills Development 13
   Interpersonal Social Work Skills Development and Community Practice 14
   Building a Framework for Examining the Role of Interpersonal Social Work Skills in Community Practice 17
   Practitioner Readiness and Self-Care in Community Practice 21
   Organization of This Textbook 23
   Key Takeaways and Summary 24
   Resources 25
   Activities 25
   Assignments 26

Part I The Preengagement Phase 27

2. **Entering the Community and Using Interviewing Skills to Understand People, Issues, and Opportunities** 29
   Introduction 29
   Defining Community 30
   Assessing Community Readiness for Social Change 30
   Entry Into the Community 31
   Learning About Community Members: One-on-One Key Informant Interviews 34
   Similarities in Using Micro Practice Skills for Conducting One-on-One Interviews in Community Practice 37
   Differences in the Use of Interviewing Skills in Community Organizing and Micro Practice 40

    Using Technology and Social Media to Engage Communities 42
    Putting Values Into Action: Cultural Competence and Cultural Humility 44
    Key Takeaways and Summary 50
    Resources 50
    Activities 51
    Assignments 51

3. **Recruiting Potential Participants** 53
    Introduction 53
    Recruiting Volunteers and Participants: Applying Engagement and Relationship-Building Skills in Nontraditional Settings 53
    Engaging, Motivating, and Appreciating Volunteers and Constituents 54
    Additional Techniques and Technologies for Recruitment 57
    Putting Values Into Action: Fostering Individual Commitment to Social Justice 64
    Key Takeaways and Summary 68
    Resources 68
    Activities 69
    Assignments 69

4. **Developing Relationships and Partnerships With Grassroots and Formal Organizations** 71
    Introduction 71
    The Purpose of Organizational Partnerships in Community Practice 72
    Models of Organization Partnerships: Establishing a Common Agenda and Communication 73
    Interpersonal Skills for Bridging Differences Among Organizational Partners 80
    Facilitating and Maintaining Partnerships With Technology 85
    Bridging Differences Through Mutual Learning and Participation 85
    Putting Values Into Action: Sustaining Mutual Learning and Partnership Among Organizations 86
    Key Takeaways and Summary 88
    Resources 89
    Activities 89
    Assignments 89

Part II The Engagement Phase 91

5. **Using Dialogue, Traditional and Digital Storytelling, and Structured Group-Work Techniques to Identify Community Issues** 93
    Introduction 93
    The Purpose of Group Dialogue 93
    Using Group Dialogue to Identify Issues, Strengths, and Resources to Solve Challenges 94
    Using Group Storytelling to Identify Collective Issues, Strengths, and Resources to Build Group Solidarity 97
    Community Conversations and Large-Group Forums 99
    Nominal Group Technique 102

Focus Groups   103
Study Circles   106
Intergroup Dialogue   107
Putting Values Into Action: Engaging Diverse Groups and Cultures Within Communities   108
Key Takeaways and Summary   109
Resources   110
Activities   110
Assignments   111

6. **Engaging Participants in the Discovery, Assessment, and Documentation of Community Strengths and Challenges   113**
   Introduction   113
   The Purpose of Community Assessments   114
   Identifying Assets and Community Capital   115
   Participatory Action Research: Working in Partnership With Communities   118
   Community-Based Participatory Research (Action Framework)   119
   Youth-Led Participatory Action Research   120
   Application of Group Methods for Conducting Participatory Action Research: Empowering Constituents to Take Action   121
   Participatory Data-Collection Methods   124
   Using Traditional Community Assessment Methods: Surveys, Focus Groups, and Interviews Within a Participatory Action Research Framework   128
   Power Analysis: Mapping Power Relations and Social Networks in the Community   131
   Strategic Compatibility: Fostering Collaboration With Intentionality   137
   Putting Values Into Action: Building on Strengths and Shared Expertise   138
   Key Takeaways and Summary   141
   Resources   142
   Activities   142
   Assignments   143

7. **Facilitating Leadership Development and Group Decision-Making: Encouraging Public Participation in Planning and Engaging Constituents in the Development of Action Plans   145**
   Introduction   145
   Ladders of Participation and Engagement   146
   Theoretical Perspectives: Community Involvement in Decision-Making   146
   Leadership Development and Training   150
   Engaging in Peer and Professional Networks   153
   Facilitating Community Participation in Public Decision-Making and Planning   154
   Engaging Community Members in the Development of Community Action Plans   156
   Putting Values Into Action: Self-Determination, Empowerment, and Cultural Competency in Plan Development   167
   Key Takeaways and Summary   170
   Resources   170
   Activities   170
   Assignments   171

8. **Taking Action: Group Processes for Implementing Action Campaigns and Change Strategies**   173
   Introduction   173
   Defining and Framing Action Campaigns and Change Strategies   174
   Charting Milestones: Theories of Change   174
   Funding and Resources for Action Campaigns and Change Strategies   179
   Components of Successful Campaigns and Change Strategies   181
   Considerations in Adjusting and Implementing Strategies and Tactics in Response to Situational Demands   184
   Using Basic Group-Work Techniques for Group Maintenance, Growth, and Cohesion   188
   Communication Using Technology and Social Media for Action Campaigns   189
   Other Interpersonal Social Work Skills Needed to Facilitate Action Campaigns   190
   Closing Campaigns   199
   Putting Values Into Action: Using Action Campaigns to Achieve Social Justice   199
   Key Takeaways and Summary   202
   Resources   203
   Activities   203
   Assignments   205

Part III The Postengagement Phase   207

9. **Working With Community Groups to Critically Reflect and Engage in Dialogue on the Process and Outcomes of Action Plans**   209
   Introduction   209
   The Process of Praxis   210
   Theoretical Frameworks for Using the Process of Praxis in Community Organizing   210
   Praxis and Knowledge Production   212
   Self-Reflection in Community Practice   213
   Reflection as a Group Process: Assessing the Roles of Participants in Community Practice   215
   Praxis as Group Dialogue: Decisions by Many Rather Than a Few   216
   Interpersonal Skills for Facilitating Praxis   217
   Using Praxis to Monitor the Community-Organizing Process and Changing Course   218
   Assessing What and Why Things Happened at the End of the Organizing Campaign   219
   Putting Values Into Action: Critical Reflection, Thinking, and Action   221
   Key Takeaways and Summary   224
   Resources   224
   Activities   225
   Assignments   225

10. **Discovering Whether and Why the Action Worked: Using Participatory Research to Conduct Formal Evaluations** 227
    Introduction 227
    The Purpose and Politics of Formal Evaluations in Community Practice 228
    Challenges in Conducting Formal Community-Based Evaluations 229
    Community Evaluations and Evidence-Based Practice 230
    Systematic Approaches for Community-Based Research: Using Logic Models to Guide Evaluations 232
    Evaluation Types 235
    Evaluation Methods for Community Practice 236
    Participatory Evaluation Methods 243
    Interpersonal Skills for Participatory Evaluations: Fostering Inclusion and Skill Building 249
    Putting Values Into Action: Mutual Learning and Partnership in Evaluations 251
    Key Takeaways and Summary 255
    Resources 256
    Activities 256
    Assignments 257

Part IV Additional Applications of Social Work Skills for Community Practice 259

11. **Using Social Work Skills to Advocate for Legislation** 261
    Introduction 261
    Defining Legislative Advocacy and Lobbying 261
    Legislative Campaigns 262
    Background Research for Legislative Campaigns 267
    The Role of Interpersonal Social Work Skills in Lobbying for Legislation 271
    The Relationship Between Legislative and Political Campaigns 278
    Putting Values Into Action: Changing Laws and Policies to Promote Social Justice 281
    Key Takeaways and Summary 284
    Resources 284
    Activities 284
    Assignments 285

12. **Social Work Skills for Community Building** 287
    Introduction 287
    Theoretical Perspectives on Community Development: Community Building, Social Capital Development, Asset Building, and Capacity Development 288
    Trauma-Informed and Resiliency-Focused Community and Economic Development Approaches 292
    Community Development Practice and Environmental Justice for Social Work 294
    Community Development Models That Strengthen Connections Among People 297

"Early Wins": Community Events, Arts, Culture, Beautification, and Greening Initiatives to Celebrate and Reimagine Community   304
Interpersonal Social Work Skills for Building Bridges and Strengthening Community Connections   305
Putting Values Into Action: Building on Strengths and Assets   310
Key Takeaways and Summary   313
Resources   314
Activities   314
Assignments   314

13. Leadership, Teamwork, and Supervision in Macro Social Work Practice   317

Introduction   317
Leadership, Teamwork, Organizational and Team Culture   317
Defining Staff Supervision, Roles, and Team Processes   320
Models of Supervision and Team Building for Community Practice   322
Specific Supervisory Skills for Community Practice in Social Work   331
Using Technology for Team Planning and Processes   339
Putting Values Into Action: Parallel Processes and Encouraging Community Practitioner and Community Member Self-Determination and Empowerment   340
Key Takeaways and Summary   343
Resources   343
Activities   344
Assignments   344

14. Social Work Skills in a Global Context: Advocating for Human Rights   347

Introduction   347
Putting Values Into Action: Human Rights   347
The Process of Globalization: Impact on Health, Well-Being, Wage Rates, and Migration   349
International Social Work and Community Practice: Applying International Federation of Social Workers Principles and Taking Action   352
Social Planning and Community Development: Applying Standards From the United Nations' Universal Declaration of Human Rights   354
Social Action and Transformative Organizing: The Antiglobalization and Environmental Movements and the Struggle for Democracy and Human Rights in the Developing World   361
The Implications of a Global Perspective for Social Work and Community Practice   364
Key Takeaways and Summary   366
Resources   367
Activities   367
Assignments   367

Index   369

PREFACE

OVERALL GOAL OF THE BOOK

While writing this book, I was teaching an introductory macro social work class. The first week of class I was approached by one of my students who shared, "I'm really excited about this course—I'm very intrigued by macro social work. However, I find it so intimidating! That is why I am planning to go into direct social work practice."

Drawing from over a decade of experiences as a social work educator for undergraduate and graduate students at three different institutions, I have come to understand that many social work students share these sentiments of intimidation or apprehension when it comes to macro practice. Macro social work is an alluring yet elusive domain within the social work field. Compounding this issue, as educators we often do not talk about macro practice enough across the social work curriculum, and, when we do, we tend to use complex terms and concepts like *systems-level change* and *action campaigns*. Also, we often present social work practice to students as an either/or choice—either you pursue a career in direct practice, or you pursue a career in community/macro practice. Further, social work students are also commonly—and unfortunately—misguided by well-intentioned instructors who perpetuate myths such as "you won't be able to get a job as a macro practitioner right out of graduate school," or, for those schools that offer specializations in community practice, "you won't be able to become a licensed social worker if you choose a macro practice specialization."

This messaging is not only problematic—as social work graduates who engage in specialized study of macro practice can indeed enter community practice or choose to pursue clinical licensure immediately after graduation; it also perpetuates a false dichotomy of micro versus macro practice, and fails to recognize the essential importance of preparing ethical and competent social work practitioners to engage in practice across micro, mezzo, and macro domains. Social workers in primarily direct-practice roles are working with individuals and families that exist within communities, within organizations, within systems, and therefore both *impact* and are *impacted by* their environments. Social workers in direct practice must be prepared to navigate those systems and to advocate for policy and systems change with and for the benefit of the consumers of their services as mandated by our professional code of ethics. Similarly, social workers in macro practice roles may be focused primarily on communities, organizations, and systems, yet the effectiveness of their work is dependent on their ability to use interpersonal social work skills with individuals and groups of people that *impact* and are *impacted by* those communities and systems. Indeed, communities, organizations, and systems are constructed and maintained by people.

Further, what is lost in this messaging is that the origins of the social work profession are often credited as rooted in macro practice, beginning with the settlement house movement of the late 19th century. The settlement house movement focused on supporting people and communities that were struggling by fostering relationships and connections to provide social supports. In today's society, social work leadership and participation in activism and social justice movements are more essential than ever. Black Lives Matter, #MeToo, the Indigenous land rights movement, voting rights, environmental justice, and the March for Our lives are all examples of recent and current social movements that require social workers trained in community organizing and macro skills. Holding social justice as a core social work value, social workers trained in community organizing and practice skills are essential to facilitating social, systems, and community change. In addition, with the American Academy of Social Work and Social Welfare's (AASWSW's) recent call to action through the Grand Challenges for Social Work initiative, social workers will need vital community practice skills to achieve social progress and meet each of the critical challenges set forth in the Grand Challenges initiative.

This book aims to prepare social workers to engage in macro community practice by providing digestible content for social work students that is enriched with practical and applicable learning experiences. This book argues that competent, effective, and ethical social work practice involves training and skills development in all domains of social work practice—micro, mezzo, and macro—and aims to bridge the existing micro–macro divide, in order that social work students are prepared for competent practice with communities, organizations, and systems regardless of whether they engage primarily in direct or community practice.

Interpersonal skills and the ability to engage with others are essential in all domains of social work practice. Community organizing has been considered germane to the social work profession dating back to the settlement house movement. However, only a small number of social workers engage in community practice (Mendes, 2008). Rubin and Rubin (2008) define *organizing* as "working with people to help them recognize that they face shared problems and to discover that by joining together they can fight to overcome these problems" (p. 5). Such activity should logically fit with social work's focus on human relationships and the resolution of social problems.

THE PURPOSE OF THE BOOK

The purpose of this book is to examine how social work skills can be used to organize communities and achieve social change. Curriculum in social work programs is based on the assumption that there is one overall set of skills that can be applied by practitioners for work with individuals, groups, families, organizations, and communities. The Council on Social Work Education (CSWE; 2022) defines *core practice competencies* for practice across each of these systems as engagement, assessment, intervention, and evaluation. Although CSWE guidelines are broad enough so that they can be applied in micro and macro settings, macro curriculum in schools of social work tends to focus on tasks such as conducting community or organization assessments, program planning, and evaluation (Johnson, 2000; Salcido et al., 2002). Although field practicum is one place in which students should be able to acquire knowledge and competency in using interpersonal social work skills, field instructors often have limited expertise in providing supervision to social work students in community-organizing and practice methods (Gamble et al., 1994; Mendes, 2008).

One of the reasons that the absence of instruction in these critical micro practice skills for macro practice is problematic is that community organizers seldom conduct community assessments, carry out interventions, or evaluate the impact of their activities by themselves. They must recruit volunteers and partners to engage in social action or community development. Organizers must have good interpersonal skills in order to build relationships with volunteers, community leaders, and local decision makers, and to facilitate group activities (Bayne-Smith et al., 2008; Staples, 2016).

These volunteers are usually encouraged to actively engage in planning and conducting assessments, actions needed to effect social change, and evaluations of those actions. For example, these participants may assist in conducting assessments of community needs and strengths by identifying community resources and mapping where community assets (such as schools, parks, businesses, and leaders) are located or pointing out trouble spots in the neighborhood (Kretzmann & McKnight, 1993; Santos et al., 2010).

CONTENTS

To emphasize the community practice and micro social work linkages described in the book, my contributing author and I use frameworks drawn from generalist social work practice as well as core practice competencies identified in the Educational Policy and Accreditation Standards developed by the CSWE. In addition, we aimed to make this book accessible to all social workers, regardless of systems focus or practice experience, by focusing on a broad range of community practice models. Content covered in this book is organized into five primary sections: Introduction, Preengagement Phase, Engagement Phase, Postengagement Phase, and Additional Applications of Social Work Skills for Community Practice.

The introductory chapter provides a detailed overview of content covered in the book, including the merging of micro, mezzo, and macro social work; models of community practice and organizing; ethics, values, and human rights; and the Grand Challenges, as well as practitioner readiness and self-care. The Preengagement Phase (Chapters 2–4) includes content covering entering the community and using social work skills for community assessment, recruiting community members for participation, and developing partnerships with grassroots and formal organizations. The Engagement Phase (Chapters 5–8) includes content to foster social work skill building in facilitation and group dialogue, group work, assessing and documenting community strengths and challenges, leadership development and capacity building, and implementing action campaigns and change strategies. The Postengagement Phase (Chapters 9 and 10) includes content to facilitate applied learning for working with communities to evaluate action campaigns and change strategies and use participatory research to conduct evaluations. The final section, Additional Applications of Social Work Skills for Community Practice (Chapters 11–14), includes content on legislative advocacy and legislative campaigns; community building; social capital development; asset building; capacity development, leadership, teamwork, and supervision; and advocating for human rights in a global context.

The content covered in this book intends to provide social work students with applied learning and skill building to:

- Lead and facilitate community engagement, dialogue, and change initiatives.
- Understand and assess community assets, challenges, and readiness for change.
- Plan for positive social change interventions, policies, and campaigns.
- Organize communities and cross-sector partnerships for positive social change.
- Advance positive social change in response to the Grand Challenges for Social Work initiative.
- Evaluate social change efforts (process and impact).
- Harness technology for understanding, planning, organizing, facilitating, and evaluating social change initiatives.
- Secure resources and fundraising for social change initiatives.
- Engage in reflective practice on positionality, intersectionality, and ethical decision-making for community practice.
- Engage in self-care and peer/professional networking for community practitioners.

DISTINGUISHING FEATURES AND LEARNING TOOLS

This book includes case vignettes and a variety of suggested applied and experiential learning activities and assignments to reinforce content and to emphasize the skill-building focus of the text. In addition, this book highlights the importance of the use of technology as a tool for social work mezzo/macro practice and provides social work learners with skill-building content and activities that are responsive to the National Association of Social Workers (NASW), Association of Social Work Boards (ASWB), CSWE, and Clinical Social Work Association's (CSWA's) *Standards for Technology in Social Work Practice* (2017). Further, each chapter includes several resources for additional learning, including videos, online tool kits, and additional readings.

INSTRUCTOR'S RESOURCES

This textbook is accompanied by an Instructor's Manual that includes the CSWE competencies covered in each chapter and suggested individual and group discussion prompts and activities. Sample PowerPoints to guide lectures and a Test Bank with multiple-choice and essay questions for each chapter are also available.

INTENDED AUDIENCE

This book is written for social work students and can be used either at the BSW or MSW level. It is intended for use in introductory macro social work practice courses and/or community practice courses. It is appropriate for on-ground (in-person), online, or hybrid course delivery.

SUMMARY

Our goal in writing this book was to make it accessible to both students who are interested in organizing and community practice careers and those who are likely to apply some of these skills in practice for tasks such as facilitating meetings, coalition building, facilitating public participation, engaging in political activism, and lobbying. This book prepares social work students to ethically and effectively work with communities, including cause-based coalitions and health and human service organizations, to promote social justice and achieve positive social change. We also hope to make a persuasive case that community practice is no different from any other form of social work practice. Interpersonal skills are essential critical components in building relationships, motivating people to engage in personal and societal transformation, and achieving social justice.

REFERENCES

Bayne-Smith, M., Mizrahi, T., & Garcia, M. (2008). Interdisciplinary community collaboration: Perspectives of community practitioners on successful strategies. *Journal of Community Practice, 16*(3), 249–269. https://doi.org/10.1080/10705420802255122

Council on Social Work Education. (2022). *2022 educational policy and accreditation standards.* Author. https://www.cswe.org/accreditation/standards/2022-epas/

Gamble, D. N., Shaffer, G. L., & Weil, M. O. (1994). Assessing the integrity of community organization and administration content in field practice. *Journal of Community Practice, 1*(3), 73–92. https://doi.org/10.1300/J125v01n03_06

Johnson, A. K. (2000). The community practice pilot project: Integrating methods, field, community assessment, and experiential learning. *Journal of Community Practice, 8*(4), 5–25.

Kretzmann, J. P., & McKnight, J. L. (1993). *Building communities from the inside out: A path toward finding and mobilizing a community's assets.* ATCA Publications.

Mendes, P. (2008). Teaching community development to social work students: A critical reflection. *Community Development Journal, 44*(2), 248–262. https://doi.org/10.1093/cdj/bsn001

National Association of Social Workers, Association of Social Work Boards, Council on Social Work Education, & Clinical Social Work Association. (2017). *NASW, ASWB, CSWE, & CWSA Standards for Technology in Social Work Practice.* National Association of Social Workers.

Rubin, H. J., & Rubin, I. S. (2008). *Community organizing and development* (4th ed.). Pearson Education.

Salcido, R. M., Ornelas, V., & Lee, N. (2002). Cross cultural field assignments in an undergraduate community practice course: Integrating multimedia documentation. *Journal of Community Practice, 10*(4), 49–65. https://doi.org/10.1300/J125v10n04_04

Santos, C. A., Ferguson, N., & Trippel, A. (2010). Engaging urban youth through technology: The Youth Neighborhood Mapping Initiative. *Journal of Planning Education and Research, 30*(1), 1–14. https://doi.org/10.1177/0739456X10366427

Staples, L. (2016). *Roots to power: A manual for grassroots organizing* (3rd ed.). Praeger.

ACKNOWLEDGMENTS

I would like to acknowledge Donna Hardina, PhD, MSW, the author of the first edition of this textbook, for entrusting me to carry her work forward in this new edition to teach future generations of social work students the skills necessary for community practice. I would like to acknowledge my many mentors and teachers in academia, health and human service organizations, and the community who generously provided me with the knowledge, skills, experiences, and support that prepared me to write this textbook. I would also like to thank my parents, who inspired me to pursue a career in social work through their own example of dedication and service to building community, and my partner, for providing me with levity and hope when the injustices and inequities of our world, systems, and society seem too great to overcome.

In addition to the many community partners to whom this book is dedicated, my contributing author and I would like to acknowledge our team members from the Arizona State University Office of Community Health, Engagement, and Resiliency (ASU OCHER)—the current and former student interns, student workers, graduate research assistants, AmeriCorps service members, staff, and faculty affiliates—for their dedication as community change agents and activist scholars in strengthening community health and resilience. They are our village and they strive and struggle with us every day in community practice to make this world a better place. Finally, we would like to specifically acknowledge and thank Mattea Pezza, Zoe Baccam, Ellen Brown, Elizabeth Hatch, and Lauren Phanawong for their contributions in the preparation of this textbook.

—*Mary-Ellen & Katie*

AVAILABLE RESOURCES

 A robust set of instructor resources designed to supplement this text is located at http://connect.springerpub.com/content/book/978-0-8261-5835-2. Qualifying instructors may request access by emailing **textbook@springerpub.com**.

Instructor Resources:

- **Instructor's Manual** containing a chapter summary, corresponding 2015 and 2022 Council on Social Work Education Competencies, learning objectives, chapter discussion questions, and activities and assignments for each chapter.
- **Test Banks** with over 100 essay questions and multiple-choice questions with full rationales, all available on Respondus®.
- **Lecture PowerPoints**

INTRODUCTION: THE APPLICATION OF COMMUNITY PRACTICE SKILLS IN MACRO SOCIAL WORK

LEARNING OBJECTIVES

After reading this chapter, students will be able to:

- Recognize community-organizing models.
- Describe how community practitioners apply the National Association of Social Workers (NASW) *Code of Ethics*.
- Define the concept of *critical consciousness*.
- Identify various skills for community practitioners.

INTRODUCTION

This introductory chapter describes macro social work and community organizing as a method of practice that emphasizes both task- and process-oriented activities; different models and approaches to community social work practice are also discussed. Cultural competency, cultural humility, ethics, values, and human rights associated with social work and community practice are examined. The Grand Challenges for Social Work (Sherraden et al., 2014) and their implications for macro practice and community practice skills are introduced. Specific social work interpersonal skills that are commonly used in community practice are described. A framework is presented that describes how relationship-building and engagement are essential for accomplishing common community-organizing tasks such as interviewing prospective community members and constituents, recruiting volunteers, creating group consensus, and conducting participatory needs assessments, planning, and evaluation. In the last section of this chapter, the organization of the book is described.

SOCIAL WORK AND COMMUNITY PRACTICE: THE MERGING OF MICRO, MEZZO, AND MACRO SOCIAL WORK SKILLS

Community practice in social work involves applying micro, mezzo, and macro practice skills in the community, organizational, and systems contexts. *Micro social work practice* typically refers to direct practice with individuals and families in a one-on-one setting, and often involves providing services such as behavioral health, mental health, psychoeducation, case or care management, or other services that are focused on and tailored to facilitating change for the individual participant or family system. *Mezzo practice* is commonly associated with facilitating change at the group level, and group systems can vary in diversity, size, and setting, such as a group of people within an organization, school, or neighborhood. Mezzo practice goals are focused on addressing a shared issue or common need among the group, can include the provision of direct services for groups, and often involve the delivery of some type of programming for the group (e.g., bullying prevention program, neighborhood watch group, veterans support group). *Macro social work* traditionally refers to facilitating large-scale change for communities, systems, and society, and often involves community organizing, social action, or community change initiatives that aim to address unjust policies, racial, health, or other inequities, systemic racism, discrimination, and other injustices, human rights, and social issues that impact minoritized and marginalized groups of people and communities.

Community practitioners use micro, mezzo, and macro social work skills to achieve social change. In all levels of social work practice, different types of skills are not only useful, but also essential to ethical, competent social work practice in diverse contexts. Although we commonly refer to micro, mezzo, and macro as separate domains of practice, they all overlap and are intertwined. Micro, mezzo, and macro social work skills are all integral to achieving our professional goals of social justice in all realms of social work practice. This book demonstrates that interpersonal social work skills are as necessary in mezzo and macro practice as they are in micro practice. In addition, the mezzo and macro social work skills discussed are also necessary for micro practitioners, as they address oppressive structures and facilitate community-level and systems change that directly impact individuals and families.

COMMUNITY PRACTICE AND ORGANIZING MODELS

Successful community practice and community organizing involves a combination of process- and task-related skills (Hardcastle et al., 2004). Although these process- and task-related skills cover the spectrum of micro, mezzo and macro social work domains, there are a number of models or approaches that have been designed for use specifically in community practice. Community practice requires attention not only to task accomplishment but also attention to the process used to achieve community change. Although both are equally important, as one is concerned with the achievement of goals and the other with building capacity, in some approaches, practitioners give more emphasis to outcomes, and in others, process is most important.

Rothman (1979) identified three primary models of community organizing: (a) community development, (b) social action, and (c) social planning. *Community development* is a process through which a variety of community residents, groups, businesses, churches, organizations, and other stakeholders come together to reach a consensus about community challenges and work cooperatively to improve the community. The primary method used to achieve results is through consensus and cooperation among group members (Korazim-Korosy et al., 2007). The emphasis of this method for the community practitioner is often on the process and capacity built by bringing people together to work cooperatively or by strengthening relationships among individuals or between individuals and community institutions rather than specific outcomes (Rubin & Rubin, 2008).

Other experts in the social work field identify several additional process-oriented community development approaches, including consensus organizing, the assets-based approach, capacity building, and community building as subtypes of the community development model (Kretzmann & McKnight, 1993; Ohmer & DeMasi, 2009; Singh, 2003). These community development and organizing models are often used to improve economic conditions in a community; increase the number of jobs or businesses in a geographic area; improve community infrastructure and the built environment; increase the supply of high-quality, affordable housing; or create, expand, or increase access to social services (Rubin & Rubin, 2008). *Capacity building*—training and engagement in activities designed to increase individual and organizational capacity and readiness to participate in community change activities—is also considered one of the main components of the process of community development practice (Cnaan & Rothman, 2008).

In contrast to the emphasis on cooperation and consensus often ascribed to community development models of practice, *social action* involves putting pressure on individuals or groups to achieve community-level, policy, or systemic change; and social action tasks may include lobbying policy makers and other governmental officials, running for political office, or engaging in social protest (Mondros, 2005). Social action is generally regarded as the most task- or outcome-oriented of the three models identified by Rothman (1979). Task activities and outcomes, especially in political and legislative campaigns, are oriented toward "winning" the campaign or social action cause. In social protest, the desired outcome is having a law, policy, practice, or program adopted or stopped (Staples, 2016). These task activities require an extensive amount of engagement and relationship building with community members, leaders, and other groups. In campaigns, candidates must persuade individual voters to support them and ask potential donors to make campaign contributions.

When advocating for or against legislation and policies, lobbyists must meet with elected officials to persuade them to support or oppose a piece of legislation. Protests in social action movements are most successful when large numbers of people and groups participate. In addition, people who participate in protest activities for social justice causes must be able to reach consensus about their goals and the strategies and tactics they are prepared to use to achieve them. Often it is necessary to form coalitions and to cooperate with and coordinate among people who may have different views about the issue or who may prefer to use different tactics and strategies to raise awareness for and to support the cause (Hardina & Obel-Jorgensen, 2011). Large alliances of groups, called *social movements*, are also formed to support collective action to advocate for the redistribution of goods; services; and civil, human, and political rights with or on behalf of minoritized and underrepresented groups or people who perceive themselves to have grievances that should be addressed by the government (Pyles, 2013). For each of these social action activities, social workers in community practice must be able to effectively engage with others, build and maintain meaningful relationships, motivate people, and generate buy-in that leads to action in order to advance the social justice cause.

The third approach identified by Rothman (1979) is *social planning*. Community planners apply skills and knowledge in a systematic way to problem-solve and create solutions for social issues. They work with communities to identify an issue; conduct an assessment; develop a program plan, community initiative, or social policy; facilitate the implementation of the plan; and evaluate the outcome and impact of their collective efforts. Social workers serving in the role of community planner are commonly employed by government agencies or nonprofit groups. Often, community planning processes solicit participation of the people directly impacted by the social issue—either likely to be affected or likely to benefit from a particular program, initiative, or policy. As a consequence, much of their work is conducted in consultation with others (Netting et al., 2008). Facilitation of citizen participation in social planning efforts is likely to be one of the primary responsibilities of the community planner (Brody et al., 2003). According to Forester (2001), it is critical that community planners have good interpersonal social work skills to keep participants engaged during the life of a typical community project, build consensus among a variety of people and groups about the choice of the best plan, and lobby government decision makers for support and funding. Therefore, the creation of the plan, the process used to create the plan, and tasks used to carry out and implement the plan are all important.

Other useful variations of models of community practice in social work have been developed to conceptualize the process, activities, and tasks identified in the community development, social action, and community planning approaches for community organizing. For example, Gamble and Weil (2010) identify eight different approaches that vary in terms of social work practice roles, scope of activities, the people served, change targets (e.g., policies or social issues), and the intended outcomes. In addition to social planning and social action, these models include neighborhood organizing, advocacy for a particular issue or a population, social/economic and sustainable development, program development, coalition building, and social movement organizing.

Additional models identified in the literature on community organizing include transformative, multicultural, and feminist organizing methods (Hardcastle et al., 2004). The transformative model is associated with the work of Paulo Freire (1970). The goal of this approach is the personal transformation of participants through education and activism. Freire's model of "popular education" was originally intended to meet the needs of individuals in Brazil who were minoritized or marginalized and did not have access to education; it focuses on using the education process to study social problems so that members of minoritized and marginalized communities can understand and analyze the political, economic, and social origins of oppression (Pyles, 2013). Once members of the group develop a "critical consciousness" about social issues and the social institutions that sustain these problems, they take action to change oppressive systems. Adapted for use in community organizing, the transformative method requires strong bonds and dialogue among group members; one of the primary methods used is called *praxis*, a group process that involves a combination of action and reflection in order to perfect social change techniques (Castelloe et al., 2002).

Multicultural and feminist organizing approaches incorporate many popular education techniques. These models are designed to address political, economic, and social oppression affecting minoritized communities, women, and other groups experiencing racial, ethnic, or gender-based discrimination. Dobbie and Richards-Schuster (2008) describe multicultural practice as going "beyond simply accepting cultural differences to explore how they are linked to struggles over material conditions to structure everyday life" (p. 329). Techniques used by community practitioners and organizers to bring people together include intergroup dialogue, forming coalitions of organizations that represent minoritized and marginalized populations, and recruiting leaders who can work to "bridge" differences among members of different backgrounds. Once consensus has been achieved among group members, participants engage in social change activities that may include social action, community development, or planning.

Feminist organizing is oriented toward the empowerment of women and addressing gender-based discrimination. Joseph and colleagues (as cited in Mizrahi, 2007) describe feminist organizing as a process:

Based on women's contributions, functions, roles, and experiences and is derived from their strengths while recognizing the limitations of their socially ascribed roles and the nature of their oppression. A women's perspective affects which issues are selected and worked on, how a problem is defined, what needs will be met, what tactics and strategies are used, and how success or victory is defined. (p. 40)

According to Hyde (2005), feminist community practice can be characterized by the importance of relationship ties among members, the link between personal difficulties and social action, and using emotions and passion for the cause as a mechanism to recruit and retain members. In one study of feminist organizers, Mizrahi (2007) found that many of the women they interviewed regarded their practice as different from male-identifying organizers in terms of their use of interpersonal skills, the emphasis placed on outcome rather than process, and the use of collective or group decision-making techniques.

Hardcastle and colleagues (2004) describe similarities among the three approaches (transformative, multicultural, and feminist), including an emphasis on group dialogue, the personal transformation of individuals and group members, intellectual freedom from traditional ways of thinking, and the self-expression of group members. All three models also require a combination of task- and process-related activities—including the building of group solidarity among members, achieving consensus, and engaging in social action to address social issues (such as protests and confrontations with people, especially those in authority, and institutions outside the group; Hardina, 2002).

Young Laing (2009) has criticized the Rothman (1979), Gamble and Weil (2010), feminist, and multicultural models as being insufficient in incorporating cultural context and practice skills such as those identified by Lum (2011): cultural self-awareness, cultural knowledge, and the ability to use culturally appropriate practice methods. Other critics have focused on the relevance or appropriateness of consensus-style or conflict-oriented organizing approaches given changes in economic or political trends and social values (Conway, 2003; Ohmer & DeMasi, 2009).

Regardless of the chosen approach or method for community practice and organizing, it is essential for social workers trained in community practice to serve in positions in government, nonprofits, and other sectors in the roles of organizers, activists, policy analysts, legislators, community developers, program managers, and community planners. Indeed, the values and ethics germane to the social work profession stipulate that the voices of the *experts* on the social issue are elevated. Those experts whose voices should be central to any social change process are the community members affected by the issue who possess knowledge about what will or will not work in their community to address the issue, and those with lived experiences relevant to the social issue.

Community members and groups hold unmatched expertise and knowledge that is essential to creating and implementing effective social solutions that are meaningful, sustainable, and culturally appropriate, and, as such, should not only be recognized for this expertise but also serve as the driving voices for social action, community development, and social planning processes. Social workers in community practice roles acting as facilitators and organizers understand the vital importance of this expertise in a way that other professionals serving in these roles may not similarly recognize, and this is one reason why community practice in social work is so important. Authentic community empowerment and engagement requires that community practitioners' approach to social action and community change initiatives occur in partnership "with" communities—not "at," "to," or "for" those impacted by the social issue and intended beneficiaries of community change. This message resonates strongly in the mantra "nothing about us, without us"—a phrase credited for its initial use in the United States in connection with the disability rights movement (Charlton, 2000). Social workers in community practice and organizing roles bring the values and ethics of the social work profession into community planning, development, and social action settings, and, as a result, can help ensure that community voices are elevated, participation in decision-making processes are inclusive, and empowering experiences are fostered, ultimately leading to meaningful and sustainable social progress and change.

INTEGRATING ETHICS, VALUES, AND A HUMAN RIGHTS PERSPECTIVE INTO MACRO SOCIAL WORK SKILLS DEVELOPMENT

Each of the models described in the previous section contains a theory about why specific actions should produce the desired outcome and a set of value assumptions about how the social work community practitioner should approach and engage in the work (Hardina, 2002). In any form of social work practice, it is essential that values and ethical principles be integrated into practice, especially because social work takes place within the context of interactions with other individuals, families, groups, organizations, and communities. Most of these values and principles are clearly identified in the National Association of Social Workers (NASW; 2021) *Code of Ethics*.

Although the NASW (2021) *Code of Ethics* describes how social workers are to conduct themselves with clients, colleagues, and supervisors in social service organizations, most community practice and organizing work takes place outside the confines of traditional social service organizations. Community organizers and practitioners work to bring diverse groups of people and organizations together. They also strive to foster community change, using both collaboration and conflict methods, depending on what the situation calls for, as an effective and necessary approach. Because community practice often involves advocacy for the reallocation or redistribution of goods, services, and political power, practitioners and organizers may face ethical dilemmas with regard to the strategies and tactics used in the field to facilitate social change. For example, tactics can include putting pressure on opponents of social justice causes or staging acts of civil disobedience to bring attention to an issue (Hardina & Obel-Jorgensen, 2011).

In some instances, community practitioners and organizers may apply principles in the NASW (2021) *Code of Ethics* in a manner that is slightly different from processes used in other types of social work practice. For example, rather than having clients sign a consent form, a social worker attempting to organize people to participate in protest will engage volunteers in detailed discussions on various organizing options so that the group chooses the method with which they are the most comfortable. If people do not participate in the protest or chosen organizing method, this is an indication that individual members have withdrawn consent (Hardina, 2004). In addition, there are some principles that are fundamental to community-organizing work that are not identified in the NASW (2021) *Code of Ethics*. For example, the establishment of equal partnerships between community-organizing staff and the volunteers/community members who participate in community-organizing and change efforts is one of the bedrock principles followed by most organizers and practitioners (Carroll & Minkler, 2000).

Values are statements of an ideal that we try to achieve, whereas *ethics* describe actions that should be taken to uphold these values (Dolgoff et al., 2012). Throughout this text, value assumptions, ethical principles associated with these values, and practice activities that can be used to put these principles into action are applied to the preengagement, engagement, and postengagement phases of community practice. The section that follows sets the stage for understanding how several key social work values (i.e., social justice; self-determination and empowerment; the strengths perspective; the development of a critical consciousness, mutual learning and partnership; anti-racism and the use of culturally competent practice methods that incorporate an understanding of cultural and social diversity, power, and oppression; and the human rights perspective) shape community practice across these phases.

Social Justice

Social justice pertains to the fair and equitable distribution of resources such as liveable wages, suitable and affordable housing, nutritious and healthy food, high-quality education and healthcare, civil liberties, voting rights, and political power. Social justice maintains that all people should have equitable access and opportunities to these resources and freedom from discrimination in order that they may achieve their full potential. People who do not have these things are considered to be at a disadvantage when compared to other individuals and groups in society (Gil, 2013). The terms *oppression, minoritized*, and *marginalization* are used to describe political, economic, or social arrangements that prevent some groups of people in society from gaining access to resources or the opportunity to acquire them. Oppression is often based on demographic characteristics that differentiate these groups from the dominant society, social stigma and discrimination based on social or economic status, or specific experiences or conditions such as being without housing (i.e., houselessness) or mental illness (Reisch, 2011). The term *minoritization* is closely connected to marginalization; when dominant groups "minoritize" other groups, they are "pushing to the margins" or "othering" groups that are different than them in an effort to maintain power using oppressive language and tactics. Black, Indigenous, people of color (BIPOC) and LGBTQIA+ groups are often considered minoritized in the United States. The term *social justice* is generally used to describe efforts to make the distribution of resources fair, equitable, or equal for oppressed, minoritized, and marginalized groups by changing laws, policies, or social institutions (Rawls, 1971). The NASW (2021) *Code of Ethics* states that:

> Social workers should engage in social and political action that seeks to ensure that all people have equal access to the resources, employment, services, and opportunities they require to meet their basic human needs and to develop fully. Social workers should be aware of the impact of the political arena on practice and should advocate for changes in policy and legislation to improve social conditions in order to meet basic human needs and promote social justice. (Section 6.04)

Self-Determination and Empowerment

The NASW (2021) *Code of Ethics* states that "social workers respect and promote the right of clients to self-determination and assist clients in their efforts to identify their goals" (Section 1.02). In practice with individual clients, therapeutic groups, and families, this clause refers to the right of clients, in most circumstances, to contract with social workers for the services they want or need. The second part of this section carves out an exception for circumstances in which the clients could harm themselves or others.

In organizing initiatives and community social work practice, the right of self-determination is often closely connected to the term *empowerment*. In its early conceptualization, empowerment was described as "a process of reducing the sense of powerlessness that resulted from discrimination" (Kam, 2021, p. 331). Empowerment involves addressing oppressive systems and policies, and creating or accessing power and pursuing social justice for marginalized groups so that people who have been traditionally disempowered have influence over their own lives—the right to self-determination (Kam, 2021; Pinderhughes, 1983; Solomon, 1976).

Empowerment is a concept that, when incorporated into social work practice, pertains to efforts to increase experiences of personal self-efficacy and self-esteem (Gutierrez et al., 1998; Rose, 2000). Zimmerman (2000) describes empowerment theory as "both a value orientation for working in the community and a theoretical model for understanding the process and consequences of efforts to exert control and influence over decisions that affect one's life, organizational functioning, and the quality of community life" (p. 43). In community practice, *empowerment* is used to refer to a set of assumptions that focus on the participation of individuals and in decision-making processes in nonprofit organizations, public institutions, and the political process. A number of studies have documented that individuals who have participated in social change-related activities have a greater sense of personal self-efficacy than nonparticipants (Checkoway & Zimmerman, 1992; Itzhaky & York, 2002; Zimmerman & Rappaport, 1988). A social worker's responsibility for ensuring that the public has an opportunity to participate in the development of social policies is also included in the NASW (2021) *Code of Ethics* in Section 6.2.

It is important to note, however, that the term *empowerment* is often abused or misconstrued when it is referred to as something—power—that is given by one individual to another. True empowerment is not a "gift" that a social worker bestows on a community member. Rather, the role, responsibility, and opportunity as it relates to empowerment and the community practitioner or organizer is to facilitate, encourage, and nurture the self-discovery and activation of the power that individuals and communities already hold within themselves. Community practitioners can assist communities in removing barriers to accessing their own power within systems, structures, and organizations, and by addressing unjust policies and inequities. Community practitioners and organizers can foster capacity-building experiences that strengthen and cultivate individual and community power. Community practitioners can encourage participation in community change initiatives and action strategies, and practice from a strengths-based perspective, in order to facilitate opportunities to illuminate experiences of one's individual and a community's collective power.

The Strengths Perspective

The strengths perspective is a set of assumptions used by many social workers to conduct assessments of the people they serve. Rather than look at people in terms of the resources they lack, any deficits, or their personal issues, social workers should focus on and identify the strengths, personal skills, and resources that people already have that can be reinforced, expanded, and used to address personal and community issues (Saleeby, 2013). This value assumption runs counter to the medical model that has been used by some social workers to describe client issues as weaknesses (Mackelprang et al., 2022). In the literature on social policies, communities with high concentrations of individuals and families living in poverty are sometimes discussed as experiencing social problems (such as unemployment, houselessness, substance abuse, violence, and crime) because of their own moral failings—rather than the myriad of things that commonly occur associated with or as a consequence of experiencing poverty, limited access and barriers to opportunity, and limited political power (Segal, 2007). Consequently, recognizing individuals, families, and communities as possessing assets, skills, and resources that can be activated to solve social issues and lead to experiences of individual and collective empowerment is critical for successful community organizing and positive social change (Hardcastle et al., 2004; Kretzman & McKnight, 1993; Ohmer & DeMasi, 2009).

Development of a Critical Consciousness

In the book *Pedagogy of the Oppressed*, Paulo Freire (1970) described the concept of *critical consciousness*. People who are oppressed and those engaged in social action should strive to understand how political, social, and economic institutions and systems interact to limit and sustain barriers to accessing resources, voting rights, and civil liberties for members of minoritized and marginalized groups (VeneKlasen et al., 2007). The first step of achieving critical consciousness is understanding how these systems and institutions serve as oppressive structures, and this is followed by taking action to address oppression based on that understanding. According to Staples (2016), community practitioners should not only increase their knowledge about how society works, but they also have a responsibility to transmit this knowledge to members and leaders of the community. These leaders should be able to "actively reflect about their personal life experience, to recognize similar experiences shared by others, to develop a political critique of systemic oppression, and to prepare to act collectively to change the conditions of their lives" (Staples, 2016, pp. 50–51).

Mutual Learning and Partnership With Community Members and Constituents

Freire's (1970) model of popular education emphasizes the creation of equal partnerships among educators, other professionals, and members of minoritized and marginalized groups. One of the primary value assumptions inherent in Freire's work is that a professional's status in a community-organizing context should be no better or no worse than that of the members of minoritized and marginalized groups with whom the professional works (Carroll & Minkler, 2000). Hierarchy is eliminated as each party is recognized for bringing valuable expertise and knowledge into the partnership. One of the basic assumptions of this approach is that participants should engage in a process of *mutual learning* from one another (Goodkind, 2006). Mutual learning takes place within the context of dialogue among all participants in the social change process, including professionals and the people who will benefit from the social change effort (VeneKlasen et al., 2007). Professionals possess formal knowledge while the other participants have knowledge that they have acquired through lived experiences. As a consequence, what each partner brings to the relationship has value and can collectively be used to facilitate and achieve social change. In community practice, these principles are applied in the creation of relationships between the practitioner and the people the organizer recruits to participate in the organizing process (Satterwhite & Teng, 2007).

The values associated with the terms *mutual learning, partnership, empowerment,* and *self-determination* are also inherent in the term generally used to refer to volunteers or participants in the community-organizing process. Rather than *clients*, the people who participate in or who benefit from community organizing are called *community members, community partners,* or *constituents*. VeneKlasen and colleagues (2007) define *constituents* as "a group of people or a community who have a common concern and whose interests are advanced by organizing and engaging in advocacy to solve a problem" (p. 59). They are considered experts with lived experience about the issues that impact their lives and their communities, and they possess the knowledge to guide the change that is necessary in order to move their own communities forward.

Anti-Racism, Cultural Competency, and Cultural Humility: Using Methods of Practice That Incorporate an Understanding of Cultural and Social Diversity, Power, and Oppression

The NASW (2021) *Code of Ethics* identifies respect for the dignity and worth of individuals as a core value of the profession and identifies actions to eliminate discrimination and oppression as one of the primary activities of social workers. The NASW (2016) has also developed a set of standards for members of the profession to follow for culturally competent practice. These standards require that social workers be aware of their own beliefs and values, develop appropriate skills for cross-cultural practice, and advocate for hiring standards, education, organization procedures (such as language services), and public policies that promote and advance diversity, equity, and inclusion. Most community practitioners view their work as an opportunity to facilitate opportunities for self- and collective empowerment with minoritized and marginalized communities; to promote racial, social, and health equity and equality; and to advocate for improvements in well-being and living conditions. Community-organizing work is conducted either in partnership with community members or on behalf of people when they are not in a position to advocate for themselves (such as children or individuals who are incarcerated) or entities (e.g., the environment or animals) that require others to speak for them (Alinsky, 1971; Bobo et al., 2010; Homan, 2016; Rothman, 1996).

It is expected that community practitioners, indeed—all social workers—will engage in a set of learning activities, beginning with training in their social work education program and continued throughout the remainder of their careers in the form of professional development and other learning experiences, that promote culturally competent practice. There is no single course that will "certify" a social worker as a culturally competent practitioner, and *cultural humility* reminds us that this is a lifelong process, requiring an acknowledgment that there is always more to learn, that culture is complex and layered for communities and for individuals and groups within communities, and challenges us to continuously reflect on our own biases and experiences that influence our approach to working with diverse individuals and cultures. Many community practitioners work cross-culturally or within groups that contain diverse groups of people who may vary in terms of age, race, ethnicity, income, gender identity, immigration status, sexual orientation, and physical/mental abilities (Gutierrez et al., 2005; Mackelprang et al., 2022). Consequently, it is imperative that community practitioners become aware of their own personal biases, strive to overcome stereotypical beliefs or values that may limit their ability to work cross-culturally, and engage in a process of lifelong learning about people who are different from them. It is also necessary to become aware that individual community members within cultures have differing identities characterized by *intersectionality*, which is the intersection of racial and ethnic identity, gender identity, class and/or religious identity, and a multitude of other self-identities that together comprise our unique view on the world and how we interact within it. Specific skills used by community practitioners to engage in cultural humility and community practice with a culturally competent approach are discussed throughout this text. For example, Chapter 2 identifies many of these skills and describes how they may be applied by macro practitioners for "getting to know" the community and the cultural groups they serve.

However, it should be noted that mere competency in delivering services to people who are demographically different from you is not sufficient. *Anti-racism* in social work practice is an imperative for the field, and necessitates that social workers acknowledge that racism exists, and to recognize the harmful historical and current impact of racism on individuals and communities, and how it is perpetuated in systems, organizations, and society through harmful and oppressive policies and practices. Indeed, social workers must continue to examine our own field and the ways in which we uphold and contribute to racial oppression and racism in society and within our own profession. Anti-racist community practice in social work requires us to challenge and advocate against racial oppression and racism, and to promote nonoppressive behaviors, practices, and policies in communities, organizations, and systems, in order to dismantle racism and promote racial justice and equitable opportunities for all people to achieve their full potential. Using a multicultural lens for community practice, including cultural awareness and cultural competency, alone falls short of engaging in anti-racist community practice (Feize & Gonzalez, 2018). Community organizers must also understand the power dynamics that contribute to the oppression and disempowerment of community members; the historical context of oppression, discrimination, racism, and stigmatization affecting cultural, ethnic, and other oppressed groups; and work in partnership with communities and groups to address the conditions that foster minoritization and marginalization (Satterwhite & Teng, 2007).

Human Rights Perspective: Toward an Integrative Framework for Ethics and Action

In addition to the NASW (2021) *Code of Ethics* and the general principles associated with popular education to which most community practitioners adhere, additional sources of values and ethical standards can be found in the *Code of Ethics* of the International Federation of Social Workers (IFSW; 2018). IFSW ethical principles include standards of professional conduct for social workers globally, and they identify two primary principles associated with social work practice: human rights and social justice. The IFSW *Code of Ethics* mandates that social workers recognize individual strengths, foster self-determination, and promote the empowerment and participation of participants in social services. Social workers are also expected to fight against discrimination and unjust policies. They are also reminded that social workers often have divided loyalties among social service participants, colleagues, and employers as well as obligations to professional organizations and the legal system that may conflict with one another; consequently, social workers should continuously engage in ethical discussions in their agencies and with colleagues to ensure that they make appropriate, values-based, and ethical decisions in their practice.

The IFSW (2018) implores all social workers to advocate for the standards set out in the United Nations' (1948) *Universal Declaration of Human Rights*. This mandate also includes a number of other charters of rights adopted by the United Nations, including the *International Covenant on Civil and Political Rights*, the *Convention on the Elimination of all Forms of Racial Discrimination*, the *Convention on the Elimination of All Forms of Discrimination Against Women*, and the *Convention on the Rights of the Child*.

In these documents, basic human rights are identified and defined. The United Nation's (1948) *Universal Declaration of Human Rights* includes provisions that mandate freedom from discrimination, the right to work, a prohibition against inhumane treatment and torture, the right to legal protection under the law, the right to an education, the right to marry, the right to an adequate standard of health and well-being, and freedom of expression. The other charters and conventions also require that the governments that have ratified these documents enforce provisions banning discrimination and mistreatment. For example, the U.N. (1979) *Convention on the Elimination of All Forms of Discrimination Against Women* includes provisions requiring governments to eliminate discrimination in employment, education, and healthcare and take action to ensure that men and women are treated equally.

According to these documents, it is the responsibility of all governments to preserve these human rights. The mandates described in the various charters are to apply to all people of all nations, including citizens, residents, and undocumented people. However, not all governments adhere to these standards and some, including the United States, have refused to ratify some of these charters. For example, the U.S. government body that must ratify all treaties, the U.S. Senate, has only approved the *Charter of Rights*, the *International Covenant on Civil and Political Rights*, the *Convention on the Elimination of Racial Discrimination*, and the *Convention Against Torture* (Wronka, 2017). Members of the Senate have opposed ratification of the other covenants and conventions for a variety of reasons, mostly ideological. For example, the *Convention on the Rights of the Child* was opposed because it was perceived to conflict with U.S. labor laws and the legal rights of parents (Wronka, 2017). It was also opposed because of a provision that prohibits the execution of children under 18 (Clifford, 2009).

In countries in which they have been ratified, the standards provide a framework for the distribution of resources and the enforcement of human rights (Fox & Meier, 2009). Each government that has ratified the charters or conventions is required to file an annual report to the United Nations documenting progress toward meeting these goals (Wronka, 2017). In addition, advocacy groups may file complaints with the United Nation against governments that fail to live up to them. For example, women's and human rights organizations in Ciudad Juárez, Mexico, were able to draw attention to the murders and disappearance of over 500 women from their city between 1993 and 2003 by requesting an investigation by the United Nations (Ensalaco, 2006).

According to Lundy and Van Wormer (2007), the human rights framework helps social workers understand that social problems are simply not attributable to individual struggles, but have their origins in social and political structures and oppressive systems. It also leads us to the recognition that social work, as a profession, cannot stop at simply helping individuals acquire resources to meet their needs, but must also work toward changing the social, economic, and political systems that perpetuate social inequities. Indeed, the human rights approach can be used to influence and drive social investments for social programs and policies that ensure people have access to the resources they need and address widespread social issues (Androff, 2018).

INTEGRATING SOCIAL WORK GRAND CHALLENGES INTO MACRO SOCIAL WORK SKILLS DEVELOPMENT

In 2013, the American Academy of Social Work and Social Welfare (AASWSW) convened a leadership group of social workers, including representatives from national social work organizations, interest groups, social work educational programs, and other areas of the field, to develop the Grand Challenges initiative. Since its inception, this initiative has led to the development of 13 Grand Challenges for the social work profession that are leading the charge to advance society through a call to action for the profession today. These challenges were designed in response to the most pressing social issues of our time, in consideration of 13 emerging global trends, including: (a) advances in information technology; (b) globalization; (c) rising inequality; (d) increased interactions across nations, races, ethnicities, religions and cultures; (e) environmental changes; (f) aging populations; (g) underinvestment in the well-being of children; (h) racial segregation in residence and schooling; (i) unemployment and disconnection; (j) mass incarceration; (k) lack of access and ineffective healthcare systems; (l) financial instability; and (m) the increasing risks for vulnerable populations (Sherraden et al., 2014).

Driven by the research that identified these emerging issues and trends, in 2016 the AASWSW adopted 12 initial Grand Challenges for Social Work organized in three overarching themes, and issued a 10-year call to action for the profession at the annual Society for Social Work and Research conference. Although eliminating racism was originally considered to be interwoven across all 12 Grand Challenges, in 2020, due to the heightened awareness across the nation for the need to end racial injustices and to stop systemic racism and violence on Black/African Americans and people of color, the AASWSW announced the addition of a 13th Grand Challenge specifically focused on eliminating racism (Figure 1.1; Grand Challenges for Social Work, 2022).

Community-organizing practice aims to achieve widespread social change. The social work profession's pursuit of actions to address the Grand Challenges for Social Work

FIGURE 1.1 Grand Challenges for Social Work.

highlights the central need for more social workers in macro practice roles (Lightfoot & Toft, 2019). Community practitioners, organizers, and macro social workers are leading the charge to address the systemic challenges our society currently faces, the root causes of social injustices, and complex social issues through participatory processes that elevate the voices of minoritized and marginalized communities (Teixeira et al., 2021). Each challenge highlights a different area of community practice that is the focus of community change strategies and policies and systems reform.

INTERPERSONAL SOCIAL WORK SKILLS DEVELOPMENT AND COMMUNITY PRACTICE

In addition to values, ethics, and principles, macro practitioners and community organizers must have good interpersonal social work skills. The ability to interact with a diverse group of people is essential. According to Staples (2016):

> The bulk of an organizer's time is spent working either with individuals—in their kitchens, on their front door stoops, and over the phone—or with small groups in an endless array of meetings for recruitment, action research, community education, leadership training, executive decisions, grassroots fundraising, strategic analysis, action planning negotiating, lobbying, and evaluating organizational actions and activities. (p. 41)

After recruiting individuals and groups, community practitioners use interpersonal social work skills to assist people from diverse groups representing a variety of interests and opinions to identify common challenges or issues that affect them (Dobbie & Richards-Schuster, 2008; Ohmer & DeMasi, 2009). The development of a consensus among group members and the establishment of alliances or coalitions among members of diverse groups are critical for the success of organizing efforts (Mulroy et al., 2005).

Korazim-Korosy and colleagues (2007) identify a number of skills needed by community organizers to help facilitate group consensus, including an understanding of personal motivation, facilitating the development of leadership skills among group members, managing conflict, and negotiation. In addition, community organizers need good communication skills to bring people together such as listening, writing, and speaking in public. The application of the community-organizing principles associated with the transformative model of community practice also requires that the social worker use group-work skills to foster partnerships among the participants regardless of social status, encourage mutual learning, and facilitate ongoing dialogue among participants (Pyles, 2013).

Community practitioners must also work with community members, constituents, and partner organizations to plan intervention or action plans. These plans consist of a primary focus or strategy and a set of individual actions or tactics that make up a typical organizing campaign (Bobo et al., 2010). In their book on the United Farm Workers, Marshall Ganz (2009) describes the use of interpersonal social work skills in organizing campaigns:

Indeed, in complex, changing environments, devising strategy requires team members to synthesize skills and information beyond the ken of any one individual, like a good jazz ensemble. And good strategy, like good jazz, is an ongoing creative process of learning to achieve a desired outcome by interacting with others to adapt to constantly changing circumstances. (Ganz, 2009, p. 10)

Community practitioners also work with community and constituent groups to carry out action plans, lobby governments, and participate in the decision-making process in nonprofit organizations and government agencies. Basic group-work skills are needed by community practitioners to coordinate activities and provide support for community leaders, who are critical for the success of organizing campaigns and planning efforts (Brody et al., 2003; Zachary, 2000).

In addition to planning and conducting campaigns, community members and constituent groups are also likely to participate in conducting community needs assessments or to join with the organizer to evaluate the outcomes produced (Hardina, 2002). One primary model for establishing partnerships among academics, community practitioners, and the beneficiaries of social change efforts is called *participatory action research* (Reason & Bradbury, 2002). In this model, community members work with a researcher or an organizer to identify a community issue or challenge; conduct an assessment; develop a research methodology; conduct the study; and analyze, interpret, and disseminate the findings (Homan, 2016). Based on the results, community members develop a social change-oriented campaign to resolve the issue affecting the community. In order to facilitate such a project, the organizer needs a number of interpersonal social work skills, including effective engagement with participants, group facilitation, conflict management, and the ability to assist the group in developing trusting relationships and in reaching a consensus around research questions, goals, methodology, and the interpretation of findings (Schmuck, 2006; Stoecker, 2013).

Many of the skills identified by community organizers and practitioners easily fit into a classification system developed by Rothman and Zald (2008). They identify three types of social work skills commonly used in community practice, including the facilitation of the process of organizing, using influence, and using interpersonal social work skills for interacting with people. Skills for facilitating the organizing process include informing people, staffing committees, encouraging participation in decision-making, and developing and training new leaders. Influencing skills include advocating, bargaining, mediating, influencing powerful decision makers, and forming coalitions with members of a variety of groups. Skills for interpersonal macro social work interactions include the personal use of self (competent practice that incorporates ethics and values), interviewing people to collect information and to persuade them about issues, and facilitating groups.

Hardina and Obel-Jorgensen (2009) have also identified a set of skills needed for social action organizing that can be applied to most methods of organizing and that incorporate engagement and relationship skills with the various phases of the organizing process. These phases are consistent with the problem-solving model that guides social work practice with individuals, groups, families, organization and communities: issue identification, assessment, intervention, and evaluation (Kirst-Ashman & Hull, 2018).

- Be self-aware and use cultural competency
- Use verbal and written communication
- Engage in dialogue with community members, constituent groups, key informants, and decision makers
- Facilitate community member and constituent self-determination and self-empowerment
- In partnership with community members and constituent groups, identify issues and appropriate assessments
- In partnership with community members and constituent groups, weigh the ethical implications of tactics and strategies
- In partnership with community members and constituent groups, plan campaigns and take action
- In partnership with community members and constituent groups, evaluate outcomes and processes (Hardina & Obel-Jorgensen, 2009)

These skills can be conceptualized as occurring in sequential order. An organizer must first exhibit self-awareness and cultural humility to work effectively in communities. The organizer must also have excellent verbal and written communication skills to engage effectively and participate in dialogue to develop relationships with community members and constituent groups, and to persuade the public and decision makers. Community practitioners and organizers must also be able to prioritize empowerment and self-determination with members of community and constituency groups; they must also be able to work with group members to develop a consensus around issue identification, assessment, weighing the ethical implications of various strategies and tactics, developing and carrying out action campaigns, and conducting evaluations of their work (Figure 1.2).

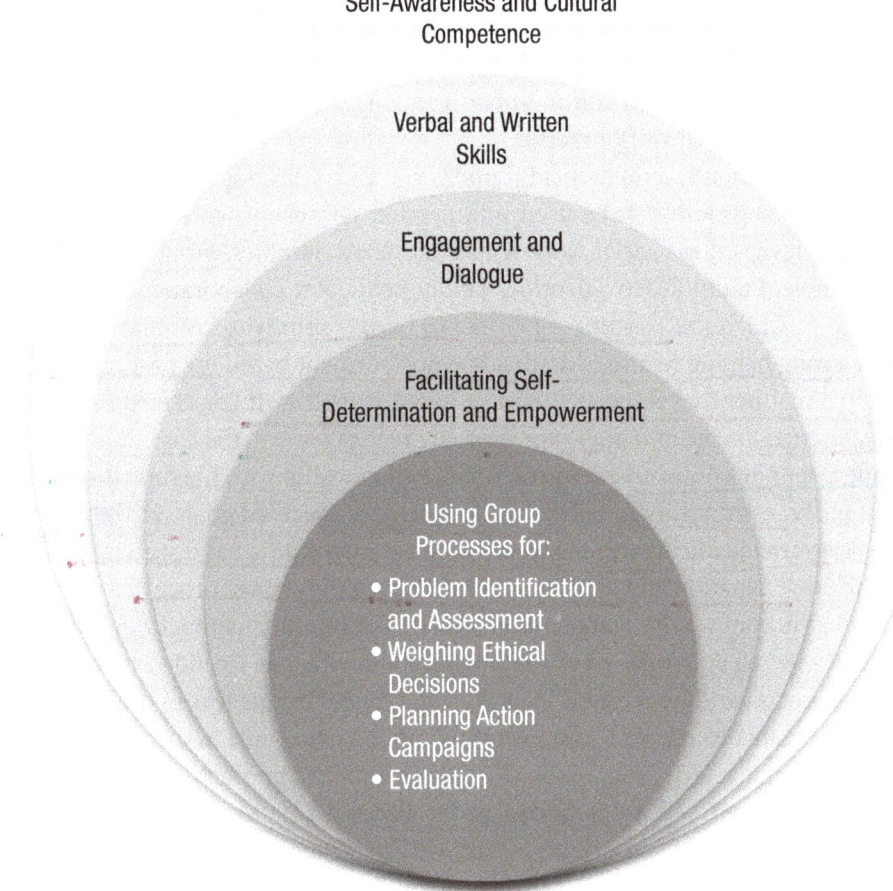

FIGURE 1.2 Progression of skills development for community-organizing practice.

BUILDING A FRAMEWORK FOR EXAMINING THE ROLE OF INTERPERSONAL SOCIAL WORK SKILLS IN COMMUNITY PRACTICE

The Council on Social Work Education (CSWE; 2015) has identified a set of core competencies that practitioners should possess, including:

- Demonstrate ethical and professional behavior.
- Engage diversity and difference in practice.
- Advance human rights and social, economic, and environmental justice.
- Engage in practice-informed research and research-informed practice.
- Engage in policy practice.
- Engage with individuals, families, groups, organizations, and communities.
- Assess individuals, families, groups, organizations, and communities.
- Intervene with individuals, families, groups, organizations, and communities.
- Evaluate practice with individuals, families, groups, organizations, and communities.

All these skills can be applied across all systems with which social workers typically practice. The remaining chapters of this book contain material about how to apply engagement skills and the process of dialogue in the facilitation of community and constituent group participation in assessment, intervention, and evaluation in community organizing. These skills can be used either in community organizing or as components of generalist or multisystem-oriented social work practice.

Using these components, a theoretical framework can be developed to understand how community-organizing skills can be used in a manner consistent with generalist practice models that are designed for social work with individuals, families, groups, and organizations. For example, Poulin (2010) identifies components of a collaborative model of generalist practice in which the practitioner works in partnership with community members to develop a strong helping relationship that is empowerment based for participants and is carried out in a manner that respects their needs and strengths. It consists of three phases: *preengagement, engagement*, and *disengagement*. In preengagement, the community member has not made a definite commitment to enter into a relationship with the practitioner. In the engagement phase, community members work to achieve specified goals. In the disengagement phase, gains made during the engagement phase are solidified and sustained. Tasks in this phase include evaluation and identifying next steps in the change process. Because these types of activities in community practice often involve community members and constituent groups in reviewing what happened in the program and whether intended outcomes were produced, this process will be referred to as *postengagement* in this text in order to emphasize the continuing involvement of volunteers and other participants in the change process.

Miley and colleagues (2017) integrate the empowerment approach within a generalist practice model. As described by Gutierrez and colleagues (1998) the empowerment approach incorporates several important aspects of Freire's popular education model, including the importance of mutual learning, equal partnerships between professionals and community members, and dialogue among members of various constituency groups in social service agencies (e.g., staff, administrators, board members, and users of social services) and community groups. Using these principles and other aspects of the empowerment model, Miley and colleagues identify three essential types of skills for generalist practice that can be used across multiple systems and in different practice arenas: *dialogue, discovery*, and *development*. They describe the concept of dialogue as a process that involves developing partnerships with and understanding the experiences of community members in order to identify intervention goals. In the Miley and colleagues (2017) model, the term *discovery* pertains to the use of the helping relationship to conduct assessments and the development phase includes both intervention and evaluation.

Using these three typologies (CSWE, 2015; Miley et al., 2017; Poulin, 2010) as a framework and adding evaluation as a separate practice component, a model can be constructed to identify engagement, dialogue, and other interpersonal social work skills that are needed primarily for community practice. The skills inherent in this model also build on previous work by Rothman and Zald (2008) and Hardina and Obel-Jorgensen (2009). The primary assumption of this framework is that organizing is not a skill that can be performed by one person alone. It must take place within a group context and requires interpersonal interaction and effective dialogue with community members, constituent groups, beneficiaries,

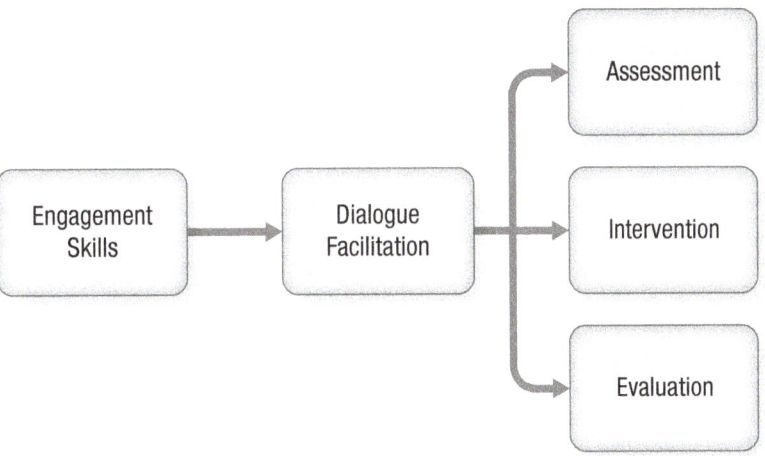

FIGURE 1.3 The relationship among engagement, dialogue, and social work practice skills for community organizing.

agency administrators, elected officials, and other decision makers. Therefore, to be successful, an organizer must have excellent engagement skills in order to facilitate dialogue with and among group members and sustain their involvement in conducting assessments, planning interventions, and evaluating whether and how they have achieved their goals (Figure 1.3). This practice framework assumes that a typical community practitioner must first engage with potential constituent groups and key informants in the community, and then facilitate dialogue with members of the community or constituent group in order to conduct assessments, plan and participate in interventions, and evaluate the process and outcomes of these action plans.

Table 1.1 identifies the interpersonal social work skills that should be used during different phases (preengagement, engagement, and postengagement) of the community-organizing process and also incorporates the types of activities needed during each phase. For example, during the preengagement phase of community organizing, dialogue-related skills focus on the recruitment of potential community members, constituent groups, and community leaders, including the distribution of flyers, tabling, door-knocking, conducting one-on-one interviews, and using technology to reach volunteers, donors, and other supporters. During the engagement process, dialogue-related skills include using group work to facilitate issue identification, assessment, intervention planning, and the implementation of the intervention. In the postengagement evaluation phrase, the organizer applies similar group-work skills in facilitating a participatory evaluation process to assess the successes, limitations, and lessons learned from the organizing process. Many of the other skills discussed earlier in this chapter (e.g., interviewing, recruitment, relationship-building with community members, constituent groups, organizations, and decision makers; facilitating participation in decision-making; and working with constituent groups to develop a consensus about strategies and tactics) can be classified based on whether assessment, intervention, or evaluation skills are used during preengagement, engagement, and postengagement phases of the organizing process.

TABLE 1.1 Types of Interpersonal Social Work Skills Used in Organizing by Engagement Phase and Type of Activity

PHASE	PURPOSE OF DIALOGUE	ASSESSMENT	ACTIVITIES AND SKILLS INTERVENTION	EVALUATION
Preengagement	Learn about the community and build relationships with constituents and organizations. Engage in outreach and recruitment of volunteers, donors, supporters, constituents, and organizational partners.	Preliminary assessment of community assets and challenges using the following techniques: Enter and observe the community. Learn about the "culture" of the community and of community residents. Identify community leaders. Conduct one-on-one interviews and develop relationships with community residents and leaders.	Part 1 Recruit constituents for participation in social change-related interventions. Part 2 Develop relationships and partnerships with organizations and groups.	
Engagement	Form and maintain task groups. Develop leadership. Dialogue with constituents to identify and prioritize community issues, conduct assessments, plan interventions, and participate in action campaigns.	Use participatory (group) methods to identify community issues and challenges and to conduct assessments, asset mapping, and power analysis. Facilitate participant knowledge and skill building.	Build and strengthen relationships with and among constituents, social networks, allies, and opponents. Facilitate participation in public and nonprofit decision-making. Use group-work skills to work in partnership with constituents and allied groups to set goals, assess ethics of plan options, choose strategies and tactics, establish evaluation criteria, implement campaigns, and lobby decision makers.	Monitor and reflect on the success/failure/process of tactics. Modify and implement tactical methods in response to what the group has learned (praxis) and its situational demands. (See also Postengagement and Assessment.)
Postengagement	Note constituent participation in evaluating the organizing campaign.	Group/constituent reflects on organizing successes and failures. (See also Engagement and Evaluation.)	Partner with constituents to identify evaluation questions and choose a research methodology.	Partner with constituents to conduct formal evaluations. Build on successes; revise unsuccessful plans.

PRACTITIONER READINESS AND SELF-CARE IN COMMUNITY PRACTICE

As discussed previously, the Grand Challenges for Social Work indicate that well-trained community practitioners are needed more now than ever. The Grand Challenges create a unique opportunity for schools of social work to strengthen an often-neglected curriculum area—macro practice—by creating new courses and actively recruiting community practitioners and organizers for enrollment in BSW and MSW programs. This calls for an increased commitment on the part of schools of social work to prepare students to assume leadership positions in community-based organizations (Mott, 2008).

> *Community change is, in short, a tough and demanding job requiring a broad background, analytic and strategic skills, and practical experience in understanding and motivating people and moving them into action on strategies which will lead to growing success. It is a tremendously challenging— and exciting—responsibility, at least as complex as any other profession. Like other professions, it requires extensive preparation, well beyond what people can learn on a job without a serious educational component, mentoring and guidance. (Mott, 2008, p. 9)*

In addition to the recognized need for skilled social workers in community practice roles and the responsibility of social work programs to prepare competent community practitioners with skills, abilities, and knowledge, community practice requires a certain level of "readiness" and professional attributes that position a practitioner for success in this type of work. Mott (2008) identifies three basic competency areas for community organizers:

- analytical skills, including the ability to examine political, economic, and social processes, the ability to conduct research, and the ability to engage in reflective practice and think strategically;
- interpersonal and organizing skills that can be used for the facilitation of collective action, including participatory methods, program development, organization management, and coalition building; and
- specialized skill development related to specific fields of practice and social issues; for example, practitioners may specialize in areas such as environmental justice, poverty alleviation, or housing.

Community practitioner readiness involves the acquisition of these competencies in preparation for work in the field and the ethical and values-based orientation to community practice work discussed earlier in this chapter, as well as professional traits or attributes that prepare the community practitioner for success. These include the ability to thrive in an adaptive work environment where priorities and goals may suddenly shift, the ability to be flexible and creative when things do not go as planned (which is not uncommon in community practice), the ability to build meaningful relationships easily and authentically, the ability to problem-solve and be self-motivated, and the ability to set healthy professional boundaries. As relationships are the most important currency in community practice and organizing, being able to establish healthy relationships and engaging in meaningful self-care is important.

There is little in the literature to guide macro social worker practitioners in regards to engaging in self-care. In clinical social work practice, professional boundaries between clinicians and their clients are more clear. In community practice, social workers often engage socially with community members and other partners in community celebrations, events, over coffee or a meal, and in the homes of community members. These relationships are key to building trust and capacity, understanding communities, and mobilizing community members to action. However, because these relationships are community-based, they extend beyond the confines of a traditional social work practice setting. The "iM-PAACT" model is a conceptual framework for self-care in community practice (Brown, 2020). The four-stage iM-PAACT model is an acronym for: (a) **i**nvest in **M**e, (b) **P**rioritize (Stage 1), (c) **A**ct and **A**ssess (Stage 2), (d) **C**onnect (Stage 3), and (e) **T**hrive (Stage 4).

The overarching premise of the model—*invest in Me*—represents the overarching emphasis of the model—that investing in oneself is a worthy and important use of time. In community practice reserving time to invest in oneself is often neglected, overlooked, or sacrificed due to the often urgent and complex demands of the work. The first stage involves the practitioner acknowledging that self-investment is not just important but rather necessary in order to be able to show up fully—with energy, motivation, and optimism—to engage in the challenging and complex work that is involved in community practice.

Once the practitioner embraces this premise, the first stage, *prioritize*, includes the goals of exploring individualized activities to promote meaningful self-care, setting practice goals for regular self-care, and incorporating self-care into one's weekly schedule. This stage includes exploring activities that promote health and well-being in the physical, spiritual, mental, emotional, and relational domains of one's life, in order to establish balance. The key at this stage is to identifying one's interests and resources to engage in activities that promote and help to achieve this balance, which is unique for each person. It is also important at this stage to consider what is not working and what is holding you back from achieving that balance, including unhealthy habits, tendencies, and/or relationships. Eliminating, addressing, or limiting the things that cause imbalance, and elevating the things that promote balance and fulfillment involves resetting personal priorities, setting realistic and achievable goals, and committing to act on these goals by establishing a written self-care plan and incorporating the plan into your routine and schedule.

Stage 2 of the iM-PAACT model, *act and assess*, involves putting your self-care plan into action. During this stage you act on concrete steps that are incorporated into your schedule (i.e., planned activities written into your calendar, specific time designated for self-care and improvement activities) and protect that time from interference from external, competing demands. If professional obligations that are time sensitive derail you from protecting that time, then the goal is to limit this interference as much as possible and to reschedule, rather than cancel, these activities only when absolutely necessary. During this time, you also assess, or take inventory of, what is working and what is not working in achieving your goals, and make adjustments as needed to make your goals more realistic or achievable, or to address barriers and issues that cause interferences.

Stage 3, *connect*, occurs once you have achieved a rhythm of acting on your self-care plan and it is fully incorporated into your routine, and involves reflecting with yourself internally and connecting with others to continue to be successful in practicing ongoing self-care. Reflecting internally requires you to consider how your interests and needs evolve over time, and adjusting your planned activities to reflect those changes and growth. Connecting externally involves engaging with people in your life and in networks that are supportive, and help keep you on track and accountable to continuing your commitment to self-care as an integral element of your community practice. Finally, Stage 4, *thrive*, is the phase you enter when you are fully engaged in your self-care routine; you continuously reflect and review your goals, plans, and commitment to self-care and growth; and maintain optimal health that helps to prevent professional burnout. It is important to note that although presented linearly, the iM-PAACT model is an iterative process, as we cannot prevent professional and personal life challenges that occur that may take us off course, and we use the various stages of this framework to continuously strive for self-growth and optimal health because when we are taking care of ourselves we can more fully show up for others and be ready to engage in challenging community work (Brown, 2020).

ORGANIZATION OF THIS TEXTBOOK

The next nine chapters of this text focus on one of the phases of the organizing process and the various practice components within each phase. For example, three chapters address activities typically conducted during the preengagement phase of the organizing process. Chapter 2 describes dialogue-related activities in the preengagement phase: Entry into the community and "getting to know you" interviews with community members. Community practitioners and organizers can only be successful using these skills when they are knowledgeable about the community and practice using a lens of cultural humility. Consequently, techniques for culturally competent practice are discussed in this chapter. In Chapter 3, techniques for recruiting future participants in organizing efforts are identified. The recruitment methods described include the distribution of flyers, tabling, street outreach, house meetings, phone banks, using the media, and more innovative methods, including text messaging and social media. In Chapter 4, a process for developing relationships and establishing partnerships with community groups, organizations, institutions, and key decision makers is examined.

In the next section of the book, the process of engagement is described in detail with an emphasis on the group-work skills necessary for working with multiple individuals and organizations. In Chapter 5, information is presented on forming and establishing dialogue with groups that can be used to identify community challenges and issues. Chapter 6 describes group-work–related methods typically used to involve volunteers, community members, and other constituents in conducting detailed community assessments. In Chapter 7, interpersonal macro social work skills used to involve community members in the planning of organizing campaigns and facilitating public participation in planning and other types of decision-making are described. In Chapter 8, the group-work skills needed to facilitate and carry out organizing campaigns and community change strategies are discussed.

In the third section of this book, postengagement skills are examined. Chapter 9 describes how to use group dialogue to assess whether campaign strategies and tactics have actually worked and whether they should be revised. This process of *praxis*, described earlier in this chapter, involves critical reflection by constituency group members followed by taking action. Praxis-related activities can occur while campaigns are being conducted or at the conclusion of the campaign. Chapter 10 describes the use of group-work–related methods to involve community members in planning and actually conducting formal evaluations of community intervention plans.

In the final section of the book, additional applications of macro social work skills are examined. In Chapter 11, the importance and use of relationship and engagement skills for lobbying elected officials and other decision makers are described. Chapter 12 provides an overview of methods used in the process of community building to develop strong bonds and solidarity among community members. Chapter 13 addresses supervisory practices that help facilitate interpersonal social work skill development among new community practitioners and organizers. The final chapter of this book, Chapter 14, examines the process of globalization, international social work, and macro skills in organizing work outside of the United States.

END-OF-CHAPTER RESOURCES

KEY TAKEAWAYS AND SUMMARY

Interpersonal macro social work skills are critical in community-organizing practice; community organizers need to be able to effectively engage community members and recruit participants for community development initiatives, social planning, and social action. Community practitioners should be able to facilitate the development of strong bonds and effective partnerships among community members, lobby decision makers, and work with groups of constituents to conduct assessments, plan interventions, and evaluate whether and why their actions have been successful. There are numerous models for community practice and community organizing that provide useful frameworks for engaging in social action, community development, and community planning initiatives. Ethics, values, cultural humility, and human rights are the foundation for community practice in social work, and, as such, social workers bring an essential lens to community work that elevates the voices of community members as equal partners in organizing efforts. Macro social work skills are essential in achieving forward movement in addressing the Grand Challenges for Social Work. Excellent engagement skills are needed to establish relationships with group members and sustain involvement in campaigns and community projects to address complex social issues. Because most community-organizing activities require the participation of multiple people for successful completion, engagement skills and the ability to facilitate dialogue among group members are essential if community practitioners are to carry out assessments, conduct interventions, and evaluate their work.

RESOURCES

- **Community Tool Box (University of Kansas):** A resource for community practitioners in organizing and community development initiatives. Accessible at: https://ctb.ku.edu/en
- **Grand Challenges for Social Work.** Accessible at: https://grandchallengesforsocialwork.org
- **NASW Standards and Indicators for Cultural Competence in Social Work Practice** (2015). Accessible at: https://www.socialworkers.org/LinkClick.aspx?fileticket=PonPTDEBrn4%3D
- **United Nations Sustainable Development Goals.** Accessible at: https://www.un.org/sustainabledevelopment
- **Grand Challenges for Social Work.** Accessible at: https://grandchallengesforsocialwork.org/

ACTIVITIES

1. Watch the movie *Invictus* (McCreary et al., 2009) about Nelson Mandela's efforts to support South Africa's Whites-only rugby team in their bid to win a world championship immediately after the dissolution of apartheid. Describe:
   a. The interpersonal skills used by President Mandela in interactions with supporters.
   b. The interpersonal skills used by President Mandela in interactions with people previously connected to the apartheid government, including government staff members.
   c. Any similarities or differences in the way President Mandela interacted with supporters and previous opponents.
   d. Techniques used by President Mandela to motivate members of the rugby team.
   e. Techniques used by President Mandela to garner support for the rugby team from both White and Black South Africans.
   f. The rationale for President Mandela's efforts to rally South Africans behind the winning rugby team.
2. Observe a community outreach activity, such as a health fair or informational event, in which organizations set up booths or tables and distribute literature about their services or community issues. Identify:
   a. Which of the booths seemed to be doing the most "business" in terms of the number of people coming by the booth, looking at the literature to be distributed, and chatting with organizational representatives?
   b. What types of things draw people to the booths that are doing the most business?
   c. Compare and contrast the behavior of the people staffing the booths that draw the most people to booths drawing the least number of people.

ASSIGNMENTS

1. Describe how you, as a social worker engaged in community practice, would put into practice the ethical principles identified in the *Code of Ethics* of the International Federation of Social Workers. Write a five-page paper that responds to the following questions: How do these principles compare with those in the NASW *Code of Ethics*? Do you think it is important to have global standards for advocacy and social justice?

 A robust set of instructor resources designed to supplement this text is located at http://connect.springerpub.com/content/book/978-0-8261-5835-2. Qualifying instructors may request access by emailing textbook@springerpub.com.

KEY REFERENCES

Only key references appear in the print edition. The full reference list appears in the digital product on Springer Publishing Connect: connect.springerpub.com/content/book/978-0-8261-5835-2/part/part00/chapter/ch01

Brown, M. E. (2020). Hazards of our helping profession: A practical self-care model for community practice. *Social Work, 65*(1), 38–44. https://doi.org/10.1093/sw/swz047

Carroll, J., & Minkler, M. (2000). Freire's message for social workers: Looking back, looking ahead. *Journal of Community Practice, 8*(1), 21–36. https://doi.org/10.1300/J125v08n01_02

Checkoway, B., & Zimmerman, M. (1992). Correlates of participation in neighborhood organizations. *Administration in Social Work, 16*(3/4), 45–64. https://doi.org/10.1300/J147v16n03_04

Dobbie, D., & Richards-Schuster, K. (2008). Building solidarity through difference: A practice model for critical multicultural organizing. *Journal of Community Practice, 16*(3), 317–337. https://doi.org/10.1080/10705420802255098

Hardina, D. (2004). Guidelines for ethical practice in community organization. *Social Work, 49*(4), 595–604. https://doi.org/10.1093/sw/49.4.595

Kam, P. K. (2021). Strengthening the empowerment approach in social work practice: An EPS model. *Journal of Social Work, 21*(3), 329–352. https://doi.org/10.1177/1468017320911348

Ohmer, M., & DeMasi, K. (2009). *Consensus organizing: A community development workbook*. Sage.

Rothman, J. (1996). The interweaving of community intervention approaches. *Journal of Community Practice, 3*(3/4): 69–99. https://doi.org/10.1300/J125v03n03_03

Segal, E. (2007). Social empathy: A new paradigm to address poverty. *Journal of Poverty, 11*(3), 65–81. https://doi.org/10.1300/J134v11n03_06

Teixeira, S., Augsberger, A., Richards-Shuster, K., Martinez, L. S., & Evans, K. (2021). Opportunities to "make macro matter" through the grand challenges for social work. *Families in Society, 102*(3), 414–426. https://doi.org/10.1177/1044389420972488

THE PREENGAGEMENT PHASE

ENTERING THE COMMUNITY AND USING INTERVIEWING SKILLS TO UNDERSTAND PEOPLE, ISSUES, AND OPPORTUNITIES

LEARNING OBJECTIVES

After reading this chapter, students will be able to:
- Describe the role of interpersonal engagement in community organizing.
- Identify skills and attributes of an effective interviewer.
- Describe how social media can be used to facilitate community engagement.
- Identify the need for cultural competency and cultural humility in community practice.

INTRODUCTION

In this chapter, the term *community* is defined. In addition, methods used by community organizers during the preengagement phase of an intervention, when they first enter a new community or start working with members of a group with whom they are not familiar, are discussed. One of these techniques involves observations of the community and the people who are residents of, or who participate in, the community. Such observations often require that practitioners gain entry to and build trust or acceptance with community members and leaders. Techniques for gaining access and observing the community are presented in this chapter. A second technique for getting to know the community, one-on-one interviews with key informants, is also described. These interviews resemble casual conversations but differ in key ways from formal interviews conducted within the context of agency-based, social work practice. Consequently, this chapter contains an overview of the skills needed for successful interviewing in community organizing and compares and contrasts these skills with techniques commonly used in micro practice. In order to initiate meaningful relationships with potential constituents and allies, the community organizer also needs to practice from a foundation of cultural competency. In the last section of this chapter, techniques commonly used by community organizers to gain knowledge about community beliefs, practices, customs, and values that facilitate cultural competence and cultural humility are examined.

DEFINING *COMMUNITY*

Communities are typically either geographically constructed or identity based, and therefore can consist of neighborhoods or political districts (i.e., geographic), or be composed of people with a shared culture, common characteristics, interests, or issues (i.e., identity-based). In addition, most communities consist of a group of people who are linked together through a pattern of social interactions or exchanges such as giving and receiving resources, advice, or support. The term used to describe these interpersonal transactions is *social networks* (Miley et al., 2017). Often, community organizers will use their skills to foster strong bonds among community members and to help community members strengthen a sense of identification with or belonging to the community (Wilson et al., 2010).

One of the requirements for defining a group of people as being part of the community is whether or not people identify themselves as community members (Longres, 2008). People may identify themselves as residents of specific neighborhoods or a group of people with common characteristics (e.g., age, race, ethnicity, income, gender identity, immigration status, or people with mental, emotional or physical disabilities) or shared interests (e.g., parents with children who have special needs or renters at risk of eviction). In addition to common experiences, members of communities share common traditions, values, behaviors, language (either formal language or the use of slang), and patterns of interaction with one another (Lum, 2011). Communities also can be characterized in terms of what resources are generated and distributed, the businesses, organizations, and institutions that are frequented or operated by community members, and how political, social, and economic decisions are made. Decision-making authority is often the key for identifying which people and groups have the power to determine what happens in the community (Netting et al., 2017). Regardless of the type of community, when working with a community, the first goal of a community organizer is to gain knowledge about the collective experiences of the community, whether people within the community view themselves as part of the community, what challenges and opportunities they face, and what they want for themselves and others in their community in the future (Pyles, 2013).

ASSESSING COMMUNITY READINESS FOR SOCIAL CHANGE

Prior to entering a community, an organizer should engage in background research to understand potential readiness for community change by the members of the community. The organizer should search for any stories or historical documentation of prior change efforts to learn about what took place, who was involved, what successes were achieved, and the challenges they faced. Community readiness involves both the belief that change is possible and the belief that the community has the capacity for change. Social work organizers must be prepared to meet people where they are, as some community members may not have hope that change is possible. It is the job of the community organizer to help foster that hope where little exists, and when it does exist, to help harness it by building relationships grounded in a shared agenda for collective change, and connecting the community with resources to build and strengthen the capacity to achieve that change. Although it may not be possible to fully ascertain community readiness prior to entry into the community, it is the organizers' ethical responsibility to ensure that they have done their due diligence to understand past community trauma, including possible harm from prior organizing efforts that were unsuccessful, in order not to repeat the mistakes of the past, and to understand past community successes that can be built on in the process of mobilizing for community change.

ENTRY INTO THE COMMUNITY

In their book *Gang Leader for a Day*, sociologist Sudhir Venkatesh (2008), a California resident and child of Indian immigrants, describes how they were able to establish a relationship with a Black/African American street gang in Chicago that allowed them to observe and even participate in some gang activities. Venkatesh stumbled across members of the gang when trying to administer a multiple-choice questionnaire in a public housing community that was actually vacant. Much of what Venkatesh did to gain acceptance by the gang was not considered standard practice among sociologists or social workers; organizers or researchers would be wise to not adopt some of their methods, for example, traveling alone and on foot to the research site, not informing anyone of their whereabouts, and bringing a six-pack of beer with them to distribute to the gang members. However, Venkatesh was able to gather valuable information for their research using a number of techniques that included conveying acceptance, respect, and humility; finding common interests with members of the gang (e.g., sports and cars); sharing meals; and altering their interviewing techniques in response to suggestions from their research subjects.

Like Venkatesh, an organizer seeking to gain entry into a community also needs to convey acceptance, respect, and humility. One also needs to find a way to communicate effectively, often with people and groups across demographic boundaries, such as race, ethnicity, age, gender identity, or social class, and differences in experiences and perspectives (Pyles, 2013). In many ways, gaining acceptance into a new community requires skills similar to those of a qualitative researcher. Berg (2017) offers the following tips for gaining entry into a community:

- Watch, listen, and, if the community of interest is a geographic space, walk around. Smile and greet the people who you meet.
- Observe people, listen to conversations, and ask questions.
- Find formal and informal groups of people in the community, and identify influential community leaders and people.

Prior to conducting an observation in the community, a community organizer needs to do their own background research, and should find out as much as possible about the community by consulting newspaper accounts, reports, local web pages, social media or blogs, and existing secondary data on community characteristics (Kirst-Ashman & Hull, 2018). The organizer should consult with supervisors and coworkers and identify people who have expert knowledge or experience working in the community. Such individuals can not only provide background and historical information, but can also connect the organizer with key people (such as informal and formal leaders) who may help them gain connections with groups and people and refer them to additional resources as they enter the community.

One, or more, of the people whom an organizer meets in any community is likely to function as a gatekeeper, someone who is protective of their community and likely to control the ability of outsiders to gain access to community members or resources (Padgett, 2017). Gatekeepers are usually well connected in the community, highly knowledgeable about community issues, and can help identify important decision makers and key organizations and groups. Gatekeepers can be formal or informal. For example, as an organizer you may need to ask permission to observe or interview people from someone in a formal role such as an administrator of a community-based organization that serves a specific population group, or let an elected official such as a city council member know that you will be working in a specific area. Informal community leaders, often people who routinely provide support to their neighbors or other community members, do not usually have a formal title but are usually highly respected and well-connected members of the community, and may also serve as gatekeepers. Most communities have several formal and informal gatekeepers. Once the organizer has built a trusting relationship with a gatekeeper, that person can help link the organizer through their social networks to other key individuals and groups (Staples, 2016).

There are a number of other helpful techniques that can be used to conduct observational research as part of your entry into the community. If you are observing a community that is based on common interests, issues, or identity, you might want to attend events, contact organizations, join a coalition, patronize a business, or find other creative methods for interacting with members of the community. For example, an ethnic supermarket or a cultural festival may provide an opportunity to observe members of immigrant groups.

As in qualitative research, organizers keep detailed notes about what they observe, who they meet, and what people tell them (ben Asher, 2002; Padgett, 2017). Although entry into a new community by an organizer does not necessarily involve a formal research study, some of the things that you may want to observe are the appearance of the people and the setting, verbal and physical behaviors, and how people interact with one another (Family Health International, 2005; Neuman, 2020). The situation or context in which behaviors or actions occur as well as the power dynamics that exist (e.g., who holds the power? how is it used?) are also important. In addition, you need to pay attention to the characteristics of the community such as the geographic size of neighborhoods, the number of people who are residents or members, the physical condition of housing and other facilities, the quality of basic city services (such as street lighting and trash pickup), and the demographic composition of the community, including factors such as racial or ethnicity diversity, age, gender identity, and disability (Homan, 2016). Physical or sociodemographic barriers that exclude some people from participation in the community are also important to note. For example, railroad tracks or highways may separate some parts of the community; participation in some organizations or at some events may be implicitly or explicitly restricted to some demographic groups, but not others (Hardina, 2002).

You may also want to map out some of the spatial characteristics of the community, for example, where assets such as parks, schools, or businesses are located and where people typically gather for community events (Netting et al., 2017). Some very small factors may be very significant, for example, a community without a major grocery store conveniently located may face challenges obtaining healthy food, contributing to an obesity problem (Suarez-Balcazar et al., 2006). Neighborhoods without gutters and curbs or with broken sidewalks may be indicative of an under-resourced community that has little political power with which to obtain these services from city or county governments (Saegert et al., 2005). Members of an identity community for which there may be no common meeting place (for youths, for example), may have few sources of social support and consequently be at risk of depression or isolation (M. Delgado & Staples, 2008).

A community organizer also needs to think about personal safety when entering new communities, especially in terms of neighborhoods or groups that are demographically different from the organizer. Strangers may not be welcomed or may be perceived as a threat (T. Clark, 2010). In such instances, organizers will find it difficult to be accepted by community residents. Until a degree of acceptance is achieved, you will need to prepare a safety plan, pairing up with another individual to walk around the community, approach people for information, or knock on doors. Also keep your supervisor aware of your schedule, route, and plans—and make sure you carry a cell phone so that you can call or send a text for assistance.

CASE VIGNETTE: PERSONAL SAFETY IN DOOR-TO-DOOR SURVEYING

In a community assessment project in a neighborhood with high rates of violent crime, social work students and community residents were trained to conduct an interview-style survey. Surveyors went door-to-door in pairs to speak with community members to learn about their perceptions of safety and ideas for tackling the violent crime issues. The student and resident surveyors wore brightly colored matching shirts that identified them as part of the local university research team, went door-knocking in pairs with other surveyor teams on the same block while a survey supervisor remained at all times on the street, all survey teams had walkie talkies to be able to communicate with the supervisor as they moved from house to house. Further, the survey supervisor communicated with the local police department in advance to let them know at what times they would be out in the community and exactly where they would be, so the police were nearby in case there were any safety concerns for residents or student surveyors. Because of these precautions and through these efforts, the social work students and residents remained safe, and many new connections were made and relationships formed with and among residents that ultimately led to a community-wide effort to reduce violent crime.

As this example illustrates, interviews can be an effective tool in getting to know the community—both the issues and the people. A skilled organizer not only gathers information through interviews with community members, but also uses this entry tactic to identify and recruit potential participants in organizing efforts requiring relationship-building skills. In addition, it requires that the organizer commit to cultural competency and cultural humility. In the remaining sections of this chapter, these skills are examined.

LEARNING ABOUT COMMUNITY MEMBERS: ONE-ON-ONE KEY INFORMANT INTERVIEWS

In addition to entering the community, organizers use one-on-one key informant interviews to build relationships with community members and learn more about the community. *This is one of the primary interpersonal skills used in community practice.* Key informants are people closely connected to a community who can provide a wealth of insight on community challenges and ideas for solutions based on their extensive knowledge of the community. Key informants can be community leaders, residents, or professionals working with the community. Ideally you will engage a diverse group of key informants to ensure representation, get a comprehensive perspective of community issues and opportunities, and reduce the potential for one-sided perspectives or bias in your findings (UCLA Center for Health Policy Research, n.d.).

One-on-one key informant interviews resemble conversations, meaning they are semi-structured with guiding questions and elicit open-ended responses rather than yes or no answers, and the organizer typically prepares an interview tool to guide the conversation. One-on-one interviews have three purposes:

- to obtain information about community assets, strengths, issues, and opportunities;
- to establish relationships with people who may have information, skills, or assets that can be used for current and future organizing campaigns; and
- to recruit potential participants for organizing campaigns or organization membership (Indianapolis Neighborhood Resource Center, n.d.; PICO National Network, n.d.; Schutz & Sandy, 2011).

One-on-one interviews may be set up in advance or the organizer may find opportunities to conduct these conversations with potential constituents at community events, meetings, or when encountering people in the community. If preparing an interview tool in advance of a one-on-one interview, the format consists of introducing yourself and the project, asking five to 10 key questions with probing follow-up questions to more deeply explore a topic, and then asking a closing question in which the key informant has the opportunity to clarify or provide any additional information not shared in previous responses (UCLA Center for Health Policy Research, n.d.). Alternatively, the interview may be conducted in a manner that resembles a typical conversation between two people—the content and direction of the discussion determine the questions asked by the organizer (Traynor, 2002).

Rubin and Rubin (2012) use the term *conversational partner* to describe "the uniqueness of each person with whom you talk, [their] distinct knowledge, and the different ways [they] interact with you" (p. 14). Schutz and Sandy (2011) describe these interviews as both public and personal. The interviews are personal in that people are sharing stories about their own lives that can be very emotional, especially when people talk about personal hardships. The interviews are public in that they are being used in a strategic way to find out about community issues and connect the individual with a larger group in order to take action for social change.

Schutz and Sandy (2011) identify three key guidelines for conducting a one-on-one interview: Develop a relationship with the participant, find out what motivates the participant, and engage the participant in follow-up (e.g., ask the participant to attend an event or volunteer for an activity). In some circumstances (such as with an interviewee with severe personal problems), it may not be appropriate to make such a request, but part of the rationale for the interview is to recruit participants for community change efforts or assess whether someone can be asked to participate in the future (Box 2.1). Another important aspect of this process is that you are trying to involve the participant in an activity that will address some type of issue and make one's life better. The Center for Community Change (2007) emphasizes the importance of active participation in these interviews by both the interviewer and the respondent:

It's a dance. When done well, there's a dance between two people doing relational meetings. The meeting should not be about the organizer asking probing questions and the other person responding. Along the way, the organizer should have awakened enough curiosity in the other person that they, too, are probing and sharing stories. (p. 30)

In order to gain access to a potential interviewee, the organizer must establish that the interviewer has "legitimacy," meaning they represent an organization or group and can be trusted (Staples, 2016). Organizers do this by indicating the individual or individuals who might have referred the organizer to the potential interviewee. Organizers also should provide people with information about the organization that employs the organizer and its past activities and successes (Bobo et al., 2010). The organizer may also share some of their own personal information with the interviewee in order to establish rapport and a bond. For example, the organizer and the prospective recruit may have common experiences, challenges, or membership in the same organization or group. Even though you are using the relationship as an opportunity to ask people to do something, it is important to be genuine, honest, and truly excited or passionate about the cause or issue that you are trying to promote.

One of the difficulties in conducting one-on-one interviews is finding key informants. Some organizers will simply identify a particular neighborhood and knock on doors (Staples, 2016). Others will participate in community meetings or cultural and other community events and approach attendees. Gatekeepers and other community leaders and experts can provide referrals. In addition, organizers may be able to gain entry into specific community networks of people who typically know, give support, provide resources, and interact with one another. Members of such networks can generally be counted upon to refer the organizer to others with similar interests or knowledge.

In some organizing efforts, conducting one-on-one interviews is not solely the responsibility of the organizer. Volunteers or paid residents may be recruited to conduct some of these interviews with their neighbors, friends, and relatives. It is important to compensate community members for their time whenever possible; you are benefiting from their time, expertise, and networks and this exchange should be reciprocal. Oftentimes organizers are working on issues at the grassroots level and may not have access to monetary resources to compensate community members for their time, and if this is the case, the organizer must be creative about providing nonfinancial compensation and incentives to demonstrate value and recognition, such as providing training and capacity-building opportunities for nonpaid interviewers.

There are a number of advantages of using community members to conduct interviews; it increases the number of interviews that can be conducted, more information is collected, and people are more likely to open up and be candid with someone they know (Homan, 2016). It also frees up staff time and resources that can be utilized for other organizing tasks (Exley, 2008).

Box 2.1

SAMPLE ONE-ON-ONE INTERVIEW

Organizer: Hi, I'm Alicia Martinez, and I just started working at the West Neighborhood Organization. We're working on an air-quality campaign in response to the school district's proposal to locate a new elementary school near a meat-rendering facility. I understand that people in this neighborhood have had concerns about air quality and its effects on the asthma rate for a long time. I've been talking to your neighbors about their concerns. I wonder if I can have about 10 minutes of your time?

Mx. Jackson: I don't have much time to talk, I'm baking cookies for a bake sale at my church, but yes, I have concerns about the location of the school. All of my children have asthma and I've considered moving out of this neighborhood, but we don't have the money to move.

Organizer: I'm so sorry to hear that your children are sick. My cousin has asthma, too, and I know how difficult things can be. How often are your children sick? Have they missed much school?

Mx. Jackson: My youngest boy, Rashid, is usually absent from school at least 2 days a month. I'm worried that he will need to repeat the third grade. My oldest son and my daughter have also had problems keeping up their grades because of their asthma problems. I expect that all three of my children will be transferred to the new school when it is finished. If it's located near the meat-rendering plant, things will only get worse.

Organizer: We've heard that the asthma rate in this neighborhood is already very high. That's one of the reasons that we're here trying to help. We're hoping that by connecting with concerned residents like you we will be able to bring attention to this issue and stand up against the school board's proposal and reduce the children's exposure to polluted air.

Mx. Jackson: The school district doesn't seem to respond to our complaints. Mx. Brown, our neighbor, attends almost every school board meeting, trying to get them to listen to our concerns. I don't think there is much we can do. Please help yourself to a cookie.

Organizer: Sometimes complaints are more successful when many people are involved. We've talked with Mx. Brown and have offered to help them make contact with the press and other people who can help them publicize the possible health effects of locating the school near the meat-rendering plant. They are helping us organize a neighborhood meeting on Tuesday night. Will you be able to attend?

Mx. Jackson: Well, I can try to be there, but I'm awful busy with baking and trying to put together the fundraiser for our church.

Organizer: Your cookies are wonderful. Would you be willing to bring some to our meeting?

Mx. Jackson: I'd be happy to. Just let me know the time and the place.

As in qualitative research, ethical practice in community organizing involves the concept of *reciprocity*—the idea that if people consent to give their time to participate in a research study, the researcher is obligated to give something beneficial to participants in return. According to Marshall and colleagues (2022), "reciprocity may entail giving time to help out, providing informal feedback, making coffee, being a good listener, or tutoring" (p. 81). This important principle also applies in community practice; organizers should be ready to participate in community events, provide information referrals, and try to address issues raised by informants as often as realistically possible. For example, providing transportation and meals to volunteers engaged in a community cleanup effort, hosting a thank-you banquet for volunteer leaders in a community change effort, or providing information about employment opportunities would be appropriate activities. Social workers are particularly well suited to be community organizers based on their training in community resources and referrals, advocacy, and promoting social justice (Brown et al., 2015).

SIMILARITIES IN USING MICRO PRACTICE SKILLS FOR CONDUCTING ONE-ON-ONE INTERVIEWS IN COMMUNITY PRACTICE

In addition to relationship building, there are a number of ways in which micro social work practice skills can be used to conduct one-on-one interviews and community observation. For example, techniques such as using open-ended questions, exhibiting empathy, and analyzing both verbal communication patterns and body language cues can be used effectively in conducting interviews (Kirst-Ashman & Hull, 2018). Other essential interviewing skills include the ability to engage in active listening, to effectively and clearly communicate thoughts and ideas, to practice reflecting back interviewee comments to ensure accuracy in interpretation, to pay attention to detail, and to exhibit comfort and confidence in talking with new people.

In most community-organizing work, the organizer needs to establish relationships with potential constituents, partners, and allies at a rapid pace. As in micro social work practice, identifying yourself, the organization that you represent, and the purpose of the interview or conversation at the beginning of the meeting is critical to establishing early rapport (Cummins et al., 2006). The organizer must convey both interest and respect for the interviewee by using verbal communication and body language. The organizer must show up with their full, authentic self, exhibiting a positive and eager attitude and offering the participant their focused attention. For example, the Center for Community Change (2007) gives new organizers the following advice for conducting a one-on-one interview:

> *Relational meetings are not a cerebral exercise. You use your whole self—eye contact with the other person that doesn't stray every time someone walks by; leaning forward or nodding the head to communicate particular interest in a story being told or point being made. (p. 30)*

Poulin (2010) identifies four major activities for the social worker during the preengagement process for service users. In organizing, these activities take place in the phase during which the organizer is trying to persuade the community member to commit to the relationship. These activities, adopted from Poulin (2010), include:

- Study (in advance) the community member's culture, and how they and their community are affected by other systems, including the economic, social, environmental, and political landscape.
- Invite the community member to share a personal story.
- Listen for emotions and feelings as well as for the meanings associated with what the community member has to say.
- Clarify how collaboration between the organizer and the community member will take place.

All of these activities are useful skills for one-on-one interviews. In any mezzo or macro practice encounter, when engaging with communities, including groups and organizations, it is imperative to have a firm understanding of how political, social, environmental, and economic conditions may contribute to the interviewee's experiences or challenges. Often, other people in the community will have experienced similar challenges and interventions can be directed toward changing policies, laws, or programs that have played a role in creating or maintaining the issue. For example, if multiple members of the community are experiencing depression due to long-term unemployment, interventions might be oriented toward improving economic conditions and access to liveable wage careers in the community. Understanding the community member's cultural context is also important. Methods for increasing the organizer's knowledge of cultural groups are discussed in the last section of this chapter.

Although the community practitioner is not seeking information about the interviewee's mental health or previous trauma, respondents may disclose personal hardships or distress. Indeed, the organizer is interested in working with a community to address an existing unjust situation or inequitable issue, and the effectiveness of that collective pursuit is dependent on relationships and trust. Therefore, it becomes increasingly important that the organizer conveys empathy and that the relationship between the organizer and the person interviewed be characterized by genuineness and warmth. Poulin (2010) identifies several components of empathy in micro social work practice, including conveying a nonjudgmental attitude, focused listening, reflective empathy, and validation, which are equally important attributes of macro practice. Because people living in poverty or members of marginalized and oppressed groups may have beliefs or engage in practices that are different from the dominant culture, it is critical that community organizers display accepting attitudes (Hardina, 2004).

The most critical component in both micro practice and one-on-one interviews is having constituents describe situations that have meaning for them. Essentially, such accounts are narratives or stories that are key for understanding individual or group motivation, culture, lived experiences, and potential solutions. Although one-on-one interviews are conversational, it is appropriate to start either with prepared scripts, checklists, or simply with some ideas or assumptions that you want to test out. However, it is important that the questions be open ended. Questions that elicit yes or no answers will result in short interviews, limited contact with the interviewee, and will miss the opportunity to dive deeply into learning about the issue. Instead, as in qualitative research, interviews should elicit as much detail as possible; longer interviews will give the interviewer a greater chance to get to know and develop a relationship with the respondent.

Nonverbal cues, such as nodding your head or making eye contact (if it is culturally appropriate), will encourage the interviewee to add detail to their remarks (Miley et al., 2017; Poulin, 2010). In addition, verbal probes requesting more information will solicit additional responses from the interviewee. Rubin and Rubin (2012) identify the following types of probes:

- *Continuation*. Encourage the respondent to keep talking about what they are saying.
- *Elaboration*. Ask for more detail.
- *Attention*. Let the respondent know you are paying attention by indicating that you understand what they are saying or conveying interest.
- *Clarification*. Ask for an explanation about what the respondent was saying.
- *Steering*. If the respondent has veered from the intended topic, remind them about the purpose of the interview and what they had said previously.

As discussed earlier, it is essential that the interviewer be actively engaged in the interview process. Focused or active listening requires that the social worker try to glean the meaning behind the community member's spoken words, nonverbal communication (such as body language), and ideas and concepts that remain unspoken (Poulin, 2010). Often the organizer must assess whether interviewees are truly interested in the organizing effort, whether—if appropriate—they can be persuaded to participate, and whether they are fearful of the potential consequences of participation. Therefore, assessment of body language and communication patterns is critical for determining whether further interaction with the participant is warranted. For example, a potential interviewee who becomes visibly angry about the presence of the organizer or the introduction of a specific topic may not be ready to be recruited for participation in the organizing effort.

The organizer can determine whether one's assessment of the situation is correct by using a technique called *reflective empathy* or *reflective responding*; this involves restating the interviewee's message, including both factual and affective content (Kirst-Ashman & Hull, 2018). According to Poulin (2010), if potential constituents feel that their feelings are understood, they have been given *validation*. Validation is a key component when building trust between the macro practitioner and the community member. In addition, part of the purpose of a one-on-one interview is to identify the potential constituent's strengths. Therefore, asking respondents about their skills and interests and providing positive feedback, conveying genuine interest, and demonstrating support are important parts of the validation process (Miley et al., 2017).

Other micro social work techniques used to verify the meaning of the potential constituent's words include *paraphrasing* (restating what the person has said using other words), *clarification* (stating what you think the other party means), and *summarization* (restating the main points of the discussion). All of these techniques should be used in the course of a one-on-one interview, but are particularly important when interviewing someone whose primary language is different from your own or someone from a different cultural background (Kirst-Ashman & Hull, 2018).

The last phase of the preengagement interview process involves clarifying what you and the potential constituent will work on together (Poulin, 2010). As noted earlier in this chapter, it may be premature to ask some interviewees to participate in the change effort depending on the interviewee's expressed readiness, preferences, and availability, as communicated in the interview or your progress in developing a relationship with the interviewee. If requesting participation is deemed appropriate, the proposed activity should be something that will benefit, build capacity, and contribute to activating the power (i.e., empowerment) of the interviewee or the community.

DIFFERENCES IN THE USE OF INTERVIEWING SKILLS IN COMMUNITY ORGANIZING AND MICRO PRACTICE

There are a number of differences between the type of interviews typically conducted in community organizing and the application of similar skills in micro social work practice. These differences include the setting in which the interviews take place, the willingness to participate or motivation of constituents, the purpose of the interviews, the type of assessments conducted, and professional boundaries.

In micro practice, most interviews take place within agency settings and are scheduled in advance. Participants are generally willing participants as they have typically made an advanced choice to receive the services the agency provides. This is not commonly the case in community organizing. Often, people with whom the organizer will interact have no previous knowledge of the organizer and no wish to be "organized." Therefore, the successful application of engagement skills is critical for building relationships with potential constituents to advance the social change effort. Rubin and Rubin (2012) describe the reaction of potential interviewees:

Once contact has been made, most people like to talk about themselves; they enjoy the sociability and sense of accomplishment, and are pleased that someone is interested in what they have to say. Still, since people may be busy, feel incompetent, or fear exposure, you may need to explain why what they say is important. (p. 78)

As such, the organizer has to be artful at uncovering common ground quickly through conversation in order to establish rapport and eventually motivate potential participants. According to T. Clark (2010), people are likely to participate in interviews or organizing campaigns if it allows them to act on a political point of view, if they feel likely to benefit from participation, or out of a sense of moral or civic obligation. Even if the individual is not interested in participating in the organizing effort or may be a potential opponent, they may still be a good source of information or an ally on another issue in the future (Hardina et al., 2009). Therefore, *it is establishing the relationship that is of primary importance*. The instrumental nature of the contact or interview (to recruit or encourage someone to do something) is often secondary.

The process of assessment in community organizing also differs substantially from micro practice. In both agency and community settings, individuals may request assistance or a referral with a personal issue or challenge. Both clinicians and community organizers generally try to determine what the individual wants; identify personal assets and strengths that can be used to address the individual's challenges; and examine how existing social networks, services, institutions, or systems contribute to the issue or can be used to alleviate it (Miley et al., 2017). Consequently, it may be appropriate to use eco-maps, social network mapping, or asset assessment tools when working in the community. Clinical mental health or deficit-based assessments are not used in community practice. In some circumstances, however, social workers engaged in organizing as a component of generalist practice may be called upon to make referrals or provide assistance to people in distress or who are at risk of harm to themselves or others. Providing this type of assistance contributes to trust, rapport, and relationship building, and, in addition, may address barriers to community members' ability to participate in the change effort.

In community organizing, assessment is most often used to determine strengths, assets, or needs of the community as a whole. This generally requires some type of formal research. It is important to note that this is often conducted using research methods that allow for the participation of community members in the assessment process (Homan, 2016). The degree of community involvement in the assessment may vary depending on the scope and goals of the change effort, but partnering with community members in the research design holds great benefit for both building community capacity and achieving meaningful research outcomes (Brown & Stalker, 2021).

In addition to assessment, organizers also need to pay attention to professional boundaries, although in most situations these boundaries are decidedly differently than those that apply in the typical relationship between client and worker in micro practice (Brown, 2020). Cummins and colleagues (2006) identify several ways in which professional relationships in social work practice differ from friendships. Friendships are characterized by trust, shared interests, similar values, similar levels of disclosure, and reciprocity. Participants in a friendship determine how much power is held by each individual. Fees are not charged for participation. Conversely, in professional relationships between clients and social workers, participants have different interests, the values of the social worker are determined by the National Association of Social Workers (NASW; 2021) *Code of Ethics*, clients are expected to disclose information, and the relationship is not reciprocal. The social worker has a position of authority and often holds some degree of power over the client.

Using this set of criteria, the relationship between the social worker as a community organizer and the community member or constituent falls somewhere between a professional relationship and a friendship. The purpose of one-on-one interviews and other recruitment techniques is to develop relationships with individuals that are characterized by trust, reciprocity, and shared values and interests. Organizers are not paid a fee directly by constituents, unless the organizer is an employee of an organizations run by members of the constituency group. The organizer also does not hold authority over the constituent, and if the constituent engages in the change effort, the power becomes shared.

Professional boundaries in community practice may be difficult to set and maintain, and may vary based on the specific organizing task, the role of the constituent, and the work-related responsibilities of the community practitioner. However, the social networks the community organizer establishes and the relationships they build with community members are necessary in order to achieve professional goals (Brown, 2020). For example, giving a constituent a ride to an event or attending a birthday party in the home of a constituent would be entirely appropriate in community practice, but engaging in these same activities with a client for whom you are providing therapy would not. Personal relationships between constituents and organizers may evolve into friendships over time, but may be problematic in situations in which the organizer is asking the constituent to participate in protests or other activities that may result in loss of employment, social stigma, or physical harm. Seek supervision or consult with peers about appropriate boundary settings in community practice (Hardina, 2004).

USING TECHNOLOGY AND SOCIAL MEDIA TO ENGAGE COMMUNITIES

Technology, and particularly social media, can be helpful tools the community practitioner can use to help build relationships and interest around a community change effort. Technological literacy has become increasingly viewed as a critical component of micro and macro social work practice (Boddy & Dominelli, 2017; NASW et al., 2017; Sitter & Curnew, 2016; Teixeira, 2018). Technological resources can be used by the community organizer to manage contact information, document participation activities, and communicate with constituents to convey change-effort progress and communicate about upcoming activities and opportunities to get involved in the change process (Brown & Dinecola, 2020). Technology can be used to host virtual meetings and informational webinars by the organizer to increase conversation around an issue for constituents and partner allies who have access to phones, tablets, and other electronic devices when meeting in person is not an ideal option. However, the community organizer must be aware of digital equity issues (e.g., lack of access to technology devices and lack of familiarity with technology tools) and provide alternatives for participation when needed (Brown & Dinecola, 2020).

Social media can be used to attract new constituents and partner allies to a community change effort. Organizers can post information about upcoming events, raise questions to spark discussion through posts, and feature stories of success from the field using video and pictures. Social media can also be an effective tool for engaging younger constituents. Social media has been found to have potential in positively connecting people, including fostering empathy, compassion, and understanding among groups (Barak et al., 2008; Brown & Dustman, 2019). An organizer can strategically engage constituents and partner allies through social media.

Brown and Dustman's (2019) model for using social media to mobilize communities, Community Mobilization through Social Media (CMSM), describes one such approach (Figure 2.1). In the CMSM, the organizer identifies a social media facilitator, a social media messenger, an active community documenter, and an intercultural communications specialist. Depending on the resources available for the project, these roles can be held by paid agency staff, residents, and community partners, or unpaid volunteers. Together, these roles ensure that optimal community engagement and the community characteristics of diversity, culture, and language are considered, promote dialogue and interaction with and among constituents, and present interesting written and visual content that includes not only what is happening and how to get involved, but also how and why it is happening—providing the meaning of the message.

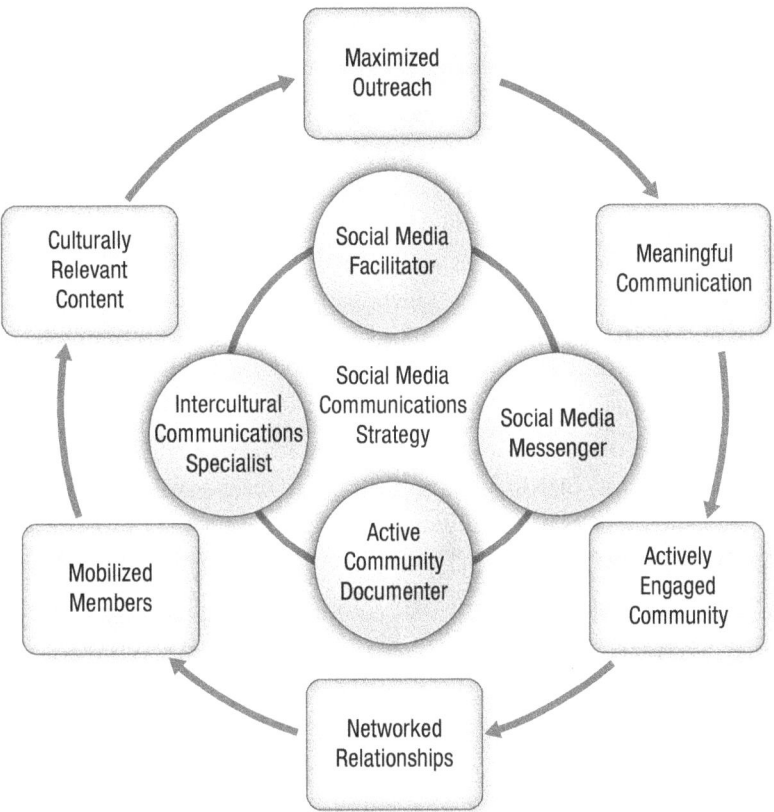

FIGURE 2.1 Community Mobilization through Social Media model.

SOURCE: Brown, M. E., & Dustman, P. A. (2019). Identifying a project's greatest "hits": Meaningful use of Facebook in an underserved community's development and mobilisation effort. Copyright © 2019 GAPS, reprinted by permission of Informa UK Limited, trading as Taylor & Francis Group, www.tandfonline.com on behalf of GAPS.

CASE VIGNETTE: DECREASING THE DIGITAL DIVIDE IN COMMUNITY ENGAGEMENT

When the COVID-19 pandemic disrupted a years-long neighborhood organizing effort led by social workers in partnership with a public housing community, and meeting in person was no longer deemed safe, organizers had to think creatively about keeping the community members engaged and motivated to carry the effort forward. The public housing community was composed of a majority of residents who were considered highy susceptible to the detrimental impacts of COVID-19—older adults and people with physical and mental disabilities. These new barriers to engagement threatened to derail the significant progress made through the organizing effort, and the priorities of the change effort were forced to shift to focus to the emerging community needs of personal health, safety, and the effects of social isolation. First, the organizers worked with resident leaders and community partners to ensure health, safety, and social isolation needs were addressed—including providing personal protective equipment and basic household cleaning supplies, launching a food and supply pantry and weekly food deliveries, and establishing a warm helpline and engaging volunteers in making social calls and wellness checks to combat social isolation. These steps allowed the organizers to maintain and be responsive to the relationships that had been built prior to the pandemic, and to build new relationships with residents who had not previously been engaged. Once critical basic needs were met, the organizers began to think creatively about engaging the community, recognizing that many of these residents did not have access to computers, tablets, or smartphones. The Thrive in the 05 project in Tucson, Arizona, launched a webinar called the *Resource Café* with the purpose of providing information to residents about services available to them from a wide array of partners during the pandemic. The webinar was conducted interview style and streamed live on social media. But recognizing the digital divide and technology limitations of many residents, the organizers arranged for a toll-free call-in number to be available for residents who were only able to join by phone, and spread the word using a weekly newsletter delivered to their doors. Further, the organizers worked with community partners to help secure tablets for interested residents, and provided training and technical assistance through the warm helpline, and later on site when it was safe to engage in person, to help promote digital literacy for residents who needed this assistance.

PUTTING VALUES INTO ACTION: CULTURAL COMPETENCE AND CULTURAL HUMILITY

Cultural competency in community practice entails many of the techniques for entry into the community, interviewing, and recruitment already described in this chapter. In learning the "story" of the community and about community residents, the community organizer should observe, listen, and build trusting relationships with people from all segments of the community, paying special attention to the cultural norms, customs, and practices of people who are not members of the dominant culture and who may be marginalized by the larger society due to factors such as ageism, ableism, racism, classism, anti-immigrant biases, adultism, sexism, and heterosexism. Cultural competence is a lifelong commitment to learning and increasing your knowledge and practice to raise awareness and consciousness of cultural norms, customs, and the practices of the communities with which you work through respect, recognition, and humility. There is no textbook or resource that can teach you everything you need to know pertaining to the culture of any specific group, and there is no process to certify a "culturally competent" practitioner. Even within communities with a shared cultural identity there exist differences in values, norms, and customs. As a community practitioner, you commit to do the best you can to practice ethically and from a lens of cultural competence, and as you learn better, you commit to doing better.

Cultural humility involves recognizing that we are not experts, but lifelong students of cultural competence committed to continuously challenging our own values, lens, and biases, and to learning from the true experts: those within the communities we serve. Skills that enhance cultural competency include self-awareness of one's own values and biases; developing knowledge about the cultural or marginalized group values, beliefs, and traditions; an understanding of historical forces and the group's status in society and how this affects their acquisition of resources; creating cross-cultural opportunities to bring diverse groups together to take action; and techniques that ensure that members of constituency groups play a primary role and hold power in community-organizing efforts.

Self-Awareness

Self-awareness is an important part of cultural competency. Organizers must be aware of their own cultural identity, how this identification affects their relationships with individuals and members of other cultural and demographic groups, their knowledge about other cultural or marginalized groups, and any biases—unconscious or conscious—they might have about others (Miley et al., 2017). Organizers also need to assess their own experiences and skills for working cross-culturally. Organizers should be aware of their own status in society, for example, whether they have experienced discrimination or are relatively privileged vis-à-vis other groups in society (Pewewardy, 2004).

One component of cultural competency is the commitment on the part of social work professionals, including organizers, to advocate for the equal distribution of resources in society and against policies and practices that discriminate or disadvantage members of marginalized or minoritized groups (NASW, 2015). Therefore, organizers should be aware of their own beliefs about what constitutes a just world and the degree to which they will engage in advocacy to remedy these injustices (Mondros & Wilson, 1994; Van Voorhis & Hostetter, 2006). Are all social groups deserving of equal access to jobs, education, healthcare, and human, political and civil rights?

Getting to Know the Cultural Community: Values, Beliefs, and Traditions

Many of the skills identified earlier in this chapter are those needed to promote cultural competence for community organizers. For example, Green (1999) identified a number of methods for "getting to know" a cultural group that are consistent with the steps described earlier in this chapter for community entry, including collecting background information about the cultural group and statistical data about the demographic composition of the community, observing members of the community, learning about leadership patterns and the way the group solves problems, and reliance on community guides. Ungar and colleagues (2004) describe community guides as "a member of the group being served, whose skills and relationship in the community is valued because of [their] social position" (p. 551). The guide can be a community gatekeeper, formal or informal leader, or simply someone knowledgeable about customs, language, and beliefs within specific cultural groups.

Organizers can also learn about the community by conducting ethnographic interviews to document cultural beliefs, values, and practices (Lum, 2011). To examine events to understand the perspectives of individuals and the personal meanings related to cultural behaviors and experiences, the focus of ethnographic interviews is on first-hand encounters through individual interviews (Marshall et al., 2022). Among the benefits of these interviews is that they provide a context for understanding the perspectives and opinions of individuals based on the shared experiences and values of the cultural group. They also serve as a reminder that there can be differences in language, values, beliefs, and social status among members of the same or similar cultural or ethnic groups (Lum, 2011).

According to J. Clark (2000), ethnographic interviews differ from the types of interviews typically conducted in micro practice by shifting the focus from understanding the individual to "a process of caring inquiry into the lived experiences of the other and a process of dialogically creating shared understanding of the cultural and conceptual meaning that shape that experience" (p. 9). J. Clark also identifies a number of principles that should be integrated into the interviewing process, including the organizer's role as a *learner* rather than an *expert*, a focus on the use of language and the meanings associated with it, an emphasis on understanding the context of the experience or situation described by the interviewee, and efforts to understand the interviewee's social status and self-perception of privilege or oppression.

Ethnographic interviews are open ended and make extensive use of probes and other questions used to clarify meaning of terms and concepts used by the respondent (Rubin & Rubin, 2012). Respondents might be asked to describe situations or sequences of events and give detailed explanations of cultural practices and experiences. Interviewers may repeat key words and phrases used by the respondent to ensure that the information collected represents the interviewee's own words and perceptions (J. Clark, 2000).

Components of the ethnographic approach can be easily integrated into one-on-one interviews. For example, Axner (2010) provides the following guidelines for organizers interested in learning about other cultures:

- Put yourself in situations where you will meet people from other cultures.
- Examine your biases about people from other cultures.
- Ask people questions about their cultures, customs, and views.
- Listen to people tell their stories.
- Notice differences in communication styles and values; do not assume that the majority's way is the right way (Axner, 2010, p. 4).

Gaining Trust and Conveying Respect

Engagement and relationship building are especially difficult among members of marginalized and minoritized communities because members have reasons to fear public officials and social service workers. For example, Kryda and Compton (2009) conducted qualitative research with people experiencing long-term houselessness to find out why they remained on the street rather than seeking shelter. Participants indicated that they mistrusted the outreach workers who were assigned to assist them because they often stereotyped people who were houseless, were not empathetic, and seldom took the time to build relationships with the people they were there to help. Interviewees indicated they were more likely to trust outreach workers who had been previously without a house themselves because they could understand the experience of being houseless. In a similar study, Pyles and Cross (2008) examined whether civic engagement and activism among Black/African Americans in New Orleans after Hurricane Katrina was sufficient to lift members of the Black/African American community out of poverty in the aftermath of this devastating event. Their findings suggest that even though civic engagement increased, the success of these groups was limited because many Black/African American participants mistrusted other community groups and institutions due to the historical context of segregation and employment discrimination in New Orleans and the slow government response to the disaster.

Organizers build trust with community members through finding out about community values and customs and conveying respect for community members. At a minimal level, one way of showing respect is for community-based organizations to incorporate culturally appropriate food and celebrations into their activities (Kahn, 1991). Organizers should also participate in customs and ceremonies if invited into the homes of community members or to cultural events. For example, if members of a Chinese family remove their shoes at the door of their home, the organizer should do so as well. If the organizer is not fluent in language, making an effort to offer a few words of greeting in the community member's language might help bridge cultural differences.

Hiring Members of the Cultural Community

In order to address issues of mistrust and fear; many organizations hire organizers or recruit volunteer leaders who are from demographic or cultural groups that share a cultural identity with members of the communities or cultural groups they serve (G. Delgado, 1997). For example, community health workers (CHWs) are community members who offer a bridge to close the gap among medical mistrust, health literacy, health access, and positive health outcomes in minoritized communities. The CHW section of the American Public Health Association (APHA; 2021) developed the following definition of a CHW (including Promotoras/es de Salud, Community Health Representatives, and other related titles), which has been adopted by APHA and the National Association of Community Health Workers:

> *A community health worker is a frontline public health worker who is a trusted member of and/or has an unusually close understanding of the community served. This trusting relationship enables the worker to serve as a liaison/link/intermediary between health/social services and the community to facilitate access to services and improve the quality and cultural competence of service delivery. A community health worker also builds individual and community capacity by increasing health knowledge and self-sufficiency through a range of activities such as outreach, community education, informal counseling, social support and advocacy. (para. 2–3)*

In Latinx communities, CHWs are described as health navigators, advisors, peer health promoters, and *promotoras*. *Promotoras* are closely connected to their communities and culture, and as such uniquely situated to understand the health literacy and service gaps, barriers to service utilization, and sociocultural contexts (Wilkinson-Lee et al., 2018). In American Indian communities, CHWs are referred to as *community health representatives*. CHWs can be essential partners for community organizers in connecting with and mobilizing communities for social change that is culturally meaningful and responsive.

Another approach for promoting the cultural appropriateness of community services involves the use of *cultural brokers*. Montana and colleagues (2010) define *cultural brokers* as advocates who are able to mediate between people of different cultural groups or backgrounds to reduce conflict. Montana and colleagues (2010) conducted a study to examine the effectiveness of Black/African American brokers who served as community representatives and advocates in the team decision-making process in a child welfare agency. Team decision-making is an approach that gives a place at the table to both family members and community representatives when parental rights are at risk of termination (Annie E. Casey Foundation, 2002). The researchers found that the cultural broker approach increased support for the families as well as communication and trust between the families and child welfare staff.

Skills for Promoting the Empowerment of Marginalized and Minoritized Communities

In addition to employing organizers who are members of the same cultural or ethnic groups, community organizers working with communities of color and other marginalized or minoritized groups should have a specific set of skills that will help them understand the effects of social stigmatization, isolation, or the lack of economic and political power (Miley et al., 2017). According to Bankhead and Erlich (2005), organizers should seek out opportunities to obtain:

- knowledge of customs, values, and social networks;
- knowledge of the community's language and the use of slang;
- historical knowledge about the community and prior organizing efforts;
- an understanding of political power and economic arrangements in the community;
- knowledge about the groups of people who are likely to be included or excluded from decision-making in community-based organizations, social networks, and cultural groups; and
- an understanding of community psychology, including the ability to assess community cohesion, the degree to which the community is hopeful that things can change, and whether there is a common problem or issue that community members can be organized to address.

This framework can be applied to any cultural, ethnic, or marginalized group. For example, applying the skills identified by Bankhead and Erlich (2005), an organizer working with the Hmong community should at minimum learn about customs and practices, learn appropriate methods to convey respect and trustworthiness to community members, take the initiative to learn about Hmong history and the development of Hmong communities outside of Southeast Asia, and be knowledgeable about the role of Hmong clan leaders in making decisions for community members (Moua, 2001). They should also be aware that until recently, Hmong women were largely excluded from participation in community decision-making, but that gender roles have been subject to change due to assimilation (Yoshihama & Carr, 2002). Organizers should also examine the research literature that indicates that members of the Hmong community in the United States have often been the targets of interpersonal and economic discrimination (Hein, 2000).

Cross-Cultural Organizing

Most organizers work cross-culturally or with a variety of different individuals or groups (Gutierrez et al., 2005). By virtue of factors such as age, physical/mental abilities, income, gender identity, religion, sexual orientation, ethnicity, race, or immigration status, some demographic groups may be relatively privileged members of society, whereas others are minoritized and disadvantaged. Therefore, it is critical that an organizer, prior to entry into a community, have some degree of insight into the relative positions of different groups in a neighborhood or how membership in a specific identity group affects community members. According to Axner (2010), these skills require active learning on the part of the organizer working cross-culturally about the community they serve, even if they make mistakes when applying cultural knowledge; organizers should also be active partners and allies with community members in social change activities.

In addition to these skills, there are a number of models of community practice that focus explicitly on cross-cultural organizing or efforts to create strong coalitions or alliances among members of diverse groups. The National Community Development Institute has developed a model for cross-cultural work that emphasizes relationship building and engagement. They recommend that organizations recruit community leaders, coordinate leadership development programs, build strong cross-cultural relationships and social networks, and engage in participatory research to document community issues and evaluate interventions. They also focus on the importance of "telling the community's story from the residents' perspective" (Satterwhite & Teng, 2007, p. 27). Some practitioners also advocate the use of study circles and intergroup dialogue to bring diverse people together and create opportunities for mutual learning about culture, minimizing differences among groups, and engaging in social change advocacy around common issues or challenges (Daley, 2007; Goodkind, 2006; Gutierrez et al., 2005).

Box 2.2

APPLYING VALUES TO COMMUNITY PRACTICE: UNDERSTANDING CULTURAL AND SOCIAL DIVERSITY, POWER, AND OPPRESSION

For Cultural Competency in Community Practice:

- Develop self-awareness about your own position in society and issues of privilege and/or marginalization vis-à-vis other individuals and groups.
- Gain entry to the community by showing respect for diverse individuals and groups.
- Conduct one-on-one interviews and ethnographic interviews with diverse individuals in the community.
- Use cultural guides to get to know the community; attend events and participate in cultural activities.
- Develop an understanding about how members of the culture or the community experience privilege or oppression.
- Identify community leaders, gatekeepers, and networks.
- Develop knowledge about the groups or leaders (inside the community and externally) who have the power to make decisions for the community.
- Establish reciprocal, working relationships with community members, leaders, and organizations.
- Involve community or cultural group members in all aspects of conducting action campaigns, including problem identification, assessment, intervention planning, implementation, and evaluation.

Transparency, Partnership, and Inclusion

It should be noted that hiring staff from the community served, promoting cultural understanding, and understanding the historical context of oppression in marginalized and minoritized communities are important, but probably not sufficient in themselves to address social inequities. It is also critical that members of these communities have a primary role in decisions that affect their lives (Wu & Martinez, 2006). For example, Young Laing (2009) argues that community organizing in ethnic, cultural, marginalized, or minoritized communities is only culturally sufficient when it is oriented toward the development of culturally specific organizing models and increases the capacity of community members to challenge the political and economic structures that oppresses them.

The principle of shared expertise makes it imperative that community organizers structure the change effort in a way that promotes participation and power sharing, if not control, of the decision-making process among members of the community (Brown & Stalker, 2021). According to Kahn (1991), organizations only achieve a high degree of cultural competency when there is equity in how resources are allocated, how they are run, and how leaders are chosen. Empowering organizations also develop decision-making processes, such as boards of directors and advisory boards, that reserve seats for community members (Hardina et al., 2006). One of the primary assumptions of this book is that constituents in community organizations should have primary roles in running organizations, identifying community problems and assets, conducting assessments, planning organizing campaigns, taking action, and evaluating the effects of these actions (Box 2.2).

END-OF-CHAPTER RESOURCES

KEY TAKEAWAYS AND SUMMARY

In this chapter, the role of interpersonal engagement and dialogue with prospective constituents has been described. Specific techniques used by organizers to explore community readiness for a change effort and conduct preliminary assessments about what happens in the community were examined, including observational studies and one-on-one interviews. The utilization of specific micro/macro practice skills, such as open-ended interviews, the use of probes, recognition and validation of strengths, and reflective empathy, is critical for the development of relationships between the organizer and community members. In addition to finding out about how a community functions, the organizer also needs to gain an understanding of the cultural identity of community members and norms, traditions, and behaviors that are characteristic of and important to members of ethnic, minoritized, and other marginalized groups that identify themselves as members of nongeographic communities.

RESOURCES

- Setting boundaries and practicing self-care as a community practitioner—see Brown, M. E. (2020). *Hazards of our helping profession: A practical self-care model for community practice.* https://academic.oup.com/sw/article-abstract/65/1/38/5673358
- National Association of Social Workers. (2015). *Standards and indicators for cultural competence in social work practice.* https://www.socialworkers.org/LinkClick.aspx?fileticket=PonPTDE Brn4%3D
- National Association of Social Workers. (2017). *Ethical principles for using technology.* https://www.socialworkers.org/includes/newIncludes/homepage/PRA-BRO-33617.TechStandards_FINAL_POSTING.pdf
- Samuels, J., Schudrich, W., & Altschul, D. (2008). *Tool kit for modifying evidence-based practices to increase cultural competence.* https://www.calmhsa.org/wp-content/uploads/2013/10/ToolkitEBP.pdf

- University at Buffalo School of Social Work (Host). (2008, December 15). Dr. Hilary Weaver, "Culturally Competent Supervision" (No. 9) [Audio podcast episode]. In *inSocialWork*. https://www.insocialwork.org/episode-9-dr-hilary-weaver-culturally-competent-supervision/
  - This episode features Dr. Hilary Weaver speaking at the Fourth International Interdisciplinary Conference on Clinical Supervision, convened in Buffalo, NY, spring 2008. Dr. Weaver discusses diversity issues in the context of supervision, highlighting the Transactional Model of Identity and the critical role supervisors have in promoting, modeling, and developing cultural competence within human service organizations.

ACTIVITIES

1. Use this scenario to answer the following questions:
   Five social work students, four males and one female, decide that they want to learn more about people who are experiencing houselessness. During Christmas break, they plan to spend 1 week living "outside" in a houseless encampment consisting of about 100 people who reside in tents and small huts composed of discarded lumber. Some of the people who live in this encampment are displaced families; others seem to experience mental health and substance abuse illnesses.
   (a) Do the students have a good plan for getting to know the people who live in this community? Why or why not?
   (b) What things should they take into consideration before putting this plan into operation?
   (c) What individuals or groups should they talk to before implementing their plan?
2. Review the sample one-on-one interview in this chapter. Identify the characteristics of a typical one-on-one interview that were evident in this example.
   (a) What elements associated with a one-on-one interview were not included in this transcript?
   (b) What micro practice-related interviewing techniques were used in the interview?
   (c) What strengths, or assets, did Mx. Jackson possess that could be used in the organizing process?
   (d) What elements of this interview made it a success?
   (e) What do you think would have happened if the respondent had not also experienced the identified problem or was not interested in becoming involved in the organizing effort?

ASSIGNMENTS

1. Conduct a one-on-one interview with one of your classmates about an issue of concern related to the social work program or the university (the interview does not need to include a specific request for action). The interview should focus on the student's experience in the program or at the university. Within this context, you should be able to discuss things that the interviewer and the interviewee have in common.

You should also obtain information about actions that could potentially be taken to improve or strengthen the program or university. Write a one-page summary describing the interview and your findings. Bring your written paper to class and compare your findings to those obtained by your classmates. Do students seem to share common problems? Do the findings suggest that an action is needed to address these problems?

2. Conduct a one-on-one interview using an ethnographic approach. Interview someone who is not a personal friend, relative, or business associate who is culturally different from you. Ask the respondent to describe an event or situation that has changed their life. Be sure to probe for customs, beliefs, values, and the cultural meanings associated with their perceptions and experiences. Write a brief paper that describes what you have learned from the interview, and how it will inform your future practice with other members who share a similar cultural identity with your respondent. Submit a copy of your interview notes or transcript and identify those aspects of the interviewer's questions and comments that are concurrent with the characteristics of one-on-one and typical social work interviews.

 A robust set of instructor resources designed to supplement this text is located at http://connect.springerpub.com/content/book/978-0-8261-5835-2. Qualifying instructors may request access by emailing textbook@springerpub.com.

KEY REFERENCES

Only key references appear in the print edition. The full reference list appears in the digital product on Springer Publishing Connect: connect.springerpub.com/content/book/978-0-8261-5835-2/part/part01/chapter/ch02

Brown, M. E., & Stalker, K. C. (2021). Assess connect transform in our neighborhood: A framework for engaging community partners in CBPR research designs. *Action Research Journal, 19,* 372–392. https://doi.org/10.1177/1476750318789484

Delgado, M., & Staples, L. (2008). *Youth-led organizing: Theory and action.* Oxford University Press.

Pewewardy, N. (2004). The political is personal: The essential obligation of white feminist family therapists to deconstruct white privilege. *Journal of Feminist Family Therapy, 16,* 53–67. https://doi.org/10.1300/J086v16n01_05

Sitter, K., & Curnew, A. (2016). The application of social media in social work community practice. *Journal of Social Work Education, 35,* 271–283. https://doi.org/10.1080/02615479.2015.1131257

Staples, L. (2016). *Roots to power: A manual for grassroots organizing* (3rd ed.). Praeger.

Teixeira, S. (2018). Qualitative geographic information systems (GIS): An untapped research approach for social work. *Qualitative Social Work, 17,* 9–23. https://doi.org/10.1177/1473325016655203

Ungar, M., Manuel, S., Mealy, S., Thomas, G., & Campbell, C. (2004). A study of community guides: Lessons for professionals practicing with and in communities. *Social Work, 49,* 550–561. https://www.jstor.org/stable/23720828

Wilkinson-Lee, A. M., Armenta, A. M., Nuño, V. L., Moore-Monroy, M., Hopkins, A., & Garcia, F. A. R. (2018). Engaging promotora-led community-based participatory research: An introduction to a crossover design focusing on reproductive and mental health needs of a Latina community. *Journal of Latina/o Psychology, 6*(4), 291–303. https://doi.org/10.1037/lat0000119

Wilson, J., Abram, F., & Anderson, J. (2010). Exploring a feminist-based empowerment model of communitybuilding. *Qualitative Social Work, 9,* 519–535. https://doi.org/10.1177/1473325009354227

Young Laing, B. (2009). A critique of Rothman's and other standard community organizing models: Toward developing a culturally proficient community organizing framework. *Community Development, 40,* 20–36. https://doi.org/10.1080/15575330902918931

RECRUITING POTENTIAL PARTICIPANTS

LEARNING OBJECTIVES

After reading this chapter, students will be able to:
- Illustrate the application of volunteer recruitment strategies to community practice.
- Describe how collective identity development applies to volunteer recruitment, engagement, and retention.
- Identify social work skills that are relevant for volunteer recruitment, engagement, and retention.
- Distinguish among different types of recruitment efforts.

INTRODUCTION

Once a community organizer learns about and gains access to a community, the organizer must begin to recruit participants for the community-organizing process. Engagement and relationship skills are essential for successful recruiting. In later stages of the organizing process, the organizer will work in partnership with participants to identify community challenges and issues, conduct assessments of community challenges and determine the strengths and resources possessed by community members, set goals, plan an organizing campaign, engage in action, and evaluate what has been accomplished. In the first section of this chapter, a general overview of the use of engagement and relationship-building skills for recruitment in nontraditional settings is presented. In the second section, theories related to the motivation of volunteers and community activists are identified. In the third section of the chapter, specific techniques for recruitment are addressed, including the distribution of flyers, tabling at events, use of phone banks, text messaging, house meetings, street outreach, using the media, word of mouth, and utilizing social media are described. In the final section of this chapter, techniques for fostering individual commitments to social justice are described.

RECRUITING VOLUNTEERS AND PARTICIPANTS: APPLYING ENGAGEMENT AND RELATIONSHIP-BUILDING SKILLS IN NONTRADITIONAL SETTINGS

Community organizing is often dependent on volunteer labor (Livermore et al., 2020). Recruitment of potential constituents occurs at all stages of the organizing process. However, applying the principles of self-determination and empowerment means that participants and potential beneficiaries should play a lead role in choosing the issue to be addressed and planning an intervention strategy. In order to have a group of people involved in leading this process, participants should be recruited during the early stages of the organizing campaign. In some instances, the community may already have identified an issue to address and has invited the organizer or community organization to assist. However, no matter who initiates the organizing process, volunteer recruitment and maintenance are ongoing challenges that need to be addressed by organizers (Staples, 2016).

Recruitment involves one-on-one meetings as well as large group events. Oftentimes, the organization plans an event or participates in an activity sponsored by another community-based organization such as a street fair, potluck, formal banquet, or cultural celebration (Kahn, 1991; National Latino Council on Alcohol and Tobacco Prevention, n.d.). Events should be used to bring diverse people together and provide an opportunity for people to have fun and acquire information about the sponsoring organization and volunteer opportunities. In many instances, people can be asked to make a commitment to participate during or at the conclusion of an event. However, additional recruitment activities may be needed to encourage people to actually attend or to follow up with anyone who may have indicated an interest in volunteering at the event (Kahn, 1991).

It is essential that community organizers use culturally appropriate methods of recruitment and relationship building; it is essential to take note of interpersonal cues such as making eye contact, personal use of space vis-à-vis others, or whether it is appropriate to call someone by their first name; these are cultural norms that must be understood and respected (Brown, 2006). In addition, the particular outreach method used should match the target constituency group (Sen, 2003). For example, door-knocking would be most appropriate when recruiting people from a particular geographic area, whereas recruitment for prospective union members would be more likely to be effective if it took place outside the workplace.

Specific recruitment activities can include the distribution of flyers; knocking on doors; house meetings (e.g., living room conversations involving small groups of people in a neighborhood); setting up an information table at an event; talking to groups at community events and meetings; using television, print, and social media; and just "hanging out" at places where people are likely to congregate (Delgado & Staples, 2008; Sen, 2003). These recruitment opportunities may provide a venue for conducting a one-on-one interview; however, one-on-ones may stop short of actually asking people to participate in an activity. As described in Chapter 2, the purpose of recruitment is to get people to actually do something: for example, attend a meeting, sign a petition, or participate in a protest. This requires specific techniques for motivating potential participants to volunteer for an activity or make a commitment to a cause (Castelloe & Prokopy, 2001).

ENGAGING, MOTIVATING, AND APPRECIATING VOLUNTEERS AND CONSTITUENTS

One essential ingredient of any successful recruitment effort is finding a way to motivate potential participants. Assessment of motivation to act is therefore as important in macro social work practice as in micro practice. A basic assumption of organizing practice is that people are motivated to act out of self-interest; they will participate in an organizing campaign that will benefit them, their families, or communities (Ohmer & DeMasi, 2009).

Delgado and Staples (2008) describe self-interest in terms of several criteria identified by Saul Alinsky (1971): "the issue must be immediate enough for people to care deeply, specific enough for them to grasp, and winnable or realistic enough for them to take the time to get involved" (p. 135). One technique commonly used to keep people motivated in community organizing is to take on a small project that is an "easy win"—for example, pressuring the city to clean a vacant lot. Once a victory is achieved, participants are motivated to tackle a much more difficult project (Bobo et al., 2010).

In addition, we know from the literature on more traditional types of volunteerism in civic and social service agencies that people are also motivated to participate by the opportunity to make new friends, socialize, develop new skills, and make employment-related contacts (Handy & Greenspan, 2008). Volunteering provides an opportunity for individuals to gain recognition from others; they may feel obligated to participate when asked or they may be motivated by a sense of social responsibility or a chance to influence programs or policies (Verba et al., 1995). Participation in community organizing or political campaigns can also be motivated by empathy for others. Appeals to morality, religious values, or a commitment to social justice also can motivate people to take action (Alinsky, 1971; Bobo et al., 2010; Haski-Leventhal & Cnaan, 2009).

Such pure or altruistic motives are not the only reason that people want to participate in social change activities. Volunteerism can also be related to the need for a sense of belonging to a group or establishing a personal bond with members of the group or people who intend to join it. Research on why people become activists has documented the strong impact of social ties among participants in protests or broad-based social movements; people are more likely to participate if asked by someone they know well and if they have the time and resources to do so (Lim, 2010; Somma, 2009). Further, research has shown that civic engagement has a positive impact on individual and community well-being (Livermore et al., 2020; Oesterle et al., 2004; Putnam, 2000). According to Haski-Leventhal and Cnaan (2009), "carrying out pro-social volunteer tasks in the presence of one's group provides strong internal rewards and incentives for persistence" (p. 66). Although relationship building and group participation are important for many volunteers, they may be particularly salient for recruiting women, who often structure work and personal lives around their friends, neighbors, and families (Ramirez-Valles, 2001; Saegert, 2006; Smock, 2004; Vaiou & Lykogianni, 2006). Women volunteers often seek out support networks in response to adversity and can often be engaged in organizing out of a desire to improve community conditions to benefit their children and people with whom they share similar circumstances.

People may also be motivated through identification with a particular minoritized or marginalized group or by experiencing issues they have in common with others (Giguere & Lalande, 2010). The term *collective identity* refers to whether people identify themselves as members of specific communities or subgroups located outside the general population, for example as a member of the LGBTQIA+ community, a person with a disability, or a resident of a geographic area. Collective identity also pertains to the degree to which people feel emotionally attached or committed to the community; an individual's attachment to the community often determines whether people will participate in group or collective action such as a protest or membership in a community organization (Little, 2010). One example of how a sense of collective identity affects individual commitment to a cause can be found in research conducted by Martinez (2008). Martinez interviewed Latinx activists who participated in the immigrants' rights movement that emerged in the United States in 2006. Findings indicate that "many Latinos found themselves either directly or indirectly targeted by anti-immigrant and anti-Latino sentiments. Still others began to empathize with immigrants' plight and what they considered unnecessarily harsh attitudes, discrimination, and attacks by extremist groups" (p. 560). In another example, the 2020 COVID-19 pandemic contributed to the rapid rise of anti-Asian racism in the United States, leading to a call to action for social workers and to unite Asian American communities to rise up against anti-Asian racial discrimination (Choi, 2020; Gao & Liu, 2021; Starks, 2021).

A concept related to collective identity, *sense of community*, also plays a role in whether a person volunteers with a community organization. Peterson and colleagues (2008) define a sense of community as "feelings that members have of belonging, of significance to one another and to groups, and as shared fate that members' needs will be met through their relationships" (p. 799). People who have a strong sense of community and commitment to neighbors or other groups with which they identify will be more likely to engage in community change efforts. Another factor that can determine whether people volunteer for a social change activity involves the degree to which individuals have a sense of personal self-efficacy (Little, 2010). *Efficacy* is the belief in oneself and pertains to whether individuals perceive themselves as able to perform a specific task, apply a certain skill, or influence others. Efficacy is one component of personal empowerment (Gutierrez et al., 1998). People are more likely to be involved in community change efforts when they feel that they have the ability to influence what happens in their community, have a high degree of a sense of community, are hopeful that things can change, and perceive that other members of the community will engage in the change effort (Brown & Baker, 2019; Foster-Fishman et al., 2009).

Unlike micro social work practice, assessment of motivation to volunteer or engage in activism in community practice does not generally rely on standardized assessment forms or psychological indicators, although researchers have used measures of personal control and self-efficacy when examining the effectiveness of social change activities (e.g., Itzhaky & York, 2002). Organizers can assess motivation through one-on-one interviews, relationship building with participants, experience (lessons learned on what works, what does not work), and feedback from constituents. Castelloe and Prokopy (2001) offer the following guidelines for operating successful recruitment campaigns:

- Use existing helping, support, or service networks (either formal or informal) to find new members. It is often helpful to ask community leaders or gatekeepers to utilize their own networks of friends, neighbors, relatives, church, or business connections to recruit volunteers.
- Develop the organizing campaign's message so that it reflects the interests and needs of community residents and delivers the message in a manner that is appropriate for the community. For example, in some immigrant communities it may be inappropriate to invite strangers into one's home; recruiting a community leader to contact residents might be more appropriate.
- Be aware that there can be both benefits and costs related to participation in an organizing campaign. For example, volunteers may need to pay for day care or

transportation. The community organization that sponsors the project can seek funding to provide babysitting or transportation assistance or set up a system of exchanges among participants to provide these services (Parker & Betz, 1996).

ADDITIONAL TECHNIQUES AND TECHNOLOGIES FOR RECRUITMENT

There are numerous methods that can be used to recruit people for social change efforts. Recruitment involves conveying a specific message to people about why their participation is important (Pyles, 2009). It may involve distributing information to people working with social networks and community groups; coordinating living-room conversations or house meetings among neighbors; conducting street outreach; and disseminating information using the media, word of mouth, and social media. Although other innovative methods can also be used to recruit, one essential element of the process is that people are asked to do something or to contribute to the organization or change effort (Schultz, 2003). Consequently, this engagement and relationship-building activity supplements and compliments the primary goals of a basic one-on-one interview, getting to know the community, and identifying community issues.

Distributing Information: Flyers and Tabling

Some one-on-one interviews are conducted by simply knocking on doors or walking around neighborhoods. However, in addition to these methods, organizers may be called upon to use other methods to recruit. Most of these activities require some form of engagement and relationship building. They may be asked to design flyers or digital images with information about the organization, the specific issue to be addressed, a time and place during which an event will be held, and contact information (Work Group for Community Health and Development, 2010).

Posters and flyers should be put in prominent places in the community, including businesses, churches, schools, and public facilities such as post offices. Distributing flyers and posters is actually an excellent "test" of engagement skills. For example, if you are asking a business or group to distribute flyers for you, you must obtain permission to leave the flyers at that location. You may need to verify who you are and your purpose before permission is granted. If you are distributing flyers at an event or on a street corner, you will want to hand the flyer to people passing by. Often individuals do not want to accept flyers from a stranger and they will quickly walk by; some people will have a legitimate fear that they will be asked to do something unpleasant or participate in a political activity that runs counter to their beliefs. Consequently, distributing a flyer requires a degree of confidence, the ability to read body language to assess whether people will be willing to accept a flyer or chat for a few minutes, and possession of the type of interpersonal skills that will permit the organizer to quickly establish a relationship with people who do accept the flyer and want to know more (Kahn, 1991).

Often there will be local events that include provisions to have groups available to inform the public about what they do. Sometimes organizers will seek out these events explicitly for recruitment purposes. Most often, each group will be assigned a table or a booth that can be used to distribute information (Work Group for Community Health and Development,

2010). Organizers and members of the constituency group will "staff" the table or booth, distributing flyers and other informational materials. Most literature tables also include a sign-up sheet for potential volunteers or people who have requested more information about the organization or campaign.

The interpersonal skills challenge that is encountered during tabling is how to attract people to your booth. Do you just sit there? What happens if no one comes over to talk to you? There are a number of techniques you can use to sell your organization. Of course, posters and banners help, but you also need to have things that interest people—perhaps you distribute candy or buttons and t-shirts with action campaign messages or slogans or offer people a chance to participate in a raffle. Staffing the table with local celebrities also helps (Work Group for Community Health and Development, 2010). But engagement is also the key; be prepared to answer questions, encourage people to tell their stories, and provide information and contacts. Tabling often provides an excellent opportunity to conduct one-on-one interviews.

Contacting People: Phone Calls and Texting

The same challenges apply to making contact with people by phone. Often people do not respond well to phone solicitations. Calls tend to be made during hours when people are having dinner or relaxing. People may have had bad experiences with phone solicitors. Many for-profit organizations make obtrusive sales calls and charitable organizations and political campaigns may call repeatedly. The challenge for an organizer making a recruitment call is to establish legitimacy quickly (within a few seconds) and explain the purpose of the call.

Many organizations will develop a script for recruitment calls, but the caller is free to improvise some of the content, depending on the recipient's response (Center for Progressive Leadership, n.d.). Calls are most effective when there is actual dialogue and relationship building between both parties in the call. In addition, some calls will be made from a "phone bank," a room with a set of phones that volunteers and staff can use to make multiple calls. The group nature of this process and the opportunity to socialize with other callers makes a task that some people find unpleasant, more tolerable.

Calls should be brief and the organizer should be ready to disengage when told that the individual does not want or is unable to talk. Unless the organizer is a real "people person," making "cold" calls to strangers is often difficult or unpleasant (Sen, 2003). Respondents may be uncommunicative, rude, or hang up on the caller. In some circumstances, volunteers may be recruited to help with these calls or asked explicitly to contact people they know with the expectation that they may have an easier time making such calls and obtaining a commitment from the prospective recruit.

Another challenge associated with making these calls is that organizations often fail to track who has actually received the call. If the respondent indicates that they have already received one or more calls from the organization or already signed up to volunteer, the organizer should quickly apologize. Even with these difficulties, it is possible for an organizer to establish a relationship with a prospective volunteer and conduct a one-on-one meeting on the phone. In some situations, the person contacted may simply look at the call as an opportunity to chat, share information, or have someone listen to their opinions and ideas

(Center for Progressive Leadership, n.d.). Often a chat, rather than reading from a script, is more likely to result in the acquisition of a volunteer.

Despite the potential for relationship building over the phone, there are some disadvantages of this recruitment method. In addition to the fact that some people will be annoyed and potentially "turned off" to the message when they receive more than one call from the same source, it also may be difficult to obtain phone numbers for potential volunteers. Some numbers may be obtained through the use of sign-up sheets at events, referrals from other volunteers, or lists from other organizations. However, privacy concerns often limit the sharing of personal information, including phone numbers and email addresses, among different organizations and groups. In addition, unless personal cell phones are used, operating phone banks requires a great deal of time and resources. Phone lines or prepaid cell phones are required. Skilled staff or volunteers are needed to supervise the phone bank.

Community organizations as well as political campaigns also send text messages to both recruit and mobilize volunteers to take action. Texting has several advantages, including the fact that one text message can be sent to groups of people at a time. In addition, sending texts may be a good way of reaching and motivating young people, who may be more receptive to a text message than a phone call (Delgado & Staples, 2008). In addition, this method is impersonal. A volunteer who may be unwilling to make a phone call to a stranger may be more than willing to send text messages to unknown persons. However, these advantages can also be disadvantages. To send a large number of text messages, organizations may need to hire a mobile messaging vendor to send "blasts" on a regular basis (Rock the Vote, 2008). In addition, the impersonal nature of a text message may limit its effectiveness as a recruiting tool. Good database management systems are required to keep track of the people who have received messages or phone calls and whether these volunteers have volunteered to participate in specific activities (Delany, 2009). The creation of these information systems is often labor intensive, requiring that volunteer contact information, including phone numbers and email addresses if available, be documented on standardized forms and that information is added to a computerized database system. Also, volunteers or paid staff must be able to make follow-up phone calls or send reminders about commitments to the new recruits (Rock the Vote, 2008).

House Meetings and Living-Room Conversations

Holding house meetings is one of the methods used to recruit new volunteers. House meetings are generally held in the home of a volunteer and involve a small number of people who have been identified as potential volunteers or people who may be interested in a specific issue that is affecting members of the community. The Virginia Organizing Project (VOP; n.d.) describes house meetings in the following way:

> *Because house meetings are small gatherings, they provide an opportunity for people to listen to each other, ask questions, share ideas and become informed. In the process, people can discuss ways to get involved in the organization that are best suited to their personal skills and interests. A successful housing meeting will inspire guests to hold their own housing meetings and help your organization grow. (p. 2)*

House meetings are often an effective way to recruit because the resident is generally the person responsible for coordinating the meeting and for inviting people one knows personally to the meeting. Consequently, existing social networks or work-related contacts are used (Schultz, 2003). People can be invited to a house meeting specifically to meet with the organizer, constituent-leader, or an expert on an issue of concern. Most of this type of recruiting operates through existing social networks. Many potential constituents are likely to be members of more than one group and can consequently serve as a link between groups and organizations.

House meetings are generally scheduled by an organizer or an interested volunteer who invites people to a meeting in someone's home to learn more about an issue. They are also organized in such a manner that they provide guests with an opportunity to socialize and have fun (Delgado & Staples, 2008). House meetings often involve sharing coffee, food, or information. Participants may also be invited to watch a video that will inform them about a particular issue (Upper Arlington Progressive Action, n.d.). In addition, they may provide an opportunity to hear from a guest speaker or a political candidate and they often serve as a prelude to asking potential recruits to make a commitment to the cause that involves time, money, or resources. House meetings are essentially an opportunity to establish dialogue with a group of potential recruits, share stories and common challenges, and to begin the problem-solving process (VOP, n.d.).

Street Outreach

Street outreach methods are typically used to reach people who are isolated or unattached to preexisting social networks or formal organizations (Hardcastle et al., 2004). Recruitment efforts may be targeted to naturally occurring groups such as preteens who congregate at local basketball courts or people patronizing the corner grocery store, bar, or beauty shop (Farrell et al., 1995; Kahn, 1991). In many neighborhoods, businesses or open spaces may serve as a gathering place for different demographic or cultural groups. For example, Delgado (1996) describes the importance of small grocery stores or bodegas in Puerto Rican communities in the United States in providing information, credit, and support. To recruit members of informal or naturally occurring groups, previous contact with leaders or community guides may be the key to gaining access. As noted in Chapter 2, street outreach may be most effective when conducted by someone who is of the same identity or community or who has had similar life experience as the people that the organizer is trying to reach (Kryda & Compton, 2009; National Council on Crime and Delinquency, 2009).

It should be noted that the term *street outreach* includes three different types of activities: linking members of socially stigmatized groups with social services (National Council on Crime and Delinquency, 2009), recruiting people for participation in research studies (Clark, 2010), and identifying and recruiting potential volunteers for participation in organizing campaigns (Corrigall-Brown et al., 2009). The third method, participation in an organizing effort, is the activity most often identified with community practice, primarily because of the potential for constituent empowerment through the involvement in community and organizational decision-making and participating in social change activities

(Delgado & Staples, 2008). However, research participation and social service delivery are also potentially empowerment-promoting situations in which constituents are involved in planning or other types of decision-making for research studies or service interventions (Wang, 2006). Research studies often serve as preludes to involving people in social change activities or developing service interventions that are culturally competent and more likely to be used by the intended beneficiaries (Silvestre et al., 2010). The other similarity among the three methods is that they all require that staff or volunteers have the skills necessary to create strong, trusting relationships with the people they try to recruit.

Research conducted with street outreach workers who work with houseless populations provides a helpful overview of the skills needed for the work. Through in-depth interviews with 12 street outreach workers, the following skills emerged as most essential to street outreach: a nonjudgmental approach to engagement, crisis-management skills, persistence, and goal and boundary setting (Lee & Donaldson, 2018). Outreach workers should also be able to establish strong relationships. It is also important that street outreach methods be culturally appropriate for reaching the target population (Schultz, 2003). For example, Silvestre and colleagues (2006) describe outreach methods for recruiting gay men of color who have sex with men for participation in a research study. A variety of approaches were used to reach members of the community and establish trust, including the establishment of advisory boards composed of diverse members to help with the creation of the recruitment plan, creating recruitment plans specific to the geographic location of each of the study sites, locating the research clinics in places considered to be safe and confidential, and hiring culturally competent staff that included gay men of color.

Using the Media

Media coverage of your organizing campaign also is an important tool for recruiting new members. Organizers generally work to develop a list of potential media contacts that they can use to publicize their organization (Schultz, 2003). Although it may not appear that this activity involves interpersonal skills, relationship building is critical for garnering publicity for your cause. Reporters and television and radio producers often seek out representatives of community-based organizations for comments on news items or information. They also look for good stories. Therefore, it is possible to establish exchange-oriented relationships with media sources (Hardcastle et al., 2004). It is legitimate to offer information or to even develop or frame the story from your organization's perspective. You also should be prepared to refer reporters and producers to additional contacts and information sources (Homan, 2016). Constituents who have experienced the challenge or issue that your organization is addressing or who will benefit from a change in a specific law or policy should be encouraged to speak to the media.

Organizers also seek out opportunities to initiate contact with reporters when they have "breaking news" or when they are seeking public support for an issue (Schultz, 2003). They send out press releases to all local media outlets to inform them about an issue and list contact information for members of the organization. Community-based organizations also hold press conferences in which the media can gather to listen to the contents of a press lease or a newly issued report and ask questions of organization members (Homan,

2016). Although press releases and press conferences are a good way to maximize media coverage, reporters are most likely to attend when they have an established relationship with the organizer and members of the constituency group or when they receive a follow-up call after the press release is distributed (Work Group for Community Health and Development, 2010).

Media coverage often results in television or radio interviews for the organizer and members of the constituency group. Members may also appear on talk shows to provide detailed information about issues (Hardcastle et al., 2004). Although some of these invitations may be issued in response to breaking news stories, it is also possible to use preexisting press contacts who know that members of your organization are available for interviews.

There are certain hazards involved in conducting media campaigns, however. Not all contacts will actually result in a story (Hardcastle et al., 2004). If printed, the story may not reflect your point of view on the subject. There are alternative means of coverage, however, including posting information and news stories related to your organization on independent media sites on the web, encouraging bloggers to report your organization's information, posting material on social media, or creating informational videos to post on YouTube (Goode, 2009; Sen, 2003). For many of these sources, contacting and establishing working relationships with reporters, editors, bloggers, and webmasters are also essential for obtaining coverage.

Word of Mouth

A recruitment method that is generally regarded as superior to all others is called *word of mouth*, or having information about your organization or campaign circulated by others. As discussed previously in this chapter, the purpose of contacting gatekeepers, service professionals such as doctors or teachers, organizations, and community leaders, is that they can spread the word about what you are doing in the community and give you legitimacy or a "seal of approval" so that others will talk to you (Schultz, 2003). If the people you have recruited indicate that they support your organization or that the events and activities sponsored by your organization are fun, informative, or involve successful action to address an issue, other potential recruits may seek you out on their own (Rubin & Rubin, 2008). Again, as with other forms of volunteer recruitment, much of the "action" takes place within social networks: People are most likely to provide information and encourage participation among friends, relatives, and neighbors.

Using Web Pages and Social Media

An attractive web page that indicates the organization's mission and a call to action can also help with recruitment. In addition, social media sites, such as Facebook and Twitter, have also been used successfully to recruit volunteers for social change activities and voter registration (Dreier, 2008). Community organizers can use social media to advertise community events, inform the community about the initiative, and present specific opportunities for community involvement. In some cases, volunteer engagement activities takes place via social media.

For instance, social media advocacy campaigns can be quite effective. Guo and Saxton (2014) summarize an advocacy organization's impact on the arrest of a war criminal:

In March 2012, Invisible Children, a San Diego-based nonprofit advocacy organization dedicated to bringing awareness to the activities of indicted Ugandan war criminal Joseph Kony, started an Internet video campaign called "Kony 2012." The goal was to make Kony internationally known in order that he be arrested by year's end. Within three days, the "Kony 2012" video quickly became one of the greatest viral successes in the short history of social media, drawing millions of viewers on YouTube. Within 3 weeks, it spurred action on Capitol Hill: Over a third of U.S. senators introduced a bipartisan resolution condemning Kony and his troops for "unconscionable crimes against humanity." (pp. 57–58)

As demonstrated by the success of the Kony 2012 campaign, social media allows for a wide range of individuals to participate in a social action initiative, and, in this case, to influence public policy in a very efficient and effective manner.

In a research study focused on how Facebook and blogs influence feminist movements, results indicated that feminist organizations used Facebook as a tool to advertise in-person events, to communicate with existing members, and to recruit new members (Crossley, 2015). This study also highlighted the utility of social media's facilitation of large and diverse friendship networks for the purpose of recruitment and mobilization (Crossley, 2015).

One example of using social networking technology for organizing involved a hunger strike held at the University of California (UC), Berkeley, in May, 2010 (Berton, 2010). A student group, Hunger for Justice, initiated action in order to demand university support for efforts to oppose anti-immigrant legislation adopted by the state of Arizona. The group also called for the UC Berkeley administration to drop charges against campus protestors arrested during demonstrations against student fee hikes and to rehire laid-off janitors. The action started with an email to the UC chancellor to which there was no response. To solicit additional support, the activists sent text messages and emails to students and the local media. They also opened a Facebook page and an account on Twitter. Within a week, the activists had acquired over 1,000 followers on Facebook and received a response (not entirely positive) from the university chancellor.

CASE VIGNETTE: CONNECTING RESIDENTS TO AGENCY CAUSES VIA FACEBOOK RESOURCE CAFÉS

Introduced in the second case vignette in Chapter 2, in 2020 the Thrive in the 05 team in Tucson, Arizona, was planning its semi-annual resource fair when the COVID-19 pandemic made in-person meetings unsafe. The Thrive in the 05 team shifted the resource fair to a "Resource Café" hosted via Facebook live. Through 30-minute interview-style videos, the Resource Café connected local residents with resources in the community, including updates on COVID-19 support and services. In addition to being an important resource for residents, the Resource Café also created a venue for volunteer recruitment. During some Resource Cafés, the Thrive in the 05 team discussed volunteer opportunities and successfully recruited volunteers. Check out some of Thrive in the 05's Resource Cafés on their website: www.thriveinthe05.com/resourcecafe

PUTTING VALUES INTO ACTION: FOSTERING INDIVIDUAL COMMITMENT TO SOCIAL JUSTICE

Much of what organizers know about recruiting people for participation in organizing campaigns is grounded in the scholarly literature on social movements (Castelloe & Prokopy, 2001). According to Snow and colleagues (2007), "social movements as a form of collective action, involve joint action in pursuit of a common objective. Joint action of any kind implies some degree of coordination, and thus organization" (p. 9). Consequently, recruitment campaigns need a structure and purpose. Klandermans (2007) identifies three reasons for participation in social movements: *instrumentality*, the use of individual participation to facilitate social and political change; *ideology*, a vehicle for finding meaning in life and expressing one's personal beliefs and emotions about specific situations; and *identity*, feelings of belonging to or personal identification with a group. Consequently, for recruitment to be effective, participants need a method or "frame" that can be used to ascribe meaning to the situation at hand and the social change desired, a sense of collective identity with the group taking action or for whom the action is taken, and a belief or sense of efficacy in their ability to affect change (Little, 2010). The role of the organizer is to facilitate the development, through interaction with volunteers and potential recruits, of a sense of collective identity through participation in groups and networks. The development of a sense of collective identity is facilitated through explicit efforts to overcome feelings of stigmatization and oppression among members of minoritized and marginalized groups. Additional techniques that can lead to empowering experiences for community members and that forge a group identity are efforts to integrate group and cultural values into the organizing campaign and to foster a sense of hope that the organizing effort will succeed (Box 3.1).

Developing Frames

Recruiting people for participation in social change activities requires both an appeal to self-interest and a call to action based on a sense of social justice, values, and morality. Saul Alinsky (1971) in *Rules for Radicals* described one of many important tactics for community organizers: "The eleventh rule of the ethics of means and ends is that goals must be phrased in general terms like 'Liberty, Equality, Fraternity,' 'Of the Common Welfare,' 'Pursuit of Happiness,' or 'Bread and Peace'" (p. 45). The use of these values in recruiting people for social activism is called *framing*. Frames are conceptual outlines used to describe challenges or issues. According to Gillian (2008), "frames relate to people's basic beliefs and attitudes; they offer direction since they are inherently action-focused, and they allow actors [participants] to understand their own position relative to others" (p. 248). Frames are often generated through interpersonal transactions as individuals struggle to place meaning on their experiences in relation to social, political, and economic institutions and discuss these experiences with others. According to Snow (2007), the theories of social constructionism and symbolic interactionism can be applied to the study of how social movements frame issues that have salience to their members, opponents, and the general public.

> **Box 3.1**

PUTTING VALUES INTO ACTION: FOSTERING INDIVIDUAL COMMITMENT TO SOCIAL JUSTICE

- Create succinct messages about challenges or issues that frame issues in ways that are consistent with the perspectives and experiences of people who you are trying to reach.
- Provide a rationale for why the issue must be addressed that includes factual evidence and other important information.
- Appeal to individual self-interest *and* social values, morality, and social justice.
- Help foster a sense of collective identity among potential supporters that facilitates feelings of group solidarity and personal empowerment.
- Use a variety of techniques, including events, flyers, house meetings, street outreach, the media, one-on-one interviews, phone calls, emails, text messages, word of mouth, and social networking technology, to reach potential recruits.
- Make sure that recruitment techniques and the message associated with the organizing campaign are culturally appropriate and that frames and symbols are used to bring people together.
- Ask the potential participant to participate in a specific action.
- Use existing social networks to "expand the circle" of contacts, resources, and potential recruits.
- Make sure that participant skills are utilized and that participants are recognized and celebrated for their accomplishments.

Community organizers use frames to recruit people around specific causes and look for ways to portray causes in a manner that has meaning for prospective participants and that can evoke strong feelings (Pyles, 2009). They also provide an opportunity to change public perceptions shaped by the dominant culture and create a means for looking at these issues that represent the perspectives of people who have been affected by the issue. Frames also appeal to an individual's sense of morality, values, and social justice or are consistent with the person's past experiences, especially those that are perceived as unfair or unjust. According to Ganz (2007), a sense of morality is often critical in motivating potential participants:

> *One of the key lessons of the social movements of the past—of the left and of the right—is that their power grew out of the moral energy of their people (not just their organizers), their readiness to take risk, and their resourcefulness—all of which was rooted in turn, not in "self-interest" in any obvious sense, but in the values at stake. (p. 1)*

Frames are used to recruit new members, raise funds, and inform the public about a problem or issue and may involve invoking moral shocks or using visual images or symbols to illustrate potential consequences associated with social policies or practices (Harris, 2010; Mika, 2006). For example, People for the Ethical Treatment of Animals (PETA) has been effective in creating ad campaigns that illustrate the harsh or abusive treatment of animals and fostering a sense of human identification with the plight of the animals (Atkins-Sayre, 2010).

Frames also can be used strategically to gain public support for a cause and involve a variety of different groups with different perspectives in the organizing campaign, especially when the message is used to put people inside the experiences of others (Gillian, 2008). For example, in June 2010, the American Civil Liberties Union (ACLU) implemented a national campaign against an Arizona law that required local police to check the immigration status of anyone they suspected of being "illegal" during any law enforcement-related encounter. Fearful that only people of Latino ancestry would be questioned by police, ACLU affiliate organizations in a number of states issued travel "advisories," warning people that they were in danger of racial profiling and arrest if they visited Arizona. One of the purposes of the advisory was to advise the people likely to be affected of their legal rights and to inform the general public about the potential impact of these policies (Associated Press, 2010).

Facilitating the Development of Collective Identity

One factor in the decision to become a community activist is whether individuals feel as if they belong to or are attached to the community or cause. As noted earlier in this chapter, this attribute is often referred to as *collective identity* or *sense of community* (Snow, 2001). Bandura (1990) defines individual perceptions of personal self-efficacy as:

> *People's beliefs that they can exert control over their motivation and behavior and over their social environment. People's beliefs about their capabilities affect what they choose to do, how much effort they mobilize, how long they will persevere in the face of difficulties, whether they engage in self-debilitating or self-encouraging thought patterns, and the amount of stress and depression they experience in taxing situations. (p. 9)*

As applied to community practice, Pecukonis and Wenocur (1994) define *collective efficacy* as "a shared perception, be it conscious or unspoken, that members of a collective hold about the group's ability to achieve its reform objectives in the face of opposition" (p. 13). Membership in preexisting groups or social networks, perceptions that members of the group are oppressed or stigmatized, the use of group and cultural symbols to foster feelings of inclusion in the group, and the perception of group members that the action will be successful are factors contributing to collective efficacy among participants in social change.

Group and Network Membership

Feelings associated with collective identity can originate in membership with a specific demographic group (e.g., gender identity, age, ethnicity, race, sexual orientation, income, culture, or physical/mental disabilities), experiences in common with other community members (such as welfare receipt or surviving a disaster), facing a common adversary, or experiencing social stigma (Taylor & Van Dyke, 2007). For example, bad treatment from a landlord who has refused to make repairs in an apartment complex may foster a sense of collective identity among the tenants. Similarly, discrimination experienced by new immigrants may bring people with a variety of ethnic backgrounds together to develop strategies in support of immigration reform (Daley, 2007).

Membership in a social network often can be used to facilitate recruitment for social change efforts. According to Della Porta and Diani (2020), people will be more likely to participate in social change activities if they are recruited through social networks. Recruitment through networks not only expands the number of people likely to participate, but also ensures that people with similar values and perspectives are involved in the process (Polletta & Jasper, 2001). This, in turn, also contributes to feelings of belonging to the group and a sense of solidarity among members. However, one disadvantage of using this method exclusively is that it is often necessary in community practice to reach out to people with different experiences, values, and perspectives in order to garner public support for the organizing effort. People who are neutral or opposed to the social change initiative must be persuaded to change their positions, requiring that potential new networks of people must be identified and brought into the organizing process.

An empowerment perspective can be helpful when working with groups toward collective action. Breton (2017) describes the concept of *consciousness raising* as a necessary component of empowerment. According to Breton (2017), consciousness raising involves the process by which groups of individuals with shared identity become aware of

- interconnections between issues and how personal issues are linked to interpersonal, political, social, economic, and cultural issues; and
- how these interconnections relate to the distribution of power.

Oftentimes, consciousness raising begins with individuals coming together and sharing their personal experiences and identifying commonalities among their experiences. These shared experiences are then analyzed as they relate to social, political, and economic structures (i.e., moving from the personal to the political). The process of consciousness raising in a group setting is a powerful process that increases group self-efficacy and sets the stage for collective action.

For example, Little (2010) describes methods used by a Center for Independent Living to facilitate the process of collective identity development and activism among people with disabilities:

Staff members also worked to establish group boundaries between those identified as disabled and the non-disabled, or between the "challenging group" and the "dominant group".... The effort included expressions of commonality among individuals with varied impairment and disability experiences. Part of the creation of "us" involved a shift in attribution for hardships experienced. Difficulties that had been ascribed to fate or tragedy were redefined as caused by social barriers and attitudes. (para. 29)

As part of the identity-development process, staff members also encouraged consumers to engage in self-advocacy, which, in turn, fostered self-esteem, self-acceptance, and feelings of personal self-efficacy among constituent group members. The process that took place with the Center for Independent Living is a good example of consciousness raising: of how shared experiences led to an examination of how these experiences are situated within the social structure. This process sets the stage for a group to examine power inequities and take collective action.

Fostering Perceptions of Success

Anticipation of positive outcomes is often central in the decision to join a group or take action (Corrigall-Brown et al., 2009). According to Goodwin and colleagues (2007), "leaders often try to arouse in participants feelings of hope or optimism, a sense that they can have a positive, transformative effect through their collective action. Optimism is associated with a heightened sense of individual and collective efficacy" (p. 421). Often, community organization recruitment efforts deliberately adopt symbols that either convey a sense of hope or explicitly reference the belief that the group can facilitate change, for example, the use of the phrase "si se puede" by the United Farm Workers or the English translation of this phrase, used by the 2008 Obama presidential campaign, "yes, we can" (Shaw, 2008).

Collective efficacy is also fostered when the group has been effective in meeting its goals and when individuals are perceived by themselves or others as instrumental in helping the group to meet its goals (Foster-Fishman et al., 2006). Consequently, celebrating goal achievement and the recognition of individual volunteers and their contributions are critical in the development of collective efficacy (Kahn, 1991; Work Group for Community Health and Development, 2010). A number of research studies indicate that involvement in successful community change projects results in increased feelings of personal and collective self-efficacy among participants (Itzhaky & York, 2002; Ohmer, 2008; Zimmerman & Rappaport, 1988).

END-OF-CHAPTER RESOURCES

KEY TAKEAWAYS AND SUMMARY

Organizing efforts rely on the recruitment of as many volunteers as possible. Participants increase the number of people who can share the work, tap into their own social networks for resources and additional recruits, disseminate information, and increase the power of the organization through their strength in numbers. Organizers seek to motivate potential volunteers by appealing to personal self-interest and providing individuals with opportunities to meet others, apply skills, make professional contacts, address wrongs, and improve conditions for community members. Participation can also be motivated by appeals based on morality, social values, or a sense of social justice. Recruitment methods must be culturally appropriate not only in terms of ethnicity, but also in terms of social status or income, age, gender identity, sexual orientation, physical/mental disability, and other demographic variables.

RESOURCES

- Rehnborg, S. J., Bailey, W. L., Moore, M., & Sinatra, C. (2009). *Strategic volunteer engagement: A guide for nonprofit and public sector leaders.* RGK Center for Philanthropy and Community Service. https://www.volunteeralive.org/docs/Strategic%20Volunteer%20Engagement.pdf

ACTIVITIES

1. Volunteer to staff a literature table or booth at a community event. What strategies did you use to attract people to your table or booth? How hard or easy was it to encourage people to take literature or sign up for a volunteer opportunity, service, or event? Why? What social work skills were you able to apply in this outreach activity?
2. Create a flyer, write a blog or news article, design a web page, or create a Facebook page for a community event or recruitment effort. Make sure you provide all the necessary critical information about the event or campaign.

ASSIGNMENTS

1. Develop a volunteer management plan for an agency in which you volunteer, work, or are completing your field placement. Be sure to include agency expectations of volunteers, what volunteers can expect from the agency, and what training or development opportunities are available to volunteers, as well as relevant policies and procedures.
2. For an organization in which you are completing your social work internship or are employed or in which you volunteer, plan a recruitment campaign or event. Turn in a paper describing the purpose of the campaign or event, your goal(s), your target population, the message that you are trying to transmit, the staff members or volunteers involved in the campaign or event and the skills and/or other resources they possessed that were applied to the requirement effort, the specific recruitment method(s) used, and why the recruitment method used was appropriate for the target population. Also describe whether you were successful and any problems or barriers encountered during the recruitment process. How could your campaign or event be improved?

A robust set of instructor resources designed to supplement this text is located at http://connect.springerpub.com/content/book/978-0-8261-5835-2. Qualifying instructors may request access by emailing **textbook@springerpub.com**.

KEY REFERENCES

Only key references appear in the print edition. The full reference list appears in the digital product on Springer Publishing Connect: connect.springerpub.com/content/book/978-0-8261-5835-2/part/part01/chapter/ch03

Alinsky, S. (1971). *Rules for radicals*. Vintage.

Brown, M. E., & Baker. B. (2019). "People first": Factors that promote or inhibit community transformation. *Community Development, 50*, 297–314. https://doi.org/10.1080/15575330.2019.1597911

Clark, T. (2010). Gaining and maintaining access: Exploring the mechanisms that support and challenge the relationship between gatekeepers and researchers. *Qualitative Social Work, 10*, 485–502. https://doi.org/10.1177/1473325009358228

Crossley, A. D. (2015). Facebook feminism: Social media, blogs, and new technologies of contemporary U.S. feminists. *Mobilization: An International Quarterly, 20*, 253–268. https://doi.org/10.17813/1086-671x-20-2-253

Foster-Fishman, P., Pierce, S., & Van Egeren, L. (2009). Who participates and why: Building a process model of citizen participation. *Health Education Behavior, 36*, 550–569. https://doi.org/10.1177/1090198108317408

Guo, C., & Saxton, G. D. (2014). Tweeting social change: How social media are changing nonprofit advocacy. *Nonprofit and Voluntary Sector Quarterly, 43*, 57–79. https://doi.org/10.1177/0899764012471585

Lim, C. (2010). Mobilizing on the margin. How does interpersonal recruitment affect citizen participation in politics? *Social Science Research, 39*, 341–355. https://doi.org/10.1016/j.ssresearch.2009.05.005

Livermore, M., Brown, M. E., & Lim, Y. (2020). Worth beyond work? Civic engagement and social support provision of benefit recipients. *Journal of Poverty, 24*(4), 300–317. https://doi.org/10.1080/10875549.2019.1703128

Putnam, R. (2000). *Bowling alone: The collapse and revival of American community*. Simon & Schuster.

Starks, B. (2021). The double pandemic: Covid-19 and white supremacy. *Qualitative Social Work, 20*, 222–224. https://doi.org/10.1177/1473325020986011

DEVELOPING RELATIONSHIPS AND PARTNERSHIPS WITH GRASSROOTS AND FORMAL ORGANIZATIONS

LEARNING OBJECTIVES

After reading this chapter, students will be able to:

- Describe the major models of organizational partnership (i.e., task forces, collaboratives, coalitions, interfaith alliances, national organizations with local affiliates, and social movements).
- Recognize the ways in which technological tools can assist community practitioners in facilitating and maintaining partnerships.
- Identify the interpersonal skills needed to facilitate collaboration among organizational partnerships.
- Summarize the process of mutual learning and partnership among organizations.

INTRODUCTION

In addition to recruiting individuals for participation in community-organizing efforts, organizers also establish partnerships with other groups and organizations. As with individuals, existing networks of people and organizations are used to make contacts and identify potential supporters and resources. Organizations provide access to other potential recruits and they can also provide resources such as facilities, information, staff support, and funding. In this chapter, theories that explain why it may be advantageous for organizations to establish partnerships with one another and the challenges often encountered when building intergroup alliances are described. Several types of structures that facilitate organizational partnerships are identified: task forces, collaboratives, coalitions, interfaith alliances, national organizations with local affiliates, and social movements. In addition, specific interpersonal skills needed for partnership building are examined, including building trust, bargaining and negotiating, developing consensus, and resource and power sharing. In the last section of the chapter, specific steps for applying the principles of mutual learning and partnership when building alliances and partnerships are described.

THE PURPOSE OF ORGANIZATIONAL PARTNERSHIPS IN COMMUNITY PRACTICE

Most community organizations seek organizational partners for social change efforts. In community development, the organizing effort is dependent on having wide representation from a variety of groups with different perspectives involved in the process (Ohmer & DeMasi, 2009). Social planners also seek to consult with diverse groups for plan development; some planning efforts may require collaboration among members, such as applying for grants or acquiring the resources needed to operate a new program or organization (Forester, 2001). In social action, successful organizing requires that as many people and organizations as possible are involved in efforts to influence or pressure decision makers to adopt a plan or pass legislation. Pressure tactics are much more successful when as many people as possible contact their legislators, attend community forums to question elected officials, or participate in protests (Staples, 2016).

Organizations can be defined as entities that engage in a set of predetermined activities arranged by and carried out by two or more people (Lohmann & Lohmann, 2002). Some of the organizations with which organizers work are relatively informal groups or gatherings of individuals with similar interests and goals such as neighborhood watch groups or friends who have started a community garden. It may not be at all clear as to whether specific individuals are affiliated with or belong to these informal groups (Chaskin, 2003; Putnam, 2000). However, formal organizations have established structures, designated decision makers, and may be legally incorporated as nonprofit or for-profit organizations or work under a government mandate, and often employ paid staff and contain clear boundaries that determine who is included in the organization (Austin, 2002). Consequently, partnerships with these organizations can be subject to legal constraints (such as contractual agreements for services offered or funder requirements); financial and legal negotiations require that the organization designate a staff person or volunteer who can enter into formal agreements with collaborative partners, board members, or elected officials. Due to the number of parties involved, the establishment of formal partnerships is often a complex and time-consuming process (Gazley, 2010).

In formal organizations and groups, recruitment of organizational partners often takes place when a gatekeeper or another previously recruited participant refers the organizer to the group. Many of the organizational techniques described in Chapter 3 can also be used in recruiting organizations; strong relationship ties are needed between the organizer and representatives of the organization (Alter, 2000). The opinions and perspectives of organizational partners should be solicited to gain insight into community issues and to develop a consensus about solutions (Emshoff et al., 2007). Existing networks of organizations should be tapped to provide additional recruits and efforts should be made via meetings and planned activities to stimulate group solidarity (Staples, 2016). In addition, any recruitment drives, organizing campaigns, or service delivery partnerships should frame community issues and potential solutions for social problems in a culturally competent manner that incorporates the values of community members, the primary missions of organizational members, and beliefs about fairness and justice (Cross & Friesen, 2005; McBeath & Briggs, 2008).

MODELS OF ORGANIZATION PARTNERSHIPS: ESTABLISHING A COMMON AGENDA AND COMMUNICATION

Theories and perspectives about how community-based organizations operate focus on both their internal and external functioning. Internally, organizational culture can be viewed as originating in the mission, structure, and interpersonal relations among managers, staff, board members, and clientele (Netting & O'Connor, 2003). However, what happens in the organization is highly associated with what happens outside the organization in terms of funding availability, laws and social policies, and public recognition and regard for the organization. An organization's relationship, or the lack thereof, with other organizations dealing with the same issues or challenges can determine whether the organization can keep its doors open, the effectiveness of its services or advocacy efforts, and its political influence (Iglehart & Becerra, 2011). Consequently, organizations form partnerships with one another to increase their capacity to address community problems. Halseth and Ryser (2007) define *partnerships* as relationships among two or more organizations in which there is an explicit agreement to work together in order to benefit all members. Ideally, all members of the partnership share responsibility for making decisions, managing the activities undertaken by the group, and sharing any risks that might be encountered.

Types of organizational alliances typically found in community-organization practice include, but are not limited to, task forces, collaboratives, coalitions, interfaith alliances, national organizations with local affiliates, and social movements. In many cases, an organization may participate in a number of these types of alliances. For example, the Faith in Action network (formerly the Pacific Institute for Community Organizing [PICO National Network]) is a national network with local affiliates and has participated in local, state, and national coalition groups and social movements (Wood, 2007).

Task Forces

Task forces are temporary structures established to address a community issue, need, or social problem that must be resolved within a short time span (Speer & Zippay, 2005). Members are generally representatives of organizations that serve a specific population group or community. However, individuals with technical expertise related to that issue or people who have experienced the problem firsthand may be included as well. Task forces may initially be informal, but if the target issue cannot be adequately addressed by existing organizations or service agencies, the task group may evolve into a collaborative effort among several organizations or an independent organization designed specifically to address the issue identified by the task group (Hardcastle et al., 2004). Task forces have some advantages that formal organizations may not. They can be flexible in structure, bringing together a diverse group of people with new ideas and a variety of skills, and may allow for the pooling of resources among different public, nonprofit, and for-profit organizations serving different populations or communities with different missions and goals. They also can be used to identify gaps in services and to address systemic issues in communities and institutions that cannot be easily addressed by one organization alone (Hooker et al., 2008). Task forces can engage in legislative advocacy or develop innovative programs or campaigns that will publicize issues, develop public support, and generate new resources to resolve problems. Task forces can also be used to quickly address new or emerging community issues for which there are limited knowledge, resources, and expertise available to develop solutions. For example, tasks forces were created in the early 2000s in Minnesota and California to address the sexual exploitation of teen runaways and an adolescent suicide epidemic in Hmong communities in both states. Both of these issues were related to the immigrant experience, but few service resources had been developed that were appropriate for the Hmong population (Hardina et al., 2008; Saewyc et al., 2007).

Similar to other types of organization partnerships, task forces can have a number of disadvantages as well. It can be difficult to reach an agreement about issue identification and goals among a diverse group of people. The time-limited nature of the task force can make this approach ineffective for addressing complex problems that require long-term changes in a variety of organizations or social policies (Saewyc et al., 2007). In addition, partners may be willing to work together, but unwilling to share their own resources, especially money and skilled staff members, on initiatives that involve risks or substantial investments of time. The issue of "protecting one's turf" rather than working collaboratively on an intractable issue often limits the success of many task force efforts, collaborations, and coalitions (Alter, 2000).

Collaboratives

Nonprofit and public organizations often establish collaborative partnerships in order to deliver services, plan programs, or engage in a specific type of joint activity (Nowell, 2009). Collaborative partnerships are often referred to as *service delivery networks* and involve complex systems of exchanges and resource sharing among multiple organizations. The use of the word *collaboration* implies that the various partners have developed a process of mutual exchange or sharing of resources and that these organizations can work together harmoniously to accomplish a task (Hardina et al., 2006). Although some community organizations do not deliver direct services to individual clients or families, they may be recruited for participation in a collaborative service partnership when the goal of the collaborative is to conduct outreach to minoritized and marginalized populations, make improvements in community services, or reform existing service delivery systems (Emshoff et al., 2007).

In some cases, organizations come together because a funding source mandates such an alliance as a condition of a grant or contract (Ivery, 2008). In other cases, organization participants serving a specific community or population group establish a partnership structure out of self-interest such as acquiring new clientele constituents, obtaining funding and other resources, or cutting costs (Halseth & Ryser, 2007). The motivation for establishing collaborative partnerships can also involve correcting gaps in service availability or adapting to changing conditions (such as funding cuts, technical innovations, or new clients or constituents with complex needs that might require different types of services or initiatives). Collaborative members often vary in organizational affiliation (nonprofit, public, service clubs, or self-help groups), budget and staff size, and the amount of power and influence they hold in the community. Participation in partnerships and networks often helps organizations adapt to fiscal, technological, or political changes in the community or the larger political environment (Alter, 2000). For example, small organizations and organizations that have lost funding often seek to join collaboratives to survive financially (Iglehart & Becerra, 2011). Larger organizations may want to join collaboratives for similar reasons; small organizations serving hard-to-serve population groups or delivering unique or specialized services may have access to staffing resources or technology that the larger organizations may want to acquire (Graddy & Chen, 2006). Collaboration may also serve as a vehicle to coordinate services so that different organizations take responsibility for different tasks or to eliminate duplication of services to the same groups of clients (Gil de Gigaja, 2001).

Although resource sharing and expansion and improvements in service delivery are two of the benefits of collaborative arrangements, a number of limitations also exist. Provan and Milward (2001) argue that for collaborative partnerships to work effectively, they must be able to establish strong relationships among member organizations and agencies and institutions outside the network, absorb new organizations as others drop out, and provide the most essential services to the target population. Often, substantial resources are necessary for these conditions to be met. Competition for funds and resources among member organizations may make it difficult for cooperation to be achieved. Also problematic is that as with task forces, members come from diverse backgrounds and often have different agendas for what they want to accomplish through membership in the collaborative. In addition, organization representatives may vary in terms of education and professional status, which can result in different perspectives on issues and solutions, thus making consensus around organizational goals difficult (Mizrahi et al., 2009).

Coalitions

A *coalition* can be defined as a group established to take joint action to achieve a specific goal by combining resources, membership, and political influence (Roberts-DeGennaro & Mizrahi, 2005). Most coalitions that are established engage in social action to lobby government or to campaign for changes in policies or institutional structures (Rubin & Rubin, 2008). However, coalition groups can also be formed to participate in joint efforts to resolve community problems or to conduct informational campaigns to encourage service utilization or health prevention. In some cases, coalitions may have multiple goals. For example, Chutuape and colleagues (2010) describe the efforts of a health-oriented coalition to educate community members about AIDS prevention, develop additional service agencies and networks, and lobby for changes in laws and policies to support risk-prevention methods (such as laws legalizing needle exchanges).

Coalitions can also be formed to bring together similar groups with similar interests, engage organizations with similar goals but varying approaches or resources with which to address the issue, or to forge relationships among diverse groups that can be persuaded to lend support to a specific cause but for different reasons (Rubin & Rubin, 2008). The primary purpose of coalitions, however, is to increase strength through numbers, the more members in a coalition, the more likely members will be able to garner political influence by pooling resources, having participants contact political representatives, gain the attention of the media and general public, and mobilize members for participation in public protests.

Unlike other types of partnership models, coalition groups generally do not establish formal, centralized structures to provide operational support and make decisions for coalition members (Wells et al., 2008). Membership is held by organizations rather than individuals; these groups come together to plan organizing campaigns in response to pressing issues. Decisions may be made by a steering committee or leadership council that consists of representatives of member organizations. Organizations do not give up their autonomy when they join a coalition and may drop out or refuse to participate in initiatives with which they disagree. As a consequence, coalition membership is often temporary and fluid; organizations may only join forces when an issue of concern requires a quick response to a government policy, legislative initiative, or social problem. However, some coalition groups are fairly well established and take on some of the characteristics of more formal organizations in response to ongoing injustices such as poverty, threats to the environment, and discrimination.

Member organizations in coalitions provide monetary and staff support for the coalition and mobilize their constituents to take action (such as lobbying government officials or engaging in protests). As a result of the loose organization structures associated with most coalitions, one of the challenges often encountered is achieving consensus on an agreement among member organizations as to mission, goals, and the strategies and tactics used to address the issue or influence social change (Conway, 2003; Hardina & Obel-Jorgensen, 2011). Ideological similarities are often critical in establishing and maintaining partnerships among coalition members. However, ideological "purity" may be abandoned in instances in which organizations with different agendas are viewed as bringing critical resources into the partnership (Roberts-DeGennaro & Mizrahi, 2005). Cultural, gender identity, ethnic, and other demographic differences can also make it difficult to forge agreements among the various groups involved in the coalition (Pyles, 2013).

Interfaith Alliances

Interfaith alliances are partnerships among organizations serving specific communities in which the lead organizations are church congregations, but include other neighborhood groups and institutions (Posadas, 2008). Often referred to as *faith-based* or *church-based community organizations*, these local groups and networks also can be affiliated with national organizations (Warren, 2001). For example, several national organizing groups have local congregation-based affiliates such as Faith in Action, the Gamaliel Foundation, and the Industrial Areas Foundation (IAF). All these organizations work for social change by engaging in lobbying and social action at local, state, and national levels (Swarts, 2008b).

Many of these interfaith alliances use an organizing approach pioneered by Saul Alinsky (1971) in which local churches are contacted and recruited for participation in organizing efforts (Posadas, 2008). Once churches and their leaders are involved, individual members are then recruited for participation (Rubin & Rubin, 2008). According to Swarts (2008a), faith-based community organizations consist of up to 30 different congregation members and sometimes include additional organizations such as unions or schools. These organizations are typically incorporated as nonprofit organizations for tax purposes. In addition to coordinating their work with national community-organizing groups, many of these local interfaith alliances are also members of local, regional, or state coalitions that are actively involved in campaigns to alleviate poverty and discrimination. For example, in 2010, priorities for organizations in Faith in Action included healthcare reform and banking reform to help people affected by foreclosure (Faith in Action, 2022).

One primary rationale for the formation of faith-based organizing groups is that congregations serve as a place for contact and recruitment of large numbers of individual members. The context of what happens in these congregations is also important. In Chapter 3, the use of moral frameworks, such as social justice and inclusion to recruit new members for organizing efforts, was described. Given that churches focus on transmitting and maintaining good moral values, organizing campaigns often link faith-based morality to church teachings and beliefs (Cnaan et al., 2005). They also are a low- or no-cost source of a number of resources typically needed in organizing efforts such as highly motivated volunteers, donations and membership dues, meeting space, community kitchens, recreational facilities, and office equipment (Swarts, 2008b).

According to Warren (2001), characteristics of faith-based community organizations include a membership base that consists of congregations rather than individuals, using religious traditions to frame social problems and organize collective action to address those problems, emphasizing relationship building rather than simply concentrating on goals or issues, and multiculturalism and diversity. In addition, many faith-based community-organizing networks provide extensive training to members, hire professional organizing staff, and engage in social action organizing and protests that often involve confrontation with public officials. One of the interpersonal skills described earlier in this book, one-on-one interviews, is used extensively in faith-based organizing to identify community issues—and in-depth training is offered to the volunteers who conduct these interviews (Swarts, 2008b).

One limitation associated with church-based community organizations includes the difficulty inherent in forging consensus among members of individual congregations and then gaining agreement among a number of diverse congregations serving the same community (Swarts, 2008a). As in other types of alliances, gender identity, income, race, ethnicity, and religious or ideological differences can make it difficult to reach agreement on issue identification, goals, and the choice of strategies and tactics used. In addition, the neighborhood focus of church-based organizing may limit the power of local congregations when the issues addressed have their roots in state or national policies. One solution for this dilemma is to form coalitions with national, state, or regional organizations that are not part of faith networks and that have the resources and staff to lobby for changes in public policy (Wood, 2007).

National Organizations With Local Affiliates

Many national organizations oriented toward improving communities and fighting for social justice also work locally with state and local chapters to carry out an agenda developed by their board of directors. Sellsky (1998) defines *federations* as structures used to mobilize collective action around shared interests. Federations often address national or regional issues and can focus on single or multiple issues. The mission of federated community organizations is to increase their political influence by increasing membership and access to funding by linking with local affiliates. As with coalitions, an increase in organizational members provides access to more volunteers, individual donors, people with power and influence, and additional networks that can be used to recruit new members. According to Sellsky, a structure in which there is a lead organization with affiliates or chapters has several advantages:

> *They establish the ground rules and articulate the values that provide a basis for affiliates to work together. They develop an image of a shared desirable future, often with a longer-term perspective than their affiliates. Finally, they provide infrastructure support, such as administrative resources, information sharing mechanisms, and project management services. (p. 287)*

One of the largest, most well-known federated community organizations is the Association for Community Organizations for Reform Now (ACORN). Started in Arkansas in 1970, ACORN focused on issues critical to the financial well-being of members of low-income communities. By the time of its demise in 2010, ACORN had affiliates in 100 cities and more than 200,000 individual members (Dreier, 2009). Agenda items included living-wage campaigns, housing and mortgage reform, regulation of pay-day lenders and currency exchanges, welfare reform, and voter registration. ACORN, in partnership with numerous local, state, and national coalition groups and powerful unions, was able to influence policies on both local and national levels. Local members, despite being low-income, were required to pay dues to the organization, helping to maintain a good financial base for the national organization. Because of its political influence and the variety of services it offered to its members (such as tax preparation and welfare case advocacy), ACORN was also able to attract state and federal and, in some instances, corporate grants and contracts that helped them recruit new members and achieve their goals (Brooks, 2005; Brooks et al., 2006; Fisher et al., 2009). In addition, confrontation and other types of protest tactics as well as the ability to register and mobilize thousands of low-income, Black/African American and Latinx voters also gave ACORN a great deal of political influence. ACORN's power was also the source of its demise—both financial mismanagement and a coordinated campaign by conservatives in 2009 to paint local affiliates as staffed by corrupt employees resulted in the loss of government grants and public legitimacy (James, 2010). This forced the national organization to shut its doors in 2010.

Most federated community organizations remain quite influential at both the local and national levels. Federated organizations with local affiliates often vary in terms of the degree to which agenda setting includes mechanisms to involve chapter members in decision-making. Some federations place the primary responsibility for decision-making with the local affiliates. However, for this type of federation to succeed, there must be some type of process for reaching agreement among a variety of local groups that may have different priorities and agendas. As an alternative, many large federations place primary responsibility for agenda and goal setting with the national organization. One advantage of top-down centralized administrative management in national organizations is that decisions can be made quickly by the national board or executive director and do not require time-consuming negotiations within local organizations or among chapter members (Swarts, 2008a).

Social Movements

As described in Chapter 3, social movements are collective efforts to achieve social change. Individuals and organizations participate in social movements through membership in broad-based coalitions and national organizations; often social movements are made of complex interorganizational relationships among numerous organizations dedicated to the same cause (Mizrahi & Rosenthal, 2001). Social movements are effective when they have a large number of members who can pay membership fees and participate in social protests or lobbying efforts. According to Sen (2003), "movements emerge from a specific set of conditions—rising expectations among the disenfranchised, a backlash against the status quo, or demographic shifts—in addition to explicit organizing" (p. 22).

Obtaining resources is critical for the success of social movements. Resources often include individual donors, grants funded by foundations, media connections, and links to influential people and decision makers (Edwards & McCarthy, 2007). Although social movements have generally been viewed as a vehicle for members of minoritized, marginalized, or otherwise oppressed groups to improve access to resources and political or civil rights, social movements can also be formed to advocate on behalf of others or for improvements in economic or environmental issues. Movements can also be formed in opposition to war or to promote ethnic solidarity or religion (Snow, 2007). In some cases, social movements advocate for the interests of affluent members of society or those who feel that their social position or income has declined as a consequence of government actions or the acquisition of rights by previously unrepresented groups (DeFilippis et al., 2010).

Although local organizations are often formally affiliated with social movements around specific issues, they may also participate in more broad-based networks of formal and informal groups. In addition, larger, formal coalitions of local, statewide, or national organizations also participate in social movements and may partner with other coalitions or national advocacy groups to sustain social movements around one or a number of causes. For example, in 2010, Faith in Action worked with large coalitions to promote healthcare and immigration reform.

Although social movements are oriented toward promoting values or rights, activities to maintain or stabilize the movement are also essential (Smock, 2004). Not only do effective movements have designated or elected (by a vote of the membership) leaders, they must also have an ongoing source of financial support, and an organizational and decision-making structure with which to operate (Clemens & Minkhoff, 2007). A single organization does not and cannot represent an entire social movement—but multiple organizations that form partnerships with one another and join coalitions around single issues that advance the mission of a social movement strengthen the movement, help generate public support, and facilitate linkages with influential public figures, politicians, and donors.

INTERPERSONAL SKILLS FOR BRIDGING DIFFERENCES AMONG ORGANIZATIONAL PARTNERS

Although the literature on the use of coalitions, alliances, and collaboratives in community practice often describes well-functioning groups, most organizers have worked in collaborative groups characterized by conflict, mistrust, few active members, ineffective leaders, and poor or no outcomes. Even when collaborative partnerships have been successful, a great deal of skill and patience are often required to maintain an organizational structure in which participants can work together to achieve their goals (Mizrahi & Rosenthal, 2001). In this section of the chapter, several specific interpersonal skills that can be used by organizers to increase collaborative capacity are described, including establishing relationships among partners; building trust; bargaining and negotiating effective partnerships; using group-work skills to develop consensus about issues, goals, action, and evaluation criteria; and power and resource sharing.

Relationship Building

Much of the work of establishing partnerships involves building both formal and informal relationships among people and organizations. Hence, some aspects of the process are informal, in which friendships are developed or common interests, values, and experiences are explored; other aspects are more formal, requiring legal or financial agreements or contracts that require commitment and follow through. In Chapter 2, one-on-one interviews were described as a process used to build "public relationships" during the organizing process. Christens (2010) describes these relationships as "respectful and civil relationships that build trust over time through action and that work to serve converging self-interest" (p. 890). However, organizing would not succeed unless these relationships happen on a large scale and are used to link groups of people together and initiate discussions with organization representatives and political decision makers. Christen conducted a research study that consisted of over 50 qualitative interviews with Faith in Action volunteers in six different organizations. Respondents identified three different benefits of relational organizing: strengthening commitments to community work, developing a greater understanding of social issues and how the world works, and establishing additional networks of relationships that can be used to facilitate social change. These changes take place at both the individual and organizational level.

Relationship building is also central to maintaining collaborative coalition decision-making structures (Carr, 2009). For example, Gil de Gigaja (2001) interviewed organization directors who coordinated collaborative efforts with other organizations. The directors viewed relationship building as a central component of their work: maintaining strong interpersonal relationships with other members to facilitate meetings and reach agreements about common goals.

CASE VIGNETTE: SENSE OF COMMUNITY RESPONSIBILITY IN COLLABORATION

Over a relatively short period of time, the Thrive in the 05 initiative grew from a small group of resident leaders and organizations to a large collaborative of residents, community leaders, local government, and cross-sector organizations, including representatives from law enforcement, education, public health, youth-focused programming, housing, and faith-based organizations. As the collaborative grew, Thrive leadership sought tools that could be used to help gauge the extent to which the collaborative was cohesive and functional. After doing some research, they identified and used the Sense of Community Responsibility (SOC-R) scale (Nowell & Boyd, 2014). This scale measures feelings of accountability for the individual and collective well-being of the community; sample scale items include "A feeling of belonging or of sharing a sense of personal connection to the other members of the collaborative" and "A sense of responsibility for the well-being of the population or geographic community that you share in common" (Nowell & Boyd, 2014). Members of the Thrive collaborative were asked to fill out the seven-item questionnaire periodically throughout the initiative. This information provided a snapshot into how individual members of the collaborative were perceiving their participation as part of the group. Coupled with other data points and reflections, insight into the sense of community responsibility of the group helped leaders decide on what activities to focus on next and when it was necessary to take a moment to take a breath and celebrate the small wins. This example highlights how collaboration among organizations ebb and flow and it is up to the community practitioner to be tuned into group process in order to ensure the highest functioning collaboration possible. Tools, such as the Sense of Community Responsibility scale, provide information to help the community practitioner in this process.

Building Trust

The establishment of trusting relationships is critical for achieving consensus among collaborative partners. According to Lambright and colleagues (2010), the two primary components of trust in interorganizational partnerships are *interdependence* and *risk*. Organizations must rely on one another to complete tasks, unless one organization completes its work, others cannot function. Risk involves putting the organization in a vulnerable position by relying on others to follow through. Previous experience in successfully working with a member organization and frequency of interaction can both be factors in the establishment of a trusting relationship.

Nowell (2009) argues that strong interpersonal relationships among members of collaborative structures increase the likelihood that these partnerships will be effective in meeting their goals. They identify five relationship qualities that are characteristic of strong partnerships, including

- the extent to which participants interact with one another in activities that are not related to the collaborative;
- individual members' perceptions of the extent to which other participants are responsive to their concerns;

- individual members' perceptions that other participants can be trusted to follow through on assigned tasks and responsibilities;
- individual members' perceptions of the degree to which other participants have "legitimacy," that is, the ability to make a unique contribution via knowledge, point of view, or skills brought to the partnership; and
- the degree to which individual members believe that other participants share a common philosophy about the goals of the partnership.

According to Graddy and Chen (2006), organizations seek trustworthy partners because they need a resource that they do not already have in order to exchange resources; they also want partners who have legitimacy or political power and connections. Therefore, they want partners who they already know something about through previous experience, common goals, or linkages through other partner organizations. Vangen and Huxham (2003) offer a number of strategies for establishing trust when organizations have no prior history of working relationships:

- Have clarity of purpose and objectives.
- Deal with power differences.
- Have leadership but do not allow anyone to take over.
- Allow time to build up understanding.
- Share the workload fairly.
- Resolve different levels of commitment.
- Accept that partnerships evolve over time.

Power and Resource Sharing

The biggest impediments to building trust in organizational partnerships involve sharing power and resources. Members of collaborative structures often worry about the degree to which they will be able to influence how decisions are made. Most organizational partnerships occur among organizations that have unequal amounts of resources and power (Sen, 2003). According to Vangen and Huxham (2003), "practitioners' perceptions suggest that unequal power relations and the need to protect individual organizations' interests by controlling collaboration agendas are inevitable difficulties pertaining to the collaborative processes" (p. 26).

Although in some types of organization, decision-making may be relatively informal, most task forces, collaboratives, coalitions, and alliances establish a formal structure for decision-making. Such structures may vary depending on available recourses, size of the membership base, ideology, and skills of the leaders. Structures may range from having one or two appointed or elected leaders who make most of the decisions, or ensuring that all decisions are made by an elected governing board, to requiring that all decisions are approved by regular assemblies of all members (Checkoway, 2007). Partnerships also require some type of structure similar to that of organizations. However, the structure may be less rigid than those used in formal organizations and somewhat more formal than those typically found in informal groups of friends or volunteers.

According to Brown (2006), aspects of structure should include a mission statement, goals and objectives, regular meetings, and rules for making decisions. Criteria for becoming an individual or organizational member, a funding source, and an explicit leadership structure are also necessary.

The governance structure for most partnerships consists of a steering committee, often selected through a vote of member organizations, with most organizations having a representative on the committee (Rubin & Rubin, 2008). Paarlberg and Varda (2009) argue that organizational partnerships require either formal governance structures, an "honest broker" who mediates relationships among members, or an informal process for governance based on shared values and practices among member organizations. A process is also required for sanctioning those member agencies that violate expectations or norms for member organizations. Transparency in decision-making, equal distribution of benefits and perks, and regular evaluations of the coalition's or collaborative's work may help minimize the harmful effects associated with power differentials among organizations (Sen, 2003).

Although a clear governance structures can minimize differences in power among members, imbalances in other resources, such as political influence or connections, monetary contributions, possession of skilled staff or technology, and the size of an individual organization's membership base or constituency group, can provide a source of informal power for some individuals and groups within the partnership (VeneKlasen et al., 2007). Consequently, one of the most problematic issues for coalitions, collaboratives, and other types of partnerships has to do with sharing resources, especially money. Sen (2003) argues that collaborations require an understanding among members that they all contribute a minimum amount of resources. Because self-interest is one of the reasons that organizations enter into partnerships, organizations often jockey to improve their own status, influence, and access to resources.

Therefore, at minimum, clear understanding is needed about the resources the various parties should contribute to the partnership and how much each organizational partner should benefit from the resources provided, gained, or exchanged. In many instances, organizations may enter into formal agreements or contracts with members of the partnership. Often a process of bargaining and negotiation is needed to facilitate these arrangements.

Engaging in Bargaining and Negotiation With Partner Organizations

Managing conflict among organizational partners is a critical skill for maintaining collaborative arrangements and facilitating consensus around the use of resources and power sharing. Rosenthal and Mizrahi (2004) maintain that a conflict resolution model should be used by partner organizations to reach agreement on contentious issues that includes bargaining, negotiations, and compromise. Rather than *majority rule*, decisions should be made by mutual consent. They identify a number of specific strategies for dealing with conflict and issues related to the protecting of *turf* among member agencies:

> *Some remedies for managing internal conflict within collaborations include appeals to rationality, diplomacy, the use of third parties, isolating disputes, excluding controversial items from the agenda, or maintaining tacit neutrality, giving each member veto power, airing and resolving disputes, or developing caucuses to facilitate inter-group negotiations. (p. 325)*

Many experts on coalition-building and partnerships advocate for the development of explicit written agreements that spell out what each of the partner organizations has agreed to contribute or do (Homan, 2016). Prospective partners can also be asked for a written letter of commitment. Staples (2016) emphasizes the need for *contracting* or specifying, either explicitly or implicitly, group norms or expectations for behavior such as meeting times, participant roles, use of agendas, how decisions should be made, and how people should behave in meetings. It is also important to set parameters about whether, and to what degree, conflict is handled in organizations.

Developing Consensus: Issues, Goals, Action, and Evaluation Criteria

The primary purpose of building trust is for individuals and organizations who make up the partnership to achieve consensus about mission, goals, actions, and evaluation criteria. Mizrahi and Rosenthal (2001) identify three critical roles for coalition leaders:

1. Sustain movement toward external goals by influencing social change targets.
2. Maintain internal relations among the core organizational representatives.
3. Develop trust with, accountability to, and contributions from the coalition's membership base.

Group facilitators should focus on building members' capacity to make decisions, relying on group dialogue and mutual learning. Often, consensus can easily be developed due to the manner in which collaborative groups or coalitions are developed—relationships are established between individuals or among organization members; prospective participants share an ideology and commitment to a cause (Rubin & Rubin, 2008; Van Dyke & McCammon, 2010). As discussed in Chapter 3, member organizations also are more likely to ban together when they perceive themselves to have a common enemy or opponent (e.g., an elected official who opposes their goals or an existing law or policy that prevents a specific action or a desired outcome).

Responsibility for facilitating discussion often falls on a staff member or designated leader of the partnership, coalition, or collaborative. Many of the interpersonal skills used to achieve group consensus are related to basic group-work skills commonly used in social work practice. For example, the Community Tool Box offers the following guidelines for facilitating group discussions (Work Group for Community Health and Development, 2022):

- Help people feel comfortable.
- Guide the group into establishing ground rules that call for respect among participants and ensure the opportunity for all group members to participate.
- Set an agenda and have specific goals for what is to be accomplished during the meeting.
- Actively lead the discussion by asking questions of group members, advancing the discussion, and asking clarifying questions.
- Make sure that everyone has a chance to speak and that one person or a small group of people do not dominate the meeting.
- Summarize the important points and ask for clarification from group members.
- Wrap up the meeting by making plans for next steps and assigning tasks to specific members.

FACILITATING AND MAINTAINING PARTNERSHIPS WITH TECHNOLOGY

Using technology effectively is an essential skill in community practice. Digital communication tools (e.g., social media, web-based video platforms) can be used to enhance community partnerships via virtual community meetings, focus groups, and interviews (Brown & Dinecola, 2020). In addition to creating opportunities for virtual meetings, there are a variety of technological tools that allow community practitioners to stay organized and communicate efficiently and effectively. For instance, web-based email marketing software (e.g., MailChimp; Whoozin) allows practitioners to design and send invitations and newsletters and consumer relationship management software (e.g., Insightly, Zoho) assists the community practitioner with tracking conversations and sharing contact information for community partners (Brown & Dinecola, 2020). Social media is also a powerful tool for community practitioners to use in recruitment (as discussed in Chapter 3) and in maintaining relationships and engagement with volunteers, residents, local leaders, community partners, and organizations.

It is important to note, however, that there are limitations to relying on technological tools to create engagement. Digital literacy and access to technology varies considerably within any community. Low-income families and older adults may be disproportionately excluded from projects that rely exclusively on technology. Thus, community practitioners must take into consideration residents' and partners' digital literacy and access to technology during the community planning phase. In addition, digital communication tools should not be implemented to the exclusion of in-person opportunities for participation. Through a balance of digital communication tools and traditional communication tools, community practitioners can maximize the participation of a diverse group of community residents, partners, and organizations.

BRIDGING DIFFERENCES THROUGH MUTUAL LEARNING AND PARTICIPATION

One of the basic principles associated with building partnerships, coalitions, and collaboratives is ensuring that membership is diverse and representative of the community. According to Checkoway (2007), community practitioners face the challenge of finding bonds among individuals, identifying issues that impact diverse groups, and creating space to foster individual and collective empowerment to take collective action.

Dobbie and Richards-Schuster (2008) describe a number of practice activities that can be used in partnerships with diverse members to help find common ground:

- Recruit leaders with multiple cultural identities and experiences who have the ability to help members of the diverse groups or constituencies "connect" with one another.
- Encourage advocacy on the part of these leaders so that the voices of people traditionally excluded (such as youth, older adults, or persons of color) will be heard in the decision-making process.
- Provide educational activities that include discussions on the negative effects of power and privilege, the value of diversity, and inequities fostered by racism, sexism, homophobia, and other forms of discrimination.

- Provide opportunities for events and celebrations that encourage informal social interactions and dialogue among participants.
- Give priority within the partnership structure for social action activities that directly affect members regardless of their perspectives.

As noted earlier in this chapter, power and resource imbalances in collaborative structures often make partnerships ineffective. Marois (2006) argues that most conflicts in collaborative partnerships originate in power imbalances related to gender identity, race, and other historical or present-day inequities in terms of who holds status in the community and within the partnership. Marois suggests a number of strategies for minimizing conflict, including shared governance, ensuring that meetings are often chaired by nonprofessionals or people who represent nondominant or minoritized and marginalized groups, and using organization self-evaluation techniques to examine whether the organization is operating in an equalitarian and culturally competent manner.

PUTTING VALUES INTO ACTION: SUSTAINING MUTUAL LEARNING AND PARTNERSHIP AMONG ORGANIZATIONS

Given that power and resource imbalances often make coalitions and other types of partnerships ineffective, it is critical that organization members agree to implement principles associated with mutuality and building trust. Foster-Fishman and colleagues (2001) identify a variety of skills needed to enhance the capacity of coalitions to foster collaboration among member organizations. They identify four components of collaborative capacity:

- *Member Capacity*: The ability to recruit and support a diverse pool of members who are motivated to work and collaborate with others and who possess the knowledge and skills needed to maintain the coalition. Maintenance includes the ability to fundraise and create an appropriate organizational structure.
- *Relational Capacity*: The ability to foster positive interactions among coalition members, establish group norms for participation, reach a consensus about goals, and maintain an inclusive decision-making structure. In addition, the coalition and its members should be able to build external relationships with individuals and groups and involve community members in the decision-making process.
- *Organizational Capacity*: The ability to foster leadership among members, formalize roles, assign and complete tasks, develop plans, foster communication among members, develop a committee structure, acquire funding, recruit skilled staff members, and monitor the coalition's ability to achieve outcomes.
- *Programmatic Capacity*: The ability to conduct needs assessments, solicit input from the community, and develop programs and organizing campaigns.

Lasker and Weiss (2003) incorporate many of these components into a management and leadership model designed to foster effective collaborative practice. In addition to encouraging participation from a diverse group of community members and organizations and an inclusive decision-making structure, they stress the importance of making all leaders, staff, and organizations accountable to the members and recognizing the contributions and skills of all participants. Leaders should also be responsible for fostering a productive group process that synthesizes member skills and resources. Lasker and Weiss also argue for ongoing efforts to expand the collaborative and build membership, actively connect the planning process to taking action, and provide technical assistance and other support.

Lasker and Weiss (2003) identify three outcomes that community collaborations should ideally try to achieve:

- Seek individual empowerment by involving community members in the problem-solving process. Furthermore, community members should have some form of actual control or decision-making power in the problem-solving process, rather than merely token influence.
- Bring diverse people together, build trust, and develop a sense of community.
- Combine knowledge, skills, and other resources to develop creative solutions to multiple community challenges.

Nowell and Foster-Fishman (2010) also identify a number of organizational outcomes associated with participation in effective community collaboratives, including increases in knowledge about community systems and how they function and awareness of community issues. In addition, participation in collaboratives should increase member access to resources and improve service delivery, facilitate community change, or influence the development of policies or legislation. It should also increase the organization's ability and capacity to resolve social problems. In addition, organizations increase their own power, influence, and reputations in the community by participating in collaborative efforts.

These collaborative activities and outcomes can be conceptualized in terms of a practice model that incorporates both process-oriented, interpersonal skills and concrete tasks or activities that must be accomplished to maintain the partnership and facilitate its work. In terms of process, participants and their designated leaders must recruit a diverse membership base that is representative of the demographic characteristics of the constituency served and includes people with a variety of skills and experiences. Group-work skills should be used to encourage mutual learning among participants about shared experiences and community issues as well as their differences in order to build an organizational atmosphere based on trust and a sense of community or collective identity. The ability to engage with one another as equal partners is essential for the development of a consensus-oriented decision-making process. Task-oriented activities should include efforts to establish a decision-making structure for the organization, obtain resources, train and provide adequate supports for leaders and staff, and assign tasks to member organizations for goal accomplishment and organizational maintenance. Other tasks should be focused on organizational goals: planning, implementation of activities, and evaluation of outcomes.

These activities should result in both process- and task-oriented outcomes. Process-oriented outcomes include individual empowerment, fostering trust and a sense of community among members, and the ability for partners to creatively resolve problems. Concrete or task-oriented outcomes should result in an increase in knowledge about how the community works; improvement in services or increases in access to services; changes in the community, policies, and legislation; and increases in the reputation of individual member organizations and their power to affect social change (Figure 4.1).

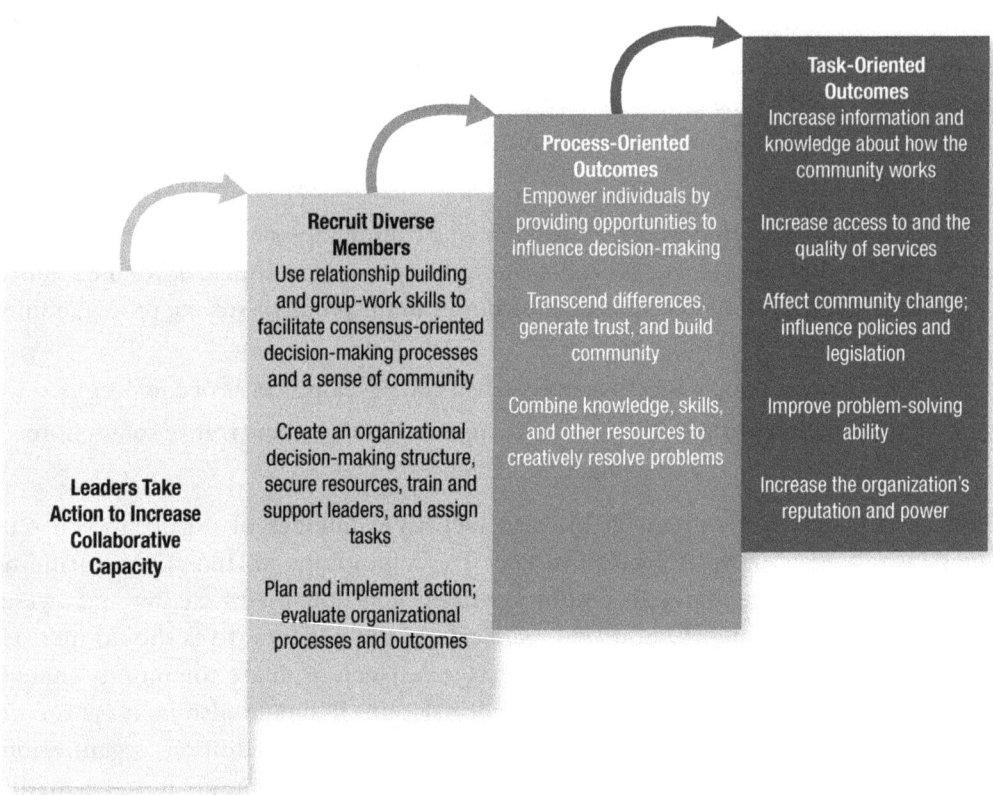

FIGURE 4.1 Conceptual model: Mutual learning and partnership among organizations.

END-OF-CHAPTER RESOURCES

KEY TAKEAWAYS AND SUMMARY

Fostering collaborative partnerships requires a combination of process- and task-related skills used to create an organizational structure that supports decision-making and performs tasks. The interpersonal skills necessary to accomplish this include mutual learning, trust, and consensus building. Many of the partnership structures established by alliances of social change-oriented organizations are complex, including a variety of organizations with different goals and motivations for participation. Decision-making takes place within individual organizations, within the context of the local partnership, and, in the case of federations, at regional, state, or national levels. Consequently, organizers coordinating organizational partnerships need to have excellent management and group-work skills to facilitate such processes. In the next five chapters, the use of group-work skills to facilitate consensus among group members (both individual and organization partners) for problem-solving, assessment, intervention planning, taking action, and evaluating the outcome and processes associated with these actions is described. The theme inherent in these chapters is the incorporation of Freire's principles of mutual learning and partnership in every phase of the community-organization process.

RESOURCES

- Cohen, L., Baer, N., & Satterwhite, P. (2002). *Developing effective coalitions: An eight step guide.* Prevention Institute. https://www.preventioninstitute.org/publications/developing-effective-coalitions-an-eight-step-guide
- Society for Public Health Education. (2022). *Coalition building resources.* https://elearn.sophe.org/coalition-building-resources

ACTIVITIES

1. In small groups, work together to develop an agenda for the very first coalition meeting focused on preventing deaths from drug overdoses. Use the process-oriented and task-oriented outcomes listed in Figure 4.1 as a guide. What specific activities might you implement to achieve these outcomes? How will you build relationships and trust among members?

ASSIGNMENTS

1. Attend a meeting of a task group or coalition and observe the verbal and nonverbal interaction among participants, the decision-making structure, and the types of decisions made by group members. Conduct a brief interview after the meeting with at least one of the participants to find out about the respondent's perception of the meeting. Write a one- to three-page paper and:
   a. Identify the participants and their organizational affiliation.
   b. Identify the participant or participants responsible for facilitating the meeting (i.e., who is in charge? Is it one person or do multiple people seem to have responsibility for ensuring that the group runs smoothly?).
   c. Describe the decision-making structure (e.g., are decisions made by majority rule or by consensus). Were there any other rules that seemed to pertain to the decision-making process?
   d. What decisions were made? If no decisions appear to have been made, why do you think this happened?
   e. Were decisions made through consensus or conflict?
   f. Does it appear that members of the group were assigned specific tasks? Were the tasks completed? If not, were reasons given? What were they?
   g. Did any member of the group seem to have a specific agenda about what was to be accomplished during the meeting? Was it similar to or different from that of other members of the group?
2. In your internship or place of employment, facilitate a task group or committee meeting that involves staff or representatives of a number of organizations. Prior to the meeting, consult with your supervisor or other staff members and discuss the history of the group, the purpose of the group, past accomplishments, and future goals. Also

make sure that you have a clear vision of what you intend to accomplish at this meeting. Prepare an agenda in advance and plan to take minutes.

For your written assignment, submit the agenda and minutes. Also submit a two- to four-page paper that:

a. Identifies participants and the organization that they represent.

b. Describes group interaction during the meeting.

c. Describes your success (or lack of success) in following the agenda.

d. Analyzes your efforts at facilitation in terms of minimizing conflicts among members, facilitating consensus, and achieving your goal for the meeting.

A robust set of instructor resources designed to supplement this text is located at http://connect.springerpub.com/content/book/978-0-8261-5835-2. Qualifying instructors may request access by emailing textbook@springerpub.com.

KEY REFERENCES

Only key references appear in the print edition. The full reference list appears in the digital product on Springer Publishing Connect: connect.springerpub.com/content/book/978-0-8261-5835-2/part/part01/chapter/ch04

Brown, M. E., & Dinecola, C. (2020). Technology and community-engaged research. *Journal of Technology in Human Services, 38*, 3–21. https://doi.org/10.1080/15228835.2019.1577790

Checkoway, B. (2007). Community change for diverse democracy. *Community Development Journal, 44*, 5–21. https://doi.org/10.1093/cdj/bsm018

Christens, B. (2010). Public relationship building in grassroots community organizing: Relational intervention for individual and systems change. *Journal of Community Psychology, 38*, 886–900. https://doi.org/10.1002/jcop.20403

Dobbie, D., & Richards-Schuster, K. (2008). Building solidarity through difference: A practice model for critical multicultural organizing. *Journal of Community Practice, 16*, 317–337. https://doi.org/10.1080/10705420802255098

Foster-Fishman, P., Berkowitz, S., Lounsbury, D., Jacobson, S., & Allen, N. (2001). Building collaborative capacity in community coalitions: A review and integrative framework. *American Journal of Community Psychology, 29*, 241–261. https://doi.org/10.1023/A:1010378613583

Lambright, K., Mischen, P., & Laramee, C. (2010). Building trust in public and nonprofit networks: Personal, dyadic, and third-party influences. *American Review of Public Administration, 40*, 64–82. https://doi.org/10.1177/0275074008329426

Mizrahi, T., Bayne-Smith, M., & Garcia, M. L. (2009). Comparative perspectives on interdisciplinary community collaboration between academics and community practitioners. *Community Development, 39*(3), 1–15. https://doi.org/10.1080/15575330809489665

Nowell, B., & Boyd, N. M. (2014). Sense of community responsibility in community collaboratives: Advancing a theory of community as resource and responsibility. *American Journal of Community Psychology, 54*, 229–242. https://doi.org/10.1007/s10464-014-9667-x

Ohmer, M., & DeMasi, K. (2009). *Consensus organizing: A community development workbook*. Sage.

Wells, R., Ward, A., Feinberg, M., & Alexander, J. (2008). What motivates people to participate more in community-based coalitions? *American Journal of Community Psychology, 42*, 94–104. https://doi.org/10.1007/s10464-008-9182-z

PART II

THE ENGAGEMENT PHASE

USING DIALOGUE, TRADITIONAL AND DIGITAL STORYTELLING, AND STRUCTURED GROUP-WORK TECHNIQUES TO IDENTIFY COMMUNITY ISSUES

LEARNING OBJECTIVES

After reading this chapter, students will be able to:
- Recognize the purpose of group dialogue.
- Distinguish among major techniques used to engage in group and community dialogue.
- Describe the application of digital storytelling to identifying community issues.
- Demonstrate skills necessary to facilitate a focus group.

INTRODUCTION

Issue identification is typically the first stage of the engagement process in community organizing, after the initial recruitment of individual and organizational members. In this chapter, a description of how dialogue among group members is used to identify the social problems or issues to be addressed in the organizing effort is provided. A number of specific techniques used for conducting group dialogues and identifying common issues are examined, including storytelling, community forums, nominal group technique (NGT), focus group interviews, and study circles. In the last section of this chapter, specific practice skills used to engage participants in the dialogue process and to facilitate the development of a critical consciousness about the origin of social problems are discussed.

THE PURPOSE OF GROUP DIALOGUE

After people and organizations are recruited for the organizing effort, they must begin to identify community issues. Because participants in the organizing effort often comprise a diverse group of people with different backgrounds, values, and perceptions, reaching agreement about the issue or issues to be addressed in the organizing effort is essential. Although organizers will have already conducted one-on-one interviews and interacted with numerous people who may have strong views about community issues, bringing individuals and organization representatives together to engage in dialogue about challenges they face is an important next step in the organizing process.

These group discussions can take many forms and may include group meetings, focus groups, and community forums. They can be informal or highly structured. Although often there is a designated facilitator (most often a community organizer or community leader), the purpose of these discussions is to encourage face-to-face interaction and to solicit diverse points of view, hence the term used to describe this process is *group dialogue*. McCoy and Scully (2002) use two different terms to describe public discussions on social problems: dialogue and deliberation. Dialogue brings people together "to listen to and understand the other" (p. 117), whereas deliberation involves the use of group processes to apply critical thinking skills to problem resolution and the development of policy alternatives. Most important, dialogue helps organizers and participants develop a collective or common understanding of an issue to be addressed in the organizing effort. It is used to find a common link among issues faced by individuals and groups and a particular "cause," institutional arrangement, policy, or practice that is sustaining or making the issue worse (Hardina, 2002). For example, people living in a community experiencing unemployment, the closure of small businesses, an increased suicide rate, and families moving out may perceive there to be a common origin for these issues such as employee layoffs from a nearby manufacturing plant.

The process of dialogue is congruent with the preliminary phases of social work practice with individuals and families. Miley and colleagues (2017) identify three primary activities for the generalist practitioner during the dialogue process: building relationships with consumers, validating the experiences of the consumer, and identifying a preliminary purpose for the worker–consumer relationship. Such issue identification helps motivate the consumer to take action and guides the search for resources needed to resolve the issue. Other social work skills needed for this process include recognition of consumer or constituent strengths, conveying respect for individual participants and their cultural values, recognizing and working through differences, active listening, and group-work skills that are used to minimize differences among participants and to develop a consensus about the issues that affect them (Gutierrez et al., 2005).

USING GROUP DIALOGUE TO IDENTIFY ISSUES, STRENGTHS, AND RESOURCES TO SOLVE CHALLENGES

One of the primary frameworks used by social workers to make decisions is the problem-solving model. This model is generally considered a component of generalist social work practice because it can be used to develop interventions across systems: individuals, groups, families, organizations, and communities (Kirst-Ashman & Hull, 2018a; Poulin, 2010). This approach, also called *the rational model*, is also used as one of the primary decision-making frameworks by organizers, planners, and policy makers. The basic assumption inherent in this model is that experts have the time, knowledge, professional expertise, and resources to make objective decisions based on available information and logic (Netting et al., 2008). It is also assumed that the decision maker (social worker, policy analyst, organizer, or planner) has the critical thinking skills necessary to make the best decision. Kirst-Ashman and Hull (2018b) define *critical thinking* as "the questioning of beliefs, statements, assumptions, lines of reasoning, actions, and experiences" as well as "the creative formulation of an opinion or conclusion when presented with a question, problem, or issue" (p. 35).

The problem-solving model typically consists of five stages: issue identification, assessment, goal setting or planning, intervention or implementation, and evaluation. Some versions of this model also include a termination phase and a feedback loop that involves modification of the original plan if it has not resulted in a successful outcome (Kirst-Ashman & Hull, 2018b).

The use of the rational or problem-solving model has some important limitations, however. One of the primary criticisms of this approach is that decision makers seldom actually have the time or resources to carefully weigh all possible alternatives to a specific plan (Rothman & Zald, 2008). Many decisions are made in the political process, based on a number of criteria, including who actually benefits from the decision and the amount of influence possessed by interest groups and campaign donors. Also, in many circumstances, the social values of the decision maker have an important role in any policy or planning recommendation made. For example, should people living in poverty be the first to benefit from any policy or plan, should benefits be distributed equally among everyone, or should government provide minimal or no benefits to people in need? Community organizers, social policy makers, and planners often use decision-making models that make such value assumptions explicit (Forester, 2001; Larkin, 2004). Most organizers also have explicit values and ideological perspectives on how social benefits should be distributed (Mondros & Wilson, 1994). Consequently, many decisions typically made by organizers will be guided by values and will not be entirely objective or value free.

In addition to concerns about values that guide decision-making, most planners and community organizers argue that it is often not solely their responsibility to make most organizing decisions (Reisch & Lowe, 2000). Colleagues, employers, board members, organization partners, beneficiaries of the action, and constituents must often be consulted or actively involved in the decision. Community organizers, planners, and policy analysts use a number of decision frameworks that guide or are used to examine how and when people are involved in making public decisions. These models include incremental (decisions are made through negotiation among political interest groups), advocacy (the planner represents the interests of one's employer), and transformative planning (Davidoff, 1973; Lindblom, 1959). The transformative approach draws heavily on the work of Paulo Freire (1970) and assumes that planning decisions should be made through dialogue and discussion between a professional or expert (planner, organizer, social worker, etc.) and constituents. In this conceptualization, the people who will benefit from the plan are actively involved in issue identification, assessment, goal setting, implementation, and evaluation (Friedmann, 1987; Kennedy, 2009). The radical planning model is also used by some community organizers, primarily to understand and critique how social and political institutions function to marginalize members of some groups and to benefit others.

In addition to these classic approaches, Netting and colleagues (2008) advocate the use of an alternative to the rational model called *interpretive planning*, which is consistent with the transformative approach and allows for the incorporation of values and the perceptions and experience of individual participants in the decision-making process. These stakeholders include people who will benefit from the plan. Issue identification, assessment, data-collection strategies, and goals emerge through the inclusion of constituents and other interested parties in the planning process and dialogue among participants. The decision-making process is characterized by relationship building, compromise, consensus, and reliance on multiple sources of data. Planning is cyclical in nature; a plan may go through several phases, and can be modified during implementation based on new information about what works and what does not. Consequently, this method contains an expectation that the parties involved sustain the dialogue and engage in ongoing learning about the issue at hand and strategies used to address it.

There is one other important way in which problem-solving in community organizing differs from generalist practice. Barretti (2009) notes that the various steps in the problem-solving model used by social workers are viewed as linear (i.e., the previous step must be completed before the next step is contemplated). However, in community practice, the process is multilayered, with many of these problem-solving activities happening simultaneously or reoccurring periodically during an organizing campaign based on situational demands and group preferences:

> *In organizing, the definition of the problem is a negotiated, shared process between organizers and consumers that is continually in flux, and it takes substantially longer than the initial assessment phase in psychotherapy. In organizing, it is not unusual for the intervention to precede the definition of the problem, though the tenants and the organizer might initially agree on the basic concrete problematic realities that brought them together; for example, it's bitterly cold outside and they have no heat or hot water.* (Barretti, 2009, p. 12)

Consequently, although there are some types of operational decisions (such as finding a location for a meeting or which individuals to recruit for participation in an organizing campaign) that may be made by a single organizer, most often decisions in community practice are made in the context of a group process. However, it is the responsibility of the organizer to help constituents define the issue and develop an understanding or "critical consciousness" about the role of social structure and power relations in the origins of the issue or barriers that must be overcome to successfully resolve the issue (Barretti, 2009). This discussion or dialogue is interactive, with both the organizer and members of the constituency group or decision makers taking part in the process. It is based on the premise, derived from social constructionism and popular education, that issues affecting individuals, groups, families, and communities are socially constructed and should be identified and examined using criteria that include the perceptions, experiences, and values of the participants.

According to McCoy and Scully (2002), there are two issues that need to be addressed before initiating a dialogue to examine social problems: How to bring people into the process and how to structure the meeting or "public conversation" in which the dialogue will take place? Several techniques used to help bring people together to identify and resolve issues include storytelling, community forums, NGT, focus groups, and study circles. Some of these methods are used to identify injustices and will require putting pressure on or confronting authorities; others are intended to foster cooperative methods for problem resolution, whereas a number of techniques can be utilized for either purpose (Hardina, 2002; Schatz et al., 2003). Regardless of how these dialogues are structured, they are often preliminary to planned organizing campaigns; group discussions take place at numerous points in time while action is planned, carried out, and evaluated. Initial meetings may be limited to issue identification or may include content on problem assessment and goal setting as well.

USING GROUP STORYTELLING TO IDENTIFY COLLECTIVE ISSUES, STRENGTHS, AND RESOURCES TO BUILD GROUP SOLIDARITY

Often when people are approached about joining a community-organizing or social change effort, potential participants will respond by sharing a story about how they were personally affected by a social problem or issue. If relevant and appropriate, the organizer may also share their own personal story to build solidarity, rapport, and trust. Participants are commonly invited to share their stories with other group members and sometimes with the media, the general public, and elected officials. Consequently, one technique that has gained national prominence through its use by the 2008 Obama presidential campaign involves storytelling. This technique involves bringing a group of people together in a small group at the beginning of an organizing campaign to discuss their connection to the problem or issue at hand and to begin the process of "getting to know" one another, to exchange information and resources, and to initiate the development of a cohesive group or organization (Stirland, 2008).

Marshall Ganz (2001), a former organizing director for the United Farmworkers during the 1960s and 1970s, currently a Harvard professor and the chief organizing architect of the Obama campaign, views storytelling as a mechanism to inspire and motivate volunteers. According to Ganz, the process of storytelling has a number of essential components, including a frame for understanding social problems; a mechanism for placing the storytelling in the context of someone who can make change happen; moral values; goals for what the storyteller hopes to achieve; a description of any barriers encountered when trying to resolve individual and social problems; and a sense of the collective identity derived from the storyteller's community, family, and culture. Ganz also describes how storytelling is used in an organizing context:

> *Arguably the most critical elements in telling a new story are the identities of storytellers and listeners. The identity of a storyteller gives credibility to the story, linking her with her listeners in a common journey. Social movements tell a new story. In this way they acquire leadership, gain adherents, and develop a capability of mobilizing needed resources to achieve success. Social movements are not merely reconfigured networks and redeployed resources. They are new stories of who their participants hope to become. (Ganz, 2001, Conclusions section, para. 1)*

In addition to recruitment and motivation, storytelling can also be a mechanism that can be empowering for members of minoritized and marginalized communities. Rappaport (1995) describes the use of storytelling in community work in the following way:

> *For many people, particularly those who lack social, political, or economic power, the community, neighborhood, or cultural narratives that are available are either negative, narrow, "written" by others for them, or all of the above. People who seek either personal or community change often find that it is very difficult to sustain change without the support of a collectivity that provides a new communal narrative around which they can sustain changes in their own personal story. Associated with such narratives are cognitive, emotional and behavioral consequences that involve social support, role opportunities, new identities, and possible selves. (p. 796)*

According to Foster-Fishman and colleagues (2005), research on storytelling and its use in community practice is designed to provide a vehicle for understanding the perceptions of meaning that people have about their own lives. More specific, storytelling allows members of minoritized and marginalized groups to describe their experiences, especially those that involve marginalization or stigmatization by the larger society (Williams et al., 2003). It also provides an opportunity for members of these groups to challenge the way in which the dominant culture describes or tells stories about minoritized and marginalized groups of people; often these accounts are not accurate descriptions of the experiences of people from nondominant groups. Consequently, storytelling by people who have traditionally been excluded allows them to assert their identities and makes their perceptions and experiences known, especially when they engage in social action to fight injustice.

Little and Froggett (2009) attribute a number of personal and community benefits that result from telling one's own story, including bonding with listeners and others who share the story or who have similar stories and the transmission of cultural values and traditions. This in turn drives the development of a complex narrative that contains numerous depictions (both good and bad) about the motivations and actions of community members. Little and Froggett also describe the contents of a typical story:

The narrative involves the protagonist engaging in a sustained period of effort which results in significant and what are often portrayed as life-changing rewards. After the period of struggle, the hero is almost unquestioningly depicted as feeling and being better. Emotional experience is, therefore, split into a before and an after. There is a teleological [purposeful] element to this narrative, an implicit sense that personal struggle will result in meaningful benefits, indeed morally just rewards. (p. 459)

The process of using storytelling for issue identification requires face-to-face dialogue guided by a skilled facilitator. Su (2009) describes the use of the storytelling process in community-based organizations as consisting of specific types of content. Typically, group members are given a series of exercises that focus on collective goals or analysis of issues. People are asked to explain how they are personally affected by an issue, but the expectation is that the exercises will not serve to exclude participants, but that all group members will be able to identify some connection to the issue or situation under discussion. Although common patterns may emerge in the stories, individual experiences may differ, making the group's common understanding of the issue or problem more complex. According to Su, disadvantages of the storytelling process are that meeting space, time, and extensive face-to-face contact is needed to facilitate these activities. In addition, although the method is often effective in producing an understanding of the perspectives of diverse community members who have actually experienced the issue, it may not result in concrete policy proposals for addressing the issue.

Storytelling also becomes a mechanism for motivating people to join the cause and take action, especially in circumstances in which resolving an issue, taking a stand, or accomplishing a goal has been achieved by an individual, group, or organization. The actual narrative of the story may be restructured or shaped in a manner that best promotes the cause or provides a moral or meaning for the general public. For example, Polletta (2006) describes how the story of Rosa Parks's refusal to move to the back of the bus in Montgomery, Alabama, in 1955 is not entirely factual. Rather than making a spontaneous decision to risk arrest, Parks's action had actually been extensively planned by a group of activists in response to a previous arrest of a passenger on a segregated bus.

CASE VIGNETTE: DIGITAL STORYTELLING

Digital storytelling infuses the power of group storytelling with multimedia tools, such as photography and video clips that are combined into a short movie. Just as traditional group storytelling can foster connections among people and lead a group toward a shared perspective, digital storytelling is a powerful process that can lead to collective action. Creative Narrations is an organization based in Tucson, Arizona, that collaborates with individuals, groups, and communities using digital storytelling to promote social change. Creative Narrations' founders were inspired by their work as adult educators, community organizers, public health advocates, and researchers to help facilitate the storytelling process (Creative Narrations, 2022a).

Creative Narrations worked with the Zaagichigaazowin Home Visiting Program at the Red Cliff Community Health Center and Tribe of Lake Superior Chippewa in Wisconsin on a digital storytelling project about birth and parenthood (Creative Narrations, 2022b). They partnered with community members to create 10 digital stories. These stories were then used to throughout the community to support new and expecting parents. Check out the Creative Narrations website for more digital storytelling projects: www.creativenarrations.net/recent-work

COMMUNITY CONVERSATIONS AND LARGE-GROUP FORUMS

Community forums are large meetings that are typically held at the beginning of the organizing process to examine community issues and set priorities for organizing campaigns. The goal of forums is generally to identify issues facing communities and set priorities for addressing these issues. A wide segment of the community and people with diverse viewpoints are generally invited to attend for the purpose of establishing a core group of volunteers to set the direction for the organizing process and to recruit others for participation. Forums also offer a good opportunity for organizers to conduct additional one-on-one or follow-up interviews to deepen relationships with potential volunteers, solicit information, and ask people to contribute time, money, and other resources for the organizing effort.

Generally, the forum is led by one or more facilitators or a steering committee and a previously determined structure is used to solicit input from the public. A number of issues need to be addressed in the planning process:

- What is the purpose of the event?
- What is the primary goal? What does the group hope to accomplish?
- What time and location will permit the largest number and best mix of people to attend?
- What size facility is needed and what equipment (such as seating, tables, or kitchen facilities) should it contain?
- What is the agenda for the event? How will the forum be structured?
- Who will be invited to attend and how will they be recruited or informed about the event?

- Are there any ground rules that should be set for participants? Some examples of ground rules are that participants are expected to be civil to one another, that they refrain from interrupting speakers, or that each speaker in the audience complies with a time limit for their questions and comments.
- Who has the skills, the leadership abilities, and reputation in the community to serve as a facilitator for the meeting?
- Should other speakers be invited to make presentations and what format should be used (e.g., should individuals speak or should there be a panel discussion? Should one or a variety of views of the issue be presented)?
- Is a budget needed for the event or can resources, such as meeting space and printing, be solicited from donors? If money is needed to pay for the event, how will these funds be obtained?
- What printed information about the topic or issue under discussion should be distributed?
- Will a sign-in or registration table be used to obtain names and contact information for participants? If not, how will organizers determine who attended?
- What other resources are needed to make sure the forum runs smoothly such as food, transportation, babysitting, and security?
- Will the media be contacted and asked to attend?
- Will public officials be contacted and asked to attend? If so, what type of help, assistance, or commitment should be requested from these officials?
- What type of help, assistance, or commitment should be requested from participants and how will commitment be determined or verified?

Agreeing beforehand on a structure for the forum is essential. The purpose of the forum and what the organizing group hopes to accomplish is the most critical decision (Lukas & Hoskins, 2003). Is the purpose to identify an issue or does the group already know or have a general idea about the organizing campaign, community development activity, or social planning process that they want to carry out? Are there several options being considered for the organizing effort and is the intent to reach a consensus about the issue to be addressed? Will a variety of groups be asked to give their input into the matter under discussion or will only people with specific views be invited to attend (Hardina, 2002)? Is the intent of the forum just to consult or inform the community about the planned activity or to solicit support for a cause (Arnstein, 1969; Sager, 2008)?

Community forums are generally a good way to mobilize support for an issue, but they could also result in the presence of skeptics or opponents. Although the hope is that forums will result in compromise, consensus, neutralization of opposing viewpoints, or recognition or respect for people with different views, forums may be easily disrupted to the degree that speakers are repeatedly interrupted, discussion breaks down, and conflict erupts. Consequently, it is often necessary to plan forums carefully and to follow a predetermined structure and an agenda. Speakers may be recruited in advance and some groups may be deliberately invited or excluded. However, exclusion conflicts with the purpose of deliberative democracy and social work principles of self-determination and empowerment. Therefore, organizers need to think carefully before planning an agenda, setting a goal for the forum, and recruiting participants (Lukas & Hoskins, 2003). They also need to consult with potential participants, constituency group members, and prospective speakers in planning the event; cultural competency may be an issue in several aspects of the event such as the selection of community representatives, appropriate greetings and introductions, the venue in which the event takes place, the food served, and the language used or the translation services provided.

Another issue to be addressed during the planning stage is whether the structure of the forum should be open and free-flowing. An example of a relatively unstructured forum would be one in which a facilitator introduces a topic, but the agenda allows for unlimited participation, perhaps in the form of making an open microphone available to all audience members who wish to speak. An alternative structure might involve inviting speakers who represent diverse viewpoints on an issue to present their opinions as part of a panel discussion. Audience members are given a predetermined amount of time to respond to these viewpoints and make suggestions. A third option might be simply to invite speakers and guests who represent a limited number of viewpoints that are consistent with the agenda or goals of the group sponsoring the forum, with the goal of the forum to be simply to mobilize supporters around a specific issue (Box 5.1).

Box 5.1

SAMPLE COMPONENTS OF A COMMUNITY FORUM

1. A community leader convenes the meeting by describing its purpose and introduces the facilitator and lists their credentials for facilitating the meeting.
2. The facilitator describes the goals for the meeting and the intended outcome. A description of the agenda is provided and ground rules are identified.
3. One or more community leaders, experts, or people who have experienced the issue are asked to make presentations or participate in a panel discussion about the community or a specific issue to be discussed.
4. Participants are given the opportunity to ask questions about the issues at hand.
5. Participants are assigned to or are asked to join breakout groups that will engage in brainstorming or a more structured type of dialogue about a specific issue, community challenge, or community resources and assets.
6. Each group has a facilitator and/or recorder who will report back to the larger group their recommendations about challenges or issues to be addressed, resources that should be used to remedy the issue, or actions that should be taken.
7. The facilitator guides the group in a discussion or structured decision-making process to choose priorities or develop a plan. If appropriate and time allows, the facilitator leads the group in an assessment of the issue, goal setting, and planning for future action.
8. The meeting concludes. Volunteers are recruited and asked to complete a volunteer card. Dates and times are set for follow-up meetings and other activities.
9. Volunteers are asked to complete a short evaluation form to assess how they felt about the meeting, the process used to conduct the meeting, and the outcome achieved.

Note: Forum agendas vary depending on the purpose of the event and the amount of time allocated to hold the forum.

Other options when structuring forums are to ask attendees to participate in small-group discussions in order to identify issues that should be addressed and report back to the larger group or to limit individual input by restricting how people are recognized to speak, requiring that people ask to be placed on the agenda in advance, or limiting the amount of time that audience members may speak or ask questions. Typically, such restrictions are put in place to limit participation, minimize disruption, or exclude potential opponents.

In meetings in which some structure is deemed essential or preferable, but individual input is desired, the small-group process is used. Group decision-making teams are established and asked to give input. In some instances, small groups may be asked to give consideration about how a specific issue or topic should be handled. In these "brainstorming" groups, participants are instructed to "think big" or come up with the best or most innovative ideas. The advantages of brainstorming is that it potentially gives all group members the chance to be involved or creative, it can be fun, and it produces a variety of ideas (Zastrow, 2015). Some of the disadvantages are that without structure or a skilled facilitator in the group, one person can dominate the discussion or group members can be without direction or specific opinions on topics that they may know little about. Alternatively, these groups can be structured in a way that provides a clear direction and goals. One such decision-making approach typically used is the NGT.

NOMINAL GROUP TECHNIQUE

NGT is used to engage a diverse group of people in the process of setting priorities among a variety of community issues that may affect participants. As with the other methods discussed in this chapter, it is used to obtain information on the perspectives and experiences of community members and, in so doing, to identify aspects of the issue that may affect a large proportion of community residents and establish a common or joint approach for addressing the issue. The process is generally guided by a skilled facilitator. Although this process is typically used in a large-group setting, at least in the first stages of the process, there is limited interaction among group members (Zastrow, 2015). Instead, the facilitator poses a general question to the participants about their perceptions of their own needs, community issues, or about how programs, policies, or services could be improved. Each participant is asked to write down one to three ideas related to the topic and to give a verbal report about these items to the other participants. These items are then written down on a blackboard, a flip chart, or a large piece of butcher-block paper by the facilitator or assistant.

It is to be anticipated that some members of the audience will list the same item; rather than writing this down again, the facilitator indicates on the board the number of people who have listed this specific item. The facilitator might choose to identify common themes among these items or suggest grouping these items together (Hardina, 2002). Three to five of the top issues chosen are identified as potential challenges to be addressed by the group or organization. After this first set of rankings is completed, time is allowed for discussion. If no consensus for a potential campaign or plan is evident, the facilitator then asks participants to assign a ranking to the top choices. For example, if three items are selected as possible priorities, each participant is asked to assign a "1" to one's first choice, a "2" to one's second choice, and so on. Based on these rankings, a mathematical calculation (averaging individual rankings of each item) is made to determine which of the final choices has the highest score. This issue is then selected as the priority for the group with the expectation that an action might be taken. The group has the option of scheduling another meeting, developing a plan to research the issue further, or to start planning some action to be taken to address the issue. As discussed earlier in this chapter, the facilitator could also lead the group in a discussion of each of the steps in the problem-solving process before the meeting concludes: Offer a brief analysis of the issue, discuss goal setting, and determine a plan for meeting the goal (Toseland & Rivas, 2008).

According to Zastrow (2015), the advantages of this method are that it is often not time consuming, that the lack of interaction among members during the issue-identification phase ensures that everyone generates their own ideas, and that participation is not limited to people who are the most vocal. This technique also has the advantage of soliciting a variety of differing viewpoints, including some new ideas or innovative proposals. Limitations of NGT include that there may not be a great deal of thought or discussion on the various options presented or a clear rationale for adopting some or rejecting others; it is also possible that group members who may talk more or have more power and status than others may dominate the process (Toseland & Rivas, 2008).

FOCUS GROUPS

Focus groups are group interviews. Participants include a facilitator and generally six to 10 participants. These groups are used to obtain detailed information about a product, social phenomena, or program; to gauge people's reactions; and to obtain information that could not be collected through an individual survey or interviews (Zastrow, 2015). Focus groups have their origins in the world of advertisement, used as a tool for businesses to test products and learn how they are viewed by the public (Toseland & Rivas, 2008). Focus groups are used extensively in political campaigns as candidates and office holders seek a means to test out campaign slogans, agendas, or public perceptions or support for specific policies.

Focus group interviews may take place as stand-alone inquiries or as a component of a community forum designed to solicit community input. These group interviews have a unique structure and format. Typically, the facilitator poses a small number of open-ended questions (about six to eight) to respondents (Royse et al., 2014). Participants answer these questions based on their own perceptions and experiences; it is expected that the group process and interaction among members will provide more detail or descriptive information about how the group perceives the issue or topic in question. Interviewers can also use probes, ask for clarification, and summarize the main points made by respondents in order to solicit more information from the participants. Designed to collect data on a common or typical view, the process works because group members not only react to the facilitator, they also react to one another; agreeing, disagreeing, or building upon comments made by other members (Berg, 2017). The process can result in identifying common needs, perceptions, or concerns about a particular issue or a clear delineation of diverse points of view (Royse et al., 2014; Toseland & Rivas, 2008; see Box 5.2 and Box 5.3).

In social work, focus groups are typically used to gain information about people's perceptions about their experiences, a particular event or phenomena, or perceptions and experiences related to a specific program or policy. The data collected can be used to develop hypotheses or supplement other types of research. Focus groups are also used to understand or evaluate how specific interventions or programs work (Berg, 2017; Linhorst, 2002). In community organizing, development, and social planning, focus groups are typically used to see how people perceive or experience life in their communities or to learn the impact of a program or policy. In addition, focus groups can be used as a component of a community assessment to understand how people experience an issue and how they perceive its root causes. Focus groups can also be used to examine the cultural context of critical community issues and to generate ideas for addressing them. For example, Affonso and colleagues (2010) conducted focus groups with teachers, parents, school children, and community leaders to examine youth violence in rural Hawaiian communities. They found that participants attributed school violence to the lack of local resources such as social services and transportation, inadequate role modeling by adults, and a diminished connection to traditional cultural values. Respondents felt that one approach for resolving these problems should involve joint efforts by schools and the local community to integrate cultural values and practices into services for young people.

> **Box 5.2**
>
> **SAMPLE FOCUS GROUP QUESTIONS**
>
> - What was your experience as a new parent like?
> - What is a typical day like for a new parent in this community?
> - Can you think of people or resources or other supports that benefit new parents in this community?
> - What about challenges for new parents in this community?
> - What do you think needs to be done so every parent is set up for success?
>
> *Note*: Focus groups should use open-ended questions. Probes and statements soliciting clarification or more details should be used to obtain detailed information from participants.

Other than surveys or formal interviews with individuals, focus groups are probably the issue-identification tool that is the most consistent with formal research studies. Consequently, the use of this group interview format requires that attention be paid to the same ethical considerations as in other types of qualitative research. Respondents should be fully informed about the purpose of the study; they should also be assured that their confidentiality will be protected, and that nothing they say will affect their later participation in programs or services (Linhorst, 2002). Participants should be asked to sign a consent form and asked for permission to record the interview. However, as Berg (2017) points out, the confidentiality agreement includes a pledge on the part of members to disclose no information discussed in the group during the interview. Invitations to participate in the interview also have ethical implications. Effort should be made to make sure that people are not put at risk by including them in a focus group that includes someone in authority (such as an employer or public official) who could retaliate against them for negative comments (Royse et al., 2014). Participants should also be assured that they can withdraw from the group at any time (Berg, 2017). As in other types of qualitative research, if responses are to be written up in a formal report, the "real" names of participants should not be used without their permission.

According to Linhorst (2002), there are several benefits of participation in focus groups, including obtaining information and support about an issue or challenge that other people in the group may also be experiencing, as well as experiences of empowerment and pride of ownership associated with being part of a social change process. Other benefits include the low cost, the limited time needed to conduct the interview, and flexibility in how the group is conducted (Berg, 2017). It is even possible to conduct a focus group using blogs, discussion boards, and other technology, although such formats eliminate the opportunity for the facilitator to observe facial expressions and body language that can help the researcher to interpret responses.

Box 5.3

SAMPLE FOCUS GROUP DIALOGUE

Facilitator: Hello, my name is Alicia and I'd like to thank you for taking time out of your busy schedules today to tell me about your experiences as a parent in your community. (Alicia explains how participant confidentiality will be protected and distributes a consent form to respondents and waits for it to be returned.) Thank you so much. I'd like to start by asking you about your experiences as a new parent in your community.

Isabel: When my second son was born, my days began in a kind of chaos. I had to get my 5-year-old ready and out the door for school while also tending to my newborn. I am a single mom so it is all on me to make sure everyone is where they need to be on time. I have to drive my son to school because the bus picks him up too far away from our house and I worry about him walking outside on his own because of crime around here.

Melissa: I can't imagine how difficult it is with two. I have just one daughter, but life with her as a newborn was so tough. I don't even think I can describe a typical day, there was no schedule or routine at all. I did not have very much help from family either.

Julia: Family support is important. But, honestly, I had my mom and aunt stay with me after my daughter was born and I am not sure how helpful they were. They had lots of advice, but didn't really listen to me about the kind of help I needed. Holding the baby was helpful at times I guess so I could get other stuff done around the house, but I really just wanted more time to bond with my baby.

Facilitator: It sounds like each of you experienced challenges with the support you needed as a new parent, although each in a very different way. . . .

There are a number of benefits of participating in focus groups. For example, the positive impact of group member interaction in generating creative or insightful ideas (Toseland & Rivas, 2008). As previously mentioned in this chapter, it can also be beneficial for participants to tell their stories—to talk about their lived experiences in a group setting. However, there are also possible negative impacts of participation in focus groups. For example, there is a chance that people could receive misinformation through group participation or feel disempowered by reliving difficult or stressful circumstances (Linhorst, 2002). Other disadvantages of focus groups include difficulties in identifying and recruiting a representative group of people for participation in the focus group, domination of the group process by a few members, concerns regarding confidentiality if sensitive topics are discussed and the time needed to administer the interview (1 to 2 hours) and analyze fairly detailed open-ended data (Linhorst, 2002; Toseland & Rivas, 2008). For all of these reasons, strong facilitation skills are needed to lead a successful focus group.

STUDY CIRCLES

Study circles involve a process of deliberative dialogue in which people agree to come together to discuss a public issue (Wilson et al., 2010). As discussed earlier in this chapter, dialogue is generally used in small groups to study issues, share diverse viewpoints, and build trust. It can ultimately lead to collective action. Deliberation, on the other hand, involves the examination of public issues by looking at different options for problem resolution and weighing the benefits and costs of each. The purpose of public deliberation is to increase the likelihood that public policy will be made through shared decision-making rather than conflict (National Coalition for Dialogue and Deliberation, 2010).

Study circles typically consist of 10 to 15 members and generally participants consist of a diverse group of community members. Study circles take place over a number of weeks or months. In some instances, the process involves larger groups of people from a neighborhood, city, or region who break off into smaller groups for discussion. Group members are expected to examine diverse viewpoints on specific issues, find common ground, share stories about their personal connections to issues, and take action to address the social problems identified in their discussions (Co-Intelligence Center, n.d.; Everyday Democracy, 1997). The purpose of these groups is to increase democratic participation, promote social networking and relationship-building across social differences, and increase civic participation and the ability of communities to make the complex decisions necessary to address the social issues that affect their lives (McCoy & Scully, 2002; National Coalition for Dialogue and Deliberation, 2010). This method is explicitly set up with the purpose of minimizing partisan conflict and working in a collaborative manner to resolve social problems; it also is intended to change individual belief systems through rational discourse, acceptance, and understanding (Schatz et al., 2003).

According to McCoy and Sully (2002), study circles emphasize both the presentation of diverse viewpoints and the importance of really listening to others. These group discussions address some of the same issues and frame them the same way as other types of community dialogue: How are individuals and the community affected by the problem and what are the causes of the problem? The National Coalition for Dialogue and Deliberation (2010) also describes study circles as a vehicle for collaborative action. Participants share the findings with the general public and policy makers and then take action to ensure that the solutions they have proposed are adopted.

Group facilitators are not professionals, but receive training in order to help members have productive discussions and work together collaboratively. Everyday Democracy (2008) provides a thorough guide to training public dialogue (and study circle) facilitators. The following skills are identified as essential for successful facilitation:

- reflecting and clarifying: feeding back or restating an idea or thought to make it clearer;
- summarizing: briefly stating themes or main points;
- shifting focus: moving the group from one topic (or person) to another;
- asking probing or follow-up questions: using additional questions to explore disagreements, multiple perspectives, and examine common ground;
- managing conflict: moving disagreements toward being productive;

- using silence: making space for reflection by pausing; and
- using nonverbal signals: understanding body language, how people communicate without words (Everyday Democracy, 2008).

It is expected that the discussion in study circles is structured in such a way that conflict is kept to a minimum and the focus is on ensuring the participation of all group members.

INTERGROUP DIALOGUE

One process for public dialogue that has gained increasing attention is called *intergroup dialogue*. Intergroup dialogue is a facilitated, face-to-face meeting between individuals from diverse social identity groups for the purpose of meaningful engagement (Zuniga et al., 2007). The purpose and outcome of these intergroup dialogues should be clearly delineated (Nagda & Zuniga, 2003). The dialogue process consists of "an intentional, sustained, and reciprocal processes of group interaction to examine ways in which group differences are situations in systems of oppression and privilege, and to explore ways to challenge the effects of such systems on intergroup relationships" (p. 113). Consequently, the primary purpose of these groups is to address cultural differences and other community and social issues that are divisive.

Intergroup dialogues are designed to minimize conflict, to promote feelings of respect and understanding, and to create strong bonds and trusting relationships among participants. These groups are often intended to address ethnic, religious, and racial differences or conflicts. Wayne (2008) describes how intergroup dialogue is expected to work:

Practitioners lead dialogues and encourage involvement, promising participants increased understanding of, knowledge about, and comfort with those different from themselves. They will develop better relationships, resolve conflicts, and work toward building fairer and more inclusive communities. (p. 451)

Nagda and Zuniga (2003) identify three components of the dialogue process that are similar to group dialogue techniques described earlier in this chapter:

- Participants become aware of their own biases and the role of social structure and oppression in shaping prejudice and group conflict.
- Participants share stories about their racial, ethnic, or cultural identities; experiences related to discrimination; and their own perceptions about others. This process is intended to help participants develop empathy for one another.
- Members build relationships with one another that can be used to minimize conflict and take joint action across oppressive systems.

Wayne (2008) identifies three different types of outcomes commonly associated with intergroup dialogue: knowledge, attitudes, and behavior. Members gain knowledge about one another, change their attitudes and adopt more positive attitudes toward individuals and groups different from themselves, and decrease negative attitudes. The changes in both knowledge and attitude ultimately lead to behavioral changes as well, increasing positive interaction with members of groups whom the participants perceive as "different from them."

Research studies have shown some positive results of intergroup dialogue processes, although challenges in study design and methods limit generalizations across studies (Frantell et al., 2019). For example, in a study of students participating in intergroup dialogues across nine colleges and universities, Nagda and colleagues (2009) found that students who participated in intergroup dialogues significantly increased their critiques of inequality and commitments to postcollege action to redress inequalities relative to students in a comparison group. In terms of communication processes, students participating in the intergroup dialogue reported using more communication focused on engaging self, appreciating difference, critical reflection, and alliance building. In another study, Wayne (2008) conducted an evaluation of an intergroup dialogue process that brought together Jewish and Black/African American high school students. The program contained several components, including cultural education, summer tours of important historical sites associated with both ethnic groups, and leadership development. The evaluation documented both behavioral and attitudinal changes, but researchers concluded that success was dependent on the degree to which participants formed strong relationship bonds with other group members. In a similar evaluation of an intergroup dialogue process among a diverse group of university students, Nagda and Zuniga (2003) found an increase in racial identity among participants, but no differences were found in communication patterns among group members or relationship building.

According to Dessel and colleagues (2006), one of the primary barriers to the success of these groups is unequal power relationship among participants: Members of dominant groups often are eager to establish relationships with other members. However, members of minoritized or marginalized populations are more likely to prefer taking action rather than talking despite the reluctance of other group members. In addition, the use of the dominant group's language or technical terms may be the prevailing method of discourse in the group and serve to alienate some members. As noted by Gutierrez and colleagues (2005), study circles or intergroup dialogues cannot be considered successful unless they fulfill two goals: creating strong bonds and understanding among members and taking action to achieve social change. They suggest that successful outcomes can be facilitated by using a combination of short- and long-term change strategies. Short-term strategies include encouraging study circle participants to get involved with established community groups and begin to advocate for changes in government policies. Action guides can also be developed for use by community volunteers. Long-term strategies include the formation of task groups and permanent organization structures to put group recommendations for change into action.

PUTTING VALUES INTO ACTION: ENGAGING DIVERSE GROUPS AND CULTURES WITHIN COMMUNITIES

The variety of engagement tools described in this chapter can be combined, adapted, and creatively used to meaningfully and authentically engage diverse communities in the problem-identification process. Whether the community practitioner is focused on a geographic community or a community of individuals who share common interests, characteristics, or challenges (as described in Chapter 2), they will undoubtedly need to develop a wide range of engagement strategies to engage the diverse groups within the community.

During the preengagement phase, the community practitioner learns a great deal about community members, groups, and cultures within the community in which they are working by developing relationships, having on-on-one and group conversations, and conducting more formal community assessments. The knowledge gained and relationships built in the preengagement phase set the stage for determining which engagement methods for issue identification described in this chapter are most appropriate for a particular group. Community members are the experts of their lived experiences and therefore should be involved in the decision-making around engagement strategies for issue identification. For example, community practitioners may consider co-facilitating focus groups with a resident or training residents to facilitate focus groups or interviews independently. There are also a variety of ways to infuse creativity into nominal group approaches, including developing a celebratory event within a community that also serves as an opportunity for community members to develop collective goals for the future of their community.

In their work describing the implementation of a participatory assessment phase of a holistic community-change project targeting crime, violence, and other determinants of health, Stalker and colleagues (2020) highlight the value of utilizing a variety of methods in the issue-identification phase. Guided by the "ACTION team" made up of researchers, residents, and community partners, they conducted interviews with law enforcement and resident leaders as well as focus groups with small groups of residents across the community. They also held "visioning sessions" across the community, which utilized a nominal group approach to obtain information from a larger group of residents from different subpopulations across the community. The following excerpt describes how the team's engagement approach took into account the diversity within the community:

> [A] significant challenge was the separation of residents within sub-communities. Despite the fact that the target community is only 1.5 square miles, residents identified strongly with smaller subgroups. For instance, older adult residents of the public housing complex mostly identified their community as being limited to within their building. Members of the urban American Indian community also held distinct cultural norms and values. In order to address these challenges and promote social cohesion, we regularly held meetings at different locations across the community to ensure that we were accessible to residents of these sub-communities. (Stalker et al., 2020, p. 401)

END-OF-CHAPTER RESOURCES

KEY TAKEAWAYS AND SUMMARY

After a community organizer becomes acquainted with a community and begins to form relationships with individuals, organizations, and groups, a particular social problem or issue should be selected for a community development effort, a social planning process, or an organizing campaign. Although an individual organizer or organization can make a specific social problem or issue a priority, organizing is, and should be a group effort. Although problem-solving is often thought of as fact finding and data gathering, the perceptions of community residents are also critical. Group methods for issue identification include storytelling, community forums, NGT, focus groups, study circles, and intergroup dialogue.

The second phase of the problem-solving model involves assessments of community issues, power and institutional arrangements that sustain oppression or marginalization, and strengths (such as skills and resources) that can be used for social change. In Chapter 6, participatory methods for conducting community assessments will be examined, with special emphasis on group methods that put participants in control of not only problem identification, but also the analysis of the issue or need, the assets that can be used to address it, and the distribution of power that can sustain the issue or be used for social change.

RESOURCES

- Everyday Democracy. (2008). *A guide for training public dialogue facilitators.* Author.
- PhotoVoice. (n.d.). *Telling stories through photos.* https://photovoice.org
- Thomas, N., & Brimhall-Vargas, M. (n.d.). *Facilitating political discussions: A facilitator training workshop guide.* Institute for Democracy & Higher Education, Tufts University. https://idhe.tufts.edu/resources/facilitating-political-discussions-facilitator-training-workshop-guide

ACTIVITIES

1. Take a picture of something in the community that has meaning for you, or use a picture in a community publication. What story or meaning does the picture have for you? Do you think the image will have different meanings for different groups of people? How would you go about reconciling them if you were facilitating a constituency group meeting? Would the meaning of the image be different based on the composition of the group (i.e., demographic profile such as ethnicity, gender, age, etc.)? Would the meaning differ depending on the purpose or mission of the group, the situation at hand, or the community or cultural context? Please explain.

2. In class, take a few minutes to think about why you decided to become a social worker or community organizer. Briefly write down some notes about how you chose your career. Share this story with your class members either in a small group or larger classroom setting. After sharing your stories, discuss with the larger group any themes or differences among these stories.

3. Spend some time looking at the digital storytelling projects on the Creative Narrations website (www.creativenarrations.net/recent-work). In class, discuss some examples of how the digital stories could lead to social action. Are there particular aspects of a digital story that you felt would be compelling to share? Who could the story be shared with—the larger community or a policy maker?

ASSIGNMENTS

1. Join a group that is planning a community forum. If you cannot join a group or initiate a planning group, attend at least one forum and conduct an interview with a planner as well as an interview with a participant. Write a three- to five-page paper that addresses how the forum was conducted and the decisions made about the format used. In your paper address the following items:
   - What was the purpose of the event?
   - What individuals or groups were included in planning the event?
   - How was the forum structured? What activities were included on the agenda?
   - What factors did the planning committee take into consideration in planning the event?
   - What resources were used to make the event successful (i.e., speakers, facilities, equipment, printed literature, etc.)? How were these items obtained?
   - To what degree was the agenda controlled by the planners? Did the structure permit a high degree of participant participation? Why or why not?
   - Was the purpose of the forum achieved? Please explain your answer. If successful, what components were well received? If not successful, why did this happen?
2. With a group of classmates or constituents from your field agency, conduct a focus group interview on an issue likely to have been experienced by members of this group. Ask someone to act as a recorder—you may also tape the interview with permission of the participants. (Assure participants that their confidentiality will be protected and that only you will have access to the tape.) Prepare an agenda and a consent form in advance. Write a brief summary of your findings that identifies major themes identified in the interview. With this assignment submit your consent form, interview guide, and a transcript or set of notes from the interview.
3. Attend an intergroup dialogue session or a training session for facilitators of these groups. Identify the interpersonal skills necessary to facilitate dialogue and/or deliberation among members with diverse viewpoints. What social work skills were evident in the facilitation process?

A robust set of instructor resources designed to supplement this text is located at http://connect.springerpub.com/content/book/978-0-8261-5835-2. Qualifying instructors may request access by emailing **textbook@springerpub.com**.

KEY REFERENCES

Only key references appear in the print edition. The full reference list appears in the digital product on Springer Publishing Connect: connect.springerpub.com/content/book/978-0-8261-5835-2/part/part02/chapter/ch05

Dessel, A., Rogge, M., & Garlington, S. (2006). Using intergroup dialogue to promote social justice and change. *Social Work, 51*, 303–339. https://www.jstor.org/stable/23721215

Frantell, K. A., Miles, J. R., & Ruwe, A. M. (2019). Intergroup dialogue: A review of recent empirical research and its implications for research and practice. *Small Group Research, 50*, 654–695. https://doi.org/10.1177/1046496419835923

Freire, P. (1970). *Pedagogy of the oppressed*. Continuum.

Linhorst, D. (2002). A review of the use and potential of focus groups in social work research. *Qualitative Social Work, 1*, 208–228. https://doi.org/10.1177/1473325002001002620

Little, R., & Froggett, L. (2009). Making meaning in muddy waters: Representing complexity through community based story-telling. *Community Development Journal, 45*(4), 458–473. https://doi.org/10.1093/cdj/bsp017

Nagda, B. A., Gurin, P., Sorensen, N., Gurin-Sands, C., & Osuna, S. M. (2009). From separate corners to dialogue and action. *Race and Social Problems, 1*, 45–55. https://doi.org/10.1007/s12552-009-9002-6

Schatz, M., Furman, R., & Jenkins, L. (2003). Space to grow: Using dialogue techniques for multinational, multicultural learning. *International Social Work, 46*, 481–494. https://doi.org/10.1177/0020872803464005

Stalker, K. C., Brown, M. E., Evans, C. B. R., Hibdon, J., & Telep, C. (2020). Addressing crime, violence, and other determinants of health through community-based participatory research and implementation science. *American Journal of Community Psychology*, 392–403. https://doi.org/10.1002/ajcp.12438

Williams, L., Labonte, R., & O'Brien, M. (2003). Empowering social action through narratives of identity and culture. *Health Promotion International, 18*, 33–40. https://doi.org/10.1093/heapro/18.1.33

Wilson, J., Abram, F., & Anderson, J. (2010). Exploring a feminist-based empowerment model of community building. *Qualitative Social Work, 9*, 519–535. https://doi.org/10.1177/1473325009354227

ENGAGING PARTICIPANTS IN THE DISCOVERY, ASSESSMENT, AND DOCUMENTATION OF COMMUNITY STRENGTHS AND CHALLENGES

LEARNING OBJECTIVES

After reading this chapter, students will be able to:

- Describe the purpose of conducting community assessments as part of community practice.
- Discuss participatory action research (PAR) and how it differs from traditional research.
- Recognize PAR methods for data collection, including Photovoice, asset mapping, and power analysis.
- Give examples of how social network analysis can be used in community assessments.
- Summarize ethical dilemmas that arise when using participatory methods in community assessments.

INTRODUCTION

After issue identification, the next step in the engagement phase is assessment. In organizing work, assessments are generally used to discover and document (a) community challenges or needs; (b) the strengths and assets available to improve the community; and/or (c) how systems, institutions, and individual power dynamics function and interact with one another to facilitate or block social change. As with issue identification, many community assessments are conducted in partnership with community members and group dialogue is often used to make research and analytic decisions.

In this chapter, the purpose of community assessments is described. The process involved in conducting participatory research studies for community assessments is also explored. The rationale for focusing on community assets, strengths, and resources—rather than deficits—is discussed. Participatory action research (PAR), a specific approach to conducting research in which community members serve as research partners, is also examined. Other topics include methods for conducting community assessments, including the use of data-collection methods such as asset mapping; using photography to document community assets and issues; surveys and interviews; collecting secondary data about the community; and mapping community power dynamics using a participatory process. The use of these methods requires collaboration on the part of organizers and community members and requires that both task-oriented and interpersonal social work skills are used to facilitate these processes. Therefore, the last section of this chapter focuses on interpersonal skills and their use in incorporating the strengths perspective into the community assessment approach.

THE PURPOSE OF COMMUNITY ASSESSMENTS

The practice of community organization within the social work profession, which dates back to Jane Addams and the Hull House, has emphasized social research as a professional skill used to scientifically document the prevalence of social issues and make a case for the adoption of sound social policies (Harkavy & Puckett, 1994). In community practice, a specific social research technique, often referred to as *needs assessment*, examines how organizations, communities, and social structures (including political, economic, and social systems) contribute to or sustain challenges and issues experienced by the many individuals, families, groups, and organizations that comprise the community (Kirst-Ashman & Hull, 2018). Community assessments have traditionally been used to document the degree to which people are affected by specific social problems; social service priorities; the geographic or spatial distribution of these issues; and gaps in the availability, accessibility, or delivery of services (Royse et al., 2014). Separate assessments are also conducted about how power is distributed in communities, how it is used, and the people or institutions that possess power. Power analysis is also a component of developing a critical consciousness, which helps us to identify oppressive power forces and address them (Freire, 1970; Harrell & Bond, 2006).

Most often, organizers have conducted formal needs assessments by distributing surveys, analyzing secondary data, or interviewing key informants among community members (Chernesky & Gutheil, 2008; Marti-Costa & Serrano-Garcia, 1995). Such studies have traditionally been considered part of the second phase of the community-organizing process. Once the organizer has conducted one-on-one interviews and consulted potential constituents about issues that should be addressed, a structured process is used to document how people experience the community and the prevalence of the challenges or issues that concern them. Although the data collected may replicate information obtained through one-on-one interviews, it is often critical to have research evidence collected through a standardized process because evidence collected in an unsystematic way may be perceived as anecdotal, and may not be representative of the entire community. Further, evidence collected in a systematic way is less likely to be biased (or perceived to be biased) and can be disseminated to a general audience (Royse et al., 2014). Often, formal needs assessment data are required as part of a funding proposal by foundations and government agencies to demonstrate a documented need for funding. Organizations that receive funding may also be asked to have some data on hand to establish whether a specific program or initiative worked. Therefore, having data collected prior to the start of the project helps to establish a baseline against which project achievements (i.e., outcomes) can be measured.

One of the primary rationales for community assessments used for organizing purposes is that they are snapshots or impressions of what is going on in the community and may not always require intensive or rigorous data collection or analysis, especially when time and resources are limited. For example, the purpose of a community assessment may be simply to find out which hours of operation for a program are likely to ensure a maximum number of community members participate in the services offered (Royse et al., 2014). Consequently, qualitative methods (e.g., interviews or focus groups) or short surveys may be the preferred data-collection methods for many organizations.

Although time and resource constraints often determine how community assessments are conducted, there are many situations in which findings will be subjected to rigorous review, especially when it is used to verify the legitimacy of "the cause," a lobbying campaign, or an appeal for more or new services (Royse et al., 2014). With adequate time and resources, it is possible to conduct studies with large randomly selected samples that are representative of the community, or to make comparisons across geographic areas using standardized measures. Randomized samples provide a scientifically sound method of ensuring the findings of your assessment are generalizable to a larger group within a population. For example, if you are conducting a survey in a neighborhood with 10,000 residents, it may not be feasible to survey every resident in the community. However, the random-sampling approach allows you to conduct what researchers refer to as a *power analysis*, which lets you know how many surveys you need to complete to achieve confidence that you have captured a representative sample of the community. Once you know from the power analysis the number of completed surveys you need to achieve, you may randomly select potential participants by their addresses using a computer program, such as the =RAND() formula in Excel. Therefore, the purpose of the assessment; the preferences and goals of people who will potentially benefit from, fund, or design the study; and how the data will be used are important considerations when developing assessment methods. Study methods will vary substantially by specific projects or organizations based on the unique time, resources, and needs of the project (Chernesky & Gutheil, 2008; Hancock & Minkler, 2009; Meenaghan et al., 2004).

A notable component in community assessments is the focus on strengths and assets possessed by community members rather than an emphasis on the problems or needs experienced by people in poverty or members of minoritized or marginalized groups. In addition, recognizing the expertise of community members and the opportunity for capacity building, community practice has moved away from previous assessment models in which the organizer or outside consultant had the primary responsibility for conducting formal assessments of community needs. Community members are involved in data collection and analysis as a means of incorporating their perspectives into the research and motivating them to take action (Hancock & Minkler, 2009). Participatory methods for community assessment rely on theories associated with social constructionism and feminist theory (Fenge, 2010; Lincoln, 2002; Wallerstein & Duran, 2008).

IDENTIFYING ASSETS AND COMMUNITY CAPITAL

Community-based research has incorporated the strengths perspective into the process of conducting research to document the experiences of community members. Kretzmann and McKnight (1993) developed an *asset-based* approach to conducting community research and facilitating community development. This model is related to the concept of social capital, the theory that interpersonal relationships and social network formation can be used to leverage resources needed to improve communities (Putnam, 2000). Methods used to assess social capital in communities focus on examining social networks.

Johnson and colleagues (2010) describe social network analysis as a method used to examine interpersonal relationships as a specific form of social structure that changes depending on the nature of the relationship: family, neighbor, friend, community, business, or organization. Within these relationships, specific types of exchanges take place in which tangible (e.g., food, housing, jobs) or intangible (such as emotional support) resources flow back and forth among the network's participants. Social network analysis also documents network strength or density (number of linkages that connect a specific group of people). Network analysis can tell us several important things about a community, including

- the degree to which individuals perceive themselves to be connected to or trust others;
- the extent to which organizations communicate or work together on issues; and
- the degree to which individuals and groups within a community are linked to organizations within and outside their community (Kay, 2006; Krishna & Shrader, 1999).

As social capital is recognized as an essential asset in communities, and members of a community have differing degrees of social capital and social networks, organizers can use "social capital profiles" to engage community members in community assessments and social change processes. M. E. Brown and Livermore (2019) identified four distinct profiles of social capital that can help organizers determine effective strategies to engage and motivate community members for participation in social change processes, based on individual community members' degrees of social trust, civic engagement, reciprocal relationships, and social ties (see M. E. Brown & Livermore, 2019).

In addition to social capital, Flora and Flora introduced the *community capitals framework* in 2008 (Figure 6.1). This framework is used by many organizers in their work with communities, and posits that there are seven key types of community capital, including: (a) social, (b) natural, (c) cultural, (d) human, (e) political, (f) financial, and (g) built. In community assessments, assets and strengths can be identified and categorized within each domain of the community capitals framework. In addition to community members, other community partners and organizations, from a variety of sectors, can be identified as assets that possess capital in each domain, and these capitals can be captured in an asset map in order to view the full picture of community strengths and assets.

Asset-based community development is a process that involves community residents documenting community capital and resources that can be mobilized for community change, such as the knowledge and skills of individual residents (i.e., human capital), local institutions (e.g., schools, churches, and businesses; i.e., financial and built capitals), or *free space* such as parks and other places in which people gather (i.e., natural and built capitals; Flora & Flora, 2008; Kretzmann & McKnight, 1993). The basic premise is that deficit-focused models that frame community assessments in the context of "problems" imply that individuals who do not have access to political, economic, or social resources and capital are responsible for the poor quality of life in some communities. This in turn minimizes the role of oppressive political and economic institutions that are responsible for minoritization and marginalization of communities, and further perpetuates the cycle of oppression, thereby limiting community power.

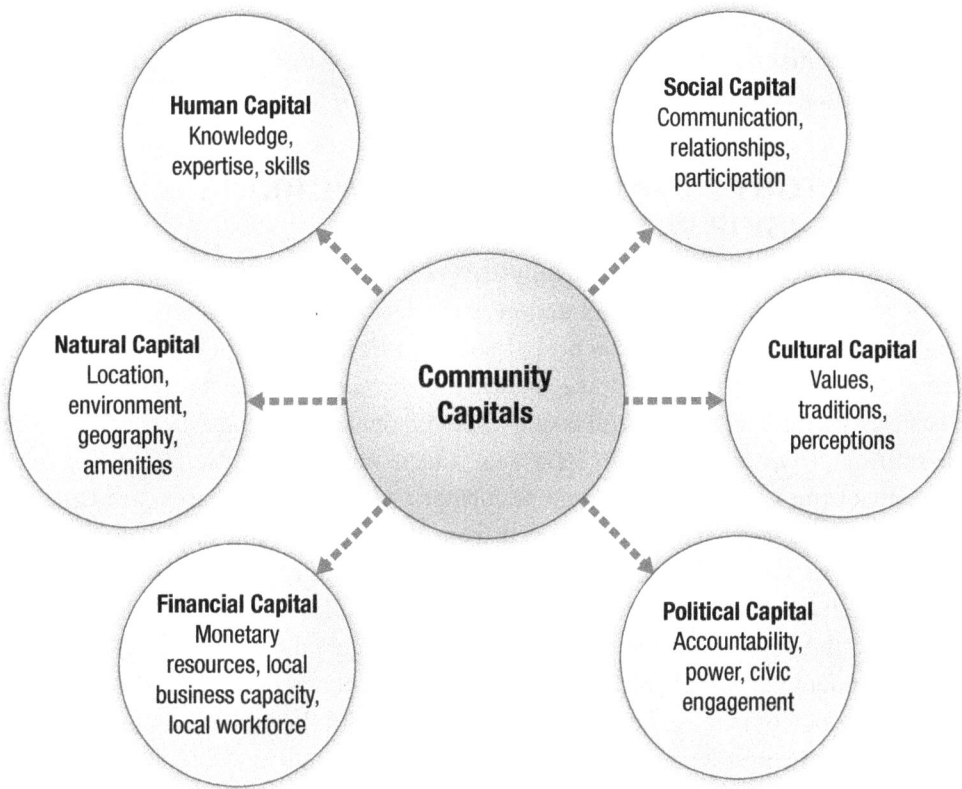

FIGURE 6.1 Community capitals.

SOURCE: Adapted from Emery, M., & Flora, C. (2006). Spiraling-up: Mapping community transformation with community capitals framework. *Community Development, 37,* 19–35; and Kelly, W. (2019). *Making sense of rural development in the 21st century—The digital capital upgrade.* Medium. https://medium.com/@wkruraldev/making-sense-of-rural-development-in-the-21stcentury-the-digital-capital-upgrade-42c3f99af10e.

McKnight and Kretzmann (2012) advocate for the use of a community development and organizing model that relies on existing resources, the skills of community members, and monetary and other resources controlled by community members. Residents come together to identify these assets, and develop a plan to use them to improve economic conditions in the community (e.g., to create more jobs or businesses). Rather than waiting for external resources to come to them, community members can leverage assets controlled by outsiders through negotiation and relationship building.

The common element in asset-based community development and participatory research methods is an emphasis on personal relationships, building community capacity, and strengthening social networks and other community capitals (Mathie & Cunningham, 2003). The focus on local control of the process and inclusive decision-making practices in the asset-based approach also corresponds to best practices in participatory research (Wallerstein & Duran, 2008). As mentioned previously, one key feature of the asset-based approach is a process called *asset mapping* in which an organizer works with community members to create an inventory of community capitals, including facilities, monetary and other resources available for community improvements, and the skills of community residents (Kretzmann & McKnight, 1993). This data-collection technique is discussed in greater detail in a later section of this chapter.

PARTICIPATORY ACTION RESEARCH: WORKING IN PARTNERSHIP WITH COMMUNITIES

PAR is the approach most often used to fully involve constituents in community assessments. With its emphasis on inclusion and action, participatory research is aligned with social work's commitment to empowerment and social justice. The method is also referred to as *action research* or *community-based participatory research* (Wallerstein & Duran, 2008). The basic assumption of the method is that a professional or external expert will work with a community group to identify an issue that affects members of the group, conduct an assessment of the issue using a variety of formal and informal research strategies, set a goal for community change that is derived from the research, and then engage in social action to achieve that goal. PAR has also been used successfully to facilitate social planning and community development processes (Sager, 2008). However, in addition to citizen involvement, this approach is intended to explicitly facilitate the use of data to advocate for changes in programs, procedures, policy, and legislation that will improve the community. Consequently, outcomes associated with PAR focus on both the individual participants and society: personal empowerment and transformation (through skill-building, power, and action) and social justice and the transformation of oppressive institutions (Sohng, 1995).

PAR is generally classified as a type of qualitative research study. However, sources of data for participatory research can range from interviews; storytelling; photography; focus groups; and art, music, spoken-word performances or theater to structured or semi-structured surveys; census data or other secondary data sources; and quantitative research designs (Grodach, 2009; Hancock & Minkler, 2009). Its classification as a qualitative study has to do with the fact that the distance between the research and participants is minimized, the research expert and community member experts have equal status and benefit equitably from participation, and that informal knowledge is valued as much as formal knowledge (M. E. Brown & Stalker, 2021; Lincoln, 2002; Stoecker, 2013). In addition, many participatory action researchers reject the notion that research should strive to be value-free or conducted in a manner that does not incorporate specific goals or a social change-oriented purpose (Fals Borda, 2002). The inclusion of community members in the research process renders it a method that relies on subjective knowledge collected, analyzed, and disseminated in a manner that reflects the perspectives and the standpoint (social status, power, and values) of participants (Wallerstein & Duran, 2008). Participatory research differs from other types of traditional research in that methodological decisions are made collectively using a group process.

According to Stoecker (2006), there are at least three ways in which participatory research differs from traditional research studies conducted by trained professionals:

- It is expected that the data will be collected and used for a specific purpose, primarily to make a change in the community.

- A number of research methods will be used. There is no one primary "right" or "wrong" approach; reliability and validity may not be as important as whether the data are useable and interpretable by research participants.
- The process involves a collaborative relationship between the researcher and members of the community and decisions are often made through group dialogue and consensus rather than simply at the expert's "recommendation."

COMMUNITY-BASED PARTICIPATORY RESEARCH (ACTION FRAMEWORK)

Community-based participatory research (CBPR), a form of PAR, is an approach that empowers communities to influence changes in policies and programs in their community through research. CBPR views community members as the experts on assets and needs related to their community, because they possess knowledge and lived experience about social issues, and they know best what will and will not work for their own community. As such, community members are actively engaged as partners throughout the research process, from research question identification to research design to interpreting and sharing results. The key components of CBPR are shared decision-making and power between researchers and community partners (Abma et al., 2017; M. E. Brown & Stalker, 2021; Kastelic et al., 2018; Wallerstein et al., 2008).

The ACTION framework is based on the CBPR approach and was developed as a guide focused on the process of implementing projects that involve partnerships between researchers and community members (M. E. Brown & Stalker, 2021). The ACTION framework consists of four domains: **a**ssess, **c**onnect, **t**ransform, and **i**n **o**ur **n**eighborhood. In addition to the four domains, there is an overarching principle of shared expertise among community partners (i.e., those individuals who live in or otherwise have a stake in the target community) and researchers. The *principle of shared expertise* acknowledges that community partners and research partners each bring unique expertise, skills, and experiences that contribute to the strength of the research project. Thus, joint decision-making and an equal opportunity to share perspectives and knowledge are essential to upholding the principle of shared expertise. Ultimately, this results in research that optimizes both scientific rigor and community authenticity. Each of the ACTION framework domains are described.

- The *assess* domain involves defining the focus of the research, identifying the research questions, and making decisions on research approach(es). As described in the principle of shared expertise, both researchers and community partners have unique expertise that must be tapped during this phase. Researchers possess knowledge on strengths and limitations of different research designs and the extent to which they are appropriate to answer specific research questions. Community partners have expertise related to community acceptability (e.g., whether residents of a community would likely prefer interviews or focus group methods), cultural knowledge (e.g., whether survey questions are culturally appropriate), and language recommendations.

- The *connect* domain refers to the relationships, information, and resources necessary to do the work. In various research projects, these assets might include connections to hard-to-reach populations (e.g., youth who are houseless), training for data analysis, individuals to serve as data collectors, equipment (e.g., tablets for door-to-door surveying), and supplies (e.g., incentives for focus groups participants). In this domain, researchers can offer training in protection of human subjects or interview protocols, as well as access to funding. Community partners can contribute by leveraging their existing relationships within the community to identify participants and volunteers. Other community stakeholders might have access to information such as crime statistics, neighborhood maps, and historical knowledge of the community.
- The *transform* domain includes the results, dissemination, and action components of the research. Given that community partners have invaluable insights about quantitative and qualitative results, they should be directly involved in interpreting the results. Results can be disseminated to the broader community for the benefit of the community and to academic audiences for the purposes of contributing to the knowledge base. In action-oriented research, activities might include the development or adaptation of interventions or sharing results with those with decision-making power.
- *In our neighborhood* refers to the fact that community research is occurring in real neighborhoods, with real people, in real time. Flexibility is key. Further, it is incumbent upon researchers and community partners to deeply consider and mitigate any potential risks or harm to research participants. Community partners also play a key role in the community trust-building process (M. E. Brown & Stalker, 2021).

YOUTH-LED PARTICIPATORY ACTION RESEARCH

Youth-Led Participatory Action Research (YPAR) is another form of PAR that has been designed specifically to engage youths and young adults in the participatory research processes. YPAR differs from other PAR frameworks based on its specific focus on issues experienced by young people, its emphasis on youth empowerment, and youth-focused capacity and skill building through the lens of positive youth development. According to the University of California, Berkeley, YPAR Hub (2015), the YPAR framework enables communities to:

- redefine who has the expertise to produce knowledge for our world to include not just professional adult researchers but young people who are living the issues they are studying;
- provide skills in inquiry, evidence, and presentation that are important to young people's development as students and agents of positive change in schools and communities;
- generate findings that provide insights into issues faced by young people that they themselves experience, as well as the resources that matter in helping solve those issues;

- promote young people's sociopolitical development and psychological empowerment such that they understand the roots of problems facing their communities and have the skills and motivation to take action; and
- evaluate programs, policies, and practices that affect young people.

APPLICATION OF GROUP METHODS FOR CONDUCTING PARTICIPATORY ACTION RESEARCH: EMPOWERING CONSTITUENTS TO TAKE ACTION

The PAR research process requires excellent use of interpersonal and group social work skills on the part of the facilitator to guide the community to achieve consensus about research goals and methodology. PAR projects may be facilitated by an organizer or a constituent. However, some of these projects employ outside experts, such as consultants or researchers, to collaborate with community members. Ongoing dialogue and discussion are the primary vehicles through which decisions are made. In many cases, training in research methodology for community members is provided by the outside expert. Issues of power and trust must be dealt with by the outside expert during the early stages of the process and good working relationships must be built with all group members. Stringer and Aragon (2021) describe the role of the researcher as minimizing conflict, showing respect and sensitivity toward group members, listening to what group members have to say, and encouraging people to perform research tasks and act for themselves.

For PAR to be effective, participants must be willing to learn and apply basic research methodology and must be enthusiastic and vocal enough to bring their own perceptions and values into the research process (Israel et al., 2008; Sohng, 1995). One of the characteristics of PAR that differentiates it from other types of research is the emphasis on Freirean methods in which group members engage in both reflection and action. Therefore, the process requires more than mere negotiation around research questions and methods, it incorporates specific values and principles into the research process. The primary goals of participatory research are to create an atmosphere characterized by trust, equality among participants, and a sense of ownership of the process by community members (Castleden et al., 2008). An organization that works to prevent police violence against women, transgender people, and gender-non-conforming people of color—Incite: Women of Color Against Violence (n.d.)—has incorporated these principles in a statement that describes its use of PAR in its advocacy work.

The incorporation of these principles into a group research process results in what Freire (1970) has described as *praxis*, the development of tacit knowledge by participants that leads to both empowerment and engagement in social change.

Often, community members have little reason to trust outside experts who have limited knowledge of the community, and many may be mistrustful of outsiders due to experiences of past harms, traumas, and oppression. According to Castleden and colleagues (2008), trust is an essential component of power sharing:

Specifically, trust is established when researchers work in an open, honest, and transparent manner. Trust is also built when researchers become involved in the community's activities, listen to and address community partners' needs, and reciprocate in some way. For example, there is a growing trend towards building capacity in the community through training and employing local people in research. (p. 1395)

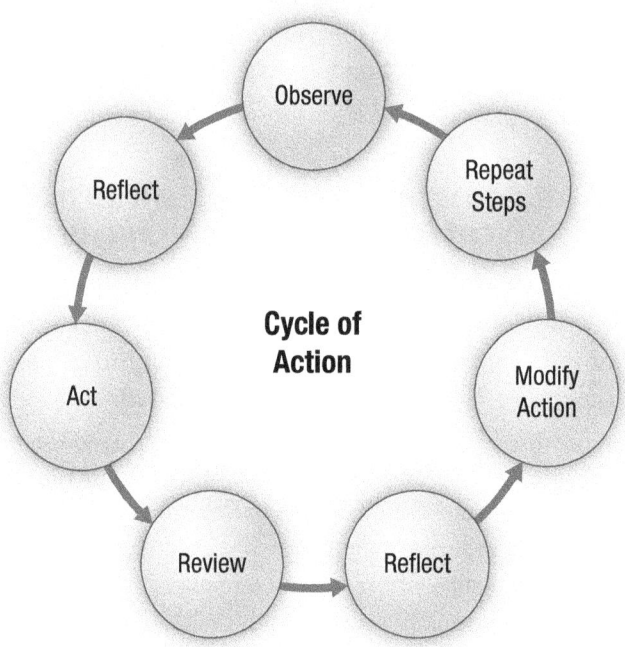

FIGURE 6.2 Cycle of action and reflection in praxis.

In addition to building trust, the application of appropriate interpersonal skills is essential for this process. Stringer and Aragon (2021) describe the components of praxis (i.e., research, reflection, and action) as a cyclical process consisting of looking, thinking, and acting:

> *As participants work though each of the major stages, they explore the details of their activities through a constant process of observation, reflection, and action. At the completion of each set of activities, they review (look again), reflect (reanalyze), and re-act (modify their actions). . . . People will find themselves working backward through the routines, repeating processes, revising procedures, rethinking interpretations, leapfrogging steps or stages, and sometimes making radical changes in direction. (pp. 10–11)*

As with issue identification, the dialogue process requires the facilitator to pose a series of *why*, *what*, *when*, and *how* questions to participants about their daily experiences; the quality of their lives; and how social programs, the economy, and the political system and other outside forces operate (Stringer & Aragon, 2021; Figure 6.2).

Advantages and Limitations of Participatory Action Research

Sager (2008) describes the difference between traditional types of university or expert-led research and PAR "as shift[ing] attitudes from stealing to sharing" or transferring power and control from researchers to community members (p. 211). A number of studies have documented that participation in PAR-related research can increase participants' experiences of personal empowerment and self-efficacy. For example, Oden and colleagues (2010) conducted a qualitative research study to document whether persons with disabilities who are members of minoritized groups felt empowered through their participation in a PAR project to increase the degree to which their community was physically accessible. Participants were interviewed about their participation in conducting accessibility assessments of local businesses. The respondents reported that the project increased their knowledge about the Americans With Disabilities Act (ADA), strategies that could be used to increase the accessibility of local businesses, and physical barriers that affect people with disabilities. They also gained a greater sense of independence in terms of dealing with the business community and increased their motivation to engage in advocacy. In a similar study, Jennings and colleagues (2006) examined the impact of a YPAR program. The participants were paired with adult leaders knowledgeable about community research and action. Once a youth received training from a mentor, the leadership dyad of an adult and young person then trained teams of youth using a process of dialogue, reflection, and action to develop community service projects. Evaluation findings indicated the youth participants experienced an increase in personal self-awareness and efficacy as well as a greater degree of engagement with the community.

Other advantages of PAR identified in the literature include the development of research methods and instruments that allow for the collection of reliable, valid, relevant or trustworthy data; increases in the number of strong social networks, improvements in neighborhood conditions or knowledge; and increases in the production of useful data easily understood by community members and disseminated to policy makers (Lincoln, 2002; Nygreen et al., 2006). Further, PAR contributes to the cultural competency of programs and services, ensures that community organizing or advocacy campaigns honor cultural or community customs and traditions, and enhances perceptions of collective identity control or political power. The cultural competency of programs, policies, and services developed through the PAR process is also enhanced, increasing the likelihood that they will actually be used by community members (Collie et al., 2010; Durst et al., 1999; Itzhaky & York, 2002; Reed & Cook, 2007; Silvestre et al., 2010; Yoshihama & Carr, 2002). PAR is also effective in the development of critical consciousness about social conditions and inequitable power relationships, and the likelihood that participants will take action to address these conditions (Carlson et al., 2006; Goto et al., 2010).

PAR processes are flexible, which allows for a variety of different types of studies, research methods, reports and dissemination techniques. In one example, Flicker and colleagues (2008) describe the use of *e-PAR* methods, using technology through the arts (e.g., photography, video production, and theater) and social media (e.g., interactive websites, blogs, and text messaging) to engage youth in issue identification, goal setting, and social action. Results of this study suggest that the e-PAR approach facilitated the development of strong social networks among the participants.

In addition to strengths, there are a number of limitations of PAR-related methods. For example, involving a large number of people in decision-making of any kind requires time (especially in terms of the time required in reaching consensus) and resources, such as a skilled facilitator (Fenge, 2010). There may be issues of power and control inherent in the group process, with group members who have more power or status dominating the process (Fenge, 2010). Group members may have hidden agendas in terms of what they want to achieve from the group and there may be a number of different groups involved in the process that have more resources, members, or the ability to make their opinions known than others (Wallerstein & Duran, 2008). There may also be external barriers that limit goal achievement, including a lack of adequate funding for the research study or political opposition to collecting information about an issue and taking action to promote social change (Chernesky & Gutheil, 2008). Power and status differentials may also play out in the group process, with people being fearful of having their say in front of an outside facilitator or general distrust of the facilitator or the process (Carlson et al., 2006). Community organizers can use tools from frameworks, such as consensus organizing (see Ohmer & Demasi, 2009), to overcome some of these challenges, foster trust, and help align community members by establishing common agendas and social change goals reflecting mutual self-interest.

PARTICIPATORY DATA-COLLECTION METHODS

As described previously, participatory research can include a variety of data-collection methods to document community challenges, needs, strengths, and assets. Some of these methods include creative methods, such as asset mapping and the use of photography, employing a specific method called *Photovoice*. Traditional methods for conducting community assessments, such as surveys, formal interviews, focus groups, the examination of secondary data about the community, and geographic mapping processes, can also be used in a manner that includes community members as central to the collection and analysis of data.

Asset Mapping

The assets approach as defined by Kretzmann and McKnight (1993) requires that participants (constituents and organizers) map or take an inventory of all the assets, resources, and skills available for use in making improvements in geographic communities. McKnight and Kretzmann (2012) contrast an asset-based conceptual model with a neighborhood "needs map" that simply lists the types of challenges experienced by residents such as poverty, unemployment, and substance abuse. The term *mapping* in this context refers to the creation of a conceptual model or picture that identifies broad categories of assets within and outside the community. However, in some circumstances, participatory community research approaches may involve using geographic maps to identify the specific locations of major community assets such as parks, schools, or businesses. Indeed, Participatory Geographical Information Systems (PGIS), or participatory mapping, is a method in which community members are trained to use geographic information systems (GIS) software in order to create their own maps, construct narratives of their lived experiences, and take an active role in community planning (Teixeira, 2018).

Asset maps used to inventory community assets contain three primary components, or what McKnight and Kretzmann (2012) identify as "building blocks."

- Primary building blocks or assets controlled by community members. These assets include personal income, individual skills, local businesses, community organizations, professional and business associations, local media, social media communication, and religious institutions.
- Secondary building blocks are community assets located within the community but controlled by people or institutions that are not located in the community. These assets may include institutions such as churches, hospitals, and schools, social service agencies, and public services such as the police, fire department, libraries and parks or recreational facilities. In this category, McKnight and Kretzmann also place vacant land, as well as unused and uninhabited housing. Such resources can be potentially used for community improvement and economic activity, for example, converting a vacant lot into a community garden or playground or a warehouse into a community center or new enterprise.
- The third-level building blocks consist of potential assets located and controlled by forces outside the community. These assets include public information such as social indicators and other secondary data that can be used to document conditions in the community and generate public support for improvements, government assistance for individuals, and government expenditures for improving buildings, parks, streets, and housing. Such assets help to generate government grants and contracts, jobs, and income for community residents.

These conceptual maps or inventories are used to guide the development process and identify individuals, agencies, facilities, and businesses that are most likely to be useful in maximizing community capacity. Other steps in the asset-building process include establishing an appropriate organization and representative decision-making structure to guide development, and identifying those organizations, government agencies, and businesses from outside the community with whom productive partnerships can be built to sustain the development effort.

Using Photovoice to Document Community Assets and Issues

Photovoice is a PAR method that involves having individuals take photos that represent their own environments and experiences and using these photos to spark critical analysis of relevant issues through guided facilitation (Wilson et al., 2007). Ultimately, Photovoice can lead to engagement in social action through community-change projects.

Photovoice draws from theoretical underpinnings of popular education, feminist theory, and social constructionism. Foster-Fishman and colleagues (2005) describe Photovoice as a type of participatory research that "puts cameras in the hands of individuals often excluded from decision-making processes in order to capture their voices and visions about their lives, their community, and their concerns" (p. 277). It builds on the concept of storytelling in that participants are given access to cameras and encouraged to take pictures of their community that have significance to their lives and capture their perspectives on community issues.

Once photos are taken, participants are asked to share stories about the photographs and what they mean to them, reflect on what the photos mean in terms of community context and issues experienced, barriers faced, and strengths possessed by community residents. Often, the pictures and these constructed stories are then shared with members of the public, the media, and political decision makers.

Photovoice was initially used in the mid-1990s by researchers interested in developing a technique to promote intergenerational dialogue about reproductive health issues in China (Wang & Pies, 2008). The technique is often designed to assist with the development of culturally appropriate health-promotion and social service programs and to facilitate multicultural understanding. In addition, it has been used extensively as a component of the community assessment process, and, in some circumstances, it may be the primary data-collection method used. For example, Mitchell (2018) used Photovoice as the primary data-collection method with American Indian community members to raise awareness of environmental justice issues and assess beliefs and perceptions of water and its meaning for Indigenous health.

The Photovoice process is congruent with techniques used in the development of critical consciousness described in Chapter 5 (Wang et al., 1998). The photos become "codes," developed by members of the community that are used to stimulate and guide dialogue among group members. The discussion is used to generate a proposed solution to a social issue, to mobilize members of the group to take action, and ultimately is used to promote changes in policies (Catalani & Minkler, 2010).

The Photovoice process includes a number of distinct components that are similar to those used in other types of PAR (Box 6.1). The dialogue process uses a set of questions that is designed to facilitate reflective dialogue from participants about the story that the picture-taker narrates about the photo, the sharing of stories among the participants, commonalities or themes identified in these pictures by participants, issues and community strengths identified, and possible solutions (Catalani & Minkler, 2010). Photovoice typically relies on a standardized set of questions posed by a facilitator called the SHOWeD method, which moves the conversation from the concrete, through critical dialogue, and ultimately to action (Wang & Pies, 2008):

- What do you **S**ee here?
- What is really **H**appening here?
- How does this relate to **O**ur lives?
- **W**hy does this issue, concern, or strength exist?
- What can we **D**o about it? (Wang & Pies, 2008, p. 188).

Numerous studies have examined the use of Photovoice in communities and have documented a number of positive effects. Participants have been found to experience increases in personal perceptions of self-efficacy and feelings of empowerment as well as increases in their knowledge about community processes and commitment to participate in social change activities (see Foster-Fishman et al., 2005; Gant et al., 2009; Wang, 2006; Wang et al., 1998). In addition, the process is also effective in helping people gain awareness about diverse perspectives and fosters a collective critical consciousness about social conditions (Carlson et al., 2006; Catalani & Minkler, 2010).

Box 6.1

STEPS IN THE PHOTOVOICE PROCESS

Wang (2006) identifies eight standard steps commonly used in Photovoice projects:

1. Recruit community leaders and other decision makers who can help take action to promote social change.
2. Recruit participants from a specific target or demographic group.
3. Provide training on safety, using cameras, and the ethical implications involved in picture taking.
4. Use established research procedures to obtain informed consent.
5. Provide some sample "themes" or ideas for the initial picture-taking process. In some cases, participants may generate their own ideas about the issues that they wish to address.
6. Distribute cameras and have participants start taking pictures.
7. Bring participants together to share the pictures and start to identify themes, or codes.
8. Develop a strategy for presenting the Photovoice project to decision makers.

It should be noted that there are a number of limitations associated with Photovoice. Catalani and Minkler (2010) conducted a review of the academic literature on the use of Photovoice; they point out several flaws in the method as well as in the available research literature; most of the research involves case studies, and there is a great deal of variation in the actual methods used and the degree of community participation in Photovoice projects. Often these procedures are not well explicated in the research literature. In addition, it is often not clearly documented as to whether action taken as a consequence of the photography and group identification of community issues actually contributed to community change.

CASE VIGNETTE: PHOTOVOICE IN JUVENILE JUSTICE SETTINGS

As part of a community-engaged research project in North Carolina, researchers invited youths who were involved in a Teen Court program to participate in a Photovoice project. Teen Court is a juvenile justice diversion program for first-time youth offenders. Rather than becoming involved in the traditional juvenile justice system, youths involved in the Teen Court program participate in a hearing in which they are judged and assigned consequences by a jury of their peers. In the Teen Court Photovoice Project, the researcher facilitated seven Photovoice sessions with a group of five adolescent girls between the ages of 15 and 17. The group decided to focus their Photovoice project on the topic of girls bullying and fighting. The youths took photos prior to each session that represented the various aspects of girls bullying and fighting and the researcher used the SHOWeD method to structure discussion around the photos. Some themes of the photo discussion included the importance of self and peer acceptance, coping skills to deal with peer pressure and bullying, the value of violence in their community (e.g., girls gaining popularity by fighting), and the power of expression and honoring their own values and beliefs. The Photovoice project culminated in a social action project designed by the participants. They ultimately chose to create a video that included some of their photos and quotes from the Photovoice discussions in order to raise awareness about the issue of bullying and violence in their community. A showcase was held and parents, community members, and Teen Court staff were invited to watch the video.

USING TRADITIONAL COMMUNITY ASSESSMENT METHODS: SURVEYS, FOCUS GROUPS, AND INTERVIEWS WITHIN A PARTICIPATORY ACTION RESEARCH FRAMEWORK

Research instruments used in most community assessments include standardized or semi-standardized questionnaires in which people are asked a series of questions about their perceptions of the community and the issues that affected them. Respondents can include community members, outside experts, other people perceived to have academic or professional knowledge about community issues, or specific interest groups such as community coalitions, cultural or religious leaders, social service providers, or business owners. In some circumstances, respondents are asked to choose among a list of community needs or to rank order their top choices. The questionnaire may include some open-ended questions to more accurately gauge their perceptions or concerns. One criticism of this method is that the survey may incorporate technical language that is not familiar to community residents (Kissane & Gingerich, 2004; Salahu-Din, 2003). Another concern about survey research is that it may allow the researcher to predetermine responses to individual questions or to reach conclusions that do not adequately reflect what community members think or feel.

Two other methods commonly used to collect data for community assessments are interviews and focus groups. The primary difference between an interview and a focus group is the number of participants involved—interviews typically happen one-on-one, whereas focus groups ideally have between six to eight participants in a small-group setting. Interviewees or focus group participants may include formal or informal community leaders, community members, members of specific cultural or identity-based groups, people providing services to community members and/or working to address an issue, or any other group of people from whom the organizer wants to learn about a social issue. Interviews differ from one-on-one, conversational interviews in that they are structured or semi-structured, meaning they generally employ a predetermined list of questions and are administered in a fairly consistent manner across respondents. Most often, community assessment interviews involve open-ended questions about the individual's perceptions of the community's assets and needs or about a specific community issue, existing services, or efforts intended to address community issues and their status, and ideas for strengthening what is already working or to develop new solutions for addressing community concerns. Alternatively, focus groups offer an opportunity to get a small group of people together to gather multiple perspectives simultaneously and spark conversations about an issue. When used in community assessments, focus groups are often made up of homogenous groups of people who have something in common such as a similar background, culture, demographic characteristics, or concern for or shared experiences with a social issue. However, sometimes the organizer may prefer to bring together a heterogenous group of people (e.g., community members representing different age groups and life stages, service consumers, and service providers) because differing perspectives and experiences can enrich dialogue about a common issue. A community assessment often includes surveys, questionnaires, interviews, and focus groups. The use of multiple methods is one of the techniques that can be used to enhance the reliability of the data collected (Royse et al., 2014).

Participatory methods can be used effectively with traditional data-collection methods; community members' expertise can be engaged to design surveys or interview protocols to capture meaningful and culturally relevant data. In a participatory process, researchers and community members work in partnership to develop community surveys or interview guides (Balcazar et al., 2009; M. E. Brown & Stalker, 2021). This type of collaborative dialogue enhances the face validity of the research instruments. The surveys or interview guides developed through this process should reflect the lived experiences of community members. It should also increase the likelihood that the language and wording of the instrument are appropriate and that people will participate in the study. Participatory methods should also increase the degree to which the study findings can be considered reliable or valid.

Capacity building is important in participatory research, and researchers often provide training to participants on how to conduct studies, design measurement instruments, analyze the data, and disseminate the findings (tell the story of what has been learned). However, and of equal importance, the process also relies on the expertise—lived experiences, knowledge, and perceptions—of participants in terms of how to approach community members for participation, the appropriateness of the research design, and the chosen method(s) of data collection. Essentially, it is often the role of the participants to *train the researcher* in culturally appropriate methods for engagement with and relationship building with members of the community. For example, if a researcher is conducting a study in the Southwestern United States of healthcare utilization among members of the Pascua Yaqui Tribe, knowledge of the Pascua Yaqui culture, history, and language would be essential. For this transborder tribal community, considerations in the design of the study would be whether households in the United States, Mexico, and enrolled members living on or off the tribal reservation should be included; the choice of language (English, Spanish, or Yaqui) or dialect to be used; actual translation of the research instrument; and the appropriateness of the questions asked.

Neighborhood Data Collection: Facilitating the Development of Social Indicators of Community Assets and Needs

Another traditional method used to document community issues is the collection of secondary data based on standardized measures about community conditions, opportunities, and needs. Both government and nonprofit service providers typically document the number of people and households with specific needs or issues as well as the number of people who receive services. Many government agencies make this information available to the public through reports that can be accessed online. The advantages of using these indicators are many; this information is often accessible to the public; people generally accept that the measures reflect the need for services, legislation, or new policies; and they provide a means to make comparisons about different communities or political jurisdictions or to examine trends in data patterns over time. Consequently, social indicator systems are important as a source of baseline and evaluation data about communities that can be used to persuade donors to fund local projects. One example of a federal data source built in response to the 2020 COVID-19 pandemic, providing real-time health-indicator data at the county level, is the Centers for Disease Control and Prevention's (CDC's) COVID Data Tracker interactive map and data dashboard (CDC, 2021). Using this tool, for example, community organizers working to increase health literacy and vaccination rates could view data trends at the local level indicating the percentage of the population that was vaccinated, how many positive cases and deaths were reported, and other relevant community characteristics. Increasingly, local communities are developing their own quality-of-life indicators that capture data related to employment and the local economy, health and well-being, safety, poverty, and other determinants of health. For example, in Tucson, Arizona, the city, the county, and a local university publish annual reports that include indicators of poverty and urban stress using a Neighborhood Vulnerability Index (University of Arizona, 2017), and in Shreveport, Louisiana, the Community Foundation of Northwest Louisiana publishes an annual "Community Counts" report that includes annual population, economics, human capital, health, social environment, and physical environment data (Community Foundation of Northwest Louisiana, 2021). Across the country, local governments, nonprofits organizations, and local foundations are important resources for acquiring secondary data, as they are increasingly generating and sharing local quality-of-life and determinants-of-health data for the benefit of their communities.

Secondary data are often used for assessment and planning purposes because they are less costly and less time consuming than primary data collection. However, there are also a number of barriers that typically limit their use in community assessment processes. For example, one primary source of data is the U.S. Census. Census data may be used to document the extent of poverty in a community, demographic composition, or household characteristics in a community. The advantage of this method is that the government collects these data at regular intervals in a standardized way and almost everyone is included (Galster et al., 2005). A major disadvantage of census data is that some groups are likely to be excluded (e.g., people who are houseless or immigrants without papers), and the full census is collected only every 10 years.

An important disclaimer regarding social indicators is that seldom are these measures used to document neighborhood assets other than income, home ownership, or the number of businesses within a specific geographic location. In fact, the emphasis on what are perceived to be "objective" measures generally contains value assumptions about how benefits are or should be distributed. In some circumstances, to make comparisons by gender, ethnicity, or social class, such objective measures may actually serve to misrepresent the experiences or interests of some groups in the community (Driscoll Derickson, 2009; Meenaghan et al., 2004). For example, research findings that indicate a large percentage of local homeowners are having difficulty paying their mortgages may be used by government officials or members of the banking industry to argue that these residents were "bad credit risks" and should not have received mortgages in the first place, ignoring the role played by limited government regulation of the home loan industry.

One effort, the National Neighborhood Indicators Partnership (NNIP), involves community residents in collecting, analyzing, and disseminating neighborhood data. Through NNIP, the Urban Institute and organizations in local communities coordinate their work to facilitate the collection of data pertaining to social conditions and determinants of health that affect neighborhoods. They also provide how-to manuals, conduct workshops, and disseminate a wide variety of technical information to other community groups (NNIP, n.d.). The data collected for use in these systems include census data as well as information obtained from a wide variety of government agencies and its use is intended to promote the development of assessment tools that look at a community or a neighborhood as a whole rather than focusing on specific types of issues (Driscoll Derickson, 2009).

Although these data systems allow neighborhood groups access to information and consequently provide a degree of ownership and control of local planning efforts, they also require a great deal of money and technical expertise. An alternative approach for using social indicators involves the development of neighborhood-level indicators of neighborhood quality and assets by community groups. This collaborative group process requires participants to identify issues of concern, examine their perceptions of the issue and its causes, and create an operational definition and a set of measures that are easy to implement. For example, in a community in which obesity is an issue, the number of walking paths or the number of parks in which it is safe for children to play may be logical indicators of the issue and reflect the perceptions of the community (Evenson et al., 2009). According to Hancock and Minkler (2009), such measures often have a high degree of *face validity* in that they reflect community values, are more accessible and understandable than academic or technical models, and can be used to convey a message or political point about the importance of taking action to remedy the issue. Other advantages of this method are that it increases community ownership of the research process, makes it more likely that both needs and assets will be measured, and that cultural values as well as community perceptions about quality-of-life issues will be incorporated into measurement procedures and discussions about possible solutions (Table 6.1).

POWER ANALYSIS: MAPPING POWER RELATIONS AND SOCIAL NETWORKS IN THE COMMUNITY

The development of critical consciousness requires that participants understand how power is distributed in their communities and how power or the lack of power affects them. Pyles (2013) describes the purpose of *power analysis* as "to determine the winners and losers of social policies and practices, identifying how social and economic power operates in order to work to undo such retrenched power" (p. 124). Traditionally, the identification of people and groups who hold power in individual communities was a task conducted by individual organizers. Knowing who has power, why they have power, and how they use it is an essential skill in community practice (Staples, 2016). There are a number of specific methods that can be used to document power arrangements. However, it is often not sufficient for community organizers to do this work in isolation. Power analysis research is often conducted in conjunction with other group assessment methods and as part of the process of praxis, working with people to develop a critical consciousness about how communities, social policies, and institutional arrangements serve to oppress, minoritize, and marginalize some groups of people while serving the interests of others.

Power in Communities

Questions typically addressed through power analysis include a focus on sources of power (such as money, votes, elected office, authority, information, social, economic, or professional status, or personal attributes such as demographic background or charisma). Power analysis also examines personal and business affiliations such as profession, employer, or memberships in clubs or seats on nonprofit organization boards. Often professional or social networks of the decision maker are examined, including asking questions such as who are their friends or relatives, with whom do they do business or socialize, and with whom did they attend school or have personal relationships? Examining relationships among businesses, corporations, or nonprofit groups is also important because overlapping memberships on boards of directors can provide evidence of networks of affiliated groups, common interests, or concentrated power (Domhoff, 2009a, 2009b; Sen, 2003).

Communities tend to be of two types: elitist or pluralist (Domhoff, 2007). Elitist communities have a well-defined group of politically, economically, and/or socially influential members who are often small in number, but hold most of the decision-making authority in the community. In contrast, pluralist communities are those in which a number of different groups hold power and interact with one another in a manner that changes in response to the issue at hand, public support, and the degree to which individuals and groups benefit from or perceive themselves to be harmed by a specific issue (Conservation Partnership, 2002; Meenaghan et al., 1982). These *interest groups* consist of members of professional, business, or advocacy organizations who have common interests and concerns (Kraft & Furlong, 2021). Interest groups typically lobby government officials to have policies and legislation adopted that reflects their values and that will benefit their own needs (vested interest), those of an unrepresented group (such as children or animals), or the general public (e.g., environmental causes or the negative effects of global warming). For example, a business association may be formed to represent the interests of downtown merchants who fear that the city will want to tear down their shops in order to build a sports stadium. A group of neighbors may come together to vote for a candidate for the school board who promises to support the building of a new middle school in their neighborhood.

The degree of social stratification in communities is also important when studying power in communities. The term *social stratification* refers to the demographic groups that are present in the community, how they interact with one another, and which of these groups actually have the power and resources to make or influence decisions (Harrell & Bond, 2006; Wolf, 2007). What groups are typically excluded, minoritized, or marginalized? What demographic group is most likely to hold political office or serve on corporate boards (Domhoff, 2009a)? What industry or industries are predominant in the community? What polices, practices, or legislation benefits them? In many cases, there are certainly important power differentials among members of identity communities as well that determine who holds power and who is typically excluded from decision-making. For example, in the Hmong immigrant community in the United States, male clan leaders who are often business or professional leaders make decisions for community members and settle personal disputes (Hardina et al., 2008; Yoshihama & Carr, 2002).

Conducting Research and Documenting Power and Influence

There are a number of ways in which organizers have worked to document power arrangements. Each of these methods contains elements in common and involves the identification of community leaders, sources of power, and groups expected to support or oppose a specific decision, policy, or piece of legislation affecting the community.

- *Identifying factors that facilitate or block change.* Two related techniques, *force field* and *SWOT* (**S**trength, **W**eakness, **O**pportunity, and **T**hreat) analysis, use a framework developed by social psychologist Kurt Lewin in the 1940s to understand the interaction of proponents and opponents of change and factors in the social, political, and economic environment that may have positive or negative effects in social change initiatives. In force field analysis, factors that "drive" or facilitate change and those forces that resist or prevent it are identified. In SWOT analysis, participants identify similar factors affecting change in organizations, identifying strengths and weakness both inside and outside the organization.

- *Interest group analysis (positional approach).* Interest group analysis focuses on the relative power of the various interest groups involved in public decision-making and their ability to negotiate and compromise with one another. The groups with most power and access to resources are believed to have greater ability to effect change. However, if there are a number of issues under discussion in any community, the degree to which the same organizations line up to support or oppose specific issues can be examined. Are the same groups always allied with one another, or do these alliances shift in response to different issues?

- *Analysis of campaign donations.* One way to document the power of interest groups is through examination of campaign donations. Candidates are required to report the names, employers, and profession of donors to local, state, and federal governments. This information can be used to link interest groups to individual politicians and specific pieces of legislation that may benefit or harm members of these groups. Information on campaign donations can be found in government offices or by going online. For example, the Center for Responsive Politics contains a database of donors to federal candidates and their industry affiliations.

- *Social network analysis to identify informal neighborhood leaders.* There are two primary approaches to conducting network analysis. The first involves conducting research to identify informal community leaders or the number and strength of informal networks that provide information, social support, and assistance to friends, relatives, and neighbors. Informal assessments of networks are generally made through observations and one-on-one interviews. More formal assessments of these helping networks involve conducting interviews with community members to see with whom they give, receive, or exchange help. Leaders can generally be identified if they are repeatedly named as helpers.

- *Social network analysis to identify formal connections between individual decision makers and organizations or among influential or powerful organizations.* Premised on Domhoff's (2009a) assertion that often there are explicit connections among powerful organizations, efforts are made to examine links among people who make decisions and their membership in organizations. This type of network analysis often involves examining membership on corporate boards, foundations, or nonprofit groups in order to document whether some of the same people sit on the same boards or whether some organizations have overlapping boards of directors and, consequently, influence decision-making in multiple organizations. Board membership lists are public information and can often be found online. Business or property ownership research using public records may also assist in the identification of these relationships or in documenting vested interests.

- *Newspaper and other media accounts of community activities and political decision-making.* Are the same individuals often identified as involved in community issues, or do these decision makers and activists vary from issue by issue? Newspaper and other print media can help organizers identify who is involved in decision-making on issues, where alignments exist between individuals and organizations in power, how they use their influence and power, and what messages are being shared with the public by people in power.
- *Postings on websites; social media; blogs; and YouTube; or candidate, office holder, or corporate websites.* These sources often provide information about the schedules for public meetings, the activities of nonprofit organizations, and meeting agendas. They often list who is involved in the decision-making process and any other businesses or organizations with which participants are affiliated. In addition, social media descriptions of policies and legislation often contain important information about the values and representation incorporated into decision-making processes, the values and perspective of the writer or person who has posted the information, policy arguments for supporting or opposing the legislation, and research evidence used to support the policy argument.
- *Personal knowledge about people with power (reputational method).* This refers to information collected through one-on-one interviews with community residents regarding their own affiliations, their personal knowledge about who has been involved in a previous decision-making processes, the people in the community who are perceived to have power, the people to whom community members typically go to for help, and the interrelationships among people perceived to have power or influence. For example, knowing that Margarita Sanchez serves on the board of the United Way, runs the constituency office for the local state senator, and is married to City Council Member Gonzalez provides important information about how contacting or persuading Margarita Sanchez to make a specific decision can be used to influence community decision-making (Conservation Partnership, 2002; Domhoff, 2009b; Hardina, 2002, 2005; Meenaghan et al., 1982; Minkler & Coombe, 2009; Work Group for Community Health and Development, 2022; Figure 6.3).

Group Methods for Conducting Power Analysis

Group methods for conducting power analysis often involve meetings in which participants working with a designated facilitator identify people, individual groups, legislation, strength in numbers, and other driving or restraining factors that can facilitate or block change. Groups can also identify weaknesses and opportunities inside and outside the organization, potential allies or coalition group partners that are already engaged in the change effort. Often a poster, whiteboard, or large piece of paper is used to record suggestions and comments from meeting attendees—space is provided to list positive and negative factors or forces that can influence the organizing effort. Sometimes conceptual or network maps can be constructed that identify driving and oppositional forces or that diagram relationships among powerful groups or people in the community (Noy, 2008; Figure 6.4).

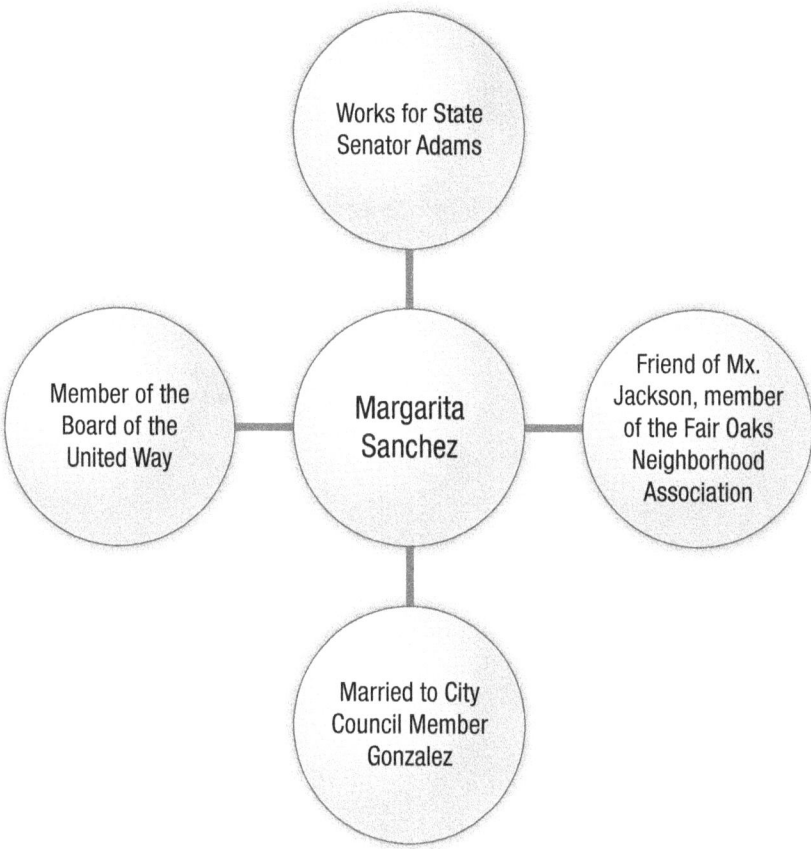

FIGURE 6.3 Simple ego-network map: Social and political network for Margarita Sanchez.

In addition, formal research studies can be conducted to supplement the knowledge of community members. If a group meeting is not sufficient to obtain all information necessary to identify community power-holders, group members can be assigned tasks and follow-up action items, such as to be asked to conduct web searches of campaign donations, board membership, or newspaper archives and social media sources. The Center for Community Engagement and Service Learning also recommends that individual group members construct a power map that illustrates their own relationships with individuals and groups in the community who can influence the decision-making process. Some of the people on these personal maps are those with whom the constituent has built relationships through one-on-one interviews (Whitcher et al., 2010).

Once the community group has a sufficient understanding of community power, the next step involves the identification of patterns or themes by participants and development of a plan for action that neutralizes the opposition or increases the power of the community group to take action and influence policy, legislation, and other public decisions. Ritas and colleagues (2008) identify a number of steps that can be used by group facilitators to

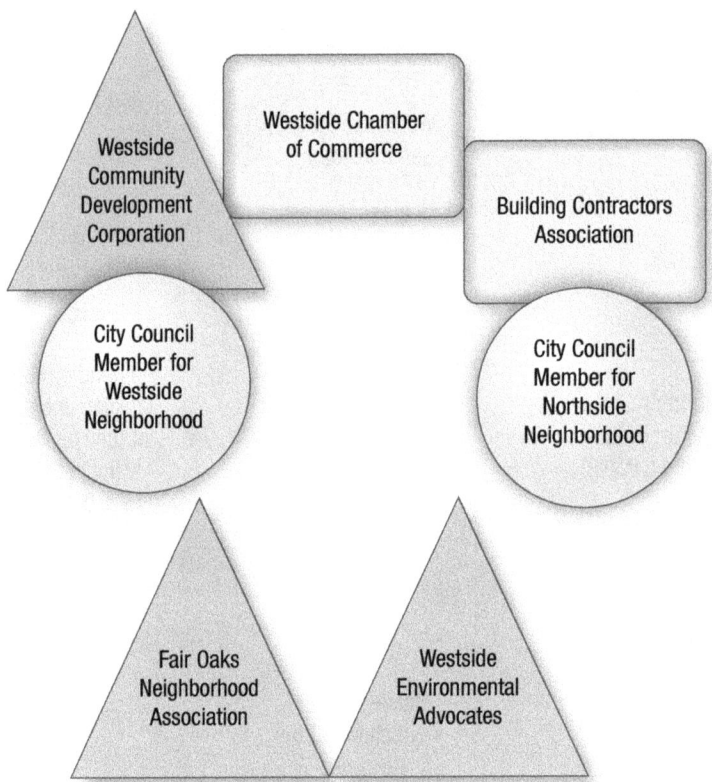

FIGURE 6.4 Conceptual map: Overlapping boards in the Westside Neighborhood. This type of map is described in Noy, D. (2008).

NOTE: Triangles = community groups; circles = government decision makers; squares = business associations.

SOURCE: Data from Noy, D. (2008). Power mapping: Enhancing sociological knowledge by developing generalizeable analytical public tools. *American Sociologist, 39*, 3–18. https://doi.org/10.1007/s12108-008-9030-5.

involve participants in power mapping. Generally, these issues can be addressed by using some of the same questions and techniques used in other types of participatory research studies—focusing on who is involved and what, why, and how things happen. Power mapping involves the following steps:

- Identify the change objective.
- Identify key decision makers and organizations.
- List these key people and groups under one of three headings: allies, opponents, and undecided.
- Choose the three most important people and groups to influence.
- Reflect on how difficult it was to identify people or choose the most influential among a number of possibilities. Determine whether group members have any relationships with these decision makers that can be leveraged in the social change endeavor.

- Conduct a force field analysis by listing the people you want to influence on a separate sheet of paper with three columns: positive factors, negative factors, and strategies for change. Identify driving or resisting forces and the relative strength of these forces.
- Begin to develop social change strategies that are appropriate for persuading or pressuring opponents, developing partnerships with potential allies, or asking potential opponents to join your coalition or engage in dialogue to seek common ground (Table 6.2).

STRATEGIC COMPATIBILITY: FOSTERING COLLABORATION WITH INTENTIONALITY

Partnerships are essential to the success of community change initiatives. As such, partnerships are another important aspect of community assessments. The collective impact framework highlights the importance of aligning cross-sector partners toward a common goal, focusing on strengths and assets, and developing mutually beneficial relationships among partners (Edmondson & Hecht, 2014; Kania & Kramer, 2011). However, establishing and maintaining partnerships and proactively engaging in collaborative efforts requires time and resources, a luxury many nonprofits do not have. Therefore, it is important that nonprofits use their time wisely, connecting with the right partners who have shared values and goals, where resources can be aligned and leveraged intentionally to respond to community challenges and facilitate positive social change.

The concept of strategic compatibility has a similar foundation to that of collective impact—the premise that interorganizational partnerships are most effective at achieving community change when they are mutually compatible and mutually beneficial (M. E. Brown et al., 2019). In one community assessment project in Baton Rouge, Louisiana, the community voiced the need for an afterschool program in their neighborhood. There was a nonprofit in the community that had access to youth, and could readily recruit them, and also program staff and volunteers to run the afterschool program, but did not have facilities to house the program or transportation to get the children to the program site and back home. Another partner had an underutilized community space, but no program staff, no relationships with youth in the community, and no transportation for the youth. A third partner had transportation, but no facilities and no relationships with the local schools or other youth-servicing organizations. Through this community assessment project, the organizers determined that a tool needed to be designed that could save these partners time and money by helping to identify where there were aligned interests and an opportunity to maximize resources through intentional collaboration. As a result, these organizers developed the Strategic Compatibility Assessment, a tool that assists community practitioners in identifying interorganizational collaborative capacities to motivate collaborative behaviors that ultimately fuel community change initiatives and enhance collective impact (M. E. Brown et al., 2019). The Strategic Compatibility Assessment involves asking potential collaborative partnership organizations to complete a simple questionnaire that asks them to identify both their organization's "assets/haves" and "limitations/needs" for 17 distinct collaboration domains (see Table 6.1).

TABLE 6.1 Strategic Compatibility Assessment Data-Collection Tool

COLLABORATIVE DOMAIN	ASSET/HAVES	LIMITATION/NEEDS
Funding	O	O
Service sharing	O	O
Facility space	O	O
Data management/record keeping	O	O
Program evaluation	O	O
Staffing	O	O
Training	O	O
Advertising/media	O	O
Market assessment	O	O
Transportation	O	O
Child/family service plan	O	O
Common committees	O	O
Emergency preparedness	O	O
Case review and shared learning	O	O
Client referrals	O	O
Voluntary written agreements	O	O
Mandatory contracts	O	O

Using network analysis once the data is collected from all potential partners in a project, the information collected from the Strategic Compatibility Assessment can then be used to identify potential mutually beneficial partnerships (i.e., partnerships in which one partner's needs are met by another partner's assets and vice versa). The researchers who developed the Strategic Compatibility Assessment found that the tool accelerated the organization and engagement process of cross-sector partners involved in the community change initiative, enabling the partners to save valuable time and more quickly respond to pressing community needs by identifying and facilitating intentional and rewarding collaborative relationships (M. E. Brown et al., 2019).

PUTTING VALUES INTO ACTION: BUILDING ON STRENGTHS AND SHARED EXPERTISE

Although the very nature of PAR seems to incorporate basic tenets associated with the strengths perspective and community empowerment, there are a number of ethical dilemmas that characterize efforts to include community members in efforts to conduct community assessments. For example, Stoecker (2008) acknowledges that the original purpose of PAR is to encourage self-sufficiency, personal and political perspectives, and promote control of the research process and knowledge production by members of minoritized and marginalized communities. However, a PAR process that assigns oversight

TABLE 6.2 Power Map and Force Field Analysis of Allies and Opponents of New Environmental Regulations Affecting Businesses in Neighborhood

PRIMARY ALLIES	OPPONENTS	UNCERTAIN OR NEUTRAL
Westside Community Development Corporation	Westside Chamber of Commerce	Westside Council of Churches
Fair Oaks Neighborhood Association	Council of Realtors	Westside Civic Organization
Consumer Rights Association	Building Contractors Association	Members of the city council
Westside Environmental Advocates	Individual business owners	
Individual homeowners		
GROUPS TO BE INFLUENCED	**POSITIVE OR DRIVING FACTORS**	**NEGATIVE OR RESTRAINING FACTORS**
Westside Chamber of Commerce	Limited power and influence	Ideology that opposes must regulations
Building Contractors Association	Actively trying to improve their image in the community	New regulations would affect building costs
Members of the city council	Can be influenced through lobbying and the prospect of votes	Westside Council Member is also a member of the Building Contractors Association

NOTE: Additional items that can be included in the analysis are the types of organizations involved and the source or amount of power possessed by the various organizations or individuals identified in the chart. Additional items that can be included in the power map are the change(s) to be made and the proposed strategies and tactics.

and most research responsibility for technical tasks or basic research design to a researcher or other consultant does not necessarily fulfill this goal. Stoecker is also concerned about the prospect of the researcher fulfilling "the educator's role," in that there is potential for the imposition of an ideological perspective or predetermined methodological stance. Control of projects and goal setting can also impose contradictions and questions about power and status in circumstances in which an outside organization approaches a community for participation in a new project or initiative. Indeed, not all researchers are equipped to participate in PAR; it requires specialized training, reflective practices, a willingness to release control, and trust in the community by the researcher as well.

Much of our knowledge about how to navigate these ethical issues comes from qualitative research. For example, Maiter and colleagues (2008) describe the importance of reciprocity in conducting PAR projects, the principle associated with ensuring that all research participants benefit directly from a community-based study as well as the researcher. They view reciprocity as a process that develops over time through relationship building, using dialogue to develop consensus among all participants and to promote the exchange of resources and knowledge. Fenge (2010) also emphasizes the importance of researcher solidarity with the participants, making sure that "the process of mutual trust works both ways. This involves a recognition that the term 'researcher' applies to both local actors and those people who contribute specialized skills, knowledge, and/or resources to the PAR process" (p. 886).

For Harrell and Bond (2006), the primary ethical challenge in community practice and research is functioning as a culturally competent professional in a diverse community. They identify a number of practice behaviors needed to put diversity principles in action, including identifying the various ethnic and other demographic groups in the community, and finding out how these groups interact with one another. Organizers should also examine community context and the historical, social, and political forces that make the community unique. They also recommend that practitioners engage in reflection about their own location in the social structure, the power and privilege they possess, and any biases that may affect their ability to work with members of the community (as discussed in greater detail in Chapter 1). Harrell and Bond (2006) argue that the appropriate stance for a culturally competent practitioner is one of "empowered" humility that is characterized by:

> *A willingness to identify limitations, to experience feelings of vulnerability and tolerate the ambiguity of "not knowing." This vulnerability is in the services of gaining greater awareness, insight and understanding. To connect, to learn, and to understand are empowering experiences that build confidence to walk in unfamiliar terrain and meet diversity challenges head on. (p. 372)*

Israel and colleagues (2008) identify practice activities that incorporate assumptions about the importance of mutual, reciprocal, and equal partnerships and cultural competence into the PAR research process:

- Members of the research partnership must be able to define the community that is to be studied, the people who are to be included in the study, and appropriate individuals and organizations who serve as the community's representatives on the research team.
- The PAR-related research methods used in specific situations may and should differ based on the research questions, the situation addressed, and the people involved. A standard methodology used for a number of different studies may not adequately reflect the preferences of participants.
- Members of the community should set research priorities and participate in the choice of research design and methodology. Researchers should not impose the specific methods to be used, but engage in dialogue with team members to explore and determine the best approach.
- Group dialogue should be used to address differences among participants in terms of culture, ethnicity, social class, gender identity, education, and other demographic characteristics. It should be recognized and acknowledged that different members have different perspectives, goals, agendas, and knowledge, both tacit (experiential) and formal. Proactive efforts should be made to bridge these differences so that participants "speak a common language" and forge a consensus about goals, methodology, and outcomes.

- All members of the research partnership have the responsibility to ensure that the process of collaboration is undertaken in a way that facilitates equity among all participants, keeping in mind that some inequities in terms of power and status are likely to exist and affect the PAR process. Such differences should be examined and addressed.
- All members will not be involved in every activity undertaken. Many tasks will be assigned to members based on skills and interests. However, all members should be involved in interpreting the data collected.
- A formative or ongoing evaluation of the degree to which the research partnership actually reflects PAR principles should be conducted, with adjustments made in procedures and activities as necessary.
- A process should be mutually agreed upon for disseminating the findings to others, either for use by the community or publication in professional journals or presentations by the researchers.

Toward this end, the Oakland Community-Based Public Health Initiative has developed a protocol that can be used to guide dialogue between researchers and other participants:

1. How will research processes and outcomes serve the community?
2. How will the community be involved in defining the objectives of the research?
3. Are researchers committed to doing the follow-up necessary to implement larger projects?
4. How will the community be involved in the analysis of the data?
5. How, when, and why should the findings be released?
6. What is the focus of the research with regard to addressing long-term community needs?
7. Are the research methods sufficiently rigorous yet true to community-based principles that incorporate perspectives and beliefs of community residents (L. Brown & Vega, 2008)?

KEY TAKEAWAYS AND SUMMARY

Community assessment is a critical step in the problem-solving process in community practice. Data help guide us to document community issues and assets; suggest changes in services, policies, and legislation that address gaps in community resources and community needs; and give us an indication of how to engage in action to strengthen assets and address community concerns. However, some of the primary questions in community assessment practice are who determines community preferences for change? Who has control of data and other information? And how, and to what degree are community residents involved in the community assessment and social change efforts? PAR provides a vehicle for incorporating basic social work and community-organizing principles, including self-determination, empowerment, the strengths perspective, respect for diverse cultures and minoritized groups, equitable partnerships, mutual learning, and shared expertise in the research process. Data-collection methods, such as Photovoice, asset mapping, participatory community mapping, and power analysis, require a commitment to these values as well as the appropriate application of appropriate interpersonal and task-related social work skills on the part of the researcher or organizer. In Chapter 7, the next stages of the problem-solving process, goal setting and planning, are examined and techniques to enhance the inclusion of community members in decision-making are described.

RESOURCES

- DePaul Asset-Based Community Development Institute: https://resources.depaul.edu/abcd-institute/resources/Pages/default.aspx
- Map the Power Toolkit by LittleSis: https://littlesis.org/toolkit
- Promoting Community Vitality and Sustainability: The Community Capitals Framework: https://pcrd.purdue.edu/wp-content/uploads/2020/09/Community-Capitals-Framework-Writeup-Oct-2014.pdf
- Data Dashboard Examples
  - Centers for Disease Control and Prevention COVID Tracker: https://covid.cdc.gov/covid-data-tracker/#datatracker-home
  - Community Counts (Shreveport, Louisiana): https://cfnla.org/data/
  - Neighborhood Vulnerability Index (Tucson, Arizona): https://mapazdashboard.arizona.edu/tucson-pima-county-housing-study

ACTIVITIES

1. In small groups, play the WE CAN Asset-Based Community Development Asset Mapping Board Game from DePaul Asset-Based Community Development Institute (instructions available at https://resources.depaul.edu/abcd-institute/resources/Pages/tool-kit.aspx).
2. In your classroom, divide members into two teams to plan and stage a debate. The topic of the debate is the "Limitations and Advantages of Qualitative (Impressionistic) versus Quantitative (Objective) Data in Participatory Research." Spend 30 minutes researching the topic prior to engaging in the debate.

ASSIGNMENTS

1. Conduct a power analysis of a geographic or identity community using at least three of the data-collection methods listed in this chapter. At least one of these data-collection methods should include either individual interviews with community members or consultation with constituency group members. Prepare a report that lists primary decision makers and their sources of power and identifies their positions on at least one issue of importance to the community. For that issue, identify driving and restraining sources and existing or potential allies and opponents. Develop a map of the power relationships (conceptual or network) that affect this community.

2. Work with constituency group members to identify a social issue and an appropriate method for conducting research using at least one of the methodological approaches identified in this chapter (e.g., constructing a survey or interview guide, creating community indicators, or using Photovoice). Once a measurement tool has been identified and created, work with the group to carry out the study and analyze the findings. Work with the group to develop a report about the findings, making sure that findings are disseminated to both community members and influential decision makers.

3. The report does not need to be written—for example, it can be a photo exhibit, a video, a play, a set of drawings, or an art installation. The report may also include the group's assessment of the research process. In addition to the "report," submit an assessment of the group process that includes a reflection of your own work and how you dealt with issues regarding group maintenance and task accomplishment.

A robust set of instructor resources designed to supplement this text is located at http://connect.springerpub.com/content/book/978-0-8261-5835-2. Qualifying instructors may request access by emailing textbook@springerpub.com.

KEY REFERENCES

Only key references appear in the print edition. The full reference list appears in the digital product on Springer Publishing Connect: connect.springerpub.com/content/book/978-0-8261-5835-2/part/part02/chapter/ch06

Abma, T. A., Cook, T., Ramgard, M., Kleba, E., Harris, J., & Wallerstein, N. (2017). Social impact of participatory health research: Collaborative non-linear processes of knowledge motivation. *Educational Action Research, 25*, 489–505. https://doi.org/10.1080/09650792.2017.1329092

Brown, M. E., Rizzuto, T., & Singh, P. (2019). Strategic compatibility, collaboration and collective impact for community change. *Leadership & Organization Development Journal, 40*, 421–434. https://doi.org/10.1108/LODJ-05-2018-0180

Brown, M. E., & Stalker, K. C. (2021). Assess connect transform in our neighborhood: A framework for engaging community partners in CBPR research designs. *Action Research Journal, 19*, 372–392. https://doi.org/10.1177/1476750318789484

Catalani, C., & Minkler, M. (2010). Photovoice: A review of the literature in health and public health. *Health Education & Behavior, 37*, 424–451. https://doi.org/10.1177/1090198109342084

Collie, P., Liu, J., Podsiadlowski, A., & Kindon, S. (2010). You can't clap with one hand: Learnings to promote culturally grounded participatory action research with migrant and former refugee communities. *International Journal of Intercultural Relations, 34*,141–149. https://doi.org/10.1016/j.ijintrel.2009.11.008

Edmondson, J., & Hecht, B. (2014). Defining quality collective impact. *Collective Insights on Collective Impact, 12*(4), 6–7.

Harrell, S., & Bond, M. (2006). Listening to diversity stories: Principles for practice in community research and action. *American Journal of Community Psychology, 37*, 365–376. https://doi.org/10.1007/s10464-006-9042-7

Mitchell, F. M. (2018). "Water is life": Using Photovoice to document American Indian perspectives on water and health. *Social Work Research, 42*, 277–289. https://doi.org/10.1093/swr/svy025

Noy, D. (2008). Power mapping: Enhancing sociological knowledge by developing generalizeable analytical public tools. *American Sociologist, 39*, 3–18. https://doi.org/10.1007/s12108-008-9030-5

Teixeira, S. (2018). Qualitative geographic information systems (GIS): An untapped research approach for social work. *Qualitative Social Work, 17*, 9–23. https://doi.org/10.1177/1473325016655203

FACILITATING LEADERSHIP DEVELOPMENT AND GROUP DECISION-MAKING: ENCOURAGING PUBLIC PARTICIPATION IN PLANNING AND ENGAGING CONSTITUENTS IN THE DEVELOPMENT OF ACTION PLANS

LEARNING OBJECTIVES

After reading this chapter, students will be able to:

- Apply the concept of ladders of participation to community practice.
- Describe methods to increase civic engagement and citizen participation.
- Discuss the process of facilitating action planning in communities.
- Explain the need to apply multiple tactics in the action-planning process.
- Recognize the importance of leadership development in community practice.
- Describe strategies to promote leadership development in community practice.

INTRODUCTION

During the engagement phase of community organizing, after issue identification and assessment, action planning must take place. This work should involve constituents, and, in many cases, be led or controlled by them. The ability of everyday people to determine what happens in their communities contributes substantially to the quality of life in neighborhoods and the well-being of individuals and families. In this chapter, the theoretical underpinnings of the philosophy associated with constituent involvement are discussed. A related concept, *leadership development* in community organizing, is also described. This activity is based on the premise that engaged citizens should have the lead role in facilitating decision-making processes in community groups and neighborhood planning, but may need information, training, and support from community organizers to do so effectively. Consequently, one section in this chapter describes techniques used to recruit and train leaders whereas another provides an overview of techniques commonly used to facilitate and support constituents involved in public decision-making and planning. In addition, this chapter also provides information on another important community-organizer role, assisting constituents and community leaders with the development of action plans for community campaigns and initiatives, and describes techniques for helping group members make choices about the strategies and tactics to be used in these initiatives. The use of group processes to weigh various tactical options and assess the ethical implications of these methods is also presented. In the final section of this chapter, specific practice techniques for incorporating principles of self-determination, empowerment, and cultural competency in action plans and community decision-making processes are described.

LADDERS OF PARTICIPATION AND ENGAGEMENT

Community participation and engagement in community planning, development, or change initiatives exists on a continuum. That is, the extent to which community members are involved in the decision-making and leadership of community projects varies considerably. In 1969, Sherry Arnstein published the seminal article "A Ladder of Citizen Participation." In this work, Arnstein (1969) offers a typology of eight levels of participation that are ordered based on the degree of citizens' decision-making power. The bottom rungs of the ladder are labeled *manipulation* and *therapy*. These levels are considered nonparticipatory in that their goal is for those individuals who hold power to "fix" in some way the participant; the citizen does not hold any power in these bottom rungs. The next rungs of the ladder are referred to as *informing* and *consultation*. At these levels, participants are involved as listeners and possibly may share some ideas, but participants hold no power to ensure that their perspectives are taken into account in the decision-making process. Moving up the ladder, *placation* is similar to *informing* and *consulting* because although participants can advise the power-holders, the lack of power to decide remains with others. The top three rungs of the ladder include varying degrees of decision-making power among participants. *Partnership* includes the power to negotiate with traditional power-holders, whereas *delegated power* and *citizen control* involve situations in which citizens have the majority of decision-making votes or full decision-making power (Figure 7.1).

Arnstein's work continues to influence the characterization of participation in community projects. In 2017, researchers reviewed the existing literature on the involvement of immigrants in community-based participatory research projects (Vaughn et al., 2017). In this study, the authors classified community engagement using a continuum from low to high based on the degree of shared decision-making, communication, and community level of involvement. The importance of decision-making power in differentiating degrees of participation cannot be understated. In the following section, we move beyond classification of participation and engagement and turn our attention to theoretical perspectives.

THEORETICAL PERSPECTIVES: COMMUNITY INVOLVEMENT IN DECISION-MAKING

Recently, the call for more citizen involvement in planning has gained traction due to the research by Putnam (2000) indicating that few people actually join nonprofit groups or civic organizations, volunteer, or even vote. As described in Chapter 6, Putnam argues that the quality of life in communities is enhanced by high levels of social capital: civic engagement and the strengthening of relationship ties among individuals and groups. Putnam

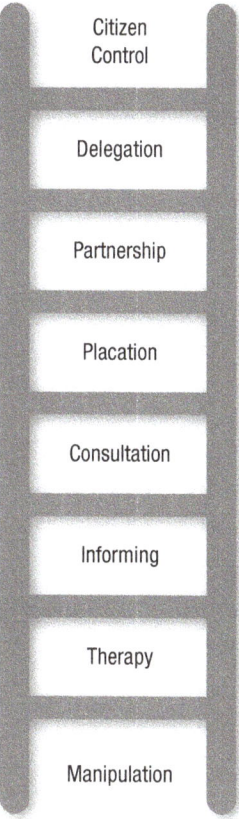

FIGURE 7.1 Arnstein's ladder of participation.

SOURCE: Adapted from Arnstein, S. R. (1969). A ladder of citizen participation. *Journal of the American Institute of Planners, 35*(4), 216–224. https://doi.org/10.1080/01944366908977225.

links current efforts to increase civic engagement to observations made by French visitor Alexis de Tocqueville in the 1830s about the role of local organizations and associations in the United States. De Tocqueville (1981) argued that the associations had a high degree of participation of ordinary citizens in nongovernment organizations and associations and that such activity was a uniquely American attribute. Putnam's work on social capital has stimulated a number of government and nonprofit efforts to increase civic engagement such as service learning requirements in high schools and universities. The literature on community practice and public participation has documented the many positive effects of civic engagement on community life and public decision-making. However, not everyone agrees as to the methods that should be used to increase civic engagement or even whether it actually needs to be increased.

Civic Engagement in Public Decision-Making: Has It Declined?

Putnam's premise has been extensively critiqued by social theorists and community organizers. Many of these critics have argued that the emphasis on social capital ignores the role of power, cultural values and norms, government, and other institutional structures in which public decision-making occurs; resource inequality; and an increasingly global economic structure in determining quality of life in individual communities (Cohen, 2001; DeFilippis, 2009; Maloney et al., 2000; Saegert, 2006; Skocpol, 2004). In addition to these factors, traditional patterns of social exclusion and oppression in minoritized and marginalized communities in the United States, Europe, and the global South may limit the degree to which strong bonds and trust can be established among community members coming from different economic and ethnic backgrounds (Hawkins & Maurer, 2010; Li Puma & Koelble, 2009; Pyles & Cross, 2008).

Despite these criticisms, many theorists agree that the decline in civic organizations in the United States is most likely to affect members of low-income communities or people of color. Institutional barriers to voting, such as identification requirements that make it hard for people who do not drive or people who move frequently to register, or laws that make it difficult for former felons to vote exclude large numbers of people from the voting process (Cohen, 2001; Piven & Cloward, 2000). Skocpol (2004) argues that declines in union participation and the growth of advocacy organizations that recruit participants primarily through social media have made participation less likely for people who are not affluent or well educated. Other scholars and community organizers argue that economic hardship and the availability of government funding for service provision in low-income communities has made it less likely that neighborhood organizations will engage in social action, preferring to address urgent needs of local residents (Brooks, 2005; Smith, 2010). Receipt of government funding may also make it difficult for organizations dependent on government funding to actually advocate against government policies and legislation (Andrews et al., 2010).

There is even some evidence that participation among low-income people may not have decreased as drastically as some scholars believe. For example, Caputo (2010) used data from the National Longitudinal Survey to compare levels of civic engagement between low-income people in the United States who received public benefits and people with higher incomes. Caputo found no difference in the degree of community activism between the two groups. Qualitative studies conducted by Green (2005) and Hunt (2007) indicate that low-income people do participate in community organizations and other types of activism although such activity may be of lower intensity (e.g., attendance at meetings or volunteering to stuff envelopes rather serving on a board) or frequency than among people with more income.

Positive Benefits Associated With Civic Engagement

As described in Chapter 3, efforts to maintain or increase levels of community engagement are critical for successful community organization. For social action practitioners or adherents of transformative approaches, membership on the boards of local organizations, involvement in social change activities and protests, engagement in lobbying for legislation, and participation in election campaigns are viewed as essential for acquiring the political power needed to improve the community's access to resources (Homan, 2016; Staples, 2016). Community developers view involvement as a mechanism for improving relationship ties among community members and developing a consensus about community goals (Ohmer & DeMasi, 2009). Social planners believe that the participation of community members in the development of programs and plans increases the likelihood that these initiatives will adequately address the needs, lived experiences, and cultural values of the people who are likely to use the goods and services produced (Brown & Stalker, 2021; Laurian & Shaw, 2009; Parker & Betz, 1996; Smith, 2010).

In addition, participation in public decision-making and service on the boards of community-based organizations have been found to increase an individual's leadership skills and experiences of personal empowerment and self-efficacy (Ayon & Lee, 2009; Gutierrez et al., 1998; Mizrahi et al., 2009; Plitt Donaldson, 2004; Ramirez-Valles et al., 2005). Some studies have also found empirical support that community inclusion on boards also improves the likelihood that community-based organizations will find the resources that they need to survive financially and that they will be accountable to the people they serve (Milam Handley & Howell-Moroney, 2010; Walker & McCarthy, 2010).

The term generally used to describe involvement in public decision-making and other types of civic engagement is *citizen participation* (Hardina, 2003; Richards & Dalbey, 2006). *Citizen participation* can be defined as efforts by residents to improve the quality of neighborhood life and advocate for changes in public policies (Ohmer & Beck, 2006). The term *citizen participation* was used extensively in the 1960s to describe government-mandated efforts to provide opportunities for clients to serve on the boards of nonprofit organizations (Marris & Rein, 1982). As proposed in the United States, the government policy of *maximum feasible participation* was intended as a tool to increase access to social services for members of low-income communities as part of the government's "War on Poverty" (Moynihan, 1969). However, the purpose of the program was often subverted when local government officials and other members of the political establishment who actually controlled the purse strings appointed their own representatives to these boards. Government officials quickly ended the program as a consequence of the few instances in which low-income participants actively engaged in protests and other efforts to increase their political power (Defilippis, 2009; Rose, 1972; Smith, 2010).

Methods Used to Increase Citizen Participation

Many government agencies and foundations that typically fund nonprofit organizations and programs require some degree of citizen or consumer participation. Most often, this manifests through organizational structures that provide seats on boards of directors or advisory councils to the users of services (Hardina et al., 2006; Linhorst et al., 2005; Mizrahi et al., 2009). Community forums, focus groups, and surveys are also used extensively by government agencies and nonprofit organizations to solicit comments and recommendations from consumers, residents, and other partner groups. Participants can also be hired as paraprofessional staff with special expertise and knowledge about how the community operates, its values, and norms, and connections with other potential constituents and community leaders (Smith, 2010).

Often, local and state governments make explicit efforts to inform program beneficiaries and taxpayers about policy proposals, plans, legislation, or budgets. Such efforts can range from public comment sessions to membership on formal citizen planning boards. Government-mandated planning councils, with appointed or elected members, have also been used extensively by governments in a variety of countries to solicit input on service decision-making, redevelopment issues, and funding priorities (Chin, 2009; Dierwechter &

Coffey, 2010; Moffat et al., 1999). As with the War on Poverty in the United States, the stated purpose of such efforts has been to counter the harmful effects of social exclusion, minoritization, and marginalization and increase the likelihood that scarce government resources will be distributed equitably. However, the track record for these planning efforts is often mixed, as different groups in society have more power than others to influence the decision-making process (Bowen, 2007; Gaventa & Valderrama, 1999; Rispel et al., 2009).

There are different opinions about and assessments of the levels and impact of citizen and client participation at the agency and community levels. Numerous research studies indicate that many government-mandated citizen participation efforts have been unsuccessful in transferring power from established political elites to members of low-income groups (Buccus et al., 2008; Claque et al., 1984; Dierwechter & Coffey, 2010; King et al., 1998; Marris & Rein, 1982; Silverman, 2003). Nevertheless, there are numerous examples of successful community-based, citizen participation efforts (Brody et al., 2003; Checkoway & Zimmerman, 1992; Itzhaky & York, 2002; Milam Handley & Howell-Moroney, 2010; Ohmer & Beck, 2006). Components of successful citizen participation efforts include an ideological commitment to create space for empowering experiences on the part of professional staff assigned to facilitate these efforts, appropriate organization structures that provide sufficient opportunities for community input, the provision of adequate information about decision-making roles and technical decision-making, and training in leadership skills for participants. Leadership training and development is generally regarded as one of the primary roles for community organizers (Hardina & Malott, 1996; Kahn, 1991; Milam Handley & Howell-Moroney, 2010). Such training often focuses on preparing constituency group members for leadership roles in community organizations or providing information and support for participants in public decision-making processes (Ayon & Lee, 2009; Kirk & Shutte, 2004; Smock, 2004).

LEADERSHIP DEVELOPMENT AND TRAINING

Often the term *grassroots leaders* are used to describe those individuals who emerge from the community-organizing process to lead community organizations and organizing campaigns. Boehm and Staples (2006) define *grassroots leaders* as "unpaid volunteers who emerge from within the community and provide direction and guidance in specific areas of its life" (p. 78). A leader may have a position as a board president or committee chairperson or may informally provide leadership and support to other members of the community (Tropman, 2012).

Andrews and colleagues (2010) argue that a special type of volunteer leader is needed for community engagement efforts. They differentiate between formal social service organizations that rely on paid staff and provide services to individual clients and civic organizations:

> Civic organizations depend upon the voluntary efforts of their members, decentralize decision making across local units, govern themselves through elected volunteer leaders, and enable their members' collective voices to be heard. They thus interact with constituents, not customers or clients. Their authority rests on moral suasion rather than economic or political coercion. Their outputs require the voluntary participation of members and supporters. (p. 1192)

The nature of these organizations makes ongoing efforts to recruit and maintain effective leaders essential. Many community organizations do more than select specific individuals for leadership roles in community organizations or organizing campaigns. They may offer leadership skills training or encourage people whom they think will be effective leaders by providing them with a series of tasks or positions that allow them to gradually develop leadership abilities. The Alliance for Justice (2010) describes the importance of leadership development in the following way:

> *Two of the key features that distinguish community organizing from other types of change efforts are [sic] its focus on developing leadership and developing constituents' sense of purpose and power. Well-crafted pathways for constituent leadership development within the organizing process (including intentional processes for consciousness raising and the development of critical analysis skills) take time, effort, and skill. Ensuring that the organizing process reinforces a healthy sense of strength among constituents is also something that requires intentional action. (p. 1)*

Effective volunteer leaders need a combination of skills similar to those of community organizers: the ability to facilitate task accomplishment; manage group processes; mediate conflicts; build relationships with individuals, groups, and organizations; hold members accountable for their efforts; plan organizing campaigns; and be able to work interdependently with other group members (Andrews et al., 2010; Kahn, 1991). Leaders also need to have communication skills that allow them to articulate a vision for the organization, inspire members, and disseminate the organization's message to others (Evans & Shirley, 2008; Homan, 2016). Grassroots leaders may also derive power from a number of sources, including their ability to give support and advice or other resources to community members such as jobs, referrals, contacts with influential people and organizations, the ability to raise funds or obtain resources for their organization, or the ability to mobilize community members to take action or vote. Power can also accrue from simply exchanging or trading off these resources with others. Boehm and Staples (2006) describe this type of power as "transactional." Power can also come via personal charisma or the ability to inspire others, articulate a vision about a just society or "right" values, and the ability to inspire others to take action to change themselves or their communities. As with the process inherent in popular education approaches, this type of power can be described as "transformational" (Boehm & Staples, 2006; VeneKlasen et al., 2007). There are also approaches to leadership that can be counterproductive. For example, ineffective or poor leaders can "take over" or lead the group without input from others, actively manipulate group members to further their own self-interests, or alternatively, provide little guidance for group members or fail to establish goals for task accomplishment (Zastrow, 2015).

Leadership training courses or workshops typically include content on board membership and responsibilities, advocacy methods, public speaking, the structure and functions of government agencies, and conflict resolution (Ayon & Lee, 2009; Delgado & Staples, 2008). Such courses can also include basic techniques for facilitating groups and conducting meetings (Kahn, 1991; Zachary, 2000). Some leadership development programs also contain a fieldwork component so that participants have a chance to apply their skills within a group context and begin the process of relationship building with others (Sen, 2003).

Some programs may also supplement field work with peer mentorship or supervision (Kaminski et al., 2000; Smock, 2004). In addition, prospective leaders may also receive technical or legal training in relation to the issues that they may wish to address and on planning or campaign-building procedures (Evans & Shirley, 2008). Training methods, derived from popular education-related approaches, may also involve workshops or institutes that provide education and information that specifically helps new leaders develop a critical consciousness about social, economic, and political forces and how they can be changed to better assist minoritized and marginalized communities (Smock, 2004).

Other components of leadership training can include opportunities for support from other constituency group members who face similar issues and concerns and relationship building with other advocates and influential decision makers (Shah & Mediratta, 2008). Sen (2003) identifies four primary principles for developing and training leaders.

1. After new leaders are recruited, community organizations should actively engage in activities to help them strengthen their skills over time.
2. Community organizations should commit resources and staff time to establish formal leadership training programs.
3. Community organizers should explicitly address issues related to culture, gender identity, and racial and ethnic equity when developing new leaders. For example, organizations in which leadership positions are disproportionately held by White males require that organizers take action to ensure equitable access to these positions.
4. In addition to training programs, community organizations need to continuously recruit new leaders, plan for leadership transitions, and seek opportunities to prevent leadership burnout and renewal such as leadership retreats or sabbaticals.

In addition to strengthening organizations, community practitioners also view leadership training as important for bringing about personal transformation. For example, Reinelt and colleagues (2003) surveyed 55 community groups to examine how leadership training programs are typically evaluated. Respondents identified a number of specific outcome measures used to determine whether these programs are successful. In addition to successful advocacy or changes in public policies and institutional systems, these outcome measures also involve changes in the leaders themselves and include

- developing new skills and knowledge;
- changes in attitudes, values, behavior, and perspectives;
- increases in self-awareness and discovery;
- an increase in the degree to which new leaders are committed to leadership roles in social justice initiatives over time; and
- improvements in ability of the new leaders to deepen their relationships and bonds with other constituents and widen their own social networks and circles of influence.

Other outcomes associated with leadership development include feelings of self-empowerment and self-efficacy or increased confidence in one's own skills (Boehm & Staples, 2006). According to Evans and Shirley (2008), effective community leaders move beyond a focus on furthering their own self-interests, to regarding activism as a "moral imperative" that requires them to act for the good of the community.

Sen (2003) also describes leadership development as a process in which the new leader progressively takes on a progression of skills and responsibilities, ranging from recruiting new members, acting as a spokesperson, raising funds, developing a critical consciousness, chairing meetings, serving on the board, helping to hire staff, supervising staff, and planning action campaigns. Boehm and Staples (2006) interviewed grassroots leaders in social action-related organizations about how they developed their leadership skills. The respondents described a process through which they became involved in social action through interest and involvement in a single issue and began to take on a number of leadership tasks over time in order to "move through the leadership ranks" and acquire more responsibility in committees and organizations. They also viewed themselves as having the ability to overcome a variety of organizing and personal challenges, learn from experience, and articulate a vision for their constituents.

CASE VIGNETTE: L.E.A.D. ACADEMY

Leadership development was at the heart of the inception of the L.E.A.D. Academy. L.E.A.D. Academy stands for **l**ead, **e**mpower, **a**ct, and **d**ecide and was co-developed in partnership with residents of public housing in Arizona. The development process was resident led; residents who had leadership responsibilities in the public housing complex researched and identified topics that they would like to focus on based on which leadership skills were most relevant and useful for them. They then worked with a community practitioner to learn leadership skills in a tangible and practical way for their daily lives. Residents chose to focus on conflict management and effective communication. Residents used these new skills within their roles as leaders in their housing complex and also in their partnership with the Thrive in the 05 community change initiative. One L.E.A.D. Academy trainee went on to serve on the mayor's task force and used their leadership skills to motivate community residents to get involved in local initiatives, was involved in planning resident participation strategies, and took on a leadership role in training other community leaders.

ENGAGING IN PEER AND PROFESSIONAL NETWORKS

Peer and professional networks are invaluable resources not only for community practitioners, but for resident leaders as well. Professional networks, including the National Association of Social Workers (NASW), Association for Community Organization and Social Action (ACOSA), Network for Social Work Management (NSWM), and the Society for Community Research and Action (SCRA), offer opportunities to engage with other social workers and community practitioners in macro leadership and community change initiatives. Peer and professional networks provide resources, information, and most important, a community of individuals engaged in community work. By engaging with peer and professional networks, community practitioners and community leaders can become involved in local and national initiatives, gain insight into new models of practice, and connect with counterparts for advice and support.

FACILITATING COMMUNITY PARTICIPATION IN PUBLIC DECISION-MAKING AND PLANNING

A major component of community-organization practice focuses on providing assistance to community residents or members of minoritized and marginalized groups who wish to increase their power and influence in public decision-making. Organizers often recruit community residents for participation on public and nonprofit boards (Gamble & Weil, 1995). They also set up organizational structures to facilitate participation on boards, advisory committees, and public planning bodies and help people who represent minoritized or marginalized groups overcome barriers that limit their participation (Daley, 2002; Hardina et al., 2006). Including the public is believed to improve the quality of government planning; make it more likely that the public will support government plans; and provide a mechanism to reduce the negative impact of economic, social, and political marginalization among members of low-income groups (Hardina, 2003; Mizrahi et al., 2009).

Barriers to inclusion of community members in organizational and government planning include the use of language (technical, formal, or inaccessible), distrust among participants, distrust of government, culture, socioeconomic status, the dominance of the professionals and other experts in the planning process, and demographic factors such as gender identity, ethnicity or race, sexual orientation, health or mental health status and disability, and age (Evans & Shirley, 2008; Hardina & Malott, 1996; Laurian & Shaw, 2009; Potter, 2010; Shah & Mediratta, 2008). Economic hardship and stigmatization may also make it difficult for members of minoritized and marginalized groups to participate in government decision-making (Green, 2005).

Another difficulty with government-mandated citizen involvement in planning is that the decision-making structures, the limited funding provided for planning purposes, the purpose of the planning process, and restrictions on the types of decisions that can be made come from government or from the "top" down. Grassroots decision-making, as defined by organizers, refers to efforts made by community residents and other constituency group members to make decisions at the local or "bottom-up" level (Mizrahi et al., 2009). Consequently, these decisions are less likely to respond to government agendas and are more likely to reflect the preferences of community members. However, it then becomes the responsibility of these participants to influence or pressure government to adopt their demands.

Social workers, organizers, and planners can play a variety of roles in the planning process. A commitment to full participation on the part of organizational leaders is often instrumental in ensuring that people who are usually excluded from decision-making are heard (Bess et al., 2009). Advocacy to ensure that decision-making groups function in a manner that allows for full participation of minoritized and marginalized groups and that planning groups have the financial and other resources needed to support effective decision-making is essential (Silverman, 2003). Supportive services needed for planning can include translation services, training for people who have not previously participated in planning efforts, recruiting from income and demographically diverse populations, the provision of technical information in a manner accessible to nonprofessionals, and support for low-income people such as transportation, day care, and meals (Beresford & Croft, 2001; Daley, 2002; Hardina & Malott, 1996; Parker & Betz, 1996).

The creation of organizational structures to support full inclusion of participants in planning is also essential. For example, Linhorst and colleagues (2005) describe explicit structures established within a public mental health facility to ensure client participation that included a formal client grievance policy and opportunities for clients to participate in the hospital's performance review team, to assess policies related to the quality of life in the facility such as the food provided to them, and to access libraries and medical records. Clients also served on a consumer council that met with the hospital director on a regular basis. Silvestre and colleagues (2002) describe a structure to enhance youth participation in HIV-prevention planning that incorporated basic values of equality and respect for all participants. Participants were elected to the planning body by members of smaller groups established to represent diverse viewpoints, cultures, and interests in the community, each member had the same voting rights, and explicit efforts were made to incorporate cultural competency in the planning and decision-making processes.

Drawing on data from interviews with local officials in 10 states that mandate citizen participation in development efforts, Brody and colleagues (2003) identify six types of strategic choices that planners typically make when designing citizen participation efforts mandated by government agencies:

1. *Resource allocation and program administration.* What staffing and other resources will be provided for the program? Will a written plan for program operation be prepared?
2. *Program objectives.* What is the purpose of the program and what degree of citizen participation will be permitted? For example, is the effort simply about complying with government requirements or is the intent to actually learn something about citizen or consumer preferences and values? Is the intent to foster actual citizen influence in the plan or to encourage the public to support government policies?
3. *Degree of citizen involvement.* When will people first be involved in the planning process? Are residents and other potential beneficiaries involved in the actual development of the plan? Are they asked to help evaluate alternative planning options, or are they only consulted after the plan has been completed?
4. *Invitations to participate.* What groups of people and organizations should be targeted for recruitment and participation in the planning process? For example, should participants be limited to business representatives, elected officials, or professional groups? Should people who own property that will be affected by the planning effort or neighborhood residents be included? Should specific demographic populations such as older adults, people with disabilities, or members of minoritized and marginalized groups who may be negatively affected by the plan be included in plan development?
5. *Soliciting input.* How will input from participants be obtained? For example, should input be limited to a survey, public meeting, or community forums? Or should more formal and inclusive processes such as workshops, advisory committees, or planning groups be utilized?
6. *Provision of information.* How should information about the problem to be addressed or the plan be provided to the general public or targeted groups? How much information should be provided and how should it be provided? For example, is posting the information on a government website sufficient or should planners give presentations or solicit media coverage for the planning effort?

Forester (1989) identifies a number of interpersonal skills that can be used to guide the decision-making process in public planning. These skills include active listening to others, recognizing the cultural identities of participants and how that affects planning preferences and values, and mediating disputes among the parties involved in the planning effort, with the intent of equalizing power relations among the participants and facilitating inclusive practices. They also view staff support for planning and decision-making as a set of choices that involve providing factual information, conveying respect for participants with less power, and ensuring that people who will be most affected by planning decisions actually have a voice in the process. Forester advocates "thinking rationally" and "acting politically" in the decision-making process, taking a number of precautionary steps to ensure inclusion of people with limited power resources:

- Establish relationships with community groups in order to obtain and distribute information.
- Engage in active listening to determine the interests of all groups likely to be involved in the process and to identify political barriers to inclusion.
- Notify people most likely to be excluded early on in the process about any planning decision that is likely to affect them.
- Educate individuals and community groups about the planning process and the "rules of the game."
- Develop skills for managing conflict.
- Inform historically excluded community groups about the importance of political pressure and having a constituency base that can mobilize politically in order to push for their interests to be incorporated into the plan.

Information provision, mediation, and conflict management also can take place in the context of group dialogue that includes both the planner or organizer and the various groups involved in the process. In the next few sections of this chapter, the process of group dialogue in creating community action plans is described.

ENGAGING COMMUNITY MEMBERS IN THE DEVELOPMENT OF COMMUNITY ACTION PLANS

In addition to participation in public decision-making, community groups influence legislation and public policy through participation in community organizations, community development and social action campaigns, or social planning activities through nonprofit organizations, service networks, or task forces. Consequently, one of the roles assumed by community organizers is facilitation of constituency group decision-making in the development of action plans or campaigns. Action plans specify goals and objectives to be addressed, the strategies and tactics used to achieve them, how tasks will be assigned, what resources will be used, and how the campaign will be evaluated.

The Purpose and Components of Action Plans

Action plans are essentially road maps that identify what activities will be undertaken during social action and community development campaigns and initiatives or how social planning processes will proceed. Decisions are most often made through dialogue between constituents and organizers or planners or through consultation among representatives of coalition, collaborative, or task group members. In some cases, decisions involving social planning may be made by professionals or other experts working on behalf of government agencies and community groups.

Action plans have a number of components: overall strategies, tactical methods, goals, objectives, desired outcomes, and an evaluation plan (Bobo et al., 2010). Because most action campaigns are carried out through coordinated actions by volunteers and other constituents, specific roles for individuals are also identified. Organizers often act as facilitators in this process and in some cases they may have assigned tasks that need to be completed so that constituents can take action. Often the organizer's responsibility may be described in a work plan as part of a formal supervisory process designed to hold the organizer accountable to the organization (see Chapters 9 and 13). However, there is also an expectation that the staff member will be accountable to members of the constituency group as well.

As described in Chapter 1, a strategy is a long-term plan of action. There are five primary types of strategies used in organizing campaigns. Each one of these methods involves different types of activities.

- *Collaboration.* A consensus for action among a variety of different groups is developed.
- *Campaign.* Participants engage in activities designed to bring opponents to the bargaining table.
- *Contest or confrontation.* Participants target opponents to achieve social change.
- *Problem-solving.* A problem and all the facts associated with it are examined to identify the best approach for resolving it.
- *Popular education or transformative methods.* As associated with practice methods developed by Freire (1970), these are activities that lead to personal and societal transformation (Brager et al., 1987; Hardcastle et al., 2004; Hardina, 2002; Ohmer & DeMasi, 2009; Pyles, 2013; Rothman, 1979, 1996, 2008).

Choices of the type of strategy used are determined by a number of factors, the situation to be addressed, the degree to which adoption of a policy or issue or the lack of a decision would harm individuals, the amount of time or resources needed to successfully address the issue, the ideology or comfort of the organizer facilitating the action, and, most important, the preferences and comfort level of the constituents involved in the action (Brager et al., 1987; Hardina et al., 2009; Mondros, 2005; Mondros & Wilson, 1994). Because some of these methods involve a great deal of time, and in some situations, entail risks for constituents (e.g., participation in protests can involve job loss), many organizers prefer to use low-intensity methods, such as collaboration, and gradually escalate their use of tactical methods if needed to bring about successful outcomes (Netting et al., 2017). Another consideration in the choice of strategies involves the people or groups who will be involved in the action, the people or systems who are the target of the action or who must be influenced to create change, and the degree of communication between the people taking action (action system) and their targets (target systems). When the same people are members of the action or target systems then collaborative approaches may be used; when members of either system do not communicate with one another or some type of action (campaigns or confrontation) is needed to bring them to the bargaining table (Brager et al., 1987). The group's analysis of the power resources available to them (see Chapter 6) and those held by members of the target group also enter into decisions about strategies (Figure 7.2).

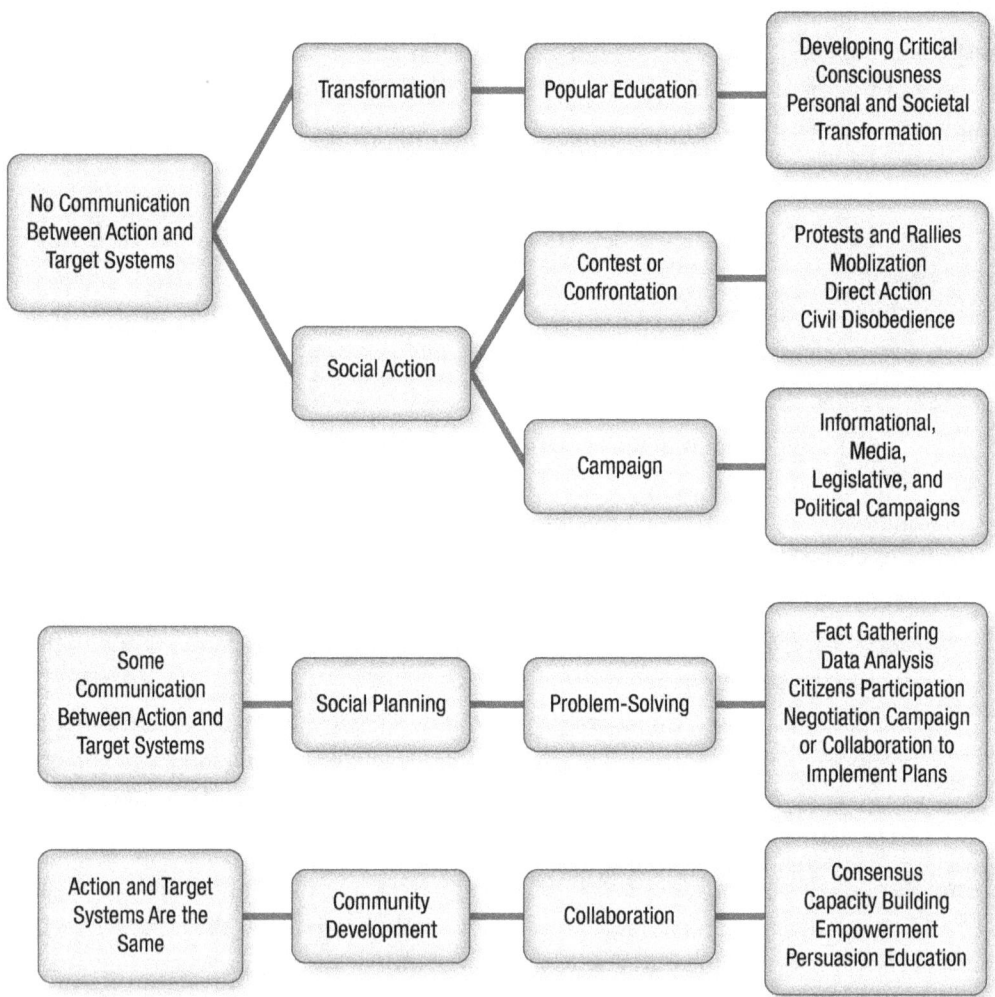

FIGURE 7.2 Choosing strategies and tactics. This conceptual model builds on models of practice identified by Rothman (1979, 1996, 2008) and strategic approaches identified in Brager and colleagues (1987) and Netting and colleagues (2017).

SOURCE: Adapted from Brager, G., Specht, H., & Torczyner, J. (1987). *Community organizing* (2nd ed.). Columbia University Press; Netting, F. E., Kettner, P., McMurty, S., & Thomas, M. (2017). *Social work macro practice* (6th ed.). Pearson; Rothman, J. (1979). Three models of community organization practice, their mixing and phasing. In F. Cox, J. Erlich, J. Rothman, & J. Tropman (Eds.), *Strategies of community organization* (3rd ed., pp. 25–45). F. E. Peacock Publishers; Rothman, J. (1996). The interweaving of community intervention approaches. *Journal of Community Practice, 3*(3/4), 69–99. https://doi.org/10.1300/J125v03n03_03; and Rothman, J. (2008). Multi modes of community intervention. In J. Rothman, J. Erlich, & J. Tropman (Eds.), *Strategies of community organization* (7th ed., pp. 141–170). Eddie Bowers.

Within each of these strategic approaches is a variety of short-term activities or tactics that can be used within the context of a long-term campaign. Most organizers agree that tactics should be chosen by community groups through mutual dialogue between the organizer and constituents. Tactics should also

- be culturally appropriate and incorporate culturally relevant terms, activities, and symbols;
- be appropriate and relevant to the lives and experience of participants/beneficiaries;
- be flexible in design, incorporating different methods in response to the situation at hand;
- take into account the amount of power held by the group taking action and the power and resources of people likely to be opposed to the plan;
- be fun for participants with opportunities for social interaction with others;
- minimize potential risks for all people likely to be involved; and
- incorporate moral principles and values that help "sell" the issue under consideration to the public or media sources (Ganz, 2009; Hardina, 2002; Homan, 2016; Kahn, 1991, 2010; Polletta, 2006; Satterwhite & Teng, 2007; Young Laing, 2009).

Tactics should also, for the most part, be consistent with the overall strategy or approach used for the organizing campaign. For example, contest- or confrontation-oriented strategies employ such tactics as protests, sit-ins, strikes, or boycotts. Collaborative strategies involve consensus, individual and community capacity building, education, and persuasion. However, as noted by Rothman (2008) most campaigns take place in several phases; therefore, it may be necessary to modify tactical methods in response to situational demands or because successful outcomes often require a shift in the type of tactics used or an escalation in the type of pressure used by decision makers. For example, a community plan, developed by consensus among neighborhood residents and local organizations, may represent an agreement among participants, but other efforts may be needed to persuade elected officials to support or approve the plan or to allocate funds and other resources that will ensure implementation (Figure 7.3).

In addition to strategies and tactics, other components of community campaigns include the following elements:

- goals or broad statements about what the action plan is intended to achieve;
- objectives or time-limited, measurable statements about the steps that will be taken to achieve the goal;
- a timeline for completing activities or objectives that place these activities in a logical sequence that will enhance their success;
- the resources needed to carry out the plan such as people, facilities, funds, media contacts, or technical support;
- specific tasks or roles assigned to constituency group members, leaders, and paid staff who will help the group execute the plan; and
- evaluation criteria used to judge the success of the action plan; criteria can include both outcomes to be achieved as well as an assessment of the process of carrying out the plan (Bobo et al., 2010; Hardina, 2002; Hoefer, 2019; Staples, 2016; Box 7.1).

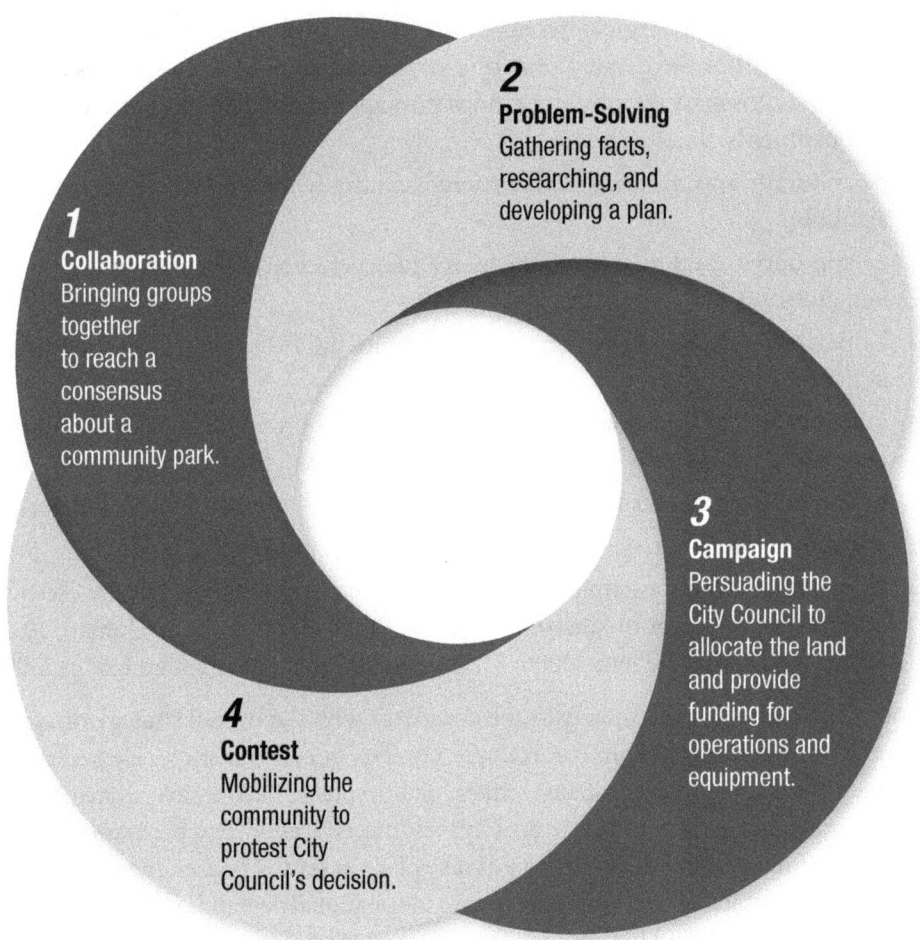

FIGURE 7.3 Mixing and phasing approaches.

Group processes are used to determine most of the components of the plan. In some instances, leaders, organizing staff or a small committee may be called upon to develop a plan or make specific recommendations that will be taken back to the group for approval. When the plan is developed within a group, a number of techniques are used to document decisions, including note-taking, formal minutes taken by one group member and reviewed for accuracy by the others, or outlining each component of the plan on a poster or a whiteboard. The advantage of this method is that it gives group members feelings of ownership about the development of the plan (VeneKlasen et al., 2007). It also assists group members in fitting together "pieces" of the puzzle by creating a timeline for goal achievement and the specific types of actions that should be taken to achieve them (Figure 7.4).

More formal methods of documentation are also used when describing plan components, especially specific goals, objectives, and evaluation criteria identified in funding proposals. Donors may also require that specific work plans be developed for the organization in which organizing activities are described in detail (Bobo et al., 2010). Written work plans can also be developed for the action campaign and distributed to members by mail or via

Box 7.1

SAMPLE GOALS, OBJECTIVES, AND EVALUATION CRITERIA

Goal: Increase Community Access to Healthy Food

Objective 1: Recruit 60 community residents for a community garden initiative by February 1.

Objective 2: Negotiate with the city to obtain permission to purchase (at a nominal price) or lease five vacant lots that can be used for community gardens by March.

Objective 3: Recruit 5 volunteer "master gardeners" to assist local residents with starting and maintaining community gardens by March 15.

Objective 4: Provide 10 "hands-on" technical workshops and demonstrations that will provide residents with the "know how" to successfully plant and maintain community gardens by March 31.

Objective 5: Start five community gardens by April 30.

Objective 6: Maintain the participation of a least 10 community residents in each community garden over a 5-month period by September 30.

Evaluation Criteria: Number of volunteers and master gardeners recruited, number of workshops held, participant satisfaction survey, number of gardens established, number of gardens maintained over a 5-month period, or the amount of food harvested from the garden.

---

the internet. However, there are a number of dilemmas inherent in formalizing long-term work plans. For example, action plans are often altered in response to unanticipated events or changes in available resources. In addition, in some types of social action and transformative organizing, keeping specific tactical plans (such as protests) confidential may be essential to their success (Considine, 2001).

It is critical that all elements of the plan fit together in some type of logical manner that links problem identification, assessment, power analysis, goal setting, action planning, implementation, and evaluation. However, the process is seldom so straightforward; successful campaigns require "fine-tuning," and ongoing dialogue among participants, in response to new information or when strategies and tactics prove to be ineffective. Therefore, action plans will continue to be modified throughout the course of a campaign as participants reflect on their experiences and work toward successful outcomes (Figure 7.5).

Using Group Methods to Weigh Ethical Decisions and Choose Strategies and Tactics

For most organizers, the involvement of constituency group members in choosing strategies and tactics is a critical component in the social change process. Constituent involvement ensures that the methods used for action campaigns have meaning for participants, reflect their values, and increase the likelihood that constituents will actually participate in any activities needed to carry them out. Organizing campaigns are similar in nature to both coalition building and other types of group activities. Members must depend on one another for the success of the plan; if one or more persons fail to perform an assigned task, the event or activity will fail. As mentioned previously in this text, there is strength in numbers: The more people who participate in an action, the better the chance that it will be successful.

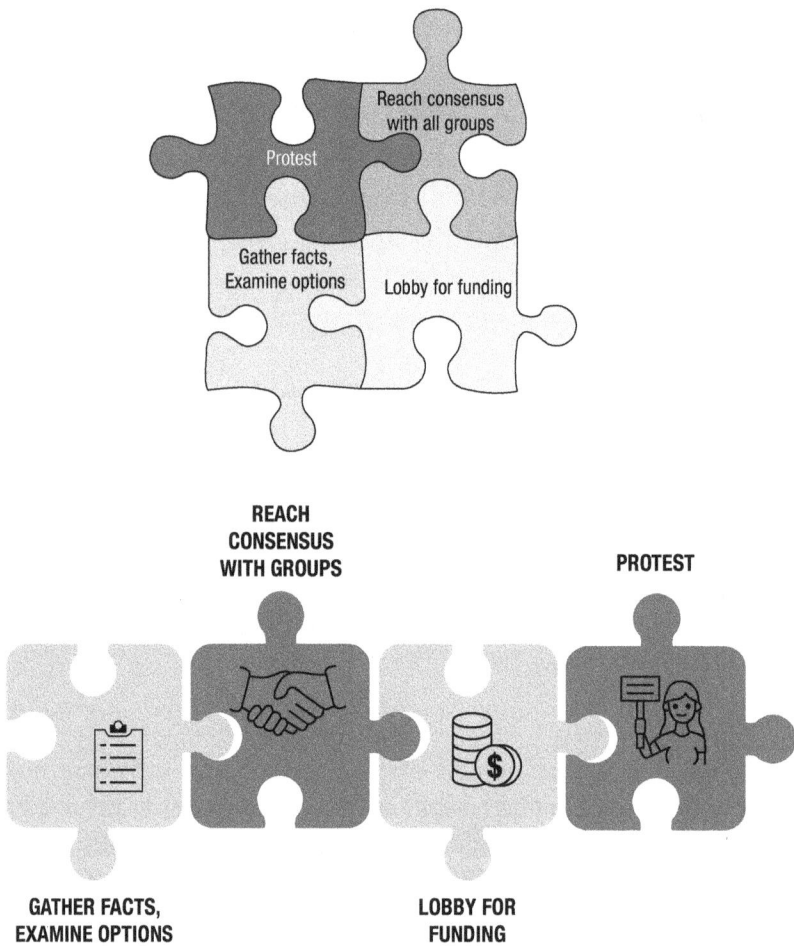

FIGURE 7.4 Putting the puzzle together: choosing tactical methods.

FIGURE 7.5 Campaign planning process.

Mondros and Wilson (1994) identify four reasons that decisions on strategies and tactics should be made in the context of mutual dialogue among organizers, leaders, and constituency group members:

- Constituents are educated about the process of organizing and the various options available to them.
- Constituents develop a sense of ownership of the organizing process and begin to feel empowered—to recognize and activate their own power—to take action.
- Constituents have the primary role in determining strategies and tactics. This serves as a "safeguard" against allowing the organizer's ideology or personal biases to determine what action will be taken.
- Constituents have an opportunity to state why they would be reluctant to participate in certain actions, especially those that may involve risks to them or their families. Consequently, the planning of strategies and tactics requires detailed discussions of the risks and potential benefits of any action to be carried out by the group.

The ethical implications of tactical methods and the consequences of choosing certain options are important considerations in the organizing process (Rubin & Rubin, 2008). Saul Alinsky (1971), "the architect" of modern organizing methods, argued that in most circumstances the potential for success should outweigh the use of offensive or unethical organizing methods. Risks are often associated with tactics such as protests, direct action or confrontation with authorities, and civil disobedience (McAdam & Tarrow, 2000). *Civil disobedience* can be defined as "the deliberate, principled, and public breaking of a law that is perceived to be unjust" (Conway, 2003, p. 508). Direct action may include legally sanctioned activities or illegal actions, but generally involves direct confrontation with authorities (Shaw, 2001).

In some instances, there may be disagreements among coalition group members about whether direct action or potentially violent tactics should be used (Conway, 2003). Another potential risk is that in some situations, authorities may choose to arrest or engage in physical confrontation with participants (Rubin & Rubin, 2008). Consequently, it is imperative that group members thoroughly discuss the potential consequences of their actions, what they are willing to risk, the benefits of undertaking the action, and processes for minimizing or preventing these risks. Such discussions serve as an informed-consent process in organizing (Hardina et al., 2009). If people find tactics inappropriate or offensive, they simply will not participate in the action. Kahn (2010) argues that it is essential that the organizer:

Be absolutely certain that the people you work with truly understand the risks they're taking, the things that could go wrong, the losses they might suffer, before they make the decision to act, individually or together. (p. 194)

Other types of tactics may also be offensive to participants or violate basic principles such as self-determination or honesty, requiring a discussion of whether the risks outweigh the costs. For example, Hardina (2000) surveyed community-organization instructors in schools of social work and asked them to identify tactics they felt were unethical. The social workers interviewed felt that harming or humiliating individuals, lying, and withholding information about the consequences of taking action were unethical practices. Hardina and colleagues (2009) conducted interviews with community organizers involved in social action organizing. They viewed as unethical any tactic that harmed individuals (allies as well as opponents), vandalism, lying, or deliberating misleading constituents.

In addition to issues specifically related to the practice of social action, other ethical considerations encountered in the organizing process involve the acceptance of funding from donors at odds with community preferences or values, or conflicts of interests on the part of individual constituents, the organizer, or the organizer's employer. Other ethical considerations involve whether the constituency group should focus solely on long-term rather than short-term gains (e.g., advocating for improvements in the minimum wage rather than helping current constituents find employment) or whether to deliberately disseminate misinformation or discredit opponents (Forester, 1989; Hardina, 2002, 2004; Minkler & Pies, 2009; Reisch & Lowe, 2000).

Facilitating Action Planning: The Art of Achieving Consensus

To choose goals, strategies, and tactics, some type of agreement or consensus must be reached among members. Although not everyone may be happy with the decision, there must be a degree of commitment to the plan on the part of the members if the action is to be implemented by the group members. The group process for developing and implementing action plans most resembles that of task groups. Interpersonal relationships are used explicitly to facilitate goal achievement. Task groups differ from treatment or therapeutic groups in that they are designed to foster the interdependence of members in a manner that allows for collective group decision-making as well as task accomplishment. Individuals within the group must rely on task completion by others if they are to complete their assigned roles (Johnson & Johnson, 2017; Kirst-Ashman & Hull, 2018). In some ways, members of effective task groups become a team in which each member has an assigned role and expectations as to what they are to accomplish in the group in order to achieve a common purpose (VeneKlasen et al., 2007).

However, although tasks have some of the same characteristics and applications as groups of individuals engaged in social action, development, or community planning efforts, there is at least one other important difference. As described by Polletta (2002), there is a dilemma inherent in the organizing process:

> *The literature on organizing is rife with injunctions against leading: organizers should rather help residents articulate their own agendas and build their leadership. Yet, in the process, organizers are often expected to help identify goals, push people to question their preferences, and rally them to act. How can they do that without thereby undermining the leadership capacities of those whom they are organizing? (p. 76)*

As opposed to leading a group, the organizer must merely assist the group leader in facilitating the group process, provide encouragement and information to members, set the stage for leadership by others, engage in mutual dialogue and learning with members, and suggest options that will lead to goal achievement. Organizers also must engage in group maintenance activities, continuing to build relationships with individual members and to help mediate or minimize conflict among members (Homan, 2016). Another difference between the typical task group and community organizing is that the purpose and goal for the group originates with members, participants may be asked to engage in recruitment of new members, and the leader is chosen by the group.

Essentially, the organizer helps the leader to do their job; provides technical information, research data, or helps identify policies, laws, or people that need to be taken into consideration in planning the campaign. The organizer also helps to guide the discussion on various campaign options. According to VeneKlasen and colleagues (2007), a nondirective approach to facilitation involves asking participants a series of questions about what they want to accomplish, how they want to achieve this, and what they perceive to be the benefits and risks of the various approaches available to them. The type of questions typically used in social work practice with both individuals and groups (reflective responding or paraphrasing, summarizing, clarification, and reframing) can be applied in this context, ensuring that all group members have a common understanding of the issues raised, goals, activities that must be accomplished, and task assignments (Kirst-Ashman & Hull, 2018; Poulin, 2010). VeneKlasen and colleagues (2007) identify the following types of questions that may be particularly effective in this group context:

- *Questions to obtain information.* For example, who will conduct the activity? When will it happen and how?
- *Questions to obtain an explanation.* For example, what else do we need to think about and how should we do it?
- *Questions to obtain a justification.* For example, why should we do it and how do you know whether this is true?
- *Questions to generate new ideas or make suggestions.* For example, is this a good idea or maybe we should think about (an alternative) as well?
- *Questions to facilitate making a choice.* For example, which of these alternatives will work the best?
- *Questions to facilitate reaching a consensus.* For example, does everyone agree that this is what we should do?

In addition to asking questions (Box 7.2), the organizer also assists the leader in developing relationships with group members, keeping the group running smoothly, and accomplishing specific tasks related to goal achievement (Schutz & Sandy, 2011).

Box 7.2

REACHING A CONSENSUS ON A TACTIC

Organizer Alicia Martinez is assisting constituents of the West Neighborhood Organization to develop a new tactic for persuading the city council to shut down the meat-rendering plant in their neighborhood. Mx. Jackson has been elected by the group members to serve as the leader and spokesperson for the group for the next few months. Mx. Smith also indicated an interest in serving as the leader in the future.

Mx. Jackson: We know that there is a proposal in the city council to grant a new permit to the meat-rendering plant. Tonight, I'd like to discuss what we can do to keep the council from giving the plant a permit. If the permit is not approved, the plant will need to shut down. Any suggestions?

Mx. Lee: We just need to rely on our city council member to make the case against the permit.

Alicia: Do you know what Council Member Gonzalez's position is on this issue? Has anyone talked to them?

(continued)

> **Box 7.2**
>
> **REACHING A CONSENSUS ON A TACTIC (CONTINUED)**
>
> *Mx. Smith:* Council Member Gonzalez is just a bum. I've talked to them and I can't get a straight answer.
>
> *Mx. Jackson:* I think the group needs to talk to Council Member Gonzalez and get them to represent our interests. We voted for them, and they won't be elected again without our vote.
>
> *Mx. Smith:* Yes, but I really think they are no good. I think we should just disrupt the city council meeting to get our point across. That should get their attention!
>
> *Mx. Lee:* I'd be afraid that we could be arrested if we disrupted a meeting.
>
> *Alicia:* Could you talk to Council Member Gonzalez first to determine their position on this issue and ask them to work with us on this issue? They seem to have a lot of influence on the other council members.
>
> *Mx. Jackson:* That seems worth a try. Can anyone else suggest an alternative?
>
> *Mx. Smith:* I like my idea better. But I'd be willing to go along with this if we come up with a good plan to persuade Gonzalez to help us.
>
> *Mx. Jackson:* Well, we have a lot of information about the asthma rates in our neighborhood and the costs involved in hospitalizing children and the number of days missed from school due to asthma-related problems.
>
> *Mx. Lee:* I'd be glad to put that information together. We just bought my son a new computer and I could use it to put together a good-looking fact sheet.
>
> *Alicia:* Do we have an agreement then?

Task groups are similar to treatment or therapeutic groups in that the stages of group development are essentially the same. For example, the Tuckman model of group development (Zastrow, 2015) can be easily applied to the type of task groups used in community organizing.

- *Forming.* Participants come together and start to think about the group's goals and start to become acquainted with one another. Members also attempt to determine their place in the group and whether there are rules that govern the operation of the group.
- *Storming.* There is a certain amount of conflict among group members. Some of this may be due to perceptions of differential status among group members due to a number of factors such as race, gender identity, ethnicity, income, professional status, knowledge, sexual orientation, or age or based on perceptions that there are differences between newcomers and "old hands." Some members may have specific agendas, either explicit or hidden, that guide their interaction with others in the group.
- *Norming.* Members set explicit rules for behavior and decision-making that are enforced in some fashion. Successful groups also develop a sense of solidarity and commitment to one another and the group as a whole.
- *Performing.* The group functions as a team to accomplish its goals. Group members also develop a sense of interdependence on one another.
- *Adjourning.* The group may end when a project is completed. What may differentiate community groups from other task groups is that the group may simply refocus its mission to achieve another goal or disband and continue in some fashion to maintain working relationships or friendships with one another.

Therefore, social workers assigned to facilitate task groups for organizing should anticipate that it is entirely normal for groups to experience some degree of distrust and conflict. The key is to move past this in order to achieve the group's goals.

Trust building and the establishment of group norms for individual and collective group behavior are critical for achieving a sense of solidarity or belonging among group members. Group consensus rather than conflict increases the odds that the group will accomplish its goals. Also of importance is whether more than one or a small number of group members actually contribute to the success of the group (Johnson & Johnson, 2017). If the leader is the only group member that performs most of the tasks, then few members will maintain their participation in the group and participant capacity will not be built in the process. Consequently, while what the group is able to achieve is one measure of success, it is equally important to understand how effective the group process was in itself, in order to understand the overall success of the group and its goals.

Most experts on group processes believe that a certain amount of conflict helps to spur innovation and creativity in decision-making (Rubin & Rubin, 2008). However, ongoing conflicts among group members based on personal issues or status differentials minimize the likelihood that group goals will be achieved (Mondros & Wilson, 1994). One of the responsibilities of the organizer or social worker is to assist the leader or, in some situations, take the lead in managing conflicts among group members.

It should be noted that task accomplishment and conflict management are not the only tasks that need to be accomplished in the community-organizing process. Plitt Donaldson (2004) views the purpose and function of groups in community organization as similar to those of empowerment groups that are established to provide social support to members experiencing common problems and increase participants' sense of personal self-efficacy and power. Donaldson argues that empowerment groups have some of the same components, in a different context, as the therapeutic groups described by Yalom and Leszcz (2021). Group members bond with and build relationships with one another, share their experiences, feel good about themselves because they are helping others, acquire technical information, and develop a sense of group cohesiveness or solidarity. As described in earlier chapters of this book, all these factors should be considered elements of a well-functioning task group in community organizing. Accomplishing a group goal, establishing a group identity and values, and banding together in the face of adversity help people develop a sense of group or collective identity (Polletta, 2002; Schutz & Sandy, 2011).

PUTTING VALUES INTO ACTION: SELF-DETERMINATION, EMPOWERMENT, AND CULTURAL COMPETENCY IN PLAN DEVELOPMENT

Leadership development, participation in public decision-making, and community control of the organizing and development process are all common methods used to apply the principles of self-determination, empowerment, and cultural competency in community practice. Constituents should have a primary role, if not complete control, in determining how social problems are addressed and be explicitly involved in actions to resolve them. Reaching this point is difficult, if not impossible, in community practice. Forester (1989) succinctly describes barriers to the inclusion of minoritized and marginalized communities in this process: "Hardly an ideal form of dialogue, real public deliberation suffers from inequalities of power, poor information, inadequate representation, histories of violence brought to the table, histories that silence the voices of many parties" (p. 9).

Toomey (2009) identifies a number of roles for community practitioners and argues that although most interventions are designed with a goal to "empower" communities, some have a negative effect, particularly when they are intended to impose assistance, "rescue," or "liberate," community members or impose reforms without their consent. This view of empowerment is problematic because it bestows the power on the community practitioner or organization, and implies that the organizer holds the power to "empower" the community. Indeed, community members *already* possess this power within themselves; the organizer is there to help illuminate the internal power that is already held by the community, and to provide tools and resources that can help strengthen community members' capacity to activate their own power in pursuit of social justice and community-desired change. The roles of "rescuer" and "liberator" are instead similar to Arnstein's (1969) description of citizen participation initiatives that are intended to provide therapy, manipulate, tokenize, or "buy off" community members. According to Toomey, organizer roles that have a positive impact on community members include that of a catalyst, helping to inspire or spark a change or as facilitator by bringing people together in observing the process, and providing support without imposing their own agenda. Other roles include acting as an advocate for what the community wants or as an ally who establishes relationships with community members and stands in solidarity with them.

Pilisuk and colleagues (2009) describe the process of being and becoming an ally as one of the primary mechanisms for engaging in mutual learning and achieving a degree of cultural competency:

The organizer's special talent lies in a willingness to understand, and an unwillingness to collude with, such internalized oppression. . . . He or she will have to earn the people's trust and establish relationships with them in their surroundings. The organizer must also suspend the power, privilege, prestige, and protection offered by his or her own background and be willing to be less safe. (p. 99)

Hence, the culturally competent practitioner needs to engage in cultural humility, abandon privilege and control, and use one's professional status and skills for the good of the community. The organizer must be willing to listen to community members and participate in dialogue as a partner of equal status.

Quaghebeur and colleagues (2004) described what they learned from their efforts to implement a community participation-related-project in Vietnam, in which the prospective participants refused to cooperate with the professional planners' proposal for the program. They described empowerment as a "double bind," in which people are offered the "opportunity" by professionals or government agencies to empower themselves:

We should pay more attention to the unexpected spaces of negotiation that go beyond the formal project. This implies the acknowledgement that project goals and objectives can be disturbed and that these spaces, which are crucial for the participatory "success" of the project, are difficult to steer, control or evaluate within classical project cycles. But this is what "real participation might be about: the contestation, discussion, struggle and negotiation about the framework offered by the "participatory project." (p. 163)

When using participatory methods such challenges may prove difficult for the organizer, social worker, or planner in situations in which the organizer sincerely believes the community's proposal is unsafe, unwise, or unethical, or the decision-making process itself is rife with competing goals and misaligned interests from different groups with a variety of agendas. Although conflict-management skills may help in such situations, there are scenarios in which organizers may ethically be required to "take sides" or walk away from the organizing effort. For example, one ethical concern in organizing is the "not in my backyard," or NIMBY, syndrome in which community residents oppose group homes for people who are suffering from mental illness, are experiencing houselessness, and are disabled or for affordable housing developments for low-income groups (Duke, 2010). Most organizers would probably support such projects as beneficial for minoritized and marginalized communities and engage in dialogue or search for common ground between constituents and proponents in order to minimize the ethical dilemma involved (Piat, 2000; Stein, n.d.). Such ethical challenges need to be weighed carefully in terms of the risks and benefits to both the organizer and group members (Reisch & Lowe, 2000). It is appropriate and necessary in such situations to seek supervision from one's employer, board members, or professional colleagues (Hardina, 2004).

To mitigate such challenges, organizers develop or seek out participatory group-work models that incorporate principles related to the community-control approach to decision-making. Often these programs are based on the premise that leadership in community groups should not try to replicate hierarchical decision-making processes in which one person has control and some people are excluded (Pyles, 2013; Smock, 2004). Instead, leadership is viewed as an inclusive process involving shared decision-making (Schutz & Sandy, 2011). Zachary (2000) describes a leadership training process, the City University of New York Parent Leadership Project (PLP), in which the organizer facilitated a shared leadership model among constituents. The purpose of the PLP project was to train community members to become advocates for school reform. Much of the theoretical framework used to develop these leadership training workshops was derived from principles such as mutual partnership and dialogue associated with popular education (Freire, 1970). The component parts of this model include

- the creation of a training curriculum in which participants take an active role in the development of learning objectives through mutual dialogue with the facilitator;
- the establishment of a group culture of shared leadership and the power to make decisions that includes both participants and the facilitator;
- the development of explicit ground rules or expectations for the behavior of members by the participants themselves; this in turn creates a sense of safety and trust among group members;
- the provision of opportunities for participants to share their stories and begin to develop an understanding of their shared experiences;
- the use of group-centered training techniques by the facilitator such as small-group discussions and role plays to convey respect for participants and their experiences and knowledge as well as high expectations for skill attainment;
- the ability of the facilitator to use "humble facilitation" techniques; the process requires that the facilitator models appropriate interpersonal skills, including the ability to make mistakes, challenges group members to improve their skills, and creates an appropriate vision for what the group should accomplish; and
- outcomes that include mutual support, trust, and respect among all participants in the training process.

According to Zachary (2000), the advantage of this model is that it transfers power from the organizer to the group as a collective entity rather than to individual leaders; limits the degree to which leadership confers special status, power, or perks to individual members; and enhances the group's capacity to use mutual dialogue to identify problems and engage in all phases of action planning.

END-OF-CHAPTER RESOURCES

KEY TAKEAWAYS AND SUMMARY

Organizers play multiple roles in community planning and decision-making. These roles include leadership development and training, facilitating citizen/constituent involvement in public planning, ensuring that constituents play leadership roles in community-organizing efforts and nonprofit organizations, and facilitating the development of social action and community development campaigns or other planning efforts. Community organizers should adhere to ethical principles, such as self-determination, diversity, and empowerment, in assisting community leaders and constituents in efforts to improve their lives and communities. Constituents should be fully involved in the decisions that affect their lives and the choice of strategies and tactics. The use of dialogue and the inclusion of multiple voices in the planning effort help to ensure that public plans and tactical methods are ethical, safe, and serve the interests of constituents. Inclusive decision-making practices are also critical if constituents are to give their informed consent in terms of the actions or activities in which they are likely to participate. In Chapter 8, group decision-making methods for implementing action campaigns are discussed.

RESOURCES

- United Nations Human Settlements Programme (UN-Habitat). (2021). *Our city plans: An incremental and participatory toolbox for urban planning.* Author. (This resource is a "global toolbox" to support local governments and planners in implementing inclusive urban planning processes.)
- Membership links to professional networks:
  - Association for Community Organization and Social Action: https://acosa.clubexpress.com
  - National Association of Social Workers: https://www.socialworkers.org/Membership
  - Network for Social Work Management: https://socialworkmanager.org
  - Society for Community Action and Research: https://www.scra27.org

ACTIVITIES

1. Interview two or more community leaders using conversational interviewing techniques. Write a short paper that describes your findings. In general, your interviews should focus on how these individuals became involved in community activism; the circumstances related to how they became leaders; how they describe their leadership roles, their current leadership responsibilities, and the pluses and minuses involved in working with group members to take action.

2. Watch the movie *Boycott* (Twain et al., 2001) about the Montgomery Bus Boycott of 1955, led by Dr. Martin Luther King, Jr. With your classmates, discuss:
   - Were the strategies and tactics used in the boycott deliberately planned or did they arise from the situation at-hand?
   - What motivated the participants (the Black/African American population of Montgomery) to comply with the boycott?
   - What power resources did the Black/African American community possess and how did they compare with those of the White community? What resources were obtained from outside the community?
   - Were all the participants committed to nonviolent, civil disobedience at the beginning of the boycott? If not, what factors motivated the adoption of this method by Dr. King and his constituents?
   - How was informed consent for risky tactics obtained?
   - Why was the Black/African American community in Montgomery successful in ending the segregation of the bus system?
3. Divide the classroom into teams or pair up with a partner to debate the ethics of the following tactical methods. In the debate, describe whether you think one of the following tactical methods is ethical and in what situations should it be used:
   a. nonviolent civil disobedience
   b. direct action involving face-to-face confrontation with authorities, for example, sit-ins or disrupting events or meetings
   c. mudslinging (i.e., calling one's opponent names or disclosing negative information about individuals or groups)
   d. deceiving constituents about the purpose or nature of a tactic, including potential risks
   e. misinforming the public about the possible benefits and consequences of specific planning decisions
   f. engaging in vandalism or violence or supporting organizations or groups that participate in such actions
   g. inviting or soliciting participation in a planning council or advisory group in which members will have limited input into making decisions
   h. offering individuals money, status, positions, or other benefits for public support of a planning decision made by others
   i. placing all responsibility for decision-making with the group leader, using charisma or coercion to motivate constituents to act

ASSIGNMENTS

1. Attend a meeting of a public agency in which the public has been invited to give input or make comments. Write a short paper that describes the purpose of the meeting, the public officials in attendance, the type of decision made, the structure of the meeting, provisions made for public comment or input, the degree to which the public was actually able to participate, and whether you think that public participation was

actually effective or had the potential to influence the final decision. In addition to observation, you may use newspaper or other news or social media reports, or interviews with public officials and members of the public who were present at the meeting.

2. Examine either a redevelopment plan developed by a government agency or a community group. Write a three- to five-page paper that analyzes the contents of the plan. What are the component parts of the plan? How did the planning agency, group, or the author describe the purpose of the plan? What information did they provide to persuade the reader that the plan was feasible, cost-effective, or oriented toward improving the lives of people living in the community? Do you think this plan should or should have been adopted? Why or why not?

A robust set of instructor resources designed to supplement this text is located at http://connect.springerpub.com/content/book/978-0-8261-5835-2. Qualifying instructors may request access by emailing textbook@springerpub.com.

KEY REFERENCES

Only key references appear in the print edition. The full reference list appears in the digital product on Springer Publishing Connect: connect.springerpub.com/content/book/978-0-8261-5835-2/part/part02/chapter/ch07

Arnstein, S. R. (1969). A ladder of citizen participation. *Journal of the American Institute of Planners, 35*(4), 216–224. https://doi.org/10.1080/01944366908977225

Hardina, D. (2003). Linking citizen participation to empowerment practice: A historical overview. *Journal of Community Practice, 11*, 11–38. https://doi.org/10.1300/J125v11n04_02

Hawkins, R., & Maurer, K. (2010). Bonding, bridging, and linking: How social capital operated in New Orleans following Hurricane Katrina. *British Journal of Social Work, 40*, 1777–1793. https://doi.org/10.1093/bjsw/bcp087

Laurian, L., & Shaw, M. (2009). Evaluation of public participation: The practices of certified planners. *Journal of Planning Education and Research, 28*, 293–309. https://doi.org/10.1177/0739456X08326532

Mizrahi, T., Lopez Humphreys, M., & Torres, D. (2009). The social construction of client participation: The evolution and transformation of the role of service recipients in child welfare and mental disabilities. *Journal of Sociology and Social Welfare, 36*(2), 35–61.

Ohmer, M., & Beck, E. (2006). Citizen participation in neighborhood organizations in poor communities and its relationship to neighborhood and organizational collective efficacy. *Journal of Sociology and Social Welfare, 33*(1), 179–202.

Smith, S. R. (2010). Nonprofits and public administration: Reconciling performance management and citizen engagement. *American Review of Public Administration, 20*, 129–152. https://doi.org/10.1177/0275074009358452

Toomey, A. (2009). Empowerment and disempowerment in community development practice: Eight roles practitioners play. *Community Development Journal, 46*, 181–195. https://doi.org/10.1093/cdj/bsp060

Vaughn, L. M., Jacquez, F., Lindquist-Grantz, R., Parsons, A., & Melink, K. (2017). Immigrants as research partners: A review of immigrants in community-based participatory research (CBPR). *Journal of Immigrant and Minority Health, 19*, 1457–1468. https://doi.org/10.1007/s10903-016-0474-3

Walker, E., & McCarthy, J. (2010). Legitimacy, strategy, and resources in the survival of community-based organizations. *Social Problems, 57*, 315–340. https://doi.org/10.1525/sp.2010.57.3.315

CHAPTER 8

TAKING ACTION: GROUP PROCESSES FOR IMPLEMENTING ACTION CAMPAIGNS AND CHANGE STRATEGIES

LEARNING OBJECTIVES

After reading this chapter, students will be able to:

- Describe theories of change, funding sources, and constraints and situational demands that may interfere with planned campaigns and change strategies.
- Describe interpersonal social work skills necessary during campaign implementation.
- Discuss the cyclical nature of campaigns and change strategies.
- Recognize the role of bargaining and negotiation in action campaigns and change strategies.

INTRODUCTION

Once community members reach an agreement on a plan for an action campaign during the engagement phase of the organizing process, the next step is to implement it. Members of the community or organizing group (i.e., people taking action; action system) should have a primary role in carrying out the overall implementation strategy for the action campaign or project. In this chapter, action campaigns are defined and components of successful campaigns are identified. Defining a theory of change and depicting the theory of change in a logic model using SMART (**S**pecific, **M**easurable, **A**chievable, **R**elevant, and **T**imebound) objectives are discussed. Securing resources for engaging in an action campaign is explored. Restraints that limit the group's ability to put plans into action and situational demands that require adjustments and the alteration of tactical methods are also discussed. A variety of interpersonal and communication skills needed by community practitioners and organizers to facilitate implementation of the plan are also described: group decision-making processes, handling logistics, facilitating and participating in formal meetings, public speaking, using the media, keeping notes and other documentation, and bargaining or negotiation. The process of ending campaigns is also examined. In addition, specific techniques for incorporating social justice-related principles in the process of carrying out action plans are identified.

DEFINING AND FRAMING ACTION CAMPAIGNS AND CHANGE STRATEGIES

When they are carried out, action campaigns and change strategies are long-term efforts to implement a specific approach to addressing an issue. Sen (2003) describes a campaign as "a sustained intervention on a specific issue; they have clear short- and long-term goals, a timeline, creative incremental demands, targets who can meet those demands, and an organizing plan to build a constituency and build internal capacity" (p. 81). Action campaigns are inclusive of community intervention programs, organizing efforts, and other change strategies. As described in the previous chapter, to be effective, campaigns should be planned in advance with assigned leadership roles for community members and a timeline that puts various activities in a logical sequence and with logistical details addressed well before the action actually takes place (Schutz & Sandy, 2011; Table 8.1).

Kahn (1991, 2010) describes an action plan as a road map that determines the starting point of the campaign, the resources to be used, and the route to be taken contingent upon anticipated as well as unexpected roadblocks that may occur during the journey. Kahn further recommends that the road map be defined by beginning at the end of the map with the end goal in mind, rather than the beginning in order to assess what is needed to accomplish the goal by a specific date. This also helps set a timeline for complying with relevant deadlines (e.g., the last day new legislation can be proposed in the state assembly, when funding and resources run out) and determining when specific campaign objectives should be achieved and what tactical methods should be used.

CHARTING MILESTONES: THEORIES OF CHANGE

Theories of change provide a logical framework for mapping the process of an action campaign. Theories of change are articulated by the community or organizing group, based on the goals and desired outcomes of the change strategy. A theory of change is a bottom-up process, meaning it is not prescriptive and is developed by the community or organizing group. Although it may be grounded in social change theories (e.g., empirically based knowledge about how and why change occurs), theories of change are project specific, providing a road map for project implementation that connects the project resources, project activities, and project outcomes or goals. In this way, theories of change are especially useful for the community practitioner or campaign organizer, as developing the theory of change is a group process that ensures the partners are in agreement about what it will take to achieve their goals. When used in project or campaign implementation, a theory of change is a road map that can help organizing groups develop a common approach to chart their path forward and identify where they are headed, including setting milestones to help the group understand what is working, what is not, and when adjustments need to be made in order to stay on track to achieve their goals.

In addition to the road map, theories of change are also described or visualized as logic models, frameworks for action, blueprints for change, pathways map, program theory, chain of causation, and models of change (Center for Community Health and Development, n.d.). Logic models are a useful tool for community practitioners and organizers to visually depict the relationships among program or campaign investments, activities, and results. Logic models are also useful because they can be applied to small projects,

TABLE 8.1 Action Plan for On-Campus Group Assisting a Statewide Coalition With a Campaign for Higher Education Funding

GOAL	OBJECTIVES	TIMELINE	ACTION SYSTEM	TARGET SYSTEM	MODEL OF PRACTICE	STRATEGY	TACTICS	RESOURCE NEEDS	EVALUATION CRITERIA
Increase funding for higher education	Form on-campus coalition with a minimum of at least 10 student clubs and local organizations to generate support for increased educational funding.	Sept. 1	Student groups and allied organizations	Members of the legislature, governor	Social action	Campaign contest	Public education, persuasion: mobilization	Volunteers; press coverage; social media; funds for travel, posters, printed material, speakers	Obtain at least 10 coalition members; obtain letters of support and resource commitment from each organization
	Recruit 20 volunteers to coordinate on-campus events and a lobbying campaign using social media techniques.	Oct. 1					Public education, persuasion: mobilization		Number of volunteers recruited
	Sponsor at least two educational forums or teach-ins on issues related to funding for higher education.	Feb. 1					Public education, persuasion: mobilization		Number of workshops held, workshop attendance; number of signed postcards sent to legislators

(continued)

TABLE 8.1 Action Plan for On-Campus Group Assisting a Statewide Coalition With a Campaign for Higher Education Funding *(continued)*

GOAL	OBJECTIVES	TIMELINE	ACTION SYSTEM	TARGET SYSTEM	MODEL OF PRACTICE	STRATEGY	TACTICS	RESOURCE NEEDS	EVALUATION CRITERIA
	Make at least 15 lobbying visits to state legislators to solicit support for increased funding for higher education.	March 1					Lobbying, persuasion		Number of visits made; number of commitments for support made by legislators
	Hold an on-campus flash mob and rally to generate media coverage and public support for the legislation.	April 15					Protest, public education, mild coercion		Attendance at rally, number of signed postcards collected to send to legislators; amount of press coverage
	Assist statewide coalition in obtaining approval for the legislation.	June 30					Bargaining and negotiation		Legislation is passed

an organizing process, or a large, multilayered action campaign. They provide an explicit picture of how an action campaign or intervention is supposed to work, and keep everyone in the organizing group moving in the same direction using a common language and a common point of reference. Logic models can be used during community assessment, planning, implementation, and evaluation phases of a change effort. They help clarify the specific strategies to be used, identify realistic and achievable campaign results, align efforts with allies and other organizations, set priorities for allocation of resources, identify gaps in needed resources, clarify timelines and milestones, negotiate roles and responsibilities for organizing group members, help focus the discussion so time spent during implementation is efficient, reduce the likelihood of unanticipated barriers or undesired outcomes, and guide the evaluation of the action campaign and change strategy (Center for Community Health and Development, n.d.).

"If–then" statements are used in a logic model to logically link resources (e.g., inputs) to planned activities; link planned activities to the anticipated outputs of those activities; and link outputs to the short-, mid-, and long-term outcomes of the theory of change. The logic behind the logic model is that all of these components of implementation should link clearly and cohesively, and, if implemented correctly, will lead to the desired goals for change.

The logic depicted in Figure 8.1 is a simple example that we all can relate to, and the logic flows as follows: *if* we are thirsty, *then* we pour a glass of water; *if* we pour a glass of water, *then* we can drink the water; *if* we drink the water, *then* we will feel hydrated and are no longer thirsty. Every person has been thirsty (i.e., the situation or issue), so what do we do about it? We know from our experience that water helps when we are thirsty, so we pour a glass of water (i.e., input), then we drink the glass of water (i.e., activity). The amount or how much we drink is the output (e.g., how the planned activity took place, how much of it, for whom; what actually occurred); as a result, we felt hydrated and were no longer thirsty (i.e., outcome). Within this example there are a number of embedded assumptions, such as that we could find the water we needed, that we would drink the appropriate amount of water to address the need, and that the consumption of water led to improvements—that we did not experience a stomachache or other negative side effect, for example. All programs and action campaigns include assumptions, and faulty assumptions are often the basis for unintended consequences, unanticipated outcomes, or not achieving our goals.

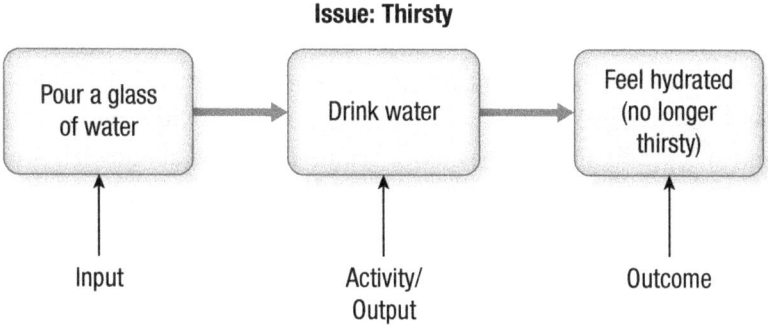

FIGURE 8.1 Everyday logic model example.

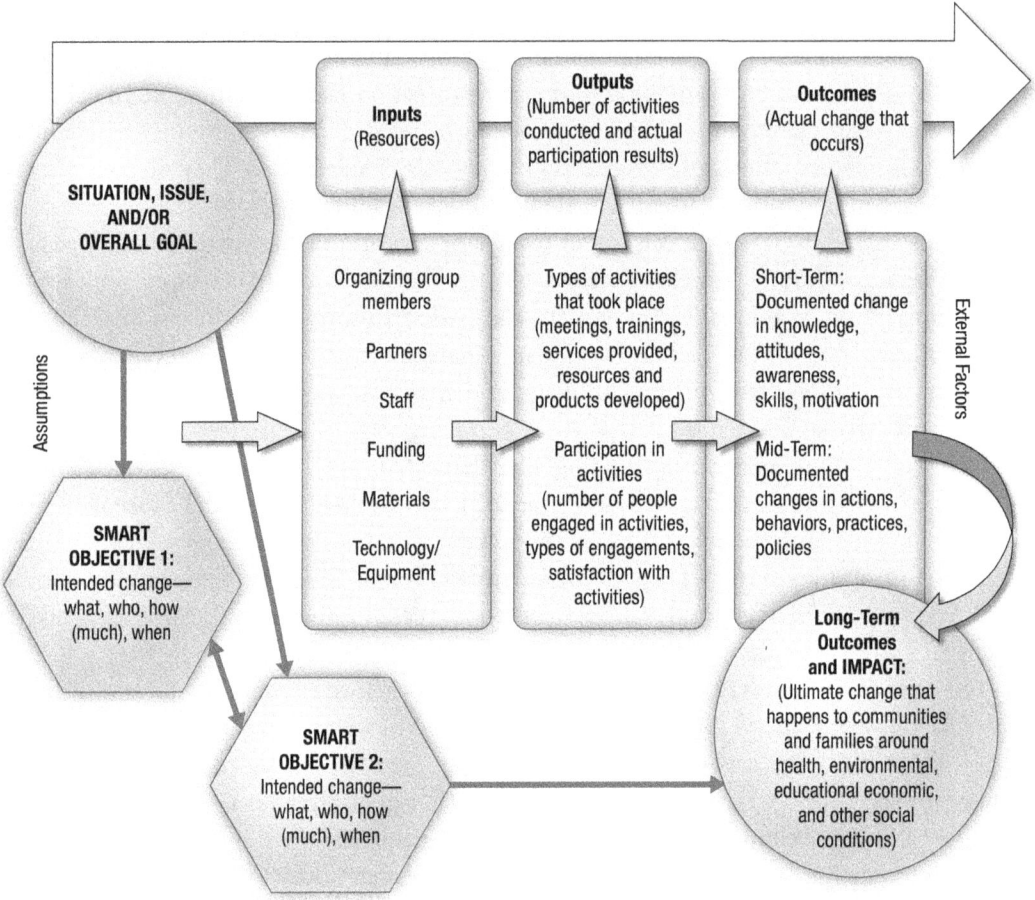

FIGURE 8.2 Detailed logic model.

Logic models vary widely in how they are visually depicted and also about what information is contained. Although nearly all logic models include the basic components of issue, inputs, outputs, and outcomes as depicted in Figure 8.2, logic models can also include information on the situation or context of the issue, underlying assumptions and how they influence or interact with resources and activities, external factors and how they may influence or interact with outcomes and impact, outcomes separated by time frames and what type of change is considered to be achievable within each time frame (e.g., short-, mid-, and long-term outcomes), and evaluation plans for each phase of implementation. Although logic models are typically depicted linearly, program implementation is not always a linear process; rather, it is a cyclical process. As a cyclical process, the logic model is considered a "living document," meaning that as new information is learned about what is working and what is not working during implementation, unanticipated barriers arise, or faulty assumptions become known, the organizing team can revisit and adjust the logic model accordingly to keep the action campaign on track toward achieving its goals.

Action campaign objectives are closely related to action campaign outcomes. With objectives, you are stating the changes that the action campaign intends to achieve. Objectives are often created based on what the organizing team anticipates is possible to achieve in the short-term, mid-term, and long-term time frames. Objectives should be directly and logically connected to the inputs (resources), program outputs (activities and participation) using if–then logic. Objectives should also be written using the "SMART" criteria so that they are actionable. The SMART acronym stands for: **s**pecific, **m**easurable, **a**chievable, **r**ealistic, and **t**ime-bound. The following questions have been adapted from the Centers for Disease Control and Prevention (n.d.) to guide the development of SMART objectives:

- Specific: What exactly are we going to do? What strategies will we use? Is the objective clear and detailed? Is the objective described with strong action verbs such as *conduct, develop, build, plan*, or *execute*? Who will be involved? Is the anticipated outcome specified? Will this objective lead to the desired results? Specific objectives are concrete, detailed, and well defined.
- Measurable: How will we know that change has occurred? Are we able to measure it? How is it currently being measured (do we have a baseline, or do we need to define one)? What types of data will be collected to measure it, how will it be collected, and who will collect it, at what intervals? How much change do we hope to see? Numbers and quantities can provide a means of measurement and comparison.
- Achievable: Can we achieve what we hope to accomplish in the proposed time frame? Are the limitations and constraints understood? Can we do this objective with the resources we have available? Is it feasible to put this objective into action?
- Realistic: Do we have resources available to achieve this objective? Is it possible to achieve this objective? Realistic objectives consider restraints such as resources, personnel, costs, and time frame.
- Time-bound: When will this objective be accomplished? What is our deadline or target date for which to achieve this objective? A time frame helps to set boundaries for the objective.

In evaluating the achievements and impact of the action campaign, objectives are translated into outcomes. Outcomes are the actual changes that occurred as measured by the framing of the action campaign objectives. They should directly connect with one another. Chapter 10 discusses logic models for assessment and evaluation outcomes in greater detail.

FUNDING AND RESOURCES FOR ACTION CAMPAIGNS AND CHANGE STRATEGIES

As demonstrated in the logic model, resources are a necessary component of executing an action campaign or implementing a change strategy. Resources (e.g., program/campaign inputs) can also be thought of as assets, and may include a variety of things such as physical resources (e.g., equipment, technology, program materials, supplies, office space, land); financial resources (e.g., grants and donations); and organizational, human, and in-kind resources (e.g., staff, volunteers, partner organizations, community members, student interns). Each action campaign will have its own unique needs with regard to the resources and inputs necessary to be able to implement the campaign as designed in order to achieve its goals. The logic model process allows an organizing group to carefully consider what resources are necessary to lead the planned activities to achieve the necessary outputs that are needed to accomplish the short-, mid-, and long-term objectives. Once the research needs have been identified, the group determines what resources and assets they already have on hand, and what gaps exist in resource needs that they will need to address before launching the action campaign.

In-kind resources are typically considered inputs that have significant value but do not require you to pay money directly for their use on the action campaign, such as volunteer time or a partner organization providing space for community meetings. In-kind resources are often a product of social capital—part of a reciprocal relationship built on established trust with community members and partner organizations that share a concern for a common social issue. When there is a gap in needed resources to launch a campaign that cannot be filled by in-kind support, such as the need to hire a full-time community practitioner to manage the campaign, then funding sources can be pursued in the form of donations or grants to secure financial resources to address the gap.

Donations can be solicited directly from local philanthropists and community members who share a concern about the issue to be addressed. Usually, these types of donations are solicited by directly approaching known philanthropists in the community, setting up a meeting, and during the meeting letting them know about the social issue, the plans to address it, the gap in funding, and making a direct request. It is helpful if you can provide an opportunity for the donor to make a donation to a tax-exempt organization (i.e., nonprofit, classified as a 501c3 organization), in order that the donor can receive a letter acknowledging their financial contribution that can be submitted to the Internal Revenue Service to claim a tax deduction. A similar approach can be used with local corporations and companies that might be interested in sponsoring the project. If approaching a corporation and offering an opportunity for sponsorship, a community practitioner might offer a reciprocal agreement so that the sponsoring company's logo may be included in communications to the public, indicating they are a sponsor. This is enticing to many businesses as they desire to be viewed as good stewards within the community, and visibility provided by this approach can increase their customer base and goodwill in the community. However, before entering into this type of arrangement an organizing team must take care to ensure that there are no conflicts of interest or concerns about aligning the action campaign with a potentially controversial sponsor that might alienate other potential partners or community members, or otherwise negatively impact the project. Beyond direct solicitations of donations, organizing groups can also host fundraising events and online giving campaigns. These types of fundraising activities serve two primary purposes, to raise money while also raising awareness of the issue and bring visibility for the cause.

Grants from sponsors can also be pursued to address funding and resource shortages. Sponsors of grant funding can include local foundations, local municipalities, national foundations, and state and federal agencies. The grant process typically involves writing a grant narrative to convey the issue; why it is important; the proposed plans to address the need with the specific action campaign, program, or change strategy and its goals; the need for funding this strategy; how the funds will be used to address the need; the evaluation plans that will be used to document the changes achieved; and to demonstrate the capacity of the organizing team in being able to successfully implement the change strategy and achieve the desired outcomes. Grant funding varies widely in what the sponsor expects or will allow funds granted to be used for in programs or campaigns, so when organizing groups decide to pursue grant funding there are three critical questions that must be asked before efforts are made to write a grant proposal:

1. Do our campaign goals match the mission and interest of the funding organization?
2. Are we eligible as an organization or group to apply for these funds?
3. Is the available funding adequate to meet our campaign needs and, if so, can we use the funds on the specific program resources we need to acquire?

To be successful in any of these fundraising approaches, specific skills and resources are necessary. All of these approaches require a great deal of time and energy. Because of this, organizers have to weigh the cost and benefit of engaging in each strategy, and the resources and skills of the organizing team in order to understand which approach will yield the highest return on investment. Organizing groups that are well known and respected in the local community, have dense social networks, and team members who possess strong communication and engagement skills might yield the highest return from soliciting direct donations from local philanthropists. Organizing groups that have team members skilled at written communication may be most successful at securing resources through writing and submitting grant proposals. Other organizing groups that have vast social media networks with high online engagement might choose to focus their energy and time with online giving campaigns. Regardless of the chosen approach, community practitioners must take care to ensure that the fundraising strategy will bring in resources of the appropriate scale to address the funding needs for the campaign, and that the approach matches the assets, skill sets, and resources available to the organizing team for the effort.

COMPONENTS OF SUCCESSFUL CAMPAIGNS AND CHANGE STRATEGIES

There are a number of ways to define *success* in social action, social planning, intervention delivery, and community development campaigns. Success will differ depending on the goals of the campaign, the perceptions of participants, situational demands, and the type of campaign conducted. As discussed in Chapter 1, organizing work involves both process- and task-related social work skills. If, for example, the focus of the campaign was community development, the emphasis of the campaign may be on the process of building relationships among community leaders, citizen participation, and community empowerment, implementing a new program, or building the capacity of neighborhood residents to facilitate improvements in community life. If, on the other hand, a social action campaign, a lobbying effort, or a political campaign was carried out with a specific purpose and intended outcome, success is most often defined as *winning* or achieving that specific outcome (Mondros, 2005). In social planning, the development of a new program, the creation of a new service delivery system, the development of a new organization, the adoption of a new policy, or improvements in existing services or facilities are generally considered to be successes. However, in some circumstances, given constraints such as legislative mandates, lack of public awareness or support, time, and resources, there may be instances in which the organizing team accepts smaller gains as measures of success. According to the Alliance for Justice (2010):

> *Gaining support for an issue from key neighborhood leaders or city council members can be an important stepping stone toward an eventual policy change sought. Some internal interim objectives might be "stepping stones" toward longer-term goals, and important "wins" in and of themselves, such as changes in constituent leadership and power, or changes in organizational capacity. An organization might lose a campaign but at the same time accomplish a "win" by building its power significantly. (p. 1)*

Consequently, campaign goals, strategies, and tactics will change in response to barriers or unexpected restraints encountered and situational demands that arise during the course of the campaign and require a response from the action system.

Restraints on Putting Plans Into Action

In some action campaigns, it simply is not feasible to achieve everything that the organizing group wants to achieve in a short time frame or with limited resources, volunteers, or power. Therefore, the organizing group can use the logic model to assess and reassess how feasible it will be to achieve their goals. One advantage of assessing power resources or conducting force field or SWOT (strengths, weaknesses, opportunities, threats) analyses (see Chapter 6) is that this process permits the organizing team to determine what resources they will need to overcome anticipated opponents to the cause and the amount of power and resources that can be marshaled by the opposition, which is particularly important when working on a legislative campaign. This also assists the organizing group in identifying and developing the activities and tactics that will be effective at counterbalancing these restraints (Homan, 2016). Other types of restraints on successful achievement of campaign goals include existing laws and regulations, incongruent community traditions and customs, the lack of public awareness regarding a new or emerging issue, and established vested interests (e.g., does someone with power stand to benefit or lose from the social change initiative?). To some degree, a well-developed action plan takes these expected barriers into consideration. Strategies and tactics for the change approach should be chosen that help the group to overcome these obstacles.

As described in Chapter 7, each change strategy involves tactics and activities that are planned approaches and action steps used to achieve a goal. Tactics are most commonly used in community-organizing processes, as they map out the approach to an action campaign, and can include *contest* or *confrontation-oriented strategies* (e.g., protests, sit-ins, strikes or boycotts), or *collaborative strategies* (e.g., consensus building, individual and community capacity building, education, and campaign-related strategies/persuasion). Activities are the steps involved in carrying out the strategy or approach, and can include planned experiences such as meetings, community events, components of program delivery, and trainings. As steps for action, activities are directly connected to the stated objectives of the action campaign. Different strategies can be adopted at different phases of the project or action campaign in response to emerging restraints and obstacles, whether anticipated or not. For expected obstacles identified in the theory of change planning process, a monitoring plan can be put in place in the event that anticipated challenges do occur (Homan, 2016). In such cases, the organization can be ready to shift or pivot to implement a "Plan B," including a number of alternative strategies or tactical methods that are responsive to the challenge.

Situational and Contextual Demands

Unintended consequences or unanticipated occurrences can also affect goal attainment during campaigns. One reason for this is that the organizing team cannot always predict what external factors will impact the implementation phase of program delivery, what targets (i.e., people or systems who are the target of the action or who must be influenced to create change) will do in response to specific tactical methods in an organizing campaign, how the public will react to a particular issue, and even what some of the members of the team or partnership will do in the course of tacking action. As with restraints, the best course of action for the organizing campaign involves *contingency planning*, that is, what options do we have if specific things happen that may veer us off course? Schutz and Sandy (2011) suggest that the best way to think about the various options for tactical implementation is using a decision tree diagram to explore the possible options and alternatives associated with each tactic. For example, if we choose plan A, these are the things that are likely to happen or that may backfire. Alternatively, if we choose plan B, the benefits and consequences may be different. The advantage of diagrams for tactical decision-making are the same as those that apply in power mapping. It allows all participants to visualize patterns and themes in the information known to the group, and to build on that information in ways that employ their own experiential knowledge. Consequently, it moves away from a reliance only on the knowledge of the organizer and places control in the hands of participants, permitting organizers to facilitate the process by providing concrete information and asking "why" questions (Figure 8.3).

In addition to consideration of the types of tactics used and activities undertaken, community practitioners and organizers can work with groups to minimize external risks prior to implementation of a change strategy by engaging community members in role plays, assisting leaders in writing scripts or scenarios to use when carrying out an activity or tactic, and make adequate preparations in the event that the action will not take place as planned (Staples, 2016). According to Sen (2003), "a good action has stages; people play roles, and everyone prepares and practices" (p. 87). Typical roles include handling logistics, leading the action, liaising with partners and the media, carrying out the action, producing and distributing posters and printed material, making sure that staff and volunteers arrive at the event or the activity in a timely manner, recruiting and engaging participants, ensuring the event or activity is accessible, and ensuring team and participant safety.

Safety is often a major concern for community organizations engaged in social action activities. For example, in many community-organizing events, there is a potential risk of disruption by opponents to the cause, outsiders simply seeking attention, or allies who may agree with campaign goals, but not the tactical methods employed. There may also be disagreements with law enforcement in terms of how event permits will be enforced or the parameters associated with free speech (Risher et al., 2010). In addition to preplanning and training, safety measures can include establishing "ground rules" for participants, asking volunteers to serve as "safety monitors" to minimize conflict and

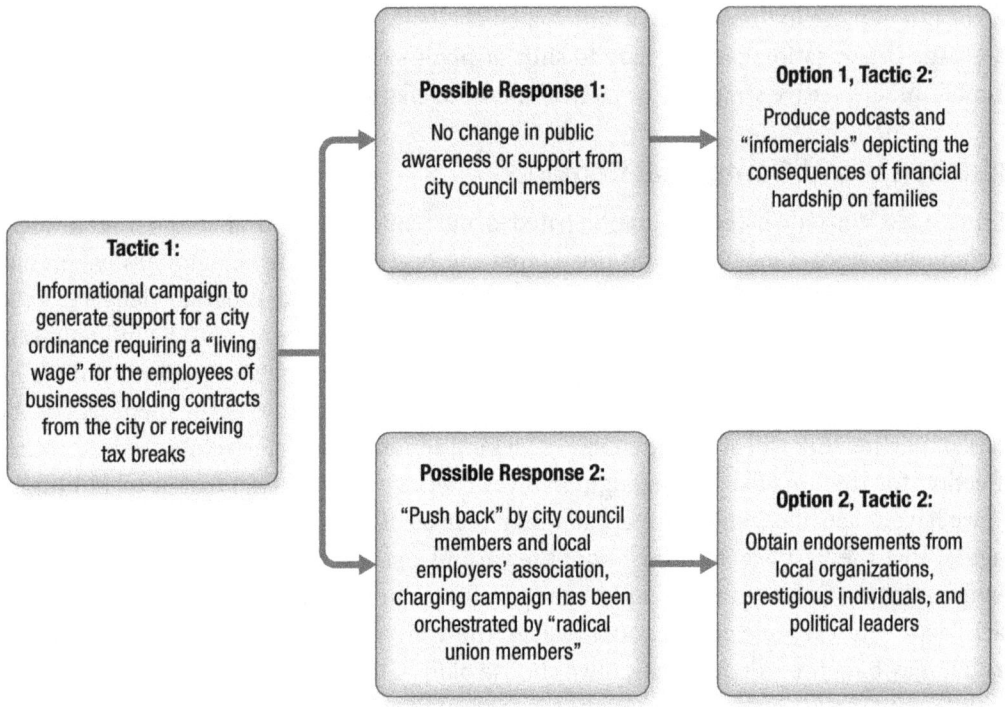

FIGURE 8.3 Decision tree diagram: developing a plan B in response to situational demands.

enforce the rules, or asking legal observers to attend the event and advise participants and local authorities about their rights and responsibilities (Hardina & Obel-Jorgensen, 2011; Maxwell, n.d.).

CONSIDERATIONS IN ADJUSTING AND IMPLEMENTING STRATEGIES AND TACTICS IN RESPONSE TO SITUATIONAL DEMANDS

Unanticipated occurrences require that some tactical methods be developed during, rather than in advance of, the implementation of the program or action campaign. In addition, the success of these new tactics and activities is dependent upon the degree to which group members participate in making decisions about adjustments and are motivated to carry them out. Consequently, group consultation sessions are necessary when developing new tactical methods and making adjustments to planned activities, in order to secure group buy-in, ensure community and cultural appropriateness of the shift in plans, and reaffirm commitment to the goal. In community-organizing campaigns, there are a number of additional factors that must be taken into consideration when making tactical choices, including whether the tactic can easily be used to frame a specific message or demand, respond to constituent preferences, minimize risks, and ensure the likelihood that success will be achieved.

Tactical Considerations: Usability and Packaging the Message

In some situations, when new or modified organizing campaign tactics are under consideration in response to an emerging situational demand, there may not be enough time available to consult everyone involved in the change strategy before the change in tactics needs to take place. Therefore, a high degree of trust among the group is necessary during the preimplementation planning phase for members to agree to delegate responsibility for decision-making to a leader or small group of leaders when the situation calls for it. Most community organizers use a set of principles that can be applied when working with members to come up with new tactical methods in response to situational demands. In addition to the criteria for appropriate tactical methods presented in Chapter 7, an effective tactic

- is easy to put into operation;
- incorporates or illustrates the principles and values associated with the issue campaign;
- provides an opportunity for community members to develop a sense of solidarity with one another;
- is unfamiliar or inconsistent with the experiences of members of the social change target group;
- minimizes risks to all participants, including members of the social change target group;
- educates participants and the general public; and
- contains a specific demand or asks someone (e.g., a policy maker, a potential organization partner, members of the public, the social change target system) to take a specific action (Alinsky, 1971; Bobo et al., 2010; Homan, 2016; Schutz & Sandy, 2011).

The chosen tactical method always presents its own unique challenges, risks, and benefits to the group; to the organization's goals; and to individual members. Much of the literature on community-organizing action campaigns focuses on the various strategic and tactical options available in different approaches to community organization. In addition to several factors identified in previous chapters of this book, such as issue identification and assessment or power resources, other considerations include:

- whether community members are minoritized or otherwise marginalized, thus potentially limiting their access to decision makers;
- the seriousness of the issue at hand;
- the amount of time available to address the issue;
- the amount of public awareness or empathy with the cause;
- the degree to which the issue matches up with the self-interest of social change targets and the general public; and
- the degree to which the tactical method is likely to generate a negative reaction from the public, including allies and possible opponents (Alinsky, 1971; Bobo et al., 2010; Kahn, 2010; Mondros, 2005; Netting et al., 2017; Schulz & Sandy, 2011; Sen, 2003).

Preferences for Tactical Methods

Community-organizing group members also need to consider whether they prefer tactical methods that are indirect or involve direct interaction with social change target groups (Rubin & Rubin, 2008). For example, filing a request for information from government agencies (i.e., public record request) or using legal resources to send "cease and desist" letters, request an injunction, or file lawsuits to stop unjust policies and laws are tactical methods that limit group member exposure to social change targets, but may also subject some individuals (such as agency employees who serve as "whistleblowers") to possible form of negative fallout, retaliation, or harassment (Greene & Latting, 2004). Alternatively, most forms of confrontational tactical methods (e.g., protests, sit-ins, strikes) involve some type of face-to-face or direct contact with social change target groups. However, in most long-term campaigns a combination of direct and indirect methods will be used.

Risk Assessment and the Likelihood That Success Will Be Achieved Using Action Campaigns and Change Strategies

There are a number of additional issues to be considered when choosing overall campaign approaches, tactical options, and activities for program implementation or other community change strategies. For example, change strategies oriented toward collaboration, consensus building, and problem-solving often are preferred methods of community practice because they involve limited risks, can build collective community capacity, are typically peaceful, and can often address needed changes in policies and practices through the inclusion, education, and engagement of people and organizations holding the power to make changes. If consensus change strategies are considered by the organizing group to be an effective approach in achieving the desired goal, while ensuring community members and constituents most affected by the social issue are driving the change process, their expertise is recognized and they have an active and powerful representative voice in the decision-making process, then it is preferable to use this approach over confrontational methods.

According to Netting and colleagues (2017), one important consideration in applying collaboration-related tactical methods is whether all or most of the relevant groups and decision makers already support the proposed change or can realistically be persuaded to do so. If more than a few friendly meetings are needed to find common ground with groups that must be persuaded to join the organizing effort, then campaign-related tactics (e.g., bringing opponents to the bargaining table) must be considered. An additional potential issue with collaboration is that more effort may go into sustaining partnership agreements with diverse organizations than actually working toward a common goal (Homan, 2016). As noted earlier in this text, from a social work perspective, community development or collaborative strategies are considered inappropriate in situations in which outside organizations impose their own agendas on community members that are incompatible with community goals or interests, or when such efforts are designed to limit dissent or sustain institutional arrangements or policies that result in resource disparities, political suppression, or adverse consequences for communities (Brager et al., 1987; Toomey, 2009; Young Laing, 2009).

Similar issues may limit the effectiveness of problem-solving approaches, especially efforts that involve consultation with numerous organizations and the public. Difficulties reaching agreements among a variety of parties with different vested interests, having sufficient time to make joint decisions, or conducting a review of all pertinent and necessary information in a collective approach may make the planning process too cumbersome and reduce the likelihood that the outcome will be satisfactory to all parties involved (Rothman & Zald, 2008). Still, community involvement is an essential mechanism for making public planning decisions rather than leaving the dimensions of the final plan to outside professionals or the political process (Heywood, 2011; Netting et al., 2017).

Although of lower intensity than confrontation-related tactics, the use of campaign-style approaches when tactics are oriented toward bringing opponents to the bargaining table can also be problematic. Netting and colleagues (2017) argue that the success of campaign-related tactics is predicated on whether people can be persuaded to adopt the organization or organizing group's position on the issue. The use of these types of tactical methods is also dependent upon how people can be persuaded to change their own position on the issue. If public pressure is needed, especially if it involves the use of a variety of tactical methods over a period of time, and the social change target has repeatedly refused to negotiate, then contest-related or confrontational tactics must be considered. Other challenges involved in using campaign-related tactics involve the length of time required for the effort, the resources required, especially if "wins" involve small incremental gains over time, and issues related to keeping all allied groups engaged in the effort, especially when agendas may differ among organizations (Kerr Chandler, 2009; Sen, 2003; Swarts, 2008).

As noted in Chapter 7, contest or confrontation strategies and the types of tactical methods used in these efforts are often fraught with hazards, especially if they involve direct confrontation with authorities. One potential consequence of confrontation involves whether an unwilling social change target can actually be forced to do something that is counter to the values and interests of that individual or organization (Netting et al., 2017). In addition, existing laws, regulations, funding limitations, or considerations about the health or safety of others may make implementing the organizing group or action system's demands less than feasible (Bobo et al., 2010; Work Group for Community Health and Development, 2022). Confrontation entails substantial risks to participants and social change targets, especially when it involves coming face-to-face with social change targets, applying pressure, and engaging in activities that could, in some circumstances, result in arrest (such as sit-ins, protests in public or private places without permission or the proper permits, deliberate disruption of meetings or events, or civil disobedience). Social change targets may "push back," make deliberate attempts to pit members of the organizing group against each other, stigmatize group members, make negative comments or false accusations in the press, take action to terminate the employment of a participant, or physically threaten or assault protestors (Kahn, 2010; Staples, 2016). Other hazards with confrontation tactics include that they can be emotionally draining; organizing participants can be easily discouraged if "wins" do not come easily or require substantial amounts of time or resource commitments (Homan, 2016). In addition, certain types of tactics (such as vandalism, threats or acts of violence, or deception) employed by some community organizations, activist groups, or allied organizations are incompatible with the ethical principles described in the National Association of Social Workers (NASW; 2021) *Code of Ethics* (Hardina & Obel-Jorgensen, 2011).

Popular education approaches also entail several challenges. Efforts to establish popular education initiatives in communities involving community education and training, health promotion, or participatory action research that are initiated from outside the community may receive a hostile or distrusting reaction from potential recruits. Trust building and overcoming differences created by the power imbalance between outsiders and community members may take substantial time and resources away from the organizing effort (Catalani & Minkler, 2010). Truly empowered community members participating in an organizing effort, once they have developed a *critical consciousness* (i.e., understanding about the role of social structure and power relations in the origin of the social problem and barriers that must be overcome to resolve it; Barretti, 2009), may wish to advance this organizing method to the next stage—involvement in social action, which may include direct confrontation with authorities. This mix of in-group consensus building and confrontation with authorities outside of the group context is used in feminist organizing (Delgado, 1997; Mizrahi, 2007). Consequently, the progression and escalation of the tactical methods require that both organizers and organizing constituents develop different skill sets appropriate for engaging in much different situations.

USING BASIC GROUP-WORK TECHNIQUES FOR GROUP MAINTENANCE, GROWTH, AND COHESION

Organizing group members who have planned the initial action campaign, community strategy, program or project should share responsibility for implementing activities and tactics, and modify them in response to situational demands. The process of doing this should result in the development of deep bonds and feelings of solidarity among group members, especially in situations in which the planning, organizing, or development effort is complex, decision-making is difficult, the use of tactical methods entails substantial risks, or the effort involves a substantial commitment of time, energy, or resources (Conway, 2003; Polletta, 2002). According to Staples (2016), for an action campaign to be successful, the organization needs to develop a group culture that consists of norms, values, and a concrete decision-making structure. They compare this process to that of a clinical social worker who contracts with a client for a specific service that has clear boundaries, role expectations, and an outcome. In an organizing group, members contract with one another; although not stated explicitly, members come to expect that the group will operate in a specific manner, with set meeting times, a location, rules for decision-making, a leadership structure, and clear roles for participants and the organizer. Basic details, such as whether food will be served, who will bring food, and whether arrangements have been made for child care or transportation, are crucial for creating a sense of group solidarity and comfort with the organizing process, as well as ensuring equitable access for participation (Bobo et al., 2010; Brown, 2006).

When discussing activities and tactical methods in a group process, the organizer and organizing group members should examine in detail the likely responses to activities and tactics and how those responses should best be addressed by the organization. For example, in a legislative campaign if an opponent retaliates against the organization, what are the possible repercussions for the organization and its members? As with the initial action plan for the campaign, the leaders of the group from the community should conduct the meeting while the community organizer provides support, resources, information, and "gentle guidance"; asking "why" questions, challenging assumptions, making suggestions, and assisting group members in weighing options, alternatives, and likely outcomes. When determining whether a tactical method fits within the experience of group members, is culturally appropriate, and will generate enough participants and public support, organizers can ask themselves the following: Are community members willing to make a commitment, take a risk, recruit friends, or provide resources that can be used for the action? A majority vote by group members may be sufficient for a tactic to be approved, but a lack of enthusiasm by those involved in the decision often indicates that few people will actually be willing to carry it out. One of the organizers interviewed by Hardina and colleagues (2009) described the informed-consent process in the organization in which they were employed:

> *There is really no formal process. Just a matter does everyone agree to it—if so does everybody agree with the tactics—what role is everyone going to play. Strategically mapping out roles and responsibilities. If it were to come down to like some kind of direct action or civil disobedience something like that. Lots of planning. It might get mundane. Reiterating why we're doing it. (p. 19)*

In addition to establishing informed consent, the group process is critical to the success of the organizing campaign in a number of ways. Participants, particularly organizing group members who have volunteered over a long period of time or organizational leaders, often have practical knowledge based on experience about what tactical methods work and the potential for these approaches to backfire (Conway, 2004). According to Polletta (2006), "as they assess different courses of action, familiar stories about what has worked or failed in the past make some options seem radical, moral, fitting, even feasible, and make others seem conservative, immoral, inappropriate, or beyond the realm of possibility" (p. 171). A number of organizers, who have written about their experiences participating in or managing large-scale campaigns, argue that the participation of people who hold a variety of viewpoints, cultural perspectives, and experiences in group decision-making increases the creativity inherent in the decision-making process, thereby leading to the development of tactical approaches that are more responsive to situational demands (Ganz, 2009; Horton et al., 1998; Kahn, 2010).

COMMUNICATION USING TECHNOLOGY AND SOCIAL MEDIA FOR ACTION CAMPAIGNS

As discussed in previous chapters, organizing groups can benefit from communication, team management, and other technology platforms, including social media. Communication platforms can be used by the organizer as a tactical approach for engaging organizing groups and constituents in messaging campaigns, including the use of e-newsletters, text messaging, websites and other forms of web-based media to convey information about community events and activities; as an informational or educational campaign to raise awareness by sharing statistics and fact-sheets on a particular social issue or current legislative action; and to share stories or testimonials related to social issues and legislative actions. Further, team management platforms (e.g., Asana, Basecamp, Slack, Microsoft Teams) can be employed by the organizer to facilitate seamless and real-time communication, keep the organizing team engaged, task-oriented, responsive to deadlines, and working collaboratively toward a common goal. Participation in community events and campaign activities and follow-up with participants can be tracked using a variety of technology tools, which can provide important information to the organizing team about who is engaged and how they are engaged, and identify which activities are more engaging than others (Brown & Dinecola, 2020).

Relationship-building, recruitment, and engagement activities of an action campaign or change strategy can also be enhanced by technology, and particularly through the use of social media and other social networking sites. Social media has been used not only to establish new connections and relationships, but also to foster empathy, compassion, and understanding among groups (Barak et al., 2008; Brown & Dustman, 2019). As detailed in Chapter 2, the Community Mobilization through Social Media (CMSM) model is one structured approach used by community organizers to harness social media to engage constituents and ally partners, promote dialogue and interaction with the organizing group, and to get the word out and encourage involvement in action events and change activities (Brown & Dustman, 2019). Models like CMSM are useful not only in the preengagement phase, but also in the engagement phase in keeping community members, participants, and organizing team members engaged, motivated, and working collectively for a common cause. Social media is an important tool for organizers in soliciting and maintaining public support and involvement in organizing action campaigns and implementing change strategies.

OTHER INTERPERSONAL SOCIAL WORK SKILLS NEEDED TO FACILITATE ACTION CAMPAIGNS

Despite the emphasis on and importance of leadership development in the organizing process, there are numerous tasks that need to be undertaken by the community practitioner or organizer. In some circumstances, the community practitioner or organizer acts as a backup if volunteers are not available or the team needs support to develop skills or carry out their responsibilities. In implementing community programs or other change strategies, the community practitioner or organizer often serves in the role of skill-builder providing trainings and connecting team members to other groups or professionals for skill-building and training opportunities as needed. Practitioner and organizer skills also include coordinating logistical support for the action campaign and specific events, the application of activity action steps or tactical methods, facilitating or participating in community or team meetings, working with the media, public speaking, keeping notes and other documentation, and bargaining and negotiation with potential partners, allies, or opponents.

Handling the Logistics

Most events or activities related to the implementation of strategies, activities for programs, and tactics require preplanning and some type of logical support to ensure that people, equipment, and printed materials or other resources are obtained, moved, used, and removed as needed (Staples, 2016). Although some of these activities can be handled by volunteers or support staff (if the organization has them), it often falls upon the practitioner or organizer to coordinate logistics. Often, the practitioner or organizer must contact volunteers prior to the event to confirm intended participation and that those people who have been assigned specific tasks in preparation for implementation of the activity or event have followed through. In some situations, relationship-building and motivational skills may be used to encourage volunteers to perform certain tasks or take on additional responsibilities. In addition, the practitioner or organizer must keep track of what other participants are doing, when events are expected to happen, and what people are supposed to be doing at various points of time (Bobo et al., 2010). Often what this means is that the person at the event carrying a clipboard or tablet and a smart phone is the community organizer. The organizer may also be responsible for making sure that equipment works, food is obtained, the room or event facility is reserved, and that participants or group members are present, physically safe, and have their needs for participation met in a timely manner (e.g., directions, rides, meals, etc.).

The community practitioner or organizer must always be ready to respond to crises or unanticipated events. What are the options if an event is rained out, volunteers fail to arrive on time, a staff or team member gets sick, a permit for a rally is not obtained or withdrawn at the last minute, or a speaker cancels hours before an event? All of these issues require back-up planning and reliance on other team members, volunteers, partners, or other supporters to pitch-in and help make the action or event successful. This is directly related to interpersonal social work skills. The practitioner or organizer should have a variety of long-standing relationships with volunteers, donors, supporters, and other community residents who can be called upon to provide resources for an event or who can be deployed in the event of a crisis. For example, if "Graham's Catering Service" cannot make a delivery of food for tomorrow's community forum, is there any chance that Mx. Jones can bake some cookies for the event or contact other volunteers to provide the food? If the plumbing breaks down in the community center in which a volunteer training workshop will be held, what are the other venue options for the event? Can Ellen Daniel, who works as a church secretary, obtain permission for the organization to use the recreation room in the church? If Mx. Brown becomes ill just before making a presentation at a city council meeting, can another team member or volunteer be found at the last minute? In such circumstances, it is also helpful to have leaders and other volunteers who can put in a call to friends, neighbors, colleagues, and business associates who may be willing to help mitigate a crisis or provide resources at short notice.

In addition to using previous relationships in handling logistics for specific actions and events, there are other interpersonal social work techniques that can be used to motivate volunteers and donors. As with other organizing situations, often volunteers are motivated based on their values, or commitment to the cause or community, opportunities to socialize with others, or the opportunity to apply their skills and special talents. It is also important to reciprocate help received, especially when someone fills in at the last minute. If Mx. Jones caters the entire meal at the community forum, they should receive recognition from the organization, thanks from the organizer, and be assured that if they ask the organization for assistance in the future, they will be listened to and if feasible, they will be supported in their request (Bobo et al., 2010).

Facilitating and Participating in Formal Meetings

Most meetings in which action planning takes place are relatively informal. Decisions may be made by consensus (such as informal general agreement) or some type of formal vote of the group members may be required based on group norms. However, in many situations, the action campaign or change strategy may need to be approved by the lead organization's board of directors. Often this involves a formal process with precise rules for attendance, voting rights, and specific roles for leaders and other board members. Other types of formal meetings in which organizing group members or the organizer may take part are annual membership meetings or delegate assemblies, neighborhood organization groups, conferences, and coalition or other organizational partnership meetings (Rubin & Rubin, 2008). In addition, group members may attend other types of formal meetings, such as government or legislative hearings, corporate board meetings, or public forums, to observe, make formal presentations, lobby for legislation, or, in some cases, to put pressure on decision makers for policy changes or to make other requests or demands of elected officials and other individuals with the power to make things happen.

Formal meetings have characteristics that differentiate them from informal groups in which participants may converse freely with one another. Although task or work groups use agendas developed by their members, formal meetings often entail additional rules or procedures for how agendas are posted or disseminated, when people may speak, who may speak, and how votes are to be taken. For nonprofit and some public decision-making bodies (such as planning boards or city councils), *Robert's Rules of Order* (Robert et al., 2011), a standard, published set of rules is used to guide meetings. Using *Robert's Rules*, the meeting is called to order by a chair (usually the president of the board), formal motions must be made by one member of the board and seconded by another board member prior to calling for a vote on an issue, and outcomes of votes follow majority rule. There are other rules that must be followed by organizations that interpret these procedures strictly such as requirements for postponing (tabling) votes on issues and the number of board members who must be present (a quorum) if official business is conducted.

Public decision-making processes are also guided by a set of rules that must be followed by elected officials, governmental staff members asked to speak regarding issues of public interest, and members of the general public. Some states have legislatively established open meeting laws that specify that state and local government bodies must follow an established set of rules that allow for public input (Nadler & Schulman, 2006). For example, typical open meeting rules include requirements that agendas are made available to the public several days prior to the meeting, that most decisions be made before members of the public, and that the public be allowed to make comments or presentations in response to the issues raised during the meeting (California Attorney General's Office, 2003). Often public comments are limited to 2 or 3 minutes per speaker (Hoefer, 2019). Open meeting laws and rules specific to various governmental bodies also allow for public comment to be structured in a way that may minimize actual input or prevent disruption, for example, allowing public comment only at the very beginning or the end of the meeting, or requiring that people apply or register to make a presentation prior to the start of the meeting (Rubin & Rubin, 2008). Consequently, participants need to know the rules and procedures before they arrive at the meeting.

For public meetings, community organizers research the issues under discussion, obtain information about meeting agendas and rules related to public participation and voting procedures, conduct background research on decision makers, and help prepare constituents to make presentations at public meetings or for service on boards, planning councils, or commissions. Both community organizers who are working with groups that intend to lobby at public meetings and practitioners employed by public organizations must have good interpersonal social work skills. According to Bernhardt (n.d.):

Meetings of one form or another are the substance behind any public participation process. They are preeminently interpersonal exercises, requiring planners not only to be approachable, personable, and professional, but also to have empathy and charisma depending on the circumstances. (Section 7.43, para. 1)

It is important to note that interpersonal social work skills are also required when working with government officials, who, in most cases, must make the final decision. Staff support roles for government agencies or for nonprofit board and committee meetings are somewhat similar. Staff members work in collaboration with decision makers to set agendas; provide up-to-date information about the types of decisions to be made; maintain written records, including agendas and minutes; provide technical information and data; and make recommendations as to the best course of action to be taken by those who have decision-making power (Hardina et al., 2006; Tropman, 2012).

A unique aspect of the organizer's role is actually ensuring successful outcomes in advance of the meeting. Staples (2016) describes the importance of using interpersonal skills to prepare for meetings in advance, talking to individuals about task assignments, what they are willing or prepared to do, and the types of decisions that will be made during the meeting. Although community practitioners or organizers may share in some of these tasks, most of the organizer's or planner's time will be spent on this type of advanced preparation work, including contacting community members by phone, discussing the issues to be addressed in the meeting, following up on previous tasks, and offering information or suggestions when appropriate. In some circumstances, board members and other constituents may need support from the organizer or encouragement to volunteer for more responsibilities. The organizer may also be called on to provide creative solutions for some of the challenges faced by the group.

Working With News Sources and Social Media

One of the most critical things to learn in the organizing process is that local media often chooses what issues or events to cover or how to report on them in ways that cannot be predicted in advance (Kirst-Ashman & Hull, 2018). Media owners are as likely to have political agendas or allegiances as anyone else, and sometimes other breaking news stories will have precedence over those that you would like covered (Sen, 2003). Consequently, one critical organizing task is to persuade media to cover your event and provide information about an issue in a manner that supports or enhances your cause. Schutz and Sandy (2011) offer a number of suggestions that increase the likelihood that the news media will cover the event:

- Maintain personal relationships with individual reporters and keep a record of updated contact information. Developing a good working relationship with reporters requires a willingness to exchange information, assisting the reporter with additional sources of information, giving referrals of other people willing to be interviewed, and offering "quotable" quotes.
- Link the story of your campaign to other breaking news stories of interest to the media. For example, Hardina and Obel-Jorgensen (2011) describe a campaign in which members of the organizing team were able to link a story about police surveillance on a university campus to a similar story that occurred in the same city about law enforcement surveillance of an antiwar group. The previous incident received national media attention and was described by Michael Moore in the movie *Fahrenheit 911*. Subsequent reporting on this issue noted the link between the two news stories and also mentioned the film (Marcum, 2006).
- Make the event so unique, unusual, or spectacular that the media would be remiss not to cover it. For example, using the arts (such murals, music, photography, videos) in a creative way to illustrate an issue, staging a mass assembly with hundreds or thousands of people, or arranging for the presence of a celebrity at the event are all tried-and-true methods for eliciting media coverage. One example of the use of this technique involved the production of a DVD for national distribution by Mayday New Orleans, an organization made up of former public housing residents in New Orleans. City government, encouraged by the U.S. Department of Housing and Urban Development, had demolished their homes after Hurricane Katrina in order to use the land for new development. The documentary film, *Coming Home: The Dry Storm*, told the story of their efforts to lobby local and federal governments for the "right of return," in this case, to federally subsidized housing in a new development in New Orleans (National Economic and Social Rights Initiative & Stephenson, 2010).
- As described in Chapter 3, other techniques often used to solicit media attention include issuing press releases directly to radio, television, and print media reporters just before the event listing basic information (what, why, who, how) and press contact information, or holding press conferences in which your members and allied organizations can be present to show their support for the issue or event (Bobo et al., 2010). Community calendars in newspapers and on websites or on local radio and television stations can be used to announce scheduled events, and local talk shows can be contacted to schedule interviews in relation to a specific event or issue.

CASE VIGNETTE: GETTING THE WORD OUT ABOUT "HELPING HANDS" CARE BAGS

In the fall of 2020, an organizing group with the Thrive in the 05 initiative sponsored a drive-through event in the Old Pascua community, an urban American Indian community in Tucson, Arizona, during the pandemic. The purpose of this event was to pass out "Helping Hands" care bags full of household goods and personal protective supplies (e.g., face masks, hand soap, hand sanitizer) in response to the COVID-19 pandemic. The team partnered with KPYT, the Pascua Yaqui Tribe's community radio station, and KPYT broadcasted live from the event site throughout the day, got the word out about the program, and attracted hundreds of families that drove through and received the care bags of supplies.

Although community group leaders should be encouraged to take on much of the media relations responsibility, community practitioners and organizers are expected to assist with this type of work. They may have up-to-date information on technical issues that can be useful in interviews or they may need to be present to guide and provide support to organizing group members. The organizer can be responsible for scheduling interviews between the media and community group leaders, ensuring that people show up on time, and helping constituents articulate a vision or message consistent with the goals of the organizing campaign. According to Sen (2003), organizers can prepare their constituents to talk to reporters by providing training for them about how to stay focused on the issue at hand and to frame the organization's message so that it is likely to have appeal to a general audience.

As mentioned earlier in this chapter, social media is a powerful tool that can be used not only to get the word out about an event, but also to document the event, activities, or use of tactical methods in an action campaign or change strategy. One of the advantages involved in using social media sites is that news organizations also use these resources when researching stories or identifying events that they want to cover (Bobo et al., 2010). Sometimes participants or by-standers may simply want to share their own experiences with their friends or relatives, sending photos or blogging about their participation in a campaign-related activity. However, many times posting information about successful applications of tactical methods, organizing campaigns, or events is part of a deliberately planned strategy to gain public support. For example, San Francisco Pride at Work posted a video of an action that they staged with the help of the Brass Liberation Orchestra (Hogarth, 2010). The event involved a "flash mob" in which the participants sang and danced in a hotel lobby to urge the public to "boycott, don't get caught in a bad hotel" due to the owners' refusal to provide healthcare benefits for their employees. The musical number used during the event "borrowed" the melody from and modified the lyrics of a song by a popular entertainer known for staging their own flash mobs to promote their music.

Public Speaking

Community organizers, practitioners, and organization leaders may also be called on to speak at rallies, protests, legislative hearings, and formal meetings. In some cases, persuading potential allies to join the cause may involve making formal presentations or speeches at board meetings or conferences. According to Homan (2016), a good speech involves preparation and knowledge of the goals and issues of the organization that the speaker represents. Good speakers are also able to relate to members of the audience, to make a connection between the issue discussed and the values and experiences of audience members, and to respond to tough questions with factual information and confidence (Richan, 2006). Hoefer (2019) recommends speakers practice their presentation prior to the event, focusing not only on content, but on the pacing of words and pauses, the use of gestures, the length of the speech (especially if time limits will be imposed), and visual aids such as PowerPoint slides, videos, props, and handouts. Effective presentations also contain personal stories or testimonials about how the speaker or other individuals and groups have been affected by the issue, social problem, or legislation under discussion (VeneKlasen et al., 2007). Personal stories of hardship or efforts to overcome adversity are particularly effective, and for community members it can be an empowering experience to have the opportunity to speak publicly about their own experiences.

An effective speech that is part of an action campaign persuades audience members to do something—to take action: Volunteer for a cause, vote for a candidate, endorse a policy proposal or issue campaign, join a coalition, or lobby their legislator. At rallies, meetings, and protests, people are often asked to sign petitions, complete letters or postcards that can be mailed to legislators, or call or visit their elected officials (Brown, 2006). Therefore, the speaker should be both informative and persuasive, urging audience members to take action and providing them with ideas for concrete action steps to take (Hoefer, 2019). As with the campaign itself, an effective speech contains an appeal to a moral framework and values. An effective community-organizing speech also is designed to evoke emotions and empathy from people, for example, concern for people who are hurting, a commitment to work with or reach out to others, or outrage about social injustice.

Keeping Notes and Other Documentation

ben Asher (2002) argues that keeping field notes is as important for community practitioners and organizers as it is for social workers who work in clinical settings. Community practitioners and organizers need to pay attention to important details regarding the individuality of each person they interact with, including preferred names, proper pronunciation of names, gender pronoun preferences, preferred spoken language and methods of communication. In addition, people may share personal things about themselves with the organizer, such as experiences, skills they possess and would like to offer for the project, or interests in involvement in and/or receiving training related to the change strategy. For a practitioner or organizer, these details are important. Due to the sheer volume of people whom the organizer may interact with on any given day or at an event, field notes can be a useful method for keeping track of that information so it can be recalled in future engagements. Field notes also serve as a method of recording what they are doing to inform their supervisors or other leadership about their activities, help the organization keep track of the process of implementing interventions (e.g., learning what works and what is not working so adjustments can be made), and can be extremely useful in an evaluation of the organizing effort (Bobo et al., 2010). Some organizers participate in regular accountability sessions with organizing group members, and reporting what the organizer did and accomplished is an important component of these meetings (Brown, 2006).

In addition, the organization will report its accomplishments and community impact to both funders and members of the community it serves or the general public. Consequently, it is important to have a written record of the tasks that are completed and the degree to which goals and objectives have been accomplished. For the practitioner or organizer, field notes can provide an opportunity for intrapersonal discovery, including self-reflection and self-accountability as well, helping them recognize any biases in behaviors or actions, any inefficient or ineffective practices they are engaged in, ensuring they are honoring the social work ethical code, and detecting any early-warning signs of professional burnout, compassion fatigue, or secondary trauma.

Other records that are important to keep include action plans; newspaper, video, and audio clips of media coverage for the organization or campaign; and accounts of lobbying contacts, legislative campaigns, and other successes and strides (or struggles) related to the actions of the organizing group or coalition partners (Family and Community Services, 2011). In addition, some of the documents maintained are useful for developing retrospective accounts of the organizing efforts. These can be published and disseminated as case studies or reports that may be helpful to organizations that are seeking to launch similar efforts; in some cases, such accounts may have historical significance and may be donated to universities or public library archives.

An additional reason for keeping records is that there should be some type of documentation of what happens in meetings. As described earlier in this chapter, *Robert's Rules of Order* is used in many organizations to guide decision-making processes. In most formal board or committee meetings, an elected or selected secretary or another volunteer takes *meeting minutes*. These consist of a written record of who is present at the meeting, motions brought to the floor for a vote, members who have proposed the various motions, and the actual vote. In many cases, minutes may also describe issues discussed for which there was no formal vote, statements made by attendees, or tasks delegated and next steps committed to by the group and individuals within the group. However, since minutes are most likely to be drawn up by volunteers, they may be brief and consequently leave out important details (note: this can be improved by providing training for the volunteer notetaker and a standardized structure for the notes). According to ben Asher (2002), it is important for the organizer to be able to describe how and why things happened and to analyze why things have occurred. This is equally as important in terms of what happens in specific meetings as during the implementation of community programs, action campaign tactical methods, community events, and overall change strategies. A practitioner or organizer should keep track of the individuals and groups involved; the perceived power, recognized authority, or ability of participants to influence specific events or outcomes; how and why decisions were made; the impact of specific tactics or overall strategies; and outcomes produced (Hardina, 2002).

Bargaining and Negotiating With Opponents

Most social action or legislative organizing campaigns involve some sort of compromise among the parties involved. The techniques used in this process are called *bargaining* and *negotiation*. Hardcastle and colleagues (2004) define *bargaining* as consisting of "(a) the division or exchange of one or more specific resources, or (b) the resolution of one or more intangible issues among the parties or among those whom the parties represent, or

(c) both" (p. 304). Bargaining takes place in the context of a negotiation. Negotiation involves a discussion that is oriented toward finding common ground or forging an agreement among participants (Homan, 2016). In the negotiation process, the parties often agree to suspend campaigns or activities designed to suppress or react to campaigns until the talks reach their conclusion.

In some cases, such as the development of a coalition or collaborative, bargaining or negotiating tactics may be used to bring opponents or nonaligned groups into an alliance with the action system. As described in Chapter 4, the groups involved identify resources to be exchanged among participants, goals to be accomplished, rules for decision-making, and specific roles and responsibilities for each group and their representatives. In social action campaigns, the last stage of the action campaign will typically involve bargaining or negotiating a resolution. When pressure tactics are used to influence people in power through public censure, humiliation, disruption of business, or other types of direct action, the purpose essentially is to force the social change target to come to the bargaining table. This necessitates that the people involved (both the social change action and target systems) actually talk to one another to develop some sort of resolution regarding the social problem or issue addressed by the action campaign (Bobo et al., 2010; Homan, 2016).

Generally, in the bargaining process, there are a set of implicit or explicit rules that are used by participants to develop compromises. For example, legislative processes and union negotiations with employers must abide by existing legal frameworks or by-laws and policies developed by the institutions involved. In some cases, provisions may be made for the conflict to be mediated by a third party, with the understanding that the groups involved will abide by the decision of the arbitrator (Jansson, 2017).

One important component of negotiations to keep in mind is that most skilled negotiators have "fallback" positions. A fallback position should be consistent with at least one of the outcomes listed in the group's action plan, but the group should be ready to acknowledge that it will not receive everything it wants (Hoefer, 2019). Group members must decide to make some concessions in order to keep negotiations moving; in such situations the organizing group may settle for something less than the original goal. However, this outcome should still advance the goals of the action campaign. For example, if the group is lobbying the city council to develop a policy to ban vendors from using Styrofoam cups and plates in concession stands in city parks, it may be to the organization's advantage to simply accept an appointment to a city commission to review policies related to contracts with private food vendors in the parks.

In organizing work that emphasizes collaboration and consensus, the bargaining process focuses on producing results that will maximize benefits for all participants if concerns about resource allocation and turf can be addressed satisfactorily. However, when contest strategies are used, without some sort of bargaining process, the resolution of organizing campaigns will involve a process of accommodation or "giving in" by one party or retreat from the conflict by the other (Hardcastle et al., 2004). According to Homan (2016), there are two basic approaches to conducting negotiations during the bargaining process:

- A positional approach in which both sides stake out their positions and try to obtain as much as possible to advance their causes; this approach is sometimes counterproductive because the emphasis on "winning" may preclude reaching a compromise.

- An outcome-based approach is used in which the parties try to reach an agreement that will result in each one obtaining at least some of what they need or wish to achieve.

In order to achieve their goals, the action group needs to do some preplanning before it enters into negotiations. Members of the negotiating team should be chosen and research should be conducted on how the opponents are likely to bargain and the composition of and power associated with their negotiating team. An accountability structure and process should also be established for reporting back to constituents about possible alternatives offered in the bargaining process and soliciting their agreement to proceed (Rubin & Rubin, 2008; Staples, 2016).

CLOSING CAMPAIGNS

One of the more challenging aspects of campaigns is knowing when and how to end them. In many circumstances, a "win," is a sufficient reason to bring a campaign to an end. In other circumstances, achieving a fallback position or winning a partial victory is sufficient. When gains have not been achieved, the group must determine whether it wants to give up or press on, modifying unsuccessful strategies and tactics. Sen (2003) recommends a debriefing session with participants at the conclusion of each action. Questions for discussion during these sessions include examining whether all intended participants attended; suggesting techniques that should be used to sustain membership, including reaching out to constituents who did not participate in the action; and determining whether and to what degree the plan was implemented as intended. Staples (2016) argues that from a strengths perspective, the first thing that the group should address is what aspects of the campaign worked as planned or were particularly effective. Challenges with the campaign can be examined during later stages of the group dialogue. In addition, constituents need to analyze what happened and, if the intended result was not achieved, why? The discussion process should serve as a kind of a feedback loop, a specific follow-up phrase identified in some conceptualizations of the problem-solving model (Kirst-Ashman & Hull, 2018). It also is consistent with the reflection phase of the organizing process identified in Lewin's (1951) model of action research as well as Freire's (1970) transformative or popular education approach. Formal evaluations can also be conducted to guide the decision-making process.

PUTTING VALUES INTO ACTION: USING ACTION CAMPAIGNS TO ACHIEVE SOCIAL JUSTICE

As noted in Chapter 5 and demonstrated in this chapter with the logic model, organizing does not necessarily conform to a linear process; action campaigns may involve multiple layers of activities and a variety of different phrases and processes. Participants and social change targets may change over time. Goals and objectives as well as tactical methods and overall strategies may be altered due to situational demands, unexpected occurrences, rising expectations, resource limitations, or the need to compromise in order to achieve results. According to Barretti (2009), many campaign activities are repeated during the organizing process in order to keep the campaign moving and to elicit new members and public support. Gilbert and Terrell (2013) conceptualize organizing campaigns as based

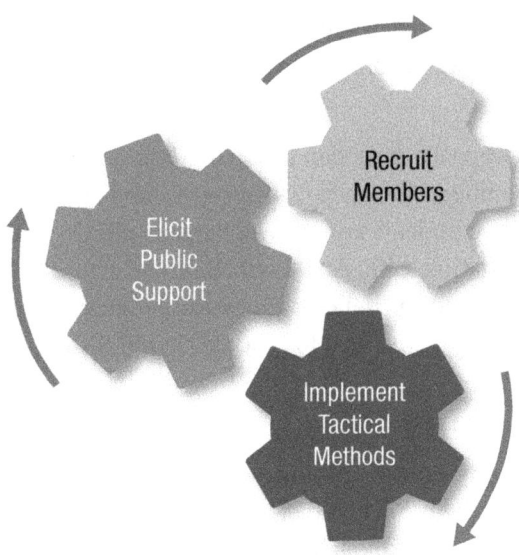

FIGURE 8.4 Component parts of a campaign.

on the problem-solving model, but incorporating activities designed to sell or "market" the campaign to others. Marketing activities include both the use of media sources and tactical methods designed to recruit and involve additional members in the action. One way to visualize the process is as a snowball that becomes larger over time, gathering more resources, support, and people as it rolls. Campaigns in which public support drops off over time or that is limited to the work of a few staff members and volunteers can ultimately be successful in some cases, but such efforts take a personal toll (including stress, time commitment, and negative impacts on the organizer's personal life; Homan, 2016; Figure 8.4).

Effective action campaigns and change strategies require careful maintenance and a mix of ingredients (people, resources, media attention, and implementation of strategies and tactics to be successful). As discussed previously in this book, campaigns also incorporate values and specify goals that are acceptable to the public and incorporate ethical, legal, or moral principles. Hardina and Obel-Jorgensen (2011) describe steps that they used to wage a successful on-campus campaign to convince university administrators to acknowledge police surveillance of a student club and adopt policies to protect civil liberties and the free speech rights of students in the future. Although the model of practice used for this campaign was social action, these steps also can be applied to other types of organizing efforts:

1. Conduct an analysis of the social problem and the specific issue addressed. Make sure the issue incorporates an important moral, ethical, or legal principle.
2. Recruit allied groups that have an interest in the issue and that can contribute to the work of the coalition.

3. Conduct a power analysis that focuses both on the power held by constituents, allied groups, and the decision makers or social change targets.
4. Identify resources held by organizing group members and their allies. Also, identify additional resources needed to launch a successful campaign and develop a plan to obtain them.
5. Engage in ongoing dialogue with constituents and members of allied groups. Schedule regular meetings as feasible, but also make sure to keep meeting times flexible in order to address unexpected occurrences. The dialogue process should be used to develop, modify, and assess strategies and tactics. These discussions should also be used to identify a variety of options and weigh the ethical implications, risks, and benefits of these methods.
6. Develop a group culture that facilitates an effective process to reconcile key differences among individual members and allied groups. Establish group norms and identify parameters for acceptable and unacceptable behavior among group members. Keep records of key decisions made by the group.
7. Establish positive working relationships with the media. Provide information on an ongoing basis to local reporters. Frame the campaign in a manner that is effective in illustrating key issues and principles that will pique the interest of the public. Be ready to use alternative media sources, including independent media sites as well as social media.
8. Implement the action campaign. Start by using low-impact methods such as sending emails or letters to decision makers and holding press conferences. If these tactics are not effective, start to slowly escalate tactical methods. Remember that tactics are to be used to illustrate the legitimacy of your cause to the public and the media and to bring decision makers to the bargaining table rather than to alienate the public or cut off dialogue with decision makers.
9. Consult with constituents and allied organizations on a regular basis, especially when changes in tactics are under consideration. Prepare campaigns as cyclical processes: recruitment, marketing, action, and reflection. Reflect on potential risks or unexpected occurrences in order to minimize risk-taking. Make sure all participants are fully informed about potential consequences and have the opportunity to withdraw or refuse to participate.
10. Be prepared to respond to unexpected occurrences and to change tactical methods in response to situational demands.
11. Be ready to negotiate with decision makers. Be open to compromise and ongoing dialogue, but have a specific goal and fallback positions in mind before negotiations start. Document all meetings or discussions with decision makers.

A 12th step in campaigns, not explicitly identified in Hardina and Obel-Jorgensen's set of guidelines, is evaluation and termination. Methods for group self-evaluation and reflection as an integral part of the campaign process and group approaches for formal evaluations of organizing campaigns are examined in the following chapters (Figure 8.5).

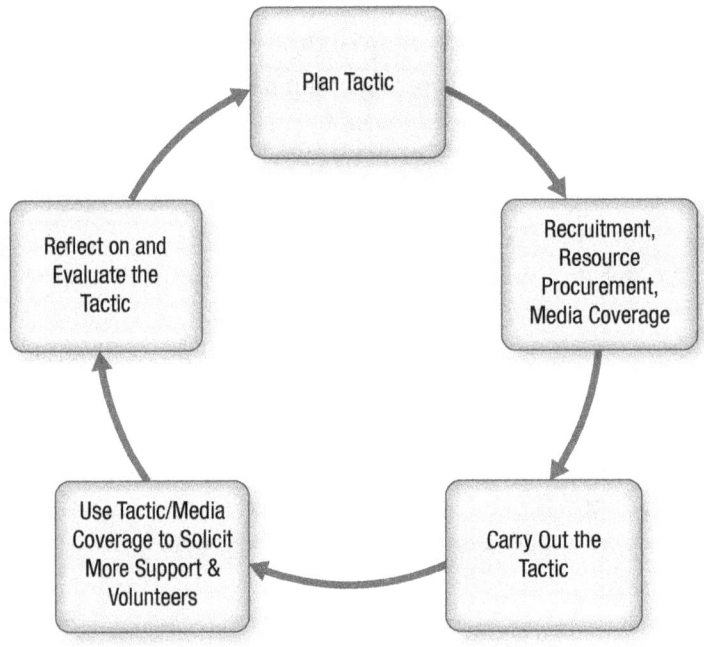

FIGURE 8.5 Campaigns as cyclical processes: recruitment, marketing, action, and reflection.

END-OF-CHAPTER RESOURCES

KEY TAKEAWAYS AND SUMMARY

Carrying out an action campaign or change strategy requires strong bonds among organizing group members, careful planning, and candid dialogue among group members. The organizer primarily serves in a support role and uses interpersonal social work skills and the relationships built with group members to motivate participants, help them weigh tactical options and respond to situational demands, and eventually, in many cases, carry out the action. In some situations, the organizer will employ interpersonal social work skills that facilitate others taking action such as providing logistical support, preparing constituents for participation in formal meetings, working with news and social media sources, giving speeches, taking notes that can be used by the organizer and group members to assess what happened, and negotiating with potential allies and social change targets. In circumstances in which the organizer does not perform these roles, the organizer may be called upon to train others or to facilitate the ability of constituents to carry them out. One essential part of this process is an assessment of the tactical method used or the overall strategic direction of the campaign. In Chapter 9, the process of critical reflection or praxis on the part of the organizer and constituents is examined. In Chapter 10, the use of formal evaluation methods to assess campaign effectiveness and processes is described.

RESOURCES

- Community Action Works' Digital Organizing Toolbox: https://communityactionworks.org/resources/digital-organizing-toolbox
- Community Tool Box: Developing a Logic Model or Theory of Change: https://ctb.ku.edu/en/table-of-contents/overview/models-for-community-health-and-development/logic-model-development/main#.UmRcAjkTHzI

ACTIVITIES

1. With your classmates, watch the movie *Walkout* (Esparza et al., 2006), which depicts efforts by Latinx students to advocate for reforms in the Los Angeles public schools in 1968. After watching the film, discuss with your classmates the following aspects of this organizing campaign.
    a. What motivated these students to take action?
    b. Were tactical methods used at the start of the campaign of low or high intensity? Why were they chosen?
    c. What situational demands motivated students to change their tactical approaches? Did you feel that these new tactics were appropriate for the situation? Were they ethical? Why or why not?
    d. Was the response to the protest by the police or the school board appropriate or excessive? Did it surprise you? Why or why not?
    e. What "safety plans" were developed to minimize potential risks to the students? In what ways were these plans sufficient or insufficient to protect the students?
    f. Did the final outcome of the campaign justify risks to the participants? Were there both short- and long-term benefits and risks associated with the organizing effort? What were they?
2. With a group of your classmates, develop a "plan B" for each of the unexpected occurrences that occur in the course of planning an on-campus rally for increased higher education funding (see Table 8.1).
    Brainstorm a number of different solutions for the issue or situation and the benefits and limitations of each option.
    a. The student who is leading the effort has called to say that that they cannot prepare for or attend the rally due to a death in the family. They have left no notes about the rally, the speakers invited, arrangements with the campus administration or police, or other aspects of the rally. No one has been designated or has come forward to take their place. Should the rally be canceled, postponed, or should arrangements be made to conduct the rally as planned? Is it likely that other volunteers will have information or knowledge about plans for the rally? What other factors should be taken into consideration in determining whether the rally should go on as planned?
    b. The day before the rally, a famous celebrity who is the relative of a student has offered to attend and give a speech on behalf of higher education funding. However, there are some conditions attached to her participation. Arrangements must be made for

security and press coverage must be guaranteed. If the campus police cannot be persuaded to provide security for her, a professional bodyguard may need to be recruited, either paid or as a volunteer. Is the potential benefit of increased media due to a celebrity participant worth potential costs? What would be lost if the offer were simply turned down?

c. The weather report indicates that the rally will be rained out. Although postponement is an option, State Assemblywoman Deana Jones plans to introduce legislation the day of the rally to increase the state's higher education budget. Consequently, it is important that the rally go on as planned. What contingency plans can be made in terms of preparing for rain or other weather-related problems?

d. The morning of the rally, the student newspaper runs an editorial stating that the rally is a waste of time and that the organizing committee is made up of people with radical viewpoints. The editorial urges students to attend a fundraiser for a children's charity sponsored by a fraternity instead. How do you respond to this and ensure that there is a good turnout for the rally?

e. The university president calls and asks the organizing committee to cancel the rally. They have been informed that the rally sponsors have a list of demands for the university administration, including a request that the university administration support Assemblywoman Jones's legislation. The president wishes to negotiate an agreement in private with the organizing group. Rally organizers suspect that the university is concerned about the possibility of negative press coverage. What are your options? Do you cancel the rally and negotiate or do you have alternatives?

3. Using the scenario in this chapter regarding on-campus organizing for higher education, conduct an exercise with your classmates involving bargaining and negotiation. Form two groups. One group consists of university administrators and the other consists of student activists. Resolve the following problem using the bargaining and negotiation principles presented in this chapter. The circumstance or situation to be resolved involves the use of the campus "free-speech zone" for the rally. The university has decided to withdraw permission for the group to hold the rally with fewer than 24 hours' notice. The position of the two groups and the vested interest of each are as follows:

University Administration: An alumnus who typically makes large donations to the university has asked that the free-speech zone be turned over to their fraternity brothers to use for a fundraising event for the local children's hospital. The donor insists that the fundraising event can only take place the next day and has threatened to withdraw their annual donation of $25,000 unless their demands are met. They also insist that the student activists sponsoring the higher education rally are dangerous radicals who must be stopped. The university president has offered to provide the activist group with a new permit for a date after Assemblywoman Jones introduces legislation on increasing funding for higher education. The university president anticipates negative publicity regardless of any decision they make, but wishes to minimize the fallout. However, they may hint to the students that there will be potential repercussions if they go ahead with the rally without their permission.

Student Activists: The students feel it is essential to hold their rally in the place designated at the predetermined time and date. They also feel that their free-speech rights have been violated. They have suggested some alternative venues for the charity fundraiser, but feel it is essential that they use the free-speech zone. Their fallback position is that the university must provide them a venue of equal size on the planned date of the rally and provide appropriate resources (such as using the university's media contacts and posting signs) to inform students, faculty, and the public about the change in venue. However, some of the group members have hinted that they want to go ahead with the rally regardless of whether or not they have a permit.

Considerations before the negotiations start:

Make sure that you have designated a leader and a have a clear goal and fallback position.

When you've concluded the role play, come back together as a group and consider:

a. What additional information would you need if you were actually conducting this negotiation?
b. Did your group obtain everything they wanted, nothing, or a portion of what they needed?
c. How easy or hard were the negotiations?

ASSIGNMENTS

1. In your field agency, take responsibility for staging a rally, community forum, a press conference or other tactic-related event. Write an eight- to 10-page paper after the event is conducted that describes:
   a. background information, the purpose, and goal of the event;
   b. how the event fits within a strategy or organizing campaign;
   c. resources needed for the event;
   d. barriers or challenges expected and actually encountered;
   e. any changes made in response to situational demands or resource limitations;
   f. how you utilized interpersonal social work skills for at least two of the eight skill types identified in this chapter as essential for conducting campaigns (group decision-making about the use of tactical methods, logistics, participation in formal meetings, the use of news and social media, public speaking, note-taking and documentation, and bargaining and negotiations);
   g. a brief narrative of what actually happened at the event; and
   h. your assessment of how processes and outcomes could have been improved.
2. Write a 10-minute speech suitable for delivery at a public event urging support for an issue, policy, or piece of legislation. In preparing your speech, conduct research on the issue, identify at least five facts that the public should know about the issue, and incorporate several moral or ethical principles that will garner public support. Make sure that in addition to facts, your speech appeals to emotions, incorporates a personal

story (either yours or someone you know or have talked to), and contains an "ask" or call to action. Present this speech in class—your grade will be based on the content and presentation of the speech as well as to what degree your presentation is perceived to be persuasive by your classmates.
3. Design a flyer, press release, or a social media page for a specific event or meeting that contains information that will persuade people to attend—make sure that this document contains information about the sponsor, purpose, day and time, and location.

 A robust set of instructor resources designed to supplement this text is located at http://connect.springerpub.com/content/book/978-0-8261-5835-2. Qualifying instructors may request access by emailing textbook@springerpub.com.

KEY REFERENCES

Only key references appear in the print edition. The full reference list appears in the digital product on Springer Publishing Connect: connect.springerpub.com/content/book/978-0-8261-5835-2/part/part02/chapter/ch08

Alinsky, S. (1971). *Rules for radicals*. Vintage.
Barretti, M. (2009). Organizing for tenants' rights: Insights and approaches from both sides of the fence. *Journal of Progressive Human Services, 20*(1), 8–25. https://doi.org/10.1080/10428230902871140
Bobo, K., Kendall, J., & Max, S. (2010). *Organizing for social change: A manual for activists* (4th ed.). Forum Press.
Brown, M. E., & Dustman, P. A. (2019). Identifying a project's greatest "hits": Meaningful use of Facebook in an underserved community's development and mobilisation effort. *Journal of Social Work Practice, 33*, 185–200. https://doi.org/10.1080/02650533.2019.1597694
Catalani, C., & Minkler, M. (2010). Photovoice: A review of the literature in health and public health. *Health Education & Behavior, 37*, 424–451. https://doi.org/10.1177/1090198109342084
Greene, A., & Latting, J. (2004). Whistle-blowing as a form of advocacy: Guidelines for the practitioner and organization. *Social Work, 49*(2), 219–230. https://doi.org/10.1093/sw/49.2.219
Kerr Chandler, S. (2009). Working hard, living poor: Social work and the movement for livable wages. *Journal of Community Practice, 17*, 170–183. https://doi.org/10.1080/10705420902856159
Mizrahi, T. (2007). Women's ways of organizing. *Affilia, 22*(1), 39–55. https://doi.org/10.2307/4022758
Toomey, A. (2009). Empowerment and disempowerment in community development practice: Eight roles practitioners play. *Community Development Journal, 46*, 181–195. https://doi.org/10.1093/cdj/bsp060
Young Laing, B. (2009). A critique of Rothman's and other standard community organizing models: Toward developing a culturally proficient community organizing framework. *Community Development, 40*, 20–36. https://doi.org/10.1080/15575330902918931

THE POSTENGAGEMENT PHASE

WORKING WITH COMMUNITY GROUPS TO CRITICALLY REFLECT AND ENGAGE IN DIALOGUE ON THE PROCESS AND OUTCOMES OF ACTION PLANS

LEARNING OBJECTIVES

After reading this chapter, students will be able to:

- Explain the process of praxis and how it applies to working with community groups.
- Recognize the theoretical frameworks that contribute to the process of praxis in community organizing.
- Describe the importance of self-reflection in community practice.
- Practice facilitating critical reflections with community groups focused on process and outcomes.

INTRODUCTION

In any problem-solving approach, the most important part of the process may be the feedback loop in which goal completion and the processes through which goals are achieved are examined (Kirst-Ashman & Hull, 2018). Consequently, the final or postengagement stage of an organizing effort involves reflection about and evaluation of the social action campaign, community development effort, or social planning process. Both these activities should take place in the context of a group process. However, reflection requires group self-analysis about how the organizing activity took place and what it achieved. It can be conducted informally, based on participant perceptions and analysis, or formally, through the collection and analysis of quantitative data or systematically collected qualitative data from interviews, observations, or content analysis.

In this chapter, the reflection stage of the organizing process, also called *praxis*, is described. The various uses and applications of praxis to assess the work of staff members and volunteers and the interpersonal skills needed by the organizer to facilitate this type of group dialogue are also discussed. In addition, the use of reflective practices to monitor the social change process and modify strategies and tactics in response to situational demands is explored. The use of critical reflection and dialogue in the final stages of a campaign or other community-organizing, development, or planning activity to critically examine the process and outcomes associated with organizing efforts is also described. In the last section of this chapter, the application of principles associated with the process of praxis is examined.

THE PROCESS OF PRAXIS

As described in Chapters 6 and 8, action and reflection are inherent components of any community practice effort, especially those that involve group consultation or decision-making and that rely on constituents and other volunteers to carry out the action. As noted by Miley and colleagues (2017), "praxis is not a linear process with a defined end point, but rather, it is a continuous looping of action–reflection–action. As the work unfolds, refection and action intertwine in praxis" (p. 98). As noted earlier in the text, although organizers tend to talk about action campaigns in terms of the problem-solving model, goal achievement, interventions and outcomes, or cause and effect, they are actually multistage, multilayered processes that constantly evolve over time as conditions on the ground change; participants are recruited or drop out; opponents react, negotiate, or retaliate; and actions succeed or fail (Barretti, 2009; Ganz, 2010; Lee, 2001). All of these changes in the various systems involved affect other aspects of the process. Consequently, the perceptions, values, and preferences of members of the action system also change over time and require dialogue and analysis of the process (Netting et al., 2017; Payne, 2021; Figure 9.1).

THEORETICAL FRAMEWORKS FOR USING THE PROCESS OF PRAXIS IN COMMUNITY ORGANIZING

As described by Freire (1970) and Lewin (1951), praxis, or the process of action and reflection, is an alternative means of constructing knowledge in which practitioners learn from past actions and use what they have learned to modify future actions. The process of action and reflection also may lead to both personal and social transformation. Social theorists, such as Bourdieu (as cited in Reed-Danahay, 2005) and Foucault (as cited in Chambon, 1999), assert that knowledge is not constant or absolute, comes out of personal

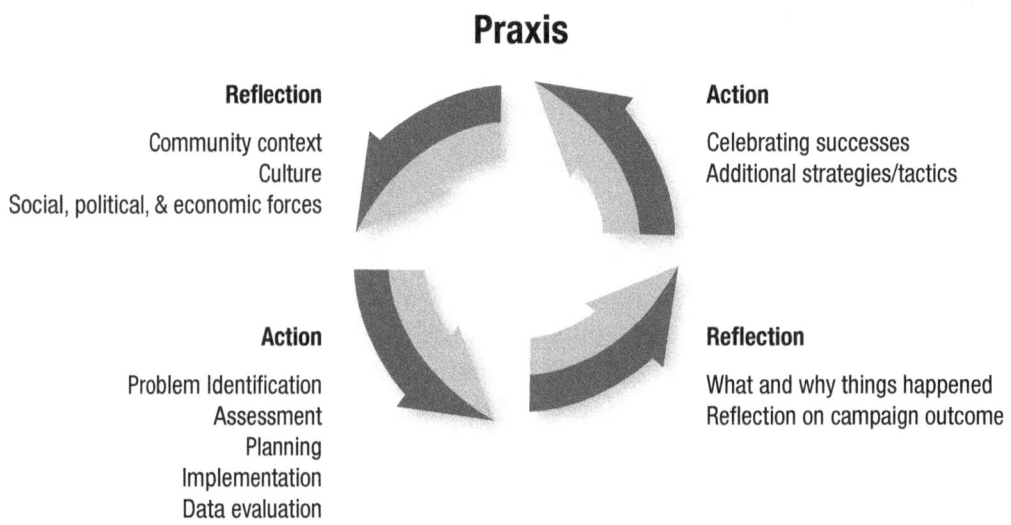

FIGURE 9.1 Action-and-reflection cycle and multistage campaigns.

experience, and shifts in relation to one's position in society and the degree of political power possessed by individuals. Consequently, the experiential knowledge of members of oppressed groups differs from other individuals and groups and may be at odds with the type of formal knowledge possessed by people with professional degrees. These authors also contend that formal knowledge often functions as a tool that serves to further oppress the powerless and that working to develop alternative sources of knowledge is the key to personal liberation. Schon (1983) argues that the recognition that knowledge varies based on experiences and social status requires that professionals working with members of minoritized and marginalized groups be able to engage in reflective practice, altering practice methods in response to situational demands and client needs. However, this should be accomplished in a structured manner that requires deliberate, systematic, and careful consideration of all the various factors and consequences associated with these alternative practice methods.

Other theoretical frameworks that guide or explain the process of reflection include social constructionism, feminist theory, critical theory, and critical race theory (CRT). These postmodernist approaches have direct links to both the process of praxis and methods of community organization. For example, the theory of social constructionism pertains to how experiential knowledge is embedded in social networks and relationships and consequently is constructed in a manner that reflects multiple understandings and shared meaning. It provides a constantly changing framework for interpreting reality that is especially relevant when a practitioner is working in a group context with diverse participants (Netting et al., 2008). Feminist approaches to both research and community-organizing practice also incorporate principles associated with social constructionism; participants in women's organizations engage in a process of consciousness-raising to examine the impact of oppressive institutions and social relations on their lives. Research studies are conducted by experts in partnership with women who have personal experiences and insight about the impact of patriarchy on their lives (Van Den Bergh & Cooper, 1995). In community practice, applying the feminist principle that "the personal is political" ensures that both personal issues and social change are addressed in the organizing process (Lee, 2001; Mizrahi, 2007).

DePoy and colleagues (1999) define *critical theory* as an approach to research that focuses on understanding what individuals actually experience in their daily lives and using this information for social change. Critical theorists view knowledge as changing over time in response to historical, social, and political forces and people's experience of their effects, especially those policies and practices that are used to minoritize, marginalize, and oppress some groups but not others (Fook, 2003). The production of new knowledge is viewed as a source of power and can be used to challenge existing ways of thinking associated with members of the power structure and to facilitate social change.

Some scholars and community organizers also use CRT in the construction of knowledge about how people of color experience everyday life and are affected by laws and social policies (G. Delgado, 1997; Young Laing, 2009). CRT applies morality and situational considerations to examine how the concept of race is socially constructed and used to minoritize and marginalize Black/African Americans and other communities of color (Su, 2007). One of the primary assumptions inherent in CRT is that persons of color have unique experiences and perspectives due to their status in society that are very different from cultural and social class-related perspectives associated with members of the dominant culture. As a consequence, one of the organizing tools used to develop experiential knowledge using the CRT approach is to provide a safe and brave "space" for people to share their own stories about what they have experienced in order to develop a counternarrative, facilitate community empowerment, and create new strategies for changing policies and laws that contribute to oppression. As discussed in Chapter 5, these stories support the collection of empirical data and the development of new theories that are relevant to the lives of people in communities of color (Stovall, 2005).

PRAXIS AND KNOWLEDGE PRODUCTION

In addition to the development of "critical consciousness" or an understanding of social problems and their environmental origins, the process of praxis provides constituents with the opportunity to develop knowledge about social change and the strategies and tactics necessary to achieve social justice. Although organizers provide information and support for the preparation of action plans, constituent input and knowledge about what works are essential parts of community practice. As stated by Freire (1997):

People have a universal right to participate in the production of knowledge which is a disciplined process of personal and social transformation. In this process, people rupture their existing attitudes of silence, accommodation and passivity, and gain confidence and abilities to alter unjust conditions and structures. This is an authentic power for liberation that ultimately destroys a passive awaiting of fate. (p. xi)

According to Conway (2004), the goal of popular education, community organizing, and participation in social movements should not only be to achieve a social change outcome. It also should produce new knowledge about how the world works and the effectiveness of various strategies used to achieve social justice. Conway identifies three different types of knowledge:

- tacit knowledge or insights that come from everyday practice and are disseminated informally through personal interaction, meetings, and group activities;
- praxis-based knowledge as described by Freire (1970), produced when practitioners and constituency group members critically reflect on and analyze what they have learned in the course of taking action; and
- research reports used to persuade the public and the academic world as to the legitimacy of their interpretation of how the world functions and how social problems should be resolved.

As described in Chapter 8, these various sources of knowledge serve as a road map in the development of strategies and tactics and allow organizers and their constituents to modify their actions in response to situational demands. Some of this knowledge is used for training purposes and may be disseminated in workbooks, brochures, and educational workshops, as well as in first-person accounts (autobiographies) of participation in community organizing and social movements (Somma, 2006). In addition to formal documents, information about organizing efforts and their effectiveness is transferred to others using Facebook,

Twitter, and YouTube, and through popular culture in music, art, videos, television, and movies (Ganz, 2010).

Reflective practice can be used for a number of purposes and at a number of system levels: self-assessment by individual practitioners, in the context of dialogue between the practitioner and supervisor, and for an evaluation of staff members, leaders, and other participants by members of the constituency group. It can also be used to modify ongoing campaigns in response to situational demands or to evaluate outcomes and processes of campaigns. In the next two sections of this chapter, organizer self-assessment, staff assessment by constituents, and constituent roles in assessing campaign processes and outcomes are examined. The assessment of staff members by supervisors is examined in Chapter 13.

SELF-REFLECTION IN COMMUNITY PRACTICE

In previous chapters, one of the most critical uses of self-assessment techniques, the practice of cultural humility, was described. Organizers must be knowledgeable about cultural dynamics in the community in which they work, how the social and institutional contexts affect community residents and intergroup relationships, and how the values and social positions of practitioners' affect their ability to interact, identify with, and form alliances with the people they serve (Harrell & Bond, 2006). In addition to this set of skills, organizers also must be able to reflect on and alter methods of practice in response to situational demands and the preferences and experiences of people they encounter, both allies and opponents. Homan (2016) refers to *reflective practice* as the process of learning from experiences, examining what happened, and thinking about what it means. Organizers engage in this activity in order to understand their own actions, why they acted in a particular manner, how those actions affected others, and how people perceived them. In addition, to self-examination, organizers often consult with other observers (supervisors, colleagues, constituents, board members and other key stakeholders) to improve their knowledge and community-organization skills.

Organizers must be aware of their own values, their comfort level with specific types of tactics, and how their previous practice experience shapes their decisions. For example, Mondros and Wilson (1994) interviewed organizers and found that they relied on ideology and a set of practice principles in choosing strategies and tactics. These practice principles were premised on a strong sense of social justice, achieving fairness for people and groups and the organizer's beliefs about how social change should be achieved. However, the respondents' preferences about strategic approaches to social change varied based on whether they believed social transformation could be achieved through politics and the legal system, through grass-roots efforts to put public pressure on decision makers, or broad-based social movements, using mass education, moral appeals to the public, or civil disobedience. In a similar study, Mizrahi (2007) interviewed female organizers in 1989 and 2003 and examined the role of feminist theory and values in the development of strategies and tactics. Mizrahi found that respondents remained committed to feminist values, including women's empowerment, building consensus, and collective decision-making, but changed attitudes toward tactical decision-making over time, recognizing the role of power and the need to use it to affect social change.

According to Burghardt (2014), an organizer also needs to be aware of one's own personality type and task versus process orientation and the degree to which these factors are compatible with various organizing styles, decision-making structures, and relationship-building skills. For example, an organizer who is people oriented rather than task oriented may excel at one-on-one interviews or conducting informal meetings, but may be relatively ineffective in terms of managing an office or completing paperwork. In contrast, an organizer who does not interact well with people may focus instead on task completion and push group members too hard or too fast in order to accomplish a goal. In addition, the organizer may feel more comfortable with certain types of strategic approaches more than others, preferring process-oriented methods such as consensus building to more conflict-oriented approaches or vice versa.

Reisch and Lowe (2000) identify a number of self-assessment questions that are designed to help an organizer resolve ethical questions related to the organizing process. In addition to the assessment of ethical dilemmas that an organizer might face, they can also be used to analyze campaign activities and decision-making processes:

- What are the ethical issues that can be identified in the situation at hand?
- What information do I (the organizer) need to have in order to clarify the ethical principles that apply in this situation?
- What ethical criteria should be used to guide what I should do?
- If there is a conflict of interest that pertains to the decision, who should make the decision and who should benefit from it?
- Is it actually my responsibility to make the decision in this situation? If not me, then who should be involved in the decision-making process?

In addition to these questions, there are other aspects of campaigns that should be assessed by organizers. Some of these questions pertain to issues involved in process that were discussed earlier in this textbook and include:

- Were my goals or the organization's goals for the meeting, event, action, or campaign achieved? If not, why did this happen?
- Were there some aspects of the process or structure used during the meeting, event, action, or campaign that could be improved? If so, what should be done?
- Is there more I need to know about participants in a meeting, event, action, or campaign? Do previous relationships or rivalries among group members affect group interactions now? Do any members have hidden agendas or goals that will affect what the group decides to do?
- Could I have acted or reacted to the situation at hand or the people involved in a different manner? What motivated me? How can I improve my approach in problematic situations?
- Were there issues related to the interaction of two or more participants at the meeting, event, action, or campaign that could be improved? What were they? Is it up to me to address this?

- What could I do to better prepare organization leaders to manage tasks, processes, or issues related to interpersonal relationships among participants (Burghardt, 2014; Gutierrez & Alvarez, 2000; Hardina, 2002; Homan, 2016; Kahn, 2010; Mondros & Wilson, 1994)?

REFLECTION AS A GROUP PROCESS: ASSESSING THE ROLES OF PARTICIPANTS IN COMMUNITY PRACTICE

Wint and Sewpaul (2000) describe praxis in community organization as a three-part process: involving all community members in defining local issues, developing strategies and tactics to resolve them, and engaging participants in critical assessments about the process and the various roles played by the participants in the social change effort. Such assessments of participant activities can be used for evaluations of staff performance as well as to assess decisions made by group leaders, the performance of various volunteers and other constituents, and the degree to which participation has contributed to personal and community transformation.

As noted in Chapter 8, one of the chief dilemmas faced by organizers is to facilitate the leadership of others and ensure that constituents have adequate opportunities to participate in tactical decision-making. Shaw (2001) views participant and staff engagement in group dialogue for the purpose of evaluating staff performance as an appropriate method to ensure constituent control. Although Shaw concedes that community organizations should rely on staff for advice about tactics, they also believe that constituents and their leaders should be the main decision makers as a safeguard against staff incompetence or refusal to carry out group decisions. They view meetings with staff as the proper venue for all organization members to thoroughly discuss work performance and the success or failure of tactical methods. According to Shaw, "the process usually takes time and requires discomforting assessments of what might have been, but the staff and the organization emerge with a clearer understanding of how to achieve social change" (p. 256).

ben Asher (2010) identifies a set of criteria for constituent evaluations of staff members. One of the primary roles of staff organizers is to facilitate the development of leaders. Consequently, they help guide the personal development of those individuals who will make policies and day-to-day decisions about community organizing and the tasks to be undertaken by volunteers rather than staff. Therefore, it is the responsibility of the organizer to prepare organization leaders and other constituents to evaluate the staff member's work. Without trained leaders who can ensure the maintenance of the organization and help set the direction of future campaigns, the community group will not be able to function, volunteer capacity to take action will not be developed, and individual participants will not feel they have the power to engage in social change (Burghardt, 2014; Lee, 2001). Therefore, constituents should examine the degree to which organizers have guided, trained, and prepared them to assume leadership roles in the organization.

In addition to constituent evaluations of staff, group processes are also utilized to assess the work of organization leaders and participants in social change activities and organization decision-making. According to Polletta (2002), during the evaluation process in community organizations, participants are often encouraged to challenge one another and make leaders accountable to the group for their choice of tactics and their actions. They describe this process as consultation "with a widening circle of community members, accountability, and a commitment to making leadership skills available to others" (p. 184).

As described in Chapter 8, group debriefing sessions after carrying out tactical actions help to minimize conflict among participants or diverse viewpoints while building a group consensus around tactical choices and conducting an assessment of their effectiveness (Mondros & Wilson, 1994). In addition, the various roadblocks and hazards faced when implementing a campaign often make people more determined to take additional action. Consequently, the analysis of these issues, the shared experiences of group members, the development of new knowledge, and group successes as well as failures increase both individual and organization capacity to keep working and striving toward social change.

The process of group praxis in community organizations may also be used as an opportunity for constituents to assess their own roles in the campaign, organization, or community. According to M. Delgado and Staples (2008):

Praxis forces the participants to tie emotions, history, and theory together in order to develop a composite picture of their own lives, as well as the life of the community in which they reside. When accomplished well, praxis represents a time for healing and for taking stock of individual and group accomplishments. (p. 142)

PRAXIS AS GROUP DIALOGUE: DECISIONS BY MANY RATHER THAN A FEW

In addition to knowledge production and assessment of participant activity, there are a number of other reasons for using group dialogue to plan and critique organizing, development, and planning efforts. According to Lee (2001), involvement in group dialogue and reflection during the community-organization process ensures that "community residents must say their own words, plan their own options, and act in ways that are their own" (p. 380). As noted previously in this text, constituent involvement in tactical decision-making ensures that the methods used are culturally appropriate and have meaning and relevance for those people responsible for carrying them out (Gutierrez & Lewis, 1999; Martinez, 2008).

In addition to cultural relevance, there are a number of other practical reasons for using group dialogue to make tactical choices and assess their impact. Polletta (2002), in describing her findings from a comprehensive study of social movement organizations, identifies several reasons for making strategic decisions using group dialogue and consensus:

- *Capacity building.* By talking through tactical options, group members are encouraged to state the reasons they supported one plan more than others. This in turn increases the knowledge of all group members. It also allows individual participants to hear different viewpoints, raise questions about what they have heard, and modify their own viewpoints.
- *Legitimatizing the authority of the group.* By requiring that the group members rather than individuals make important decisions, the degree to which one person or a handful of people with more power than others can make decisions that affect the group as a whole is limited. This also helps increase the power, resources, and

public recognition that accrue to the organization as a whole when they make recommendations on behalf of community members (Conway, 2004).
- *Ownership.* Having a say in the decision-making process will increase commitment and participation in the group over the long haul. People who feel that their opinions are always ignored are more likely to drop out or refuse to carry out tasks with which they do not agree.

In addition to organization structure and participant knowledge, Ganz (2009) argues that it is the interaction among group members with diverse backgrounds, experiences, connections, and values that generates the energy and creativity necessary to develop innovative tactical methods. According to Hofmann-Pinilla and colleagues (2005), the collective identity of group members is one of the key components that determines how they "make sense of their actions, frame issues, and handle moments of crisis" (p. 3). Collective identity also shapes relationships in the group, which in turn determine how decisions are made, who makes them, and what is decided (Conway, 2004). According to Ganz (2010):

A good campaign can be thought of as a symphony of multiple movements, each with an exposition, development, and recapitulation, but which together proceed toward a grand finale. A symphony is also constructed from the interplay of many different voices interacting in multiple ways but whose overall coordination is crucial for the success of the undertaking. (p. 559)

The ability of the constituency group to engage in collaborative dialogue is dependent not only upon the interpersonal skills of constituent leaders and staff members, but upon the structure of the organization developed to carry out the campaign. Ganz (2009), in describing the past successes of the United Farm Workers (UFW), identifies those components of organizing campaigns that contribute to a group's ability to make good tactical decisions. Strategic capacity is related to the tactical knowledge, previous experiences, and the social networks in which decision makers are members. It can also be enhanced or impeded by the decision-making and organization structures established to carry out the campaign. The organizations should be able to find and use resources and have a means of making sure constituents and staff members are held accountable for their actions. Ganz describes the ability of participants to learn from their mistakes as critical for the adoption of successful tactical approaches. This process involves "managing the tension between generating ideas and making choices, between creative dissent and organization disunity, between change and continuity" (Ganz, 2009, p. 253).

INTERPERSONAL SKILLS FOR FACILITATING PRAXIS

There are a number of interpersonal skills that can be used by organizers to guide group dialogue and analysis of organizing, development, and planning efforts in order to facilitate the process of praxis. For example, Gutierrez and Lewis (1999) describe the types of skills required for developing a consensus around tactics and managing conflicts in community practice. They argue that conflict is often a necessary by-product of organizing work, especially for White organizers working with groups consisting primarily of people of color. Group members may "test" where the organizer stands in relation to the group and one's willingness to take a stand against oppressive practices as an ally of the community.

Successfully navigating this process is often an important part of entering into a community for organizers who are different in terms of ethnicity, social class, gender identity, age, physical/mental abilities, and sexual orientation from group members. Myles Horton, the founder of one of the first community-organizing training centers, the Highlander School, describes the technique he used to engage with Black/African American leaders in the South during the civil rights struggles of the 1950s and 1960s:

> *You can't be accepted by people if you're trying to be what you're not. You've got to be genuinely what you are, but from what you are you've got to have empathy with and understanding of people and their situations, and you've got to relate as human beings in such a way that color isn't a factor in the relationship. (Horton et al., 1998, p. 1996)*

In addition to building trust, other skills for the organizer in situations that involve conflict include basic social work skills such as engagement, active listening, and the ability to step back from confrontation, even when it seems personal, in order to facilitate dialogue and reach consensus (Gutierrez & Lewis, 1999). The organizer must also be able to view the situation from a variety of perspectives, acquiring the ability to understand the views of others from their standpoint (such as personal histories and social status) in order to facilitate group consensus. In addition, the organizers also need to create a safe environment for people to engage in critical reflection. According to Kahn (2010):

> *One of the greatest skills an organizer can have is the ability to frame and ask questions in ways that make people not only want to answer them, but also to think deeply, and in unexpected ways, about what the answers might be. (p. 194)*

Gutierrez and Lewis (1999) recommend that all members of the constituency group should participate in these sessions (as feasible) and be encouraged to provide ideas, recommendations, and assessments of tactical methods during the dialogue process. Both leaders and organizers should contribute to the transparency of the group process by being explicit about the decisions that were made, who made them, and the situational factors that guided the decision. Even in these group dialogues, the organizer's role involves a dual purpose, not only facilitating a thorough discussion on tactical methods and their failures or successes, but also building up the capacity of group members to assume leadership roles, acquire tactical knowledge, develop skills, and work independently to support the organization and its actions (Zachary, 2000). One of the ethical principles incorporated into the capacity-building process is the commitment to facilitating the development of leaders who can act autonomously to plan and conduct campaigns as well as the development of new organizations, controlled and operated by members of the constituency group (Gutierrez et al., 1998).

USING PRAXIS TO MONITOR THE COMMUNITY-ORGANIZING PROCESS AND CHANGING COURSE

Most organizers advise that constituents, other participants and allies, and staff members should continuously engage in a process of action and reflection or active learning in order to assess the effectiveness, impact, and process involved in conducting events, the implementation of individual tactics, and the entire campaign (Chambers, 2004; M. Delgado & Staples, 2008; Ganz, 2009; Homan, 2016). As noted in Chapter 8, situational demands and the reactions of opponents, the general public, policy makers, and potential allies often make it necessary for tactical methods and negotiating demands to be modified throughout the campaign (Barretti, 2009). According to Ganz (2009), the ability to change tactical and strategic decisions is essential because "actors do not suddenly acquire more resources or devise a new strategy, but find that resources they already have give them more leverage in achieving their goals" (p. 21).

Chambers (2004) recommends that group evaluations be conducted for every event or action that takes place in the course of a campaign because:

Thinking and calculating go into preplanning an action, but not much thinking goes on during the action itself. We cannot think and act simultaneously. Try rubbing your belly and patting your head at the same time. Unless leaders draw off immediately after an action and evaluate it, little or no education takes place.... The same event is evaluated two weeks, two months, and sometimes two years later, providing ongoing food for learning and growth. (pp. 86–87)

Wendel and colleagues (2018) developed a useful framework for critical reflexivity at the community level. This framework is broken down into a four-step process: reflect, assess, specify changes, and implement and evaluate. As is the case with the concept of praxis described earlier in this chapter, this framework does not follow a linear process, but instead is cyclical. Wendel and colleagues' critical reflexivity framework underlines the need to focus on shared goals, developing collective meaning through reflection, and using the reflection process as an opportunity to collectively brainstorm changes. The Framework for Critical Reflexivity at the Community Level is summarized in Table 9.1.

ASSESSING WHAT AND WHY THINGS HAPPENED AT THE END OF THE ORGANIZING CAMPAIGN

During the final stages of a campaign, group assessment is essential for examining whether goals were achieved, why the campaign succeeded, why it failed, or if a partial victory is acceptable to group members. Both constituents and staff members are typically involved in these end-of-the campaign evaluation sessions simply because participants can view the same event differently and have diverse reactions. In some circumstances, members of the community may also be invited to give comments about their perceptions of the campaign and the outcomes produced (Gutierrez & Lewis, 1999). In addition to outcomes, aspects of the campaign that are likely to be examined include the behavior of all participants; the context in which campaign activities took place; the reaction of opponents, allies, and the general public; and what could be improved upon the next time a similar campaign takes place (Chambers, 2004; Staples, 2016).

In some cases, opponents or allies may weigh in with their assessment of the campaign and its effects. The end of the campaign may be preceded by successful negotiations or concessions from opponents. There may also be media coverage associated with some types of outcomes that provide an opportunity for constituents or the organizer to comment about the campaign or receive credit for its success. Media reports also provide an additional source of information that can be used to document the organization's work, obtain funding for future campaigns, and increase public awareness of the organization.

TABLE 9.1 The Framework for Critical Reflexivity at the Community Level

STEP	FUNCTION	KEY QUESTIONS
1. Reflect	Intentionally, systematically examine outcomes in context related to shared goals and of processes and representation of diverse perspectives.	Outcomes: What did we set out to accomplish? What did we accomplish? What do the data tell us? Are there areas where we did not achieve intended outcomes? What were unintended or anticipated outcomes from our efforts? Processes: What did we do collectively? What did each of us do in the process? Are there voices missing from the process that should be included?
2. Assess	Collectively make meaning of the process and determine why certain processes or actions led to success or failure.	Outcomes: Were our outcomes what we want(ed)? Processes: What specific actions or processes led to our outcomes? If something worked well, why did it work? If something did not work, what assumptions were we making that we need to change? Are there structures in place that are inhibiting success?
3. Specify changes	Explore feasible options for strengthening successful processes and altering unsuccessful ones; document a specific plan of action.	Outcomes: How do we need to modify our actions to achieve the desired outcome(s)? Processes: What options are feasible given our resources? What changes do we need to make to processes and actions? Are there broader structures that need to change? What are the specific actions that need to be taken? Who is going to do them, when, and with what resources?
4. Implement and evaluate	Implement and evaluate the planned changes; cycle back to step 1.	Outcomes: Is there evidence that our changes are having the intended effect(s)? Processes: How are we doing? Are changes being implemented as planned? Are we communicating regularly? Are we being accountable to the community for our efforts?

SOURCE: Adapted from Wendel, M. L., Garney, W. R., Castle, B. F., & Ingram, C. M. (2018). Critical reflexivity of communities on their experience to improve population health. *American Journal of Public Health, 108*(7), 896–901. https://doi.org/10.2105/AJPH.2018.304404.

In group assessment meetings, results from formal evaluations may also be incorporated into the group assessment process (see Chapter 10). Ganz (2010) argues that outcome evaluation is an essential part of any campaign and can be structured in a manner that allows participants to both monitor campaign processes and determine how far they have come and what they still need to do. He suggests constructing charts and graphs in the campaign office that illustrate progress toward meeting group goals such as the number of volunteers recruited, the number of elected officials supporting a piece of legislation, or the number of homes repaired in neighborhood clean-up efforts.

The qualitative data obtained during these group evaluation meetings can also be used to supplement data from more formal evaluations. According to Stovall (2005), personal and group narratives about the community-organizing process and the roles of participants constitute an "unspoken history" about social change efforts and consequently strengthen empirically derived evaluation data and facilitate the development of leadership skills, personal transformation, positive self-images, and experiences of empowerment among constituents.

One critical component of the group assessment process is whether the campaign has resulted in victory or defeat. According to Staples (2016), one of the questions that should be asked at the end of a campaign is "where do we go from here?" (p. 203). Members need to decide whether a victory means the end of the campaign or the start of a new one. If campaigns are to be viewed as a series of reoccurring steps that permit a group to make small gains over a long period of time, then victory often leads simply to the next phase of the process. Many community organizations engage in multiple campaigns at the same time, so completion of one set of activities will just mean that resources are shifted to other initiatives.

It should be noted that all tactical methods or campaigns are not successful. However, Gutierrez and Lewis (1999) point out the success of a tactic is often not as important as what people have learned from the experience and how they will use that knowledge in the future. Consequently, an unsuccessful tactic or campaign may simply be an opportunity to modify tactical methods or regroup (Ganz, 2010). In those cases in which a tactic or strategic approach was unsuccessful, it does not necessarily mean that other approaches will not work. According to Barretti (2009):

> *If a chosen strategy such as a tenant's meeting with a landlord about hazardous building conditions doesn't succeed, tenants will think the game is over. The organizer's job is to get the group to see the road ahead, to reframe the dilemma as a temporary setback, simply one play in the game, and an opportunity to restrategize. By the same token, the organizer must caution tenants about battles won. Just as the game may not end when tenants lose a battle, it isn't over when the battle is won either. (p. 18)*

After the group reaches a consensus about the campaign outcome, it must "wrap up" the campaign. During this last phase of the campaign, people often need a chance to let off steam, which is an opportunity to increase personal bonds and solidarity with other members, or say their goodbyes, and be honored for their work. Consequently, participants often come together to celebrate their success or commiserate when results are not quite what was expected. This final gathering might be a dinner, a party or picnic, or a formal rewards ceremony that honors leaders, volunteers, and allies for their hard work (Alliance for Justice, 2010; Chambers, 2004; Kahn, 1991). In circumstances in which constituents have diverse backgrounds, these ceremonies may offer an opportunity for participants to learn about and honor the culture and traditions of their new friends and colleagues.

PUTTING VALUES INTO ACTION: CRITICAL REFLECTION, THINKING, AND ACTION

Gardner (2003) describes the process of critical reflection for evaluating social change initiatives as incorporating a number of principles and practices consistent with postmodernist theories and qualitative research methods:

- Construct new knowledge from personal histories and storytelling.
- Ensure that diverse viewpoints are incorporated into the evaluation process, including the views of people who are seldom consulted or included in the process.

- Help people connect personal experiences with an analysis of the impact of social structure and the process of oppression.
- Incorporate values and principles into the evaluation process.
- Foster the ability of participants in the evaluation process to question and explore existing phenomena and to tolerate some degree of uncertainty in one's level of understanding. In many situations, data collection can consist of gathering information on individual experiences and perceptions rather than using formal knowledge to test hypotheses.
- Facilitate a sense of collective efficacy or belief among the participants in their ability to effectively engage in social change.

Successful campaigns generate good stories. Often the narrative reflects personal, organization, or community experiences, focusing on hardships and overcoming adversity through "struggle" via participation in one or more organizing campaigns, development efforts, or planning processes. Thus, these stories serve several purposes. In addition to the identification of issues and their impacts, they often contain a source of knowledge about how to organize. They also provide personal "testimonies" about an empowering experience that has changed the life of the narrator or improved the community. These stories provide a context for sharing experiences, developing common bonds, and transmitting knowledge about the organizing process (VeneKlasen et al., 2007; Williams et al., 2003). Increasingly, not only are stories and knowledge about social action campaigns, development efforts, or social planning processes simply shared with other community members, when formally or informally documented, they provide other groups with an organizing knowledge base from which to draw (Conway, 2004; Polletta, 2006). As described by Ganz (2010), a large part of the organizer's job is facilitating a process that changes the individual stories of hardship or struggles over adversity to "stories of us," how members of the group have bonded together to resolve collective issues and successfully challenged the odds to improve their own lives and their communities.

The story of campaigns often becomes one concerned not only with success or failure but also with how people interacted with one another, what happened to them after the campaign concluded, and how that experience may have contributed to additional organizing efforts. Did two participants meet and marry during the organizing campaign or development project? Did former opponents with different perspectives, positions, and values form a bond and become life-long friends? Did the idealist university student, hired as the neighborhood's housing organizer, become president of the United States? Did participants in a long-term struggle for labor rights become inspired, go back to school and become teachers, lawyers, judges, professional social workers, or community organizers (Shaw, 2008)? It is the relationships and experiences that people have and their personal transformations that become part of the "story" of the campaign and its successes.

Stories about campaigns and community projects, their failures and successes, and relationships or bonds among participants not only pertain to constituents but are also catalogued and described by organization board members and in the written campaign descriptions they disseminate and in the training material and organizing models they develop (Conway, 2004). These models and training materials incorporate both the experiences and values of participants and change and evolve over time in response to the recruitment of new members, development of new leaders, and the implementation of campaign strategies. Hence these models become a means to illustrate how values are translated into action, cultural traditions are honored, and the "story of us" is described. Descriptions about the organization's approach to change, strategic preferences (e.g., an emphasis on consensus rather than conflict), and the degree to which constituents are consulted about, guide, or control the action are also important parts of the story about how campaigns are viewed by participants and how the story of the campaign is presented to the public.

For example, the Asian NGO Coalition for Agrarian Reform and Rural Development (ANGOC; n.d.), an organization based in the Philippines, but operating throughout Southeast Asia, has developed a model of community-organization practice that combines traditional Western methods for social action with Asian cultural practices. ANGOC's mission is to assist members of rural communities to obtain rights to land that they have traditionally farmed, but have lost through corporate control or commercial exploitation of natural resources. The organization routinely sends organizers into rural areas in a variety of Asian countries to employ culturally appropriate tactics for social change. ANGOC describes its work as consisting of a 10-stage process:

- *Integration.* The organizer enters into the community and establishes trust through the provision of assistance with agricultural tasks, meeting with people in their homes or common areas, and attending events and ceremonies.
- *Community Study.* The organizer conducts interviews, focus groups, and group dialogues; analyzes secondary data; and observes community life before developing a tentative organizing plan. Participatory research methods may also be used for this assessment.
- *Issue Analysis.* The felt needs of the community are determined and priorities for the campaign are set. The strategic approach used may involve only self-help efforts if people are reluctant to confront authorities.
- *Formation of the Organizing Group.* Participants and leaders are recruited for the organizing campaign.
- *Recruitment of Participants.* The organizer and members of the core organizing group use one-on-one interviews and other techniques to recruit participants and ask them to participate in a community meeting. At the meeting, campaign strategies and tactics are developed.
- *Role Plays.* The organizer prepares participants to take action by having them engage in role plays and exercises for situations that may occur in discussions, confrontation, or negotiation with members of the target group.
- *Action Phase.* The participants engage in an action or activity that they have planned. In some circumstances, this may involve a group project or cooperative endeavor rather than direct confrontation.

- *Reflection and Evaluation.* Participants examine what has been achieved and what has been unsuccessful in order to improve actions in the future. This can also involve a review of the strengths and weaknesses of the process.
- *Organization Development.* In addition to developing individual capacity through leadership development, social action, and agricultural projects, capacity development also focuses on developing a formal organization structure for carrying out further actions.
- *The Last Phase.* During the last part of the campaign, ANGOC and the organizer leave the community and transfer responsibility for the project over to local residents. Clear criteria are established for assessing whether the time is right for the transfer, including whether sufficient members have been recruited, leaders have been trained, and goals for future work have been established.

END-OF-CHAPTER RESOURCES

KEY TAKEAWAYS AND SUMMARY

The process of critical reflection, or *praxis,* is an essential component of social work practice. During the initial phases of the organizing process, constituency group members work together to develop a "critical consciousness" in order to understand how political, economic, and social forces have an impact on their lives and their communities. During the final stages of organizing campaigns, critical reflection is used to examine and modify strategies and tactics used in social action, community development, and social planning and other types of community interventions. Organizers engage in critical self-reflection in order to examine their own practice activities, choices, values, and reactions, and the interpersonal skills they use to facilitate group dialogue and leadership development and to identify areas in which personal performance can be improved. Constituency group members engage in critical reflection about how individual participants (leaders, other volunteers, and staff members) functioned in campaigns, the choices available to them, and how campaigns can be improved to make them more effective. They also use reflective processes to evaluate the outcomes associated with campaigns and to examine the implementation process for campaign components. Often data from these "informal" evaluations are used to supplement formal evaluations that involve systematic collection of data. In Chapter 13, methods used in community organizing to facilitate participatory evaluations are discussed.

RESOURCES

- Asian NGO Coalition for Agrarian Reform and Rural Development: https://angoc.org/
- Highlander Research and Education Center: https://highlandercenter.org/

ACTIVITIES

1. Conduct a focus group interview with participants in previous campaigns or a group of long-term volunteers about their experiences in the campaign or organization. Your interview should focus on the respondents' perceptions of both processes and outcomes, specific experiences or critical events during their participation in the campaign or organization that have meaning for them, their personal contributions to the organizing effort, and how participation affected them and their relationships with others.
2. Keep a journal of your experiences and reactions in organizing a campaign, an event, a community forum, or another activity. Use the list of self-reflection questions presented in this chapter to analyze your work and identify your values, personality traits, and strengths and weaknesses associated with your performance.

ASSIGNMENTS

1. Using the key process and outcome questions from the Framework for Critical Reflexivity at the Community Level (see Table 9.1; Wendel et al., 2018), conduct a group dialogue with participants after an event, as part of the process of monitoring what is happening during a campaign or project, or as the "first-stage" of an evaluation at the conclusion of a campaign or project. Write a three- to five-page paper summarizing the discussion and identifying strengths and weaknesses of the methods used to facilitate the action or activities undertaken.

A robust set of instructor resources designed to supplement this text is located at http://connect.springerpub.com/content/book/978-0-8261-5835-2. Qualifying instructors may request access by emailing textbook@springerpub.com.

KEY REFERENCES

Only key references appear in the print edition. The full reference list appears in the digital product on Springer Publishing Connect: connect.springerpub.com/content/book/978-0-8261-5835-2/part/part03/chapter/ch09

Barretti, M. (2009). Organizing for tenants' rights: Insights and approaches from both sides of the fence. *Journal of Progressive Human Services, 20*(1), 8–25. https://doi.org/10.1080/10428230902871140

Gutierrez, L., & Alvarez, A. (2000). Educating students for multicultural community practice. *Journal of Community Practice, 7*, 39–56. https://doi.org/10.1300/j125v07n01_04

Harrell, S., & Bond, M. (2006). Listening to diversity stories: Principles for practice in community research and action. *American Journal of Community Psychology, 37*, 365–376. https://doi.org/10.1007/s10464-006-9042-7

Homan, M. (2016). *Promoting community change: Making it happen in the real world* (6th ed.). Cengage Learning.

Mizrahi, T. (2007). Women's ways of organizing. *Affilia, 22*(1), 39–55. https://doi.org/10.1177/0886109906295762

Stovall, D. (2005). A challenge to traditional theory: Critical race theory, African American community organizers and education. *Discourse: Studies in the Cultural Politics of Education, 26*(1), 95–108. https://doi.org/10.1080/01596300500040912

Su, C. (2007). Cracking silent codes: Critical race theory and education organizing. *Discourse: Studies in the Cultural Politics of Education, 28*, 531–548. https://doi.org/10.1080/01596300701625297

Williams, L., Labonte, R., & O'Brien, M. (2003). Empowering social action through narratives of identity and culture. *Health Promotion International, 18*, 33–40. https://doi.org/10.1093/heapro/18.1.33

Young Laing, B. (2009). A critique of Rothman's and other standard community organizing models: Toward developing a culturally proficient community organizing framework. *Community Development, 40*, 20–36. https://doi.org/10.1080/15575330902918931

Zachary, E. (2000). Grassroots leadership training. *Journal of Community Practice, 7*(1), 71–93. https://doi.org/10.1300/j125v07n01_06

DISCOVERING WHETHER AND WHY THE ACTION WORKED: USING PARTICIPATORY RESEARCH TO CONDUCT FORMAL EVALUATIONS

LEARNING OBJECTIVES

After reading this chapter, students will be able to:
- Define *participatory evaluation*.
- Describe the challenges associated with evidence-based practice when working with communities.
- Discuss the utility of logic models and theories of change in the context of community practice.
- Apply the principle of shared expertise to social work practice with communities.

INTRODUCTION

The final, postengagement stage of community organizing, development, and planning efforts involves evaluation. Evaluations can include determining the outcomes that were achieved as well as examining the process in which the intervention was implemented. In some contexts, evaluation may be conducted by a single practitioner or a small group of experts. However, in community practice, evaluation takes place within the context of collaboration among constituency group and community members, organization staff, outside consultants or researchers, and organization or coalition partners. Consequently, it involves complex decision-making processes and procedures.

In this chapter, the purpose of formal evaluations in community practice is examined, with an emphasis on the political nature of evaluation mechanisms that often involve diverse voices and viewpoints. Also discussed are some of the challenges associated with performing formal evaluations of community-organizing projects. In addition, the applicability of evidence-based practice approaches for evaluations of community interventions are discussed and contrasted with the use of a systematic research method, called *logic modeling*, to evaluate community-organizing work. Specific types of community-based evaluations are described, including goal-attainment assessments, quantitative research and descriptive studies, critical incident analysis and case studies, process and implementation analysis, and other qualitative evaluation methods. Specific methods for conducting group or participatory evaluation studies are also discussed. In addition, the skills that organizers and community-based researchers must possess in order to facilitate group evaluations are examined. In the last section of this chapter, ethical issues associated with participatory evaluation are considered, with an emphasis on mutual learning and partnership.

THE PURPOSE AND POLITICS OF FORMAL EVALUATIONS IN COMMUNITY PRACTICE

Formal evaluations provide information about whether an intervention, community plan, development effort, or a campaign worked, and, if so, why and how it worked (Homan, 2016). Formal evaluations also help determine whether the benefits associated with goal achievement outweigh the costs of the intervention (McNutt, 2011). In community practice, the purpose of evaluation is to examine the effectiveness, efficacy, quality, cost-benefits, and implementation process of community organizing or development efforts, programs, or initiatives (Ginsberg, 2001; Hardina, 2002; Royse et al., 2014).

Evaluation in community practice is distinct from evaluation at other levels of practice. Specifically, compared to traditional forms of evaluation, evaluation in community practice is more likely to involve constituency and community group members throughout the research process, including planning, implementing, and analyzing results (Brown & Stalker, 2021; Stringer & Aragon, 2021). As previously noted in Chapters 6 and 8, the types of knowledge produced may be formal, based on previous theories and objective forms of evidence, or informal and socially constructed, derived from practice experience (tacit knowledge) as well as knowledge developed through critical reflection or praxis by individuals or groups. The meaningful involvement of constituency group members throughout the formal evaluation process ensures that results accurately represent the lived experiences of those who were involved in the community initiative or program (Brown & Stalker, 2021).

Evaluation is a critical component of all types of community practice. All organizing, development, and planning efforts focus on attaining a specific goal, regardless of whether the activity is process or task oriented. In a political or legislative campaign, the goal is electing someone to office or achieving a legislative victory. In social action and transformative organizing approaches, the purpose is to change public opinion, policies, and laws and improve the ability of community members to obtain access to resources and political power. In community and economic development, goals include improvements in the quality of life, health, and economic resources for local residents. In social planning, improvements are made in the goods and services produced by public and nonprofit organizations; access to these programs is increased for the people who are likely to need or use them (Gjecovi et al., 2006; Ohmer & Korr, 2006). Evaluation is used by community practitioners to determine the extent to which those goals were achieved. Further, evaluation of the *process* by which these goals were achieved (i.e., the *how* and *why*) allows community practitioners to fine-tune strategies and make adaptations to ensure continued success. For instance, a community organizer might use evaluation methods to determine which strategies are most successful in recruiting community members to participate in social action campaigns. Likewise, evaluation methods can be used to examine social networks within neighborhoods in order to develop and implement strategies to increase social cohesion.

As noted in Chapter 9, "hard data" on goal attainment can be used to motivate participants and other community members to keep working toward their goals. Statistics and other concrete or standardized measures also allow community groups to document their success, provide a means through which to recruit people for the cause, provide persuasive evidence of hardship or deprivation, and make a case that laws and policies must be changed. Unlike tacit or praxis-derived knowledge, data collected through established, formal, standardized and systematic processes, most often involving quantitative methods, is viewed by scholars as "objective" or value free. Such data provide a vehicle for communicating information about community needs and the resolution of local issues or social problems in the common "language" used by political, academic, media, professional, corporate, and other powerful decision makers (Stoecker, 2013).

Evaluations are also often required by funders. Although it is possible for some community groups to engage in social change in organizations with volunteers, most organizations cannot sustain organizing efforts without a larger paid staff force. Thus, community-organizing, development, and planning efforts require that the organization obtain grants and contracts from foundations, government agencies, and, in some cases, corporations or unions. In some instances, funders may only require simple documentation that the organization accomplished what it set out to do. In other circumstances, funders may require that a formal evaluation be conducted to fulfill the terms of the contract (Foster & Louie, 2010; Neighborhood Funders Group, 2011). Donors may differ, however, in terms of whether they provide additional funds for evaluation purposes; require that the recipient uses a standardized approach predetermined by the funder to collect, analyze, and report data; or insist that an outside expert be hired to conduct the evaluation rather than permit organization staff or constituents to do so (Mott, 2003; Stoecker, 2013).

Some funders may require that organizations provide only data from outcome evaluations, whereas others also want information about campaign, intervention, or development processes that describe how and why results were achieved or why the effort failed to produce the desired goals. They often want this type of evaluation in order to facilitate the dissemination of findings about *best practices* and their effects on community members, organization constituents, and social conditions to other organizations; in many instances training manuals, curriculum models, formal research reports, and internet resources become the vehicle for distributing this information to the public (M. Delgado & Staples, 2008).

CHALLENGES IN CONDUCTING FORMAL COMMUNITY-BASED EVALUATIONS

There are numerous challenges in conducting credible evaluations in community practice. Mott (2003) identifies a number of challenges faced by community organizations that choose to or are required to conduct evaluations by funders, including:

- Limited resources, including skilled staff or outside consultants, are available to facilitate evaluation studies and donors are reluctant to actually provide explicit funding for the evaluations that they require.

- Donors may have requirements that only certain types of evaluations be conducted, limiting constituent participation in evaluation design, choice of research questions, and whether data will be produced that can actually be used to assess community needs.
- Timelines given to the organizations to produce results are limited; funders frequently may change their priorities in terms of goals to be accomplished, outcomes to be produced, and what measures success.

Mott (2003) also questions whether donors actually understand that most organizing work may not consist of a linear process that progresses in a logical manner over time, but one in which the organization and its members must continually reassess, regroup, and change course in response to situational demands. According to Gjecovi and colleagues (2006), "outcomes for community organizing will vary based on the campaign, the sociopolitical context, and the skills and levels of cohesiveness that exist in the community. Therefore, no single template for evaluating organizing campaigns exists" (p. 21).

Such contextual factors also limit the degree to which experimental designs or standardized measures can be used to assess campaign outcomes (Stringer & Aragon, 2021). Delgado and Staples (2008) identify several additional limitations involved in formal evaluations of community practice: exclusive emphasis on outcomes rather than processes, a tendency by organizers to value the process rather than the outcome, and the tendency of organizers and donors to value only short-term achievements rather than goals that can only be achieved over time. Another methodological concern is that often the ability of donors to adequately assess the success of community change efforts is limited by the lack of adequate indicators to determine whether process objectives have been achieved, the quality and intensity of community or constituent participation, or the actual impact of the organization in facilitating social change (Neighborhood Funders Group, 2011).

COMMUNITY EVALUATIONS AND EVIDENCE-BASED PRACTICE

Calls for social workers to use *evidence-based practice* (*EBP*) are increasingly common. *EBP* refers to a process by which practitioners incorporate empirical research evidence with both clinical judgment and consumer preferences and values (Sackett et al., 1996). Although EBP is most often applied in clinical social work practice with individuals, groups, and families, some have also argued for the use of EBP models in macro practice and policy (Briggs & McBeath, 2009; Gambrill, 2007; Mulroy, 2008; Roberts-DeGennaro, 2011). EBP generally involves a five-step process:

1. A practitioner identifies a research question about the best course of action to choose.
2. The practitioner identifies available evidence from empirical research studies that employ rigorous methods to test hypotheses and collect data.
3. The practitioner examines the research studies that have been conducted and determines whether the evidence produced is reliable and valid.

4. The practitioner combines evidence from well-conducted, rigorous studies; one's clinical experience; and the unique characteristics and values of the client to make the appropriate decision regarding what intervention method to use.
5. The practitioner implements the intervention and conducts an in-agency evaluation of the outcomes produced, generally using a single-system design to produce new empirical evidence that the intervention works (Rubin & Parish, 2007).

Incorporating EBP into community practice may not fit neatly into these five steps. Nonetheless, EBP provides guidance community practitioners can use to critically review available research and make decisions based on existing research, practitioner expertise, and community preferences and values. Although there are challenges to assessing the macro practice evidence base given a lack of scientific rigor in community-based evaluations and challenges in adequately describing complex, multifaceted interventions (Ohmer, 2008), when combined with practitioner expertise and authentic community engagement, the existing research base is a valuable tool for community practitioners (see case vignette).

CASE VIGNETTE: THRIVE IN THE 05 PLANNING AND ASSESSMENT USING RESEARCH TO GUIDE PRACTICE

The Thrive in the 05 (Thrive) community-based initiative to reduce violence and address other determinants of health in the Southwestern United States used the EBP process to select and implement a community-level intervention. During the assessment phase of the Thrive in the 05 project, social issues, including community crime/violence, drug use and dealing, concern for the lack of opportunities for youth, and lack of trust between residents and law enforcement, were identified (Stalker et al., 2020). Community practitioners worked alongside community members and other community partners to identify interventions to address these community issues. Identifying an intervention that would address the interconnected issues of crime/violence and drug use and dealing was particularly challenging.

In line with the EBP process, they examined the literature by conducting a systematic review of crime and violence prevention initiatives in order to assess the existing knowledge base (Evans et al., 2021). A systematic review is similar to a literature review, except that the search for literature in a systematic review is exhaustive and seeks to gather *all* relevant literature on a given topic. The systematic review led them to identify the Drug Market Intervention (DMI), an intervention that involves collaboration across law enforcement and social service sectors in order to shut down open-air drug markets. The practitioners and community partners spent time reviewing the intervention and its available evidence and ultimately decided that the DMI (a) targeted the crime and drug issues that were identified in the community assessment, (b) was aligned with the values of the community and would be acceptable to community members, and (c) had sufficient evidence supporting the effectiveness of the intervention.

SYSTEMATIC APPROACHES FOR COMMUNITY-BASED RESEARCH: USING LOGIC MODELS TO GUIDE EVALUATIONS

Although EBP is the gold standard, its use is not always practical in all community settings. Even in situations in which EBP is not practical, organizations and groups that receive funding must provide actual evidence that their processes work. Most government agencies and foundations require organizations to submit funding proposals that contain goals and objectives, established timelines, and a specific set of activities that are intended to produce clearly articulated outcomes. Such a plan is often referred to as a *logic model*. It contains implicit assumptions about the relationship between what the organization intends to do and what it will produce. According to Ginsberg (2001), logic models are designed:

> *To show on one piece of paper, the logical connections between the conditions that contribute to the need for a program in the community, the activities aimed at addressing these conditions, and the outcomes and impacts expected to result from the activities. (p. 181)*

Techniques for involving consumers of services and constituency group members in identifying the links among program goals, objectives, activities, and outcomes have their origins in a process called *evaluability assessment* or *utilization-focused evaluation* (Patton & Campbell-Patton, 2021; Stoecker, 2013). In this approach, an outside evaluator meets with organization stakeholders to identify the program goals that they feel are the most important and the outcomes associated with them. It is important to note that these goals may not be the same ones specified in the organization's mission or preliminary campaign or project goals. Instead, the evaluator tries to determine what participants perceive to be the actual goals that currently motivate them or that they think they are trying to accomplish. This process also requires that participants come to a consensus about goals, the activities to be undertaken to reach them, and the outcomes to be produced. Consequently, evaluability assessment establishes a link between practice-based knowledge and formal, more objective approaches-based expert knowledge. It also allows for the development of a *program theory*, *theory of change*, or *theory of action* about how and why the program or plan works and the outcomes it is expected to produce or actually achieves; consequently, this approach established the type of cause-and-effect relationship required for quantitative approaches to evaluation (Patton & Campbell-Patton, 2021). Anderson (n.d.) identifies several primary components associated with the process of working with a group of participants to develop a theory of change:

- Develop a map of the relationship between expected outcomes and the preconditions necessary to reach the project or campaign's goals.
- Use the group process to develop measurable indicators that can be used to determine whether goals have been achieved.
- Facilitate a process in which group members identify specific interventions or actions necessary to achieve the outcomes needed to achieve the goal, and create a map that illustrates the linkages between each set of activities and the outcomes.
- Encourage group members to identify the basic assumptions associated with their theory of change, essentially asking them to describe why and how these activities are expected to produce the outcomes and subsequently lead to goal achievement.

Program design should not simply describe a logical chain of events that lead to an outcome (Patton & Campbell-Patton, 2021). Instead, there needs to be an explanation or set of assumptions about why the program works in a particular manner. In other words, what do participants believe is happening in the program, project, or organizing campaign to produce a relationship between cause (process) and effect (outcome)? Another way to describe a set of assumptions about why a particular campaign or program works is in terms of the activities undertaken (specific strategies, tactics, and supportive actions such as media campaigns or efforts to facilitate citizen participation). Why do we expect such activities to have an impact? What kind of effect do we think these activities will have on opponents, allies, organizational partners, legislators, or the general public (Homan, 2016)? Essentially, the final product of group efforts to identify a theory of action is a logic model that describes how and why the program should work (Savaya & Waysman, 2005).

Logic models also conceptualize programs, projects, and organizing campaigns as consisting not only of a series of activities, but as a combination of resources, people, organization structure, policies or procedures, or inputs that create a process in which people interact with one another to produce results (Royse et al., 2014). Results are most often described as outputs (what is produced by the campaign or program) or immediate objectives. In addition, intermediate and long-term goals describe things or events that happen as a consequence of the outputs produced by the campaign or program (Mulroy & Lauber, 2004; Patton & Campbell-Patton, 2021). These components are put together in a written framework or graph to describe a logical sequence of events: inputs; program or campaign activities; outputs produced; and short-, mid-, and long-term effects or outcomes.

For example, Zimmerman and colleagues (2011) describe the theory of action they developed, using elements of empowerment and ecological theories, for an after-school violence prevention program. The theoretical assumptions associated with these theories include that increasing the skills and capabilities of youth and increasing their ability to engage with other people and organizations in social change activities would produce immediate goals such as youth participation in community change, youth attachment to positive adult role models, and the development of new community resources that could be used to sustain antiviolence efforts. The researchers also assumed that youth violence in the community would decrease and that there would be improvements in the health and well-being of these young adults. In their conceptual model about how the program should work, the researchers identified six curriculum models for the program: youth leadership, learning about the community, making community improvements, creating intergenerational partnerships, planning for community change, and reflection and action. The activities within each program component were explained and linked to both theories and specific program goals. With such a model, program goals and activities can easily be converted into a set of measurable objectives that must be accomplished within a specific time frame. A specific theory of action also allows for additional outcome criteria to be specified prior to program implementation.

It should be noted that the Zimmerman and colleagues (2011) theory of action pertains to a new program. Programs are designed using procedures and methods associated with social planning techniques. Often theories of action and logic models are based on formal theories about why specific types of social work or health-related interventions should work. In community-organization practice, theories of action may be less explicit; however, there are distinct models with different theories of change that drive action. For example, two distinct approaches to community organizing include consensus organizing and conflict organizing. Consensus organizing assumes that social change will be achieved by uniting interests within a neighborhood and aligning those interests with political, social, and economic interests outside of the neighborhood (Eichler, 2007). Some specific theory-of-change assumptions associated with consensus organizing include: (a) that power can be created through mutual self-interests, (b) community members and outside people in power can work together toward social change, and (c) relationships and collaboration is a critical strategy to create and sustain change (Ohmer & DeMasi, 2009). Conflict organizing, on the other hand, emphasizes that shifts in the power structure are necessary in order to achieve social change (Alinsky, 1971). Specific theory-of-change assumptions include: (a) neighborhood residents generally lack power and must take it from those outside of the neighborhood; (b) confrontation and other forms of conflict yield changes in the power structure; and (c) once the existing power structure is disrupted, redistribution of resources can occur (Mackie & Leibowitz, 2013). Often these assumptions are implicit, rather than explicit in the logic models and list of objectives included in action plans. In some situations, theories about why these approaches should work are simply derived from everyday practice and experience about what works in particular situations, and the process of praxis (Figure 10.1).

FIGURE 10.1 Theory of action for a home foreclosure prevention group.

EVALUATION TYPES

Given that evaluations can serve multiple purposes and can have multiple goals, it is helpful to distinguish among different types of evaluations. Three common evaluation types include formative evaluation, process/implementation evaluation, and outcome/effectiveness evaluation (Table 10.1).

Formative evaluation is conducted to help inform the specifics of a program or initiative *before* it is implemented. Formative evaluations might include assessments of conditions in a particular community with a focus on how these conditions might impact the implementation of the planned programs or initiatives. Process/implementation evaluations occur in the early stages of strategy implementation and are focused on understanding and documenting the details of how the program or initiative is being implemented. Process/implementation evaluation also helps individuals determine the extent to which a program or initiative is being implemented as intended. Finally, outcome/effectiveness evaluations focus on the *effect* of the program or initiative. At the most basic level, an outcome/effectiveness evaluation provides insight into whether and to what extent the program or initiative is meeting its goals. It is important to note that community practitioners do not need to (and should not) wait until a program or initiative is complete to begin activities associated with an outcome/effectiveness evaluation. Rather, data should be monitored throughout program implementation to determine the need for further refinement of programs or initiatives if data suggests little effect of the strategies chosen.

TABLE 10.1 Types of Evaluation

EVALUATION TYPES	WHEN TO USE	WHAT IT SHOWS	WHY IT IS USEFUL
Formative evaluation	During the development of a new program or initiative	Whether the program or initiative is needed, understood, and accepted by the community	Allows for refining programs and initiatives prior to implementation
Process/implementation evaluation	When program or initiative implementation begins	The extent to which the program or initiative is being implemented as intended Acceptability to the community	Provides early monitoring of potential problems
Outcome/effectiveness evaluation	After cohort of participants have completed the program or once community initiative has reached its first members of the community	Extent to which the program or initiative is having an effect on participants or community members	Suggests whether the program or initiative is meeting goals

SOURCE: Adapted from: Salabarría-Peña, Y., Apt, B. S., & Walsh, C. M. (2007). *Practical use of program evaluation among sexually transmitted disease (STD) programs.* Centers for Disease Control and Prevention.

EVALUATION METHODS FOR COMMUNITY PRACTICE

Many of the techniques used to conduct formal evaluations are consistent with methods used to collect quantitative data for community assessments: collecting data using internal or external indicators and surveys. In community assessment, methods are used that essentially fit techniques to the situation at hand or the research questions that community members or other stakeholders want to address. Consequently, most of these methods result in studies that are unique to different communities. In well-funded projects, there may be some effort to conduct systematic or standardized evaluations that allow for comparisons among different communities with different demographic characteristics and economic, social, or political challenges.

In addition, formal evaluations of community campaigns or other types of interventions involve the use of qualitative data, collected in a systematic manner as part of a formal documentation process to examine what happened during the project to make it successful or explain the lack of success. There are a number of additional reasons for using qualitative methods in community-based evaluations, including the emphasis on process rather than task-related goals and the expectation that participatory methods should be used to incorporate the preferences, experiences, and values of constituents in the research process (Foster & Louie, 2010; Royse & Dignan, 2008).

Goal Attainment

The easiest, fastest, and most accessible way to conduct an evaluation study to examine campaign, program, or project-related outcomes is simply to determine when the program has achieved its goals. One of the primary reasons for including a list of measurable objectives and a timeline in any intervention plan is that they provide a mechanism through which goal accomplishment can be assessed. Measurable objectives also permit the organization to track its accomplishments over time and to modify strategies and tactics that do not appear to work. Predeveloped objectives also permit organizations to collect data prior to the start of the campaign and consequently can be employed as pretest measures. At the conclusion of the campaign, the final count of activities, events, participants, and other indicators of success, are essentially posttest measures. Comparison of pre- and posttest data provides some useful information on the impact of the campaign, program, or project. However, it is important to note that without a comparison group, we cannot infer causality; in other words, we cannot be confident that the change between pretest and posttest was due solely to the community intervention.

Stoecker (2013) describes assessing goal attainment simply as identifying goals, identifying things to count that can be used to count the degree of goal achievement, determining how to find the things that should be counted (contained in organization records, obtained from other sources, or that will need to be collected), and deciding whether there is something that is not as easily countable that can be acquired. Brown and Stalker's (2021) Assess, Connect, Transform, In Our Neighborhood (ACTION) framework guides community practitioners in meaningfully engaging community members in assessing goal attainment. The *Assess* domain describes how community members' lived experience should be viewed as community expertise that is essential to making decisions about:

- What type of data and information are to collect (e.g., quantitative, qualitative, or both)?
- From whom will the data be collected?
- How will the data be collected (e.g., surveys, structured or unstructured interviews)?
- Is the community amenable to use of the particular assessment strategy (will the community be willing to engage in a particular type of data collection)?
- What is the cultural relevance of particular methods or questions (e.g., are particular survey or interview questions appropriate and relevant given the culture of the community)?

Social Indicator Analysis and Survey Data

Some of the data used to construct indicators for measuring goal attainment will come from information that has already been collected by local organizations or government agencies. Other measures will need to be constructed by community participants or consultants. One of the simplest methods, which can easily be adapted for use by community groups, is to survey community members, organizations, and other key stakeholders in the community. As with community assessments, it is critical that community group members participate in constructing surveys in order to verify that questions and response categories are consistent with local community cultural norms, traditions, and language. In addition to surveys, observational studies of community characteristics can also be conducted by research participants using some of the techniques used in Chapter 6. The key difference between surveys and other indicators used purely for assessment purposes is that there must be some degree of standardization in their use and interpretation that allows for pre- and posttest comparisons to be made. This may require that constituency group members be provided with training to ensure that data-collection procedures are consistent among research participants and across the various time periods in which data will be collected (Minkler, 2000).

Social indicators can also be used and incorporated into a program plan, campaign, or project goals and objectives. As described in greater detail in Chapter 6, there are some disadvantages and advantages related to using social indicators. The inaccessibility of neighborhood-level data and costs involved in hiring outside experts or employing computer technology to extract data or construct geographic boundaries are two of the biggest drawbacks (Stoecker, 2006). In addition, standardized, preconstructed measures may not reflect the complexity of the challenges or social issues facing the community or be adequate to measure social conditions (Hardina, 2002). Some participants may find standardized indicators irrelevant in that they may not reflect their values or culture or are inconsistent with their lived experiences or personal knowledge about what happens in their community (Fraser et al., 2006). Bowers Andrews and colleagues (2005) offer an example of the reaction of an evaluation participant to a standardized indicator:

> *A Latino staff member working in a program to improve relations between Latino immigrants and the police reported that he knew that the program had made a difference because community members (police and citizens) had informally told him. He viewed a survey, suggested by the grantmaker, to "capture" this change as redundant and potentially interfering with the relationships he had built. (p. 96)*

However, there are also advantages associated with the use of social indicators. For example, census data and the majority of information drawn from public databases about the prevalence of social problems, public benefits, or service utilization is easily obtained online, from government agencies, or public libraries for successive time periods so that posttest outcome data can be acquired (Royse et al., 2014). These data are particularly valuable for evaluation purposes because data-collection methods are standardized and can be used over multiple time periods (Hardina, 2002). In addition, supplemental indicators can be developed using administrative data from both nonprofit and public agencies to examine changes that occur at different intervals in population groups served, people requesting and receiving services or referrals made to other agencies (Green & Kleiner, 2011). For example, in areas with high poverty rates, there are likely to be high levels of demand for government food assistance programs and services from nonprofit food pantries and soup kitchens. Other advantages of social indicators are that there is often public consensus about what a particular measure means; such data are easy to understand and report; and it can be communicated easily, disseminated to the press, and used as an effective tool to persuade policy makers to change their minds about a particular issue or policy (Ben-Arieh, 2008).

Quantitative Research

Complex community change efforts involving multiple interventions, a variety of research sites, or diverse population groups often use standardized methods to make comparisons and test hypotheses. The research methods used may involve predeveloped surveys or standardized instruments that allow for comparisons among different demographic groups, organizations, or settings (Boothroyd et al., 2006). For example, Speer and colleagues (2011) conducted a pre- and posttest study of the Pacific Institute for Community Organization (PICO) National Network-affiliated church congregations that examined the degree of member participation in organizing activities, civic engagement, and feelings of psychological empowerment using standardized scales. They also used a community without a PICO-affiliated organization as a control group. Findings indicated that respondents in the community in which PICO was present had higher rates of civic engagement and personal empowerment on posttest measures than members of the comparison group.

Some of the community research studies that involve comparisons and standardization of measurement tools are "comprehensive community initiatives," large, well-funded projects in which a number of interventions related to housing, infrastructure, economic development and jobs, and family well-being are conducted simultaneously, often with the help of multiple government and foundation partners (Baum, 2001; Chaskin, 2001). In such studies, funders seek to test specific interventions and determine whether results are consistent (and consequently can be generalized) across communities and different population groups regardless of the unique context in which the project is conducted (Coulton, 2005).

Experimental studies and quasi-experiments are also conducted to help researchers and government agencies and foundations determine the long-term impacts (or achievement of ultimate goals) of large-scale social experiments and community initiatives. Impact evaluations examine the long-term effectiveness of specific programs or components of programs over time; evaluations are generally used to test hypotheses about whether the intervention, and only the intervention, has produced the intended results; consequently, its use may require random sampling, use of experimental and control groups, and pre- and posttests or other types of experimental or quasi-experimental designs (Boothroyd et al., 2006; Washington, 1995).

The overall impact of programs can also be determined using cost-efficiency or cost-benefit analysis. To determine cost-efficiency, program planners examine the amount of goods and services produced by a particular program option in relation to the cost. The program that produces the most for the least cost is then recommended as the preferred option (Hardina et al., 2006). Cost-benefit analyses examine whether the dollar costs of social programs exceed their potential benefits and the distributional effects of programs and policies on different population groups (Meenaghan et al., 2004). One of the difficulties inherent in this process is how to measure the economic value of social services, education, or mental health or healthcare on individuals and families (McNutt, 2011; Royse et al., 2014). However, in projects designed to produce specific economic benefits or the impact of housing, transportation, or infrastructure improvements, the dollar value of the jobs or goods and services produced is fairly easy to measure. Cost-benefit and cost-effectiveness approaches also have the advantage of producing information in a fairly simple, easy-to-understand manner that can be used to persuade decision makers and the public about the value of different policy options or services, especially when options are recommended that will save taxpayers money and provide future benefits. For example, C. Delgado (2004) describes how cost-benefit analysis could be applied to the evaluation of a controversial program, such as needle exchange for drug users, despite the difficulties associated with measuring health effects:

> *What value can be assigned to prevention? How does one accurately measure the number of people who do not get AIDS from contaminated needle use? We can estimate the number of IDUs [intravenous drug users] in a target population and relate this to estimates that the HIV infection rate of IDUs is approximately 50%, with additional infections in their sex partners and children. The costs of drug treatment, medical care, supportive social programs, and other nondirect costs can be calculated. (p. 176)*

As noted earlier in this chapter, there are disagreements among researchers as to whether randomized experiments can or should be implemented in community settings. Although acknowledging the need for empirical evidence of intervention evidence, some researchers believe that it is difficult to implement experimental and quasi-experimental designs in community settings due to time, effort, the lack of control groups and random samples, and challenges associated with retaining research subjects over time (Roberts-DeGennaro, 2011; Royse & Dignan, 2008). According to Boothroyd and colleagues (2006), in most community-based projects, researchers also face a dilemma in terms of whether "scientific methods" that meet criteria for internal and external validity should be more or less important than the significance of the study for community members and the consistency of top-down interventions imposed by foundations or community agencies, with local preferences and culture. Obtaining convincing evidence may result in sacrificing community control, relevance, and use of data or new intervention techniques.

However, Coulton (2005) argues that despite the difficulties inherent in applying "one size fits all" methodology in community settings, it is vital that researchers are able to document whether community interventions are effective across multiple settings and situations, requiring the use of standardized indicators, experimental and control groups, and randomized research designs. They assert that such techniques are essential so that effective intervention plans can be replicated by others, but also note that it is difficult to ensure that the same interventions will be implemented in the same way in all communities.

Process and Implementation Analysis

Process and implementation analysis involves the use of qualitative or a mixture of qualitative and descriptive measures to examine what happens in a program or campaign, how it happened, or why it happened (Patton & Campbell-Patton, 2021). Although oftentimes it is difficult to examine campaign processes because of the challenges in anticipating what happens in complex, real-time situations involving numerous people, evaluators and community organizations have increasingly adopted specific process-oriented indicators that help participants understand how resource acquisition; the number of volunteers; the degree of participation; the number of events, workshops, or other activities; the use of the internet and other technology; media coverage; the degree of diversity in the organization or campaign; and relationship building have on the organizing process (Butterfoss, 2006; Foster & Louie, 2010). Often, quantitative indicators can be developed to measure some of these factors, permitting them to be incorporated into the organization's formal list of task and process objectives (Hardina, 2002). Identification of process measures also facilitates the creation of pre- and posttest indicators or the implementation of an ongoing tracking system. In addition, qualitative types of data collection are often employed to assess campaign or project activities and decision-making processes, including individual and focus group interviews with staff, participants, and other key stakeholders; observational studies by external consultants; and a review of meeting notes and other internal documents by members of the research team (Butterfoss, 2006; Royse et al., 2014). Process analysis may be employed for one of three purposes:

- to help develop a new project or campaign by observing what happens as a new set of expectations or activities are implemented,
- to monitor what is happening in a project or campaign on a regular basis, or
- to supplement outcome studies by finding out how and why a successful project or campaign worked and why and how unsuccessful projects and campaigns failed (Baum, 2001; Royse et al., 2014).

Another type of qualitative or mixed-method evaluation involves implementation analysis (Patton & Campbell-Patton, 2021). Such evaluations focus on how resources (including funds, staff, and volunteers) were utilized in a program; how participants communicate with one another; how people move in and out of a program, project, or campaign; and whether the project was operated in the manner originally intended. Implementation analysis can also be used to determine whether the internal logic of the program makes sense or is consistent with its mission or goals. It can also focus on looking at the different parts of a project or campaign in order to determine whether these components overlap, limit the effectiveness of other units or projects, or actually complement one another (Baum, 2001). In some instances, implementation analysis can document whether a program exists only on paper or whether it has enough resources with which to realistically obtain its goals (Patton & Campbell-Patton, 2021). For example, if a new program has a substantial budget surplus at the end of the year and there is no consistent record of project activities, an evaluator might conclude that the program is not actually in operation. Similarly, if local community groups are recruited to help publicize and conduct outreach for a breast cancer awareness campaign on behalf of a local health clinic and the number of referrals made exceed expectations and results in requests for assistance from people outside the target population group of women living below the poverty line, aged 40 to 70, evaluators would want to assess how the campaign is functioning and how it could be modified to help people with other health-related needs.

In projects or campaigns that take place in two or more settings, implementation analysis can examine whether interventions, projects, or campaigns are consistently implemented across locations or whether there are contextual (social, political, environmental, and economic differences), organizational, or demographic variations that are affecting or could affect how the program is operating. Such an analysis may be required if monitoring data reveal serious fluctuations across sites or if local policies and procedures differ substantially from one another (Patton & Campbell-Patton, 2021). Implementation issues may be particularly problematic in the case of large-scale research studies or quasi-experiments that are taking place to test the effectiveness of interventions in various locations or establishing the generalizability of findings across population groups, regions, or countries. In such cases, implementation differences can mask or exaggerate findings from different locations and consequently make accurate assessment and generalization of the findings difficult (Mowbray et al., 2003).

Case Studies and Critical Incident Analysis

One technique often used to understand the process (e.g., what took place) and the perceived outcomes (e.g., the immediate and the lasting impacts) of a community intervention or change activity is a case study. Case studies are a qualitative method used to tell the story of an intervention or action campaign. Ideally, case studies are initiated at the start of a project so that external researchers have the opportunity to examine how community interventions are delivered, capture lessons learned along the way, and ascertain whether or not they achieved the goals they set out to achieve. To gather data for a case study, researchers may attend community or organization meetings, interview participants, facilitate focus groups, administer questionnaires, study organizational documents, examine archival data, review media reports, and talk to other community partners who are knowledgeable about what happened during the course of the campaign or intervention. In some cases, researchers may actually be embedded in the community as participant observers or active members of the intervention planning and implementation (Conway, 2004); in other instances, they may be outside partners observing what happens in order to add to the formal knowledge available about community processes, participation, or the impact of an intervention. Members of the community group may collaborate with researchers or conduct their own case study by keeping careful records of their experiences with a particular campaign, development effort, intervention, or planning process and then publish a report, facilitate media coverage, produce a video, or use social media to tell the story of what they accomplished and how it was accomplished (Brown & Stalker, 2021; Clover, 2011; Hume-Cook et al., 2007).

Although some case studies are conducted while the activity is taking place, data can also be collected years after the activities occur, using historical documents and interviews with participants (Polletta, 2006). These are called *retrospective case studies*, and they allow researchers to understand what happened during a particular event, campaign, or community change process over time; examining the historical, economic, social, cultural, environmental, and political context of what happened and how it impacted participants, the general public, public policies, or subsequent community change efforts (Delp et al., 2002; Vanderkooy & Nawyn, 2011). Most of the formal knowledge about how community organizations and social movements recruit members, frame their message, and carry out campaigns comes from case studies (Clemens & Minkoff, 2007; Speer et al., 2011). For example, Smock (2004) conducted intensive case studies of 10 different types of place-based community organizations in order to identify a set of capacity building, governance, strategies, and outcomes associated with five different community-organizing models: transformative, woman-centered, community-building, power-based, and civic engagement-oriented approaches. Smock's case study added to the knowledge base by analyzing and classifying the community-organizing strategies used by these organizations and identifying strengths and weaknesses inherent in each of the models.

One of the approaches for conducting a retrospective case study is a *critical incident analysis*. The critical incident technique (CIT) is useful in identifying and understanding the key activities and strategies that are necessary in a change process in order to have the greatest likelihood of achieving an intervention's goals (Flanagan, 1954; Viergever, 2019), and, because of this, it is a useful methodology for the development of theory (Bott & Tourish, 2016). Critical incident analysis can be used a short time after the event has occurred or in a historical context to examine the perspectives and feelings of participants (Hardina et al., 2008). A critical incident is an event, crisis, opportunity, or behavior associated with specific sets of circumstances that constitute a "significant contribution, either positively or negatively to an activity or phenomenon" (Gremler, 2004, p. 66).

The CIT methodology is a flexible technique that collects, analyzes, and classifies observations and stories of a critical incident in order to understand what took place and its perceived effects on a community. Data-collection techniques can include observations, questionnaires, interviews, focus groups, or field notes captured by participants, and this makes it feasible for use by community groups. Community members and partners can be encouraged to keep field notes or personal journals to document their participation and reactions to events in real time as they occur. At the conclusion of the event or community change activity, participants are interviewed about what they experienced; the degree to which the strategies, tactics, and other methods employed helped them to achieve their goals; lessons learned; and the perceived impact it had on participants and the community (Sitt-Gohdes et al., 2000). Consequently, this method of using interviews and field notes helps document the type of knowledge generated through practice activities or through the process of praxis (Ross, 2010; Treleaven, 2001).

Other Qualitative Approaches

Often community-based research simply intends to measure the perceptions of community members about their lives; the people they know and interact with; local services, organizations, and institutions; and the quality of life, assets, and challenges within their community. Consequently, a host of qualitative methods can be used to assess perceptions, including focus groups; one-on-one interviews with community members, leaders, organization staff, other allies and partners; or community forums conducted at the conclusion of an intervention (Vanderkooy & Nawyn, 2011). Observational studies or document analysis using contemporary or archival sources to tell the "story" of the organization, intervention, or campaign are also useful and are often employed as one component of more comprehensive case studies.

Another qualitative approach to evaluation is often referred to in the literature as *emergent* or *constructivist evaluation* (Guba & Lincoln, 2001; Lincoln, 2002; Netting et al., 2017). Patton and Campbell-Patton (2021) describe this approach as consistent with the process of reflective practice. A practitioner or evaluator facilitating a constructivist evaluation asks community members or agency participants to respond to a series of questions and take action, for example:

- What is the issue or challenge to be addressed?
- Can you agree to try something together to resolve this problem?
- Can you observe what you and others are doing to address this challenge, and report back to the group about what was done and what it accomplished?
- Can you identify themes or patterns in the separate reports made by each of the participants?
- Can you decide what to try next based on these findings?

As described by Stringer and Aragon (2021), the constructivist approach is based on the assumption that although diverse participants may have different experiences, values, and preferences, they will agree about evaluation outcomes and recommendations for actions. In the constructivist evaluation process, group members engage in extensive dialogue and reflection to work out their differences in order to reexamine or restate the issue in a manner in which participants can mutually agree. According to Stringer and Aragon (2021):

> [. . .] *the primary purpose of action research is to assist people to find solutions to real-life problems experienced by people in their community, professional, and social lives—contributions to the general body of knowledge being a secondary purpose, though an important one.* (p. 96)

PARTICIPATORY EVALUATION METHODS

One of the primary ways in which community-based evaluations are unique is that instead of a small number of researchers making decisions about research questions, methodology, data analysis, findings, and recommendations, a participatory approach necessitates that members of the community and other partners share power and decision-making for the planning, implementation, and dissemination of participatory evaluations. Therein, however, also lies the strength of this type of evaluation, as it recognizes that community members and other partners have equally important expertise to share due to their knowledge of the community and lived experiences—referred to as the *principle of shared*

FIGURE 10.2 Principle of shared expertise.

SOURCE: Brown, M. E., & Stalker, K. C. (2021). Assess Connect Transform In Our Neighborhood: A framework for engaging community partners in community-based participatory research designs. *Action Research Journal, 19*(2), 372–392. https://doi.org/10.1177/1476750318789484.

expertise (Brown & Stalker, 2021). The challenge of this approach is for community members and research partners to collaborate in a way that engages and maximizes the expertise of all team members so that the evaluation optimizes both the rigor of the research as well as the meaning of the findings to the community (Figure 10.2).

Researchers engaged in participatory evaluations must possess adequate facilitation, group-work, conflict- management, and other relevant interpersonal skills to conduct evaluations in partnership with communities (Roe et al., 2009). Further, researchers with skills in coalition building, partner development, and training community members add value to the participatory process (DiGirolamo et al., 2012). Stoecker (2013) identifies two traditional types of evaluation approaches in community practice: (a) those in which external evaluators who are considered "experts" in their field are hired to assess the project or intervention, or (b) internal evaluations in which a designated staff person is responsible for monitoring the progress or outcomes of a campaign or program at regular intervals. Stoecker argues that whether or not an external or internal evaluation is conducted is not as important as whether or not, and to what degree, community members participate in the process. In some cases, an external evaluator may be hired who uses participatory methods to facilitate constituent involvement in the study. Whatever method is used, it can be considered participatory only if constituents are actively involved in every aspect of the study. According to Coombe (2009):

> *Participatory evaluation also departs from traditional evaluation by rethinking who owns and controls the process, of creating, interpreting, and applying knowledge and to what end. In the emancipatory stream of participatory evaluation, both the process and products of evaluation are used to transform power relations and promote social action and change. (p. 369)*

Although the degree of participation and control can vary by organization, setting, and community preferences and needs, the literature on participatory methods typically identifies at least three different approaches: participatory action research (PAR), empowerment evaluation, and agency self-evaluation (Hardina et al., 2006). The following evaluation models contain different assumptions about the role of staff or external evaluators and the degree of constituent and community control of the research process.

Participatory Action Research and Participatory Evaluation Methods

As described in Chapter 6, PAR is a community-based approach to research in which community members, organizations, and other community partners work collaboratively with researchers to conduct research studies designed to identify community assets, challenges, and opportunities, and to co-create and assess solutions. The primary goal of PAR is positive social change for the community of focus. PAR methodology is used extensively for public health or health promotion-related projects, and in that context is often referred to as *community-based participatory research* (*CBPR*). Viswanathan and colleagues (2004) define *CBPR* as "collaborative approach to research that combines methods of inquiry with community capacity building strategies to bridge the gap between knowledge produced through research and what is practiced in communities" (p. v). Consequently, one of the rationales for participatory methods is to ensure that community assessments, intervention plans, and evaluations reflect the values, perceptions, and interests of community residents. It is important to note that although a number of CBPR principles exist to guide the research design process, CBPR projects vary widely to the degree that community partners are engaged and participate. Therefore, evaluators and community partners are encouraged to jointly consider the level of participation, power, and control that is appropriate based on the project goals (Bogart & Uyeda, 2009; Brown & Stalker, 2021).

In the assessment phase of the PAR-related studies, the focus is on developing a critical consciousness or understanding of social, economic, environmental, and political processes that impact the community. The researcher must gain the trust of community partners, gain insight into community dynamics and culture, and work with community partners to develop research knowledge in a manner that is understandable and meaningful to participants, and that allows community members to have some degree of input and sense of control of the project (Clover, 2011; Stoecker, 2013). The process of research question development, data collection, and analysis should produce actionable and translatable findings that can be utilized by constituency group members to advocate for community change.

As described in Chapter 9, participatory research methods and reflection combine formal knowledge with praxis-based knowledge in a manner that can be used as a source of activation for constituent empowerment, group inspiration, and as a tool to acquire public recognition and legitimacy for a cause (Minkler et al., 2008). Transformative participatory evaluation (T-PE) is most closely aligned with CBPR, and is a framework used to guide the design, process, and methods of the conduct of participatory evaluation research that allows for a decolonizing approach to evaluation. "It empowers communities to set evaluation agendas; incorporate historical, cultural, spiritual, social, environmental, and emotional 'data'; and have their evaluation findings returned to their communities" (Wiggins et al., 2018, p. 254). The following is an eight-step process for engaging in the cycle of T-PE (Coombe, 2012; Wiggins et al., 2018):

1. Identify the purpose and commit to participatory evaluation (e.g., commit to conducting the research in a group-controlled process).
2. Build the participatory evaluation team (e.g., recruit participants, obtain resources, assign roles).
3. Agree on what to evaluate (e.g., identify the goals, objectives, and measures of change).
4. Create a plan for collecting data (e.g., select a research design and methods that are useable, culturally relevant, capacity building, and values multiple ways of knowing).
5. Collect data and track progress (e.g., provide training to ensure that members collect data in a systematic way; members document change projects and impact).
6. Prepare feedback and interpret findings collectively (e.g., data are analyzed and interpreted by group members; specific findings and recommendations are identified by group consensus).
7. Communicate results to relevant audiences (e.g., identify key insider and outsider audiences; share findings with organizations, participants, the public, donors, and other interested parties; consider accessibility of dissemination by using creative outlets, in addition to reports and presentations).
8. Apply findings for action (e.g., findings and lessons learned are used to make transformative change in the community, organizations, systems, policies, and to plan future actions).

In some cases, the evaluation process may be more complex, with the methodology used for PAR intended as part of a pre- and posttest assessment of community conditions. Pretests consist of formal community assessments, an intervention plan is developed in response to the data collection, and a formal evaluation is conducted during the posttest phase to assess the impact of the intervention. The data are explicitly intended for use in social and personal transformation (Chatterton et al., 2007; Freire, 1970; Lewis, 2002). Community participants and constituency group members are included, and in some cases they control all phases of the project.

Empowerment Evaluation

Another approach for involving service consumers and constituency group members in assessments of interventions, programs, or campaigns is empowerment evaluation. In general, power is a core focus of and consideration for participatory research, and this is especially true of empowerment evaluations. Empowerment evaluation recognizes that power inequities exist between dominant and oppressed communities, systems, and organizational structures, and aims to promote equity by shifting and balancing power through the research process. The process of empowerment is "not a process that is done by the powerful to or for those lacking power, but rather as a process that communities most affected by inequities do for and with themselves" (Wiggins et al., 2018, p. 253). The role of the researcher in an empowerment evaluation process is to ensure community partners have the support and resources they need to activate and harness the power they hold within themselves and in their community, and to co-create space for that power to be shared.

The empowerment evaluation method originates from the work of David Fetterman (2001), an anthropologist who maintained that involving the people who will benefit from improvements in programs and services in the evaluation will help ensure that the outcomes are optimal for those people. Empowerment evaluation incorporates the principle of reciprocity into the research process; ensures that the data collected are useable, increases self-efficacy, self-determination, promotes experiences of empowerment, and builds capacity among participants; and makes it more likely that programs and services will be more effective and meet the needs of the people who use them (Roe et al., 2009).

This method typically relies on the services of external consultants to facilitate the research process and provide training on research methodologies to participants (Fetterman et al., 2015). In addition to the researchers, participant partners generally include a mixture of individuals with varying interests in the organization and its programs, including service consumers, program participants, program staff, board members, and other constituency group members. Empowerment evaluation is thought to not only benefit the organization and evaluation goals, but also to benefit individuals by increasing skills, capacity, self-confidence, and experiences of personal empowerment (Miller & Campbell, 2006).

Fetterman and associates have continued to refine the empowerment evaluation method over time, making the approach both more systematic in terms of methods and methodology, suitable for use in a variety of research contexts, and focused on the increasing participation and skills among members of minoritized or oppressed groups (Fetterman, 2001; Fetterman & Wandersman, 2007). Fetterman (2001) describes the role of the researcher in empowerment evaluation as that of a "coach," providing training in evaluation methods and motivating participants to move through and complete various stages of the evaluation process. The facilitation of empowerment evaluation studies requires that the researcher ask a series of questions of group participants that focus on their resources, goals, existing evidence, and best practices related to the type of intervention that they wish to adopt, the skills necessary for participants to start a new project and evaluate its effects, how the project will be implemented, and how the participants will find out whether it worked or how well it worked (Fetterman & Wandersman, 2007). The principles of empowerment evaluation are described in Box 10.1.

Box 10.1

TEN SPECIFIC PRINCIPLES OF EMPOWERMENT EVALUATION

1. Improvement—Helps people improve program performance.
2. Community ownership—Facilitates community control.
3. Inclusion—Promotes involvement, participation, and diversity.
4. Democratic participation—Participation and decision-making are transparent and fair.
5. Social justice—Addresses social inequities in society.
6. Community knowledge—Respects and values community knowledge.

(continued)

> **Box 10.1**
>
> **TEN SPECIFIC PRINCIPLES OF EMPOWERMENT EVALUATION (CONTINUED)**
>
> 7. Evidence-based strategies—Respects and uses the knowledge base of scholars (in conjunction with community knowledge).
> 8. Capacity building—Enhances stakeholders' ability to conduct evaluation and to improve program planning and implementation.
> 9. Organizational learning—Data are used to help organizations learn from their experience.
> 10. Accountability—Evaluation is focused on outcomes and accountability; did the program achieve its objectives?
>
> SOURCE: Reproduced with permission from Fetterman, D. (2019). Empowerment evaluation: A stakeholder involvement approach. *Health Promotion Journal of Australia, 30*, 137–142. https://doi.org/10.1002/hpja.243.

Methods to Facilitate Participation in Large, Multisite Evaluations: Standardized Agency Self-Assessments

As described earlier in this chapter, some types of community-based research are conducted to examine the effectiveness of new intervention models or social policies in different neighborhoods, geographic regions, or identity-based groups. Consequently, such evaluations are often funded by government agencies or large foundations; in order to ensure that scientifically adequate comparisons can be made, external evaluators are hired, and standardized data-collection methods are used. Although some of these studies fit traditional prototypes for large-scale experimental or, more often, quasi-experimental designs, many funders also require that there be some degree of effort to include community members in project oversight, consultation, or participatory research activities (Coulton, 2005; Stoecker, 2013). Indeed, community groups, organizations, and funders are increasingly recognizing the value of participatory research, and how participatory research can result in both strengthening the knowledge base and promoting ethical community-level protections for groups that have historically been oppressed or minoritized. Although empowerment evaluation promotes equity, inclusion, self-determination, and protection through participation, it is also an approach that can be used to facilitate standardized evaluations that incorporate provisions for local participation in multisite evaluations (Bowers Andrews et al., 2005; Fetterman & Wandersman, 2007).

One of the mechanisms used to facilitate agency self-evaluation involves the creation, often by the grantmaker, of evaluation templates that include checklists or predeveloped evaluation tools, such as surveys or databases, in which specific social indicators or measures of success are to be entered (Bowers Andrews, 2004; Kubisch et al., 2010). Specification of data points and evaluation techniques may be spelled out in formal agreements between donors and recipients of research funding or predetermined in face-to-face meetings between the various organization partners and community participants.

Although this technique seems to be fairly straightforward there are some difficulties. One limitation inherent in standardized, multisite approaches is the issue of implementation consistency, also called *fidelity* (Mowbray et al., 2003). Castro and colleagues (2004) argue that although program fidelity in comparison studies is important, it is equally, if not more, critical that programs be adapted for use in specific cultural and ethnic communities that may have unique preferences related to language, traditions, and values, and communities that may have unique considerations or needs based on socioeconomic status, identity status, geographic location, and other factors that place families at risk of poverty, instability, and other social problems. Hence, some national and regional research efforts deliberately use program planning, implementation, and evaluation models that encourage participation of local residents and service consumers and that "fit" the final details of program design and evaluation criteria to local values and preferences. Such efforts also address issues related to participant mistrust of researchers due to power and status differentials.

In addition to cultural competency, the use of in-agency self-evaluation may cause concern that the research methods used will be decided by the grantmaker rather than the community (Quaghebeur et al., 2004). External evaluators hired by the funding source to facilitate onsite evaluations may conduct evaluations in a manner consistent with donor demands rather than community wishes (Bowers Andrews, 2004). Grassroots community groups and organizations are often "resource poor," and therefore may not have governance structures, technical capacity, or organizational culture that provide an "easy fit" for formal, multisite evaluation studies. Sufficient funds from the donor may not "filter down" to the local level for recruitment of participants or supports, such as training, transportation, or food allowances, that could help sustain involvement in these projects over the long term (Maiter et al., 2008). It should be noted, however, that many local organizations often welcome such grants or contracts as a means of increasing their access to funding, even if it may not be consistent with their own goals. Consequently, mission drift or goal conflict can be one of the biggest barriers to the completion of evaluation projects.

INTERPERSONAL SKILLS FOR PARTICIPATORY EVALUATIONS: FOSTERING INCLUSION AND SKILL BUILDING

Participatory evaluation is a "bottom up" process that has a number of purposes. Participatory evaluation can be used to develop organizational capacity to conduct richer internal evaluations and it can be used to produce data that can inform improvements in intervention delivery and organizational practices. Participation in evaluations should have a transformative effect on community participants of participatory evaluation teams, not only fostering the development of research-skills but also enhancing individual and group problem-solving abilities. It can also increase participant commitment to the organization and to the evaluation process and findings (Patton & Campbell-Patton, 2021)

Despite the potential of positive impacts from using participatory methods, there are a number of difficulties inherent in facilitating community evaluations with a diverse group of participants. For example, M. Delgado (2000) identifies a number of issues that external consultants and community organizers often encounter when coordinating such efforts, such as how to:

- Keep constituents actively involved in the research process.
- Provide appropriate training and guidance to participants during the course of the evaluation.

- Make sure that data collection and analysis, if these activities are to be performed by community members, are realistic, feasible, and culturally relevant and appropriate. In addition, participants should be able to easily interpret and use the information collected to make improvements in the intervention and to communicate their achievements to others.
- Make sure that evaluation procedures and the data collected are also relevant and appropriate for the funding agency and can be easily described and disseminated to a variety of audiences.

Royse and Dignan (2008) note additional challenges, including that there is no guarantee community residents will choose to be actively involved in these projects, or that local agencies will have the time, resources, or ability to share responsibility for conducting the research. Further, they acknowledge that researchers do not make the best partners in some circumstances:

And to be fair, professionals can make serious mistakes affecting data collection and interpretation when they ignore the culture of community ..., fail to make sure that their instruments are culturally sensitive, or assume that the "community" research or evaluation they want to conduct, is in fact, supported by the local residents. (p. 509)

In response to these types of challenges, there are a number of approaches and techniques that can be used to increase participation, facilitate participant skill building, minimize conflict, and produce usable data. Determining the readiness of an organization or community to engage in and commit to a participatory evaluation is a crucial first step. Stoecker (2013) identifies several preconditions that can be used to determine whether participatory research methods can be used in specific situations, including the ability of constituency group members to work cooperatively with one another, the time and resources available for conducting research, and the ability of the evaluator or staff members to provide support and guidance for the evaluation process. In addition, constituency group members must be able to devote a substantial amount of time for the research and deliberation process. There must also be a collective commitment by members of the organization to actually use the data to improve the organizing process, intervention, or project. Minkler and colleagues (2008) also identify preconditions or factors that minimize conflict among participants, such as the ability of all participants to engage in dialogue and critical reflection, a commitment to a shared set of values, and a process through which all research partners establish a "shared sense of community" (pp. 134–135).

There are also a range of interpersonal social work skills that can be used to facilitate group processes, accomplish tasks, and resolve member disagreements or conflicts. A group facilitator can use the following skills to promote a productive group process (adapted from Schmuck, 2006):

- Foster group feelings of solidarity, trust, and a sense of community by helping members get to know one another and develop relationships.
- Rotate facilitation, leadership, and group responsibilities among members, ensuring everyone has an important and valued task to accomplish.

- Reinforce the perception that all group members are part of a team, ensuring everyone has space to speak (e.g., "everyone participates, no one dominates"), and collectively establish group norms that emphasize equity, friendliness, and cooperation.
- Address differences in power and status among members by ensuring everyone is treated equitably, with dignity and respect.
- Work with group members to co-create standards for the group process that provide an agreed-upon structure and reinforce the formal aspects of conducting a meeting (e.g., such as distributing an agenda in advance, rotating responsibility for taking notes, setting meeting times and establishing expectations for member behaviors).
- Promote a consensus-driven decision-making process, and ensure all members have the opportunity to voice their thoughts and opinions.
- Conduct a debriefing session after each meeting to assess how members perceive group functioning and to give participants a chance to suggest improvements.
- Establish accountability procedures for determining whether each group member has completed the tasks that they were assigned between meetings. The group as whole should determine how to proceed if tasks are not accomplished.

Schmuck (2006) also encourages facilitators to use basic interviewing and group-work-related communication skills, such as clearly defining group goals, tasks, and the work that must be accomplished; paraphrasing the words of group members in order to foster strong communication, understanding, and establish clarity about meaning and intent; and making summarizing statements about group decisions and what the team has accomplished.

PUTTING VALUES INTO ACTION: MUTUAL LEARNING AND PARTNERSHIP IN EVALUATIONS

There are a number of ethical issues that must be taken into account in participatory evaluation. The traditional concerns in research about confidentiality, anonymity, informed consent, and the protection of human subjects—"do no harm"—must be addressed in participatory evaluations just as they would in any research study (Stoecker, 2013; Stringer & Aragon, 2021). In addition, there are often questions about how researchers should relate to and interact with participants, the reporting of negative findings, the integrity of the research process, and control of any data produced. Patton and Campbell-Patton (2021) recommend having written agreements for evaluation plans, including how human subjects will be protected. Further, they maintain that evaluation findings should be impartial, comprehensive, and should be shared with transparency. When conflicts of interest arise, they should be disclosed and addressed directly and openly.

Evaluators have an ethical responsibility to refrain from altering findings or manipulating the research process in response to funder or organization demands, and to ensure that the voices of members of underrepresented groups are included and clearly heard throughout the research process (Patton & Campbell-Patton, 2021).

Stringer and Aragon (2021) note that part of the researcher's ethical responsibility is to ensure that data, both quantitative and qualitative, be collected and analyzed in a manner that ensures the authenticity and trustworthiness of the data. They identify four critical elements that characterize information collected through participatory evaluation processes that originate from a description of fourth generation or constructivist research developed by Guba and Lincoln (1989, 2001).

- *Credibility.* A study is credible if the interpretation of data is plausible, gathered using established qualitative research trustworthiness techniques (e.g., member checking), using concepts in the study that emerge directly from the experiences of the people studied, using multiple data sources to establish the accuracy of findings (e.g., triangulation), developed from prolonged engagement with the community, and includes participant debriefing to examine how feelings and emotions may influence and affect perceptions.
- *Dependability.* A study may be considered dependable if the researchers conduct it in a systematic and rigorous manner that can be verified through an independent audit of the research process, and it is replicable. Question to consider: Was there a sound reason that certain methodological choices were made?
- *Confirmability.* A study may be regarded as trustworthy if it can be independently verified that the chosen techniques and data-analysis procedures of the research design were those actually used by members of the research team. Question for consideration: Did the researchers keep adequate field notes or documentation? And did they keep journals, maintain an audit trail, or capture a description of decision-making processes used during the analysis of data?
- *Transferability.* Although generalizability to other communities is highly valued in quantitative research, findings from a nonrandom sample in a qualitative study or research conducted in a unique context cannot be readily generalized. However, some of the processes and results in qualitative research may still be relevant to other people or settings. Transferability is enhanced when researchers provide an in-depth description of the circumstances and settings in which a study was conducted. This allows other communities, organizations, policy makers, or researchers to determine whether the findings are relevant to their own context.

Many researchers have developed procedures and measurement tools to increase both the credibility and trustworthiness of qualitative data and the reliability and validity of quantitative methods. For example, Foster and Louie (2010) identify a number of steps to guide community organizations in facilitating participant involvement in evaluation decision-making, evaluation delivery, and using evaluation findings to improve organizing processes and outcomes:

- Develop clear indicators of successful outcomes associated with community campaigns or projects that include not only specific victories, but also measures of processes—such as improvements in organization capacity, volunteer recruitment and retention, leadership development, and the sharing of power.

- Set specific benchmarks or standards to be achieved for each of the outcome measures. Develop a monitoring system that allows for data to be collected at a variety of points in time during the campaign or intervention so that appropriate adjustments can be made in strategies and tactics to keep on track toward achieving your goals.
- Establish measurement tools that are consistent with activities of the project and that can be easily used by both staff members and constituents. Incorporate debriefing procedures and other qualitative data-collection techniques (e.g., field notes, journaling, observations) to capture systematic data about the organizing or intervention process for monitoring purposes. Data should be collected during the course of the campaign/intervention and can be used in a retrospective analysis once the campaign or project has concluded.
- If external evaluators are hired to facilitate the evaluation, they must actively take steps to ensure organizer and constituent trust and shared ownership of the evaluation process in order to promote and maintain participant involvement and meaningfully implement evaluation procedures.

Newman (2008) notes that participatory evaluators cannot be set on using a specific methodological approach; rather, they should be prepared to employ a mixture of process and outcome measures, flexible enough to reflect the preferences of all participants. Further, the evaluation should be designed to focus on both the project's objectives and to promote values traditionally associated with participatory research, including the promotion of democratic processes and the achievement of social justice. According to Lennie (2006), the legitimacy and authenticity of qualitative data are also enhanced through the process of dialogue and critical reflection by all research participants as well as participant review of the "end products" produced by researchers, including data analysis, formal reports, case studies, and publications.

The Center for Evaluation Innovation has proposed that to enhance the reliability, validity, and trustworthiness of quantitative and qualitative evaluation data, documents—produced by participants in the campaign or a by-product of the organizing effort—should be integrated into the evaluation process. Such documents include notes from one-on-one interviews, group debriefings, and meetings among participants (Foster & Louie, 2010). Participant documents can supplement process- and task-oriented indicators requested by funders resulting in more robust data sources while ensuring that participant perspectives are captured and heard, thereby increasing the usability and rigor of data collected for the evaluation. Other indicators of organizing success can be integrated into the evaluation process that are consistent with specific strategic-organizing approaches, models of practice, the community's cultural norms, and the organization's mission (Table 10.2). Such measures are comprehensive and flexible; respond to funder requirements for documentation; and reflect participant values, goals, and actions. They also allow participants to choose measures that are most consistent with what they want to achieve and how they will know they have achieved it.

TABLE 10.2 Measurement Strategies for Evaluation of Community-Organizing Campaigns and Projects

ORGANIZING ACTIVITY OR OUTCOME	OBJECTIVES	MEASURES
Recruitment and relationship building	People recruited Attendance at meetings Participation in events Social networks identified, developed, or strengthened	Internal tracking system that documents the number of people recruited, organizations represented, and attendance at meetings Documenting results of one-on-one interviews (written notes and oral debriefings) Social network mapping
Leadership, skill development, and personal empowerment	Number of leaders developed New skills acquired Changes in feelings of personal empowerment and self-efficacy	Number of leaders recruited "Career development" of new leaders, i.e., increases in responsibilities and progression through the ranks both inside and outside the organizations Participation in strategy sessions, serving on the evaluation team, lobbying for legislation, or chairing an event Standardized measures of self-efficacy, personal empowerment, and skill development Focus groups and interviews with leaders and constituents
Organization capacity	Increases in the number of staff, staff skills, and new board members Growth in financial and other organizational resources	Formal assessments of organization capacity Organizational "check-ins" or meetings with organizing staff, board members, and constituents Quantitative measures and classification of staff hired, new board members, skills obtained, workshops or trainings attended, and grants acquired
Power resources developed	Changes in organization influence or legitimacy Development of partnerships and coalitions Development of relationships with powerful decision makers Media contacts Electoral participation of constituents and other community members Organization capacity to sponsor events, protests, meetings with public officials and other activities to facilitate social change	Number and quality of relationships and formal partnerships; number of meetings with decision makers and legislators Amount of media coverage; effectiveness of framing and messaging efforts Internal dialogue about organizational influence and community visibility Critical incident analysis of organizing efforts Impact of the organization on legislative or policy decisions Number of voters registered; election turn out Number of events, protests, meetings, and other activities; number of people that participate

(continued)

TABLE 10.2 Measurement Strategies for Evaluation of Community-Organizing Campaigns and Projects (continued)

ORGANIZING ACTIVITY OR OUTCOME	OBJECTIVES	MEASURES
Ability to reflect on strategies and tactics and modify actions in response to situational demands	Development of a critical consciousness Use research data to modify interventions	Organizational "check-ins" or meetings with organizing staff, board members, and constituents Increases in participant knowledge about social processes and community conditions Development of new models or organizing approaches Production of training and curriculum materials
Ability to achieve results (successful campaigns or projects)	Increasing successful events, activities, protests, campaigns, and projects Successful organizing campaigns or policy/legislative advocacy Improvements in community capacity, infrastructure or housing, quality of life, or economic activities Improvements in service delivery External funding received by community groups or invested in the community	Number of events or activities Organization documents that describe the organizing effort and the decisions made Social indicator analysis that documents factors such as increases in new housing units, new businesses, poverty and unemployment rates, and the number of services provided Organization debriefings, community forums, surveys, or focus groups to examine community perceptions about the effectiveness and impact of campaigns and projects The amount of money obtained

NOTE: The objectives and measures included in this table were derived from a number of different sources: Foster and Louie (2010), Gjecovi et al. (2006), Kay (2006), and Speer et al. (2011).

SOURCE: Adapted from Foster, C., & Louie, J. (2010, March). Grassroots action and learning for social change: Evaluating community organization. Center for Evaluation Innovation. http://www.innonet.org/client_docs/File/center_pubs/evaluating_community_organizing.pdf; Gjecovi, S., James, E., & Chenweth, J. (2006). Immigrant-led organizers in their own voices: Local realities and shared visions. Catholic Legal Immigration Network, Inc. https://cliniclegal.org/file-download/download/public/5184; Kay, A. (2006). Social capital, the social economy, and community development. *Community Development Journal, 41*(2), 160–173. https://doi.org/10.1093/cdj/bsi045; Speer, P., Peterson, N. A., Zippay, A., & Christens, B. (2011). Participation in congregation-based organizing: A mixed method study of civic engagement. In M. Roberts-DeGennaro & S. Fogel (Eds.), *Using evidence to inform practice for community and organizational change* (pp. 200–217). Lyceum Books.

END-OF-CHAPTER RESOURCES

KEY TAKEAWAYS AND SUMMARY

Formal evaluations are a critical component of community practice efforts that supplement information collected through the process of action and reflection. Data collected systematically can be used to motivate participants, assess staff performance, assess program or intervention effectiveness, monitor ongoing organizing efforts, and document the organization's capacity to reach its goals. Evaluation findings also provide hard evidence that can be used to persuade funders, policy makers, prospective volunteers, and the media about the legitimacy, power, and effectiveness of the organization and its members. A variety of qualitative and quantitative research techniques can be integrated into participatory research processes that facilitate the participation of constituency group members in evaluating their own work. This process can also be used to facilitate and institutionalize knowledge production, moving it from a simple process of action and reflection to one in which knowledge is packaged in a manner that allows it to be disseminated and used by others. For evaluation efforts to be successful, organizers must be prepared to employ research, group work, conflict resolution, and other interpersonal social work skills to enhance the capacity of constituents to engage in such efforts.

RESOURCES

- Centers for Disease Control and Prevention Framework for Program Evaluation: https://www.cdc.gov/evaluation/framework/index.htm
- Empowerment Evaluation—An Interview with David Fetterman: https://www.youtube.com/watch?v=BGwVDfJg6R0
- Community Tool Box: Developing a Logic Model or Theory of Change: https://ctb.ku.edu/en/table-of-contents/overview/models-for-community-health-and-development/logic-model-development/main

ACTIVITIES

1. Working with a group of constituents, develop a set of evaluation procedures for a project, campaign, or event in which you are involved in your field practicum. Your paper should include the following:
    a. a set of goals and measurable objectives with a specific timeline for accomplishing objectives;
    b. outputs and outcome measures;
    c. an evaluation plan that specifies who should participate, overall methodology, data-collection methods, data-analysis procedures, interpretation of findings, and dissemination of a final report (written report, oral presentation, video, play, art installation, etc.); and
    d. a description of who should participate in the evaluation, carry out specific roles and tasks, and facilitate group meetings.
2. Examine a research report that describes a participatory research project. Write a critique of the report that:
    a. Describes how constituency group members were recruited for participation in the evaluation.

b. Describes the role of the facilitator or researcher.

c. Indicates whether the project involved a "top-down" or "bottom up" approach to community practice. For example, who initiated the project? Was it something community members wanted or needed? How is intended to assist them?

d. Explores the degree to which constituency group members were involved in the research.

e. Indicates whether you think participant involvement and control were sufficient. What actions should the researchers have taken to strengthen participation?

f. Describes who you think stands to benefit from the project and why.

g. Explains the end results. Were community improvements made, did individuals learn new skills, did group members "bond" with one another, were existing community networks strengthened, were individuals or organizations transformed or empowered, and were specific improvements made in the quality of life in the community? Were PAR participants able to use the results to engage in social change? Why or why not?

ASSIGNMENTS

1. Analyze an empirical journal article that describes a participatory evaluation of a community-based intervention. Write a three- to- five-page paper that describes the following aspects of the study:

   a. the purpose of the evaluation and the goal of the intervention, project, and campaign;

   b. the participants and how they were recruited or selected;

   c. the overall approach used to conduct the evaluation;

   d. the methodology, including sampling, data collection, instruments, and quantitative research design and/or type of qualitative study;

   e. ethical considerations, including human subject procedures and methods used to facilitate participation;

   f. major findings;

   g. major weaknesses or strengths of the study; and

   h. overall, do you think this was a useful study? Why or why not?

A robust set of instructor resources designed to supplement this text is located at http://connect.springerpub.com/content/book/978-0-8261-5835-2. Qualifying instructors may request access by emailing textbook@springerpub.com.

KEY REFERENCES

Only key references appear in the print edition. The full reference list appears in the digital product on Springer Publishing Connect: connect.springerpub.com/content/book/978-0-8261-5835-2/part/part03/chapter/ch10

Bowers Andrews, A. (2004). Start at the end: Empowerment evaluation product planning. *Evaluation and Program Planning, 27*(3), 275–285. https://doi.org/10.1016/j.evalprogplan.2004.04.002

Brown, M. E., & Stalker, K. C. (2021). Assess connect transform in our neighborhood: A framework for engaging community partners in CBPR research designs. *Action Research Journal, 19*(2), 372–392. https://doi.org/10.1177/1476750318789484

Fetterman, D., & Wandersman, A. (2007). Empowerment evaluation: Yesterday, today, and tomorrow. *American Journal of Evaluation, 28*(2), 179–198. https://doi.org/10.1177/1098214007301350

Maiter, S., Simich, L., Jacobson, N., & Wise, J. (2008). Reciprocity: An ethic for community-based participatory action research. *Action Research, 6*(3), 305–325. https://doi.org/10.1177/1476750307083720

Ohmer, M., & Korr, W. (2006). The effectiveness of community practice interventions: A review of the literature. *Research in Social Work Practice, 16*(2), 132–145. https://doi.org/10.1177/1049731505282204

Savaya, R., & Waysman, M. (2005). The logic model: A tool for incorporating theory in development and evaluation of programs. *Administration in Social Work, 29*(2), 85–103. https://doi.org/10.1300/J147v29n02_06

Stalker, K. C., Brown, M. E., Evans, C. B. R., Hibdon, J., & Telep, C. (2020). Addressing crime, violence, and other determinants of health through community-based participatory research and implementation science. *American Journal of Community Psychology, 66*(3/4), 392–403. https://doi.org/10.1002/ajcp.12438

Viergever, R. F. (2019). The critical incident technique: Method or methodology? *Qualitative Health Research, 29*(7), 1065–1079. https://doi.org/10.1177/1049732318813112

Wiggins, N., Chanchien Parajón, L., Coombe, C., Alfonso Duldulao, A., Rodriguez Garcia, L., & Wang, P. (2018). Participatory evaluation as a process of empowerment: Experiences with community health workers in the United States and Latin America. In N. Wallerstein, B. Duran, J. Oetzel, & M. Minkler (Eds.), *Community-based participatory research for health: Advancing social and health equity* (3rd ed., pp. 251–264). John Wiley & Sons.

Zimmerman, M., Stewart, S., Morrel-Samuels, S., Franzen, S., & Reischel, T. (2010). Youth empowerment solutions for peaceful communities: Combining theory and practice in a community-level violence prevention curriculum. *Health Promotion Practice, 12*(3), 425–439. https://doi.org/10.1177/1524839909357316

ADDITIONAL APPLICATIONS OF SOCIAL WORK SKILLS FOR COMMUNITY PRACTICE

USING SOCIAL WORK SKILLS TO ADVOCATE FOR LEGISLATION

LEARNING OBJECTIVES

After reading this chapter, students will be able to:

- Discuss the role of social workers in the legislative and political process.
- Describe the goals and components of legislative campaigns.
- Recognize common roles and tasks of organizers in legislative and political campaigns.
- Summarize the social work skills involved in legislative advocacy.

INTRODUCTION

A number of factors contribute to successful lobbying for legislation, including timing and opportunity, political influence, public or voter support, and election procedures. Social work skills are also important, including the ability build relationships with legislators and interest groups and to communicate issues in a manner that elicits popular support and puts pressure on legislators to take action. In this chapter, the terms *legislative advocacy* and *lobbying* are defined and the structure and context of legislative campaigns are examined. A description of the background research necessary to effectively lobby for legislation improvements is also provided. In addition, the skills required for participation in successful lobbying campaigns are described, including written and electronic communication, building relationships with decision makers, components of successful lobbying visits, and the provision of testimony at public hearings. The relationship between legislative and political campaigns is also examined in terms of the types of skills needed for each of these social action approaches, and barriers (such as legal regulations) that limit the engagement of social workers, community practitioners, and community organizers employed by public and nonprofit agencies in these activities are explored. In the last section of the chapter, lobbying campaign procedures used to change laws and social policies in order to achieve social justice are described.

DEFINING *LEGISLATIVE ADVOCACY* AND *LOBBYING*

Legislative advocacy can be defined as promoting or working for a cause that can be addressed by the passage of a new law or approval of a policy or regulation (Avner, 2013). *Lobbying* is a specific form of advocacy that involves putting pressure on lawmakers or government bureaucrats to pass or block a legislative proposal, policy, or regulation (Kirst-Ashman & Hull, 2018; Richan, 2006). Lobbying can be direct, involving face-to-face meetings with legislators, members of their staffs, and other government officials. However, in most cases, lobbying involves indirect contact with others (through letter writing, phone calls, emails, faxes, or social media) or simply urging constituents to contact their legislators. Engagement in activities that focus on urging other individuals and groups to lobby their legislators is called *indirect* or *grassroots lobbying* (Bergan, 2009; Haynes & Mickelson, 2010).

Legislative advocacy is generally considered to be a form of social action due to the fact that it often involves activities related to persuading, influencing, pressuring, or some form of mild coercion to change the minds of potential opponents (Mondros, 2005). For example, offering to give an elected official something or to withhold tangible or intangible benefits, such as votes, donations, or public good will or support, can be used to persuade legislators to adopt specific positions on an issue. It should be noted, however, that outright bribery or instances in which elected officials vote for bills from which they will financially benefit are legally prohibited (Briffault, 2008; Savage, 2011). Therefore, most lobbying takes place in a more subtle manner, in the context of the exchange of information, legal donations, and gifts (such as meals or tickets to sports or entertainment events), and political support (Kraft & Furlong, 2021; Wise, 2007). Absent access to large amounts of cash for campaign donations, community organizers involved in lobbying look for alternative means to advocate for policies and legislation that would benefit their constituents. According to Amidei (2002), it takes only about a dozen calls to a single legislator to make one take notice that the public is concerned about a particular issue or piece of legislation.

As with other types of social action, constituents often have the primary role in legislative campaigns, meeting with public officials, providing testimony at public hearings, and organizing rallies or protests to garner public support or persuade legislators to take action. Although organizers provide support for constituents in direct lobbying-related activities, they may also be called upon to manage grassroots legislative campaigns, give expert testimony at public hearings or conduct research on public issues, explain the impact and content of specific pieces of legislation, or the vested interests and power associated with the various groups and individuals involved in the legislative process (Hardina, 2002; Haynes & Mickelson, 2010; Mondros, 2005). In addition, organizers often facilitate trainings and workshops on legislative procedures and lobbying skills (O'Neill et al., 2008; Szakos & Szakos, 2007).

LEGISLATIVE CAMPAIGNS

As with other forms of action campaigns (as described in Chapters 7 and 8), members of the action system develop a predetermined approach to advocate, support, block, or request modifications in legislation that may affect them, the groups they represent, or people or issues for whom they are concerned. Legislative campaigns can differ in terms of participants, goals, and components, depending on the issue involved, the amount of power held by proponents and opponents, the salience of the issue for the public, and the structure or rules that guide the legislative process.

Participants in Legislative Campaigns

Most lobbying campaigns are conducted, not by a single organization or constituency group alone, but by coalitions of organizations. One of the most important tenets of any form of organizing is there is "strength" in numbers; the more people and organizations involved in an organizing effort increases the amount of power, resources, skills, information, and media attention that can be used to influence an issue (Bergan, 2009; Jackson-Elmore, 2005). Because these communications are tracked (and in many cases responded to) by legislative staff, they can be viewed as expressions of support or withdrawal of support by individual voters. Consequently, a legislator may change their support or opposition to an issue if enough letters or phone calls are received (Haynes & Mickelson, 2010). In addition, the various groups involved in legislative coalitions have a variety of resources that can be applied to the lobbying effort—money, media contacts, previous relationships with politicians, and social networks that can be mobilized for the lobbying effort (Mosley, 2010). They can also shape legislation by negotiating the parameters of the laws and policies that they wish to see passed with members of the coalition or other allied groups.

Many of the organizations participating in legislative campaigns are interest groups. Interest groups can be defined as groups composed of people with some shared values and policy objectives who are active in the political process (Hrebenar, 2016). As in social movements, sometimes interest groups are formed to represent the interests of those considered "voiceless" (e.g., children) or to advocate for the group's vision for the public good (e.g., reducing the public debt, environmental protection, or ending houselessness).

Often, interest groups have multiple goals that they wish to achieve for their members. For example, social work lobbying is conducted through local and state chapters of the National Association of Social Workers (NASW). NASW typically advocates for legislation that improves work conditions for social workers, (e.g., wages, benefits, or social work licensing requirements), funding for the agencies in which they are employed, and to increase access to services or the well-being of the people they serve. A study by Brown and colleagues (2015) found that NASW state advocacy agendas prioritized both professional self-interest (e.g., improvements to wages, professional licensure) and social justice issues (e.g., efforts to improve legislation related to poverty, healthcare, child welfare, mental and behavioral health, etc.). Other professional, trade, and business groups also form associations to fight for their own interests in the legislative process. Other powerful interest groups include the Sierra Club, the National Association of Manufacturers, the National Rifle Association, and AARP. The groups actually involved in lobbying on behalf of a specific issue will vary, based on the vested interest of the organization and the amount of resources and power they have to influence the decision-making process. According to Jansson (2017), legislative coalitions are often necessary to mitigate the influence of powerful interest groups, most often associated with businesses or corporations, with many members, financial resources, and long-term relationships with elected officials. Such alliances are believed to have substantial influence on the development of legislation, the awarding of government contracts, and the outcomes of election campaigns.

Because membership in coalitions supporting various pieces of legislation can shift in response to the issue at hand or the vested interest of participant organizations, today's ally can become tomorrow's opponent, requiring that good relationships be maintained with both prospective allies and opponents (Richan, 2006). These relationships can be employed later on in the legislative process when negotiations take place among politicians and the interest groups with which they are allied, as well as opposition forces. The ability to compromise or reach common ground on new legislation helps to ensure "win-win" situations in which many of the groups and elected representatives involved achieve at least a portion of their goals in the final draft of the legislation (Kraft & Furlong, 2021).

Goals in Legislative Campaigns

Goals in legislative campaigns generally focus on alleviating a specific problem or addressing a social issue. For example, a legislative goal may be to increase the amount of healthy food available to school children. Adopting new legislation or changing current legislation may simply be one of many methods for achieving the goal (Avner, 2013). Although passing a specific bill is often the primary focus of legislative campaigns, there can also be other reasons for lobbying for legislation. An organization or coalition group may wish to:

- Campaign for a specific package of interrelated measures designed to address a specific long-term goal. For example, child welfare advocates may submit several bills designed to increase funding for and services provided by independent living programs for foster children during a single legislative session.
- Campaign for increases (or in some cases decreases) in funding allocations to be set in annual budgets or changes in tax policy. Most often, community groups will request increases in funds to benefit individuals and families living in poverty, community-based organizations, or communities.
- Defeat or delay a piece of legislation viewed as harmful to individuals, organizations, or communities.
- Amend legislation that is viewed as likely to pass or that the organization may wish to support, deleting provisions viewed to be harmful or otherwise counterproductive (Amidei, 2002; Gelack, 2008; Kingdon, 2011; Richan, 2006).

The following issues to be considered in deciding whether to engage in a legislative campaign include the issue to be addressed, whether there have been other attempts to address the issue legislatively, and what options exist for addressing the issue through legislation (Gelack, 2008; Jansson, 2017). In addition, the types of provisions that should be contained in proposed legislation, positive benefits or negative consequences associated with the prospective legislation, potential opponents and allies, and those decision makers or targets who will need to be persuaded to sponsor or vote for the legislation should be examined. In legislative advocacy, targets are almost always individuals, for example, a specific elected official, government bureaucrat, or a member of a specific committee or legislative body who will need to make a decision on the legislation (Richan, 2006).

In some cases, targets can include members of the press, influential people, and the public (Kraft & Furlong, 2021). For example, the coalition or lobbying team may engage in activities to persuade an influential newspaper columnist, TV commentator, or a newspaper editorial board to publicize or take a stand on an issue or present information that can be used to persuade the public and elected officials that legislation should be adopted or defeated. Influential citizens (business people, church leaders, union officials, or members of specific professional groups) can be asked to sign letters or have their names listed in the press as supporters of a proposed piece of legislation. Often a good way of obtaining press coverage of an issue is asking a prominent person or a celebrity to endorse or serve as an ambassador for the cause, and give interviews about the issue, staging a rally, testifying at a public hearing, or sending out information about the legislation via email or social media (Marlantes et al., 2006; Schultz, 2003).

The greater the press coverage, public awareness, and support for the issue from voters (i.e., public pressure), the more likely decision makers can be influenced. Because many legislative campaigns have multiple components and may involve a lengthy time commitment, organizations are likely to have long-term, intermediate, and short-term goals. As with other types of campaigns, outcomes may be considered "wins" or partial "wins" if the legislative campaign educates the public about an issue or a bill that has been defeated or contributes to the likelihood that the bill is amended or passed in the next legislation due to increased legislative support or public awareness. In addition, legislative campaigns also include fallback positions if it seems unlikely that goals will be achieved (Richan, 2006).

Components of Legislative Campaigns

Typical roles for social workers, community practitioners, or community organizers in legislative campaigns include advocating for changes in local, state, and federal policies, proposing legislation, lobbying for or in opposition to legislation, protesting unjust laws and policies, and using the media to inform the public about these issues or problematic policies (Jansson, 2017). The component parts of legislative campaigns are similar to those of action campaigns and may involve a specific strategic approach or a multistage process (Avner, 2013; Gelack, 2008). For example, if an organization is seeking to improve safety standards for playground equipment in their community, it may first need to advocate for state legislation that establishes such standards or for a funding stream that provides financial assistance so that city and county governments can afford to purchase this special equipment.

As in other types of campaigns, it is critical that the action system develops a strategic approach with goals and objectives and identify specific targets to be utilized at different phases of the campaign. Tactical methods used in legislative campaigns can include a variety of activities:

- Conduct research on an issue and providing elected officials, the public, and the media with facts and figures that provide a rationale for the adoption or defeat of a particular bill; release a "fact-finding" report on the issue or the likely impact of proposed legislation.
- Draft a legislative proposal that reflects the constituency group's or coalition's interests.
- Find a sponsor for a piece of legislation or work collaboratively with an elected official to draft a piece of legislation. Bills can have multiple sponsors or can be supported by a political party. However, bipartisan support that crosses party lines makes it more likely that a piece of legislation will have sufficient support to pass.
- Conduct news and social media campaigns to present the coalition's position on the issue and to persuade the public to support it. Media campaigns can also be used to put pressure on lawmakers to change their positions on the issue or to ensure that others continue their commitment to your cause.
- Schedule individual and group meetings with legislators.

- Make phone calls or send letters, emails, or social media messages in order to advocate a specific position on an issue. These communications are addressed to specific individuals in the legislative process, most often the individual's own elected representative. This tactical method requires that people outside the "lobbying team" be motivated and mobilized to take action.
- Present testimony at legislative hearings.
- Persuade legislators to introduce, support, or oppose specific amendments to a piece of pending legislation or to identify compromises that can be made in order to obtain approval of the final bill (Avner, 2013; Haynes & Mickelson, 2010; Jansson, 2017; Mondros, 2005; Richan, 2006).

Most campaigns use multiple methods to ensure success. Often lobbying efforts require that the action system continually monitor the legislative process and be able to respond to situational demands and unique opportunities that can be used to persuade elected officials and the public to support their goals (Jansson, 2017; Kingdon, 2011). For example, in 2011, after an earthquake and tsunami struck Japan and destroyed several nuclear plants, antinuclear groups worldwide stepped up efforts to persuade governments to substitute green energy for nuclear power (Betigeri, 2011; Cowell, 2011). In addition to the situation at hand, factors affecting tactical choices are similar to those in other types of social action and include:

- the extent of policy change desired;
- specific objectives for the legislative campaign;
- whether the action system is supporting or blocking the change;
- the time frame involved;
- the current positions of decision makers on the issue;
- the power of the decision makers, the amount of influence possessed by opponents, and the amount of power held by the group taking action; and
- the importance of the issue to decision makers and the public (Avner, 2013; Baumgartner et al., 2009; Jansson, 2017).

According to Mondros (2005), the choice of strategy often depends on the degree of access that members of the action system have to decision makers. They identify two primary ways to plan strategy: the insider approach (i.e., working through the system and approaching decision makers directly) and the outsider approach. The outsider approach requires that the action system put pressure on decision makers using protest-related tactics and, in some situations, legal action, including lawsuits, public records requests, and injunctions or restraining orders. Mondros (2005) argues that most lobbying groups want to have influence comparable to other insiders; consequently, collaboration, compromise, and consensus are often preferred tactical methods. As in other approaches to community practice, legislative advocates often start out using collaboration and then escalate their tactical methods over time. Other factors to think about when developing a strategy are similar to those considerations taken into account in other types of action campaigns:

- Adapt a strategy that is appropriate for the setting and the policy actors involved. For example, using the same strategy to lobby a city council and the state assembly would not produce the same results. Keep in mind that the interests of elected officials as well as decision-making rules are not the same in different venues.
- Constituents (people involved in the change effort or those who will benefit) should also have a leadership and decision-making role in developing the strategy.
- The people who carry out the strategy should be comfortable with the style and intensity of tactics chosen.
- Frame the issue in a manner that will solicit the most support from decision makers and the public.
- The choice of strategies and tactics are situational and often must be changed as conditions "on the ground" change (Jansson, 2017; Kingdon, 2011; McGrath, 2007).

BACKGROUND RESEARCH FOR LEGISLATIVE CAMPAIGNS

Successful lobbying relies on both interpersonal relationships with elected officials and background research. Often, the role of the community organizer is to use web research, newspaper accounts, literature and policy reviews, and personal interviews to obtain information about the content of proposed legislation, as well as knowledge about the legislative process, including how decisions are made and who has the power to make them. The lobbying team also needs to identify the vested interests and power resources associated with individual decision makers and the interest groups involved in influencing the policy debate on the legislation.

Content of the Legislation

Advocates and policy analysts examine the content of a new policy to determine policy goals, the individuals or groups who will be affected by a policy, who will benefit or lose from it, how it will be funded, and what it is expected to do, and to anticipate what will actually happen as a consequence of a policy (Chambers & Bonk, 2013; Gilbert & Terrell, 2013). They also examine how the policy will be put into operation or implemented. If there are specific alternatives to a policy, the potential benefits, costs, and impacts of each alternative can be compared (Dobelstein, 2003; Kraft & Furlong, 2021). After a policy is adopted, they assess the impact of the policy, the degree to which it has benefited or harmed members of the general public, specific demographic groups, members of minoritized and marginalized communities, whether it has been implemented in the manner intended, and whether policy goals have been achieved (Davis & Bent-Goodley, 2004; Meenaghan et al., 2004; Weaver, 2010).

Often policy analysis is a matter of conducting research on the effects or anticipated effects of a policy. Because most public programs publish information about the number of people who receive benefits from a policy and the amount of funds allocated or spent in association with the policy, much of this information is accessible to the public. As with a needs assessment, secondary data and information about community conditions is often obtainable using the web and other public sources (Meenaghan et al., 2004). Although constituency groups can do some of this research, interest groups and advocacy organizations often conduct policy research and make their data available to the public, disseminate reports, and give press conferences and media interviews (Jackson-Elmore, 2005). The availability of data in reference to a specific piece of legislation often increases as the bill advances through the legislative process (Gelack, 2008). Stories and testimonials about how individuals and groups are affected by a specific piece of legislation or how new legislation may affect them can also be used in the legislative process, included in letters to legislators, media stories, and in public testimony presented by constituency group members, or formal reports.

Often, one of the ways in which a persuasive argument is built for or against a policy is by articulating a frame (similar to those used in other types of community organizing) that includes specific values important to the public such as equality, efficiency, equity, self-determination, adequacy of the benefits provided, and justice (McGrath, 2007; Stone, 2012). Policy analysis is often a matter of examining whether the policy is expected to uphold these values—based on the available facts, the amount of funding to implement the policy, the people it is expected to serve, how benefits will be distributed, and how it is expected to operate (Chambers & Bonk, 2013; Kraft & Furlong, 2021).

Another type of information needed for policy analysis is an examination of policy alternatives. This requires a review of other pending policy or legislative proposals. Have alternative bills been introduced and how does the bill differ from the one that you propose? It is also helpful to determine whether similar bills have actually been proposed, passed, or implemented in other jurisdictions or countries or if alternative measures have been taken to address the issue. Often this information can be found in the professional or peer-reviewed research literature on a topic, in newspaper and other media accounts, or through online searches. Such reports generally include valuable information on the benefits and costs of these policy alternatives, whether policies can feasibly be implemented, and any side effects or consequences associated with them (Glover Blackwell et al., 2009; Kraft & Furlong, 2021).

For community groups with few resources, obtaining basic facts about the social problem to be addressed, and proposed legislation as well as exploring how people have been affected by the issue may be sufficient to launch a policy campaign. It is also very feasible to rely on coalition partners, legislative allies, or national organizations for fact sheets, policy briefs, and prepared campaign materials. If constituency group members initiate a campaign, basic steps in the content analysis process include:

- Identify social problems or issues of concern.
- Find out how individuals and the community have been affected by the social problem. Obtain data from other advocacy groups, government agencies, or elected officials or document how people in the community have been affected by the social problem or prior legislation.
- Identify a set of value criteria for viewing the contents of legislation and weigh alternative approaches in terms of these criteria, as well as the costs, benefits, feasibility, and consequences associated with each option.
- Determine the outcome to be achieved and any fallback positions.

- Determine whether the specific approach constituency group members have chosen is feasible, given funding and other restraints.
- If supporting a specific bill, find out the bill number, who has introduced the bill, potential allies and opponents, and how the bill will move through the legislative process.
- Ask one or more constituency group members whether they would be available to send a letter to their elected representatives or speak on how they or people they know have been affected by the social problem (Avner, 2013; Glover Blackwell et al., 2009; Haynes & Mickelson, 2010).

Legislative Processes

In order to lobby successfully, organizers and their constituents must understand the legislative process. It is necessary to be able to identify the key decision makers, the types of decisions that can be made, how the decision-making process is structured, and specific steps required for a bill to become a law. Essentially, advocates must determine the "rules of the game" and assess where and when they can have the most influence. For example, it may not be sufficient to have a majority of votes to achieve a legislative victory. In understanding how the U.S. Senate works, a successful lobbyist must be aware that 60 votes (out of 100 votes) are needed to bring a piece of legislation to the floor for debate (Davis, 2007).

In the United States, the federal and state governments have similar structures with bicameral (two-house) legislatures, a chief executive (president or governor), and an independent judicial system. In this type of system, there are a number of points in the legislative process at which members of constituency groups can influence legislative decision-making:

- when bills and amendments are proposed;
- when bills are introduced in both legislative and budget committees;
- when bills are advanced to the floor of the house/assembly or senate;
- during the budgeting process, when funds for specific policies and programs are allocated;
- when bills are finalized by conference committees that reconcile differences between bills approved by bicameral (two-house) legislatures; and
- when the governor, president, or other chief executive is considering whether to sign a new bill (Amidei, 2002; Gelack, 2008).

As noted in Chapter 8, advocates can also appeal to the courts in some cases to block unjust legislation or to take other legal action when people are harmed by a policy (Chambers & Bonk, 2013). Lobbyists need to have good working knowledge about how the legislative process works, the procedures available to introduce or amend legislation, technical aspects of the budgeting process, and how to contact elected officials and their staff members in order to influence the process.

For example, most legislative bodies establish standing committees that handle specific types of issues: budgets, public services, taxation issues, healthcare, transportation, and so on (Haynes & Mickelson, 2010). Legislative advocates need to know how this structure operates, the membership composition of the committees, and who is responsible for chairing or staffing them. Often it is in these committees that members of the public will be able to provide public testimony about the bill. According to Amidei (2002), discussions in committees and on the floor of the legislative body are oriented toward addressing whether the bill is based on a good idea, if it makes appropriate use of government funds, and whether the public can support it. Consequently, committee hearings provide legislative advocates with a good opportunity to influence the contents of proposed legislation or to block it from proceeding to a vote on the floor of the legislative body.

Power Analysis: Decision Makers and Interest Groups

An important step in the lobbying process is assessing the power of individual decision makers and groups. This type of power analysis is similar to the background research on potential allies and opponents discussed in Chapter 6. Members of the constituency group should be able to identify sources of power that they can use to lobby for legislation, the power resources held by individual legislators, potential allies and opponents, and the degree to which the various groups involved have the power to influence the legislative process.

Some of the critical things to know in terms of a specific policy or piece of legislation are the legislative positions, values, political agendas, and vested interests of individual decision makers. Although rules of ethics prohibit politicians from benefiting financially from legislation, they may have other reasons for supporting an issue (Savage, 2011). For example, a social worker elected to political office can probably be expected to support legislation that benefits the profession, people who receive social services, or organizations that provide services. Similarly, if a piece of legislation that makes it easier for couples to adopt a child is under consideration, legislators who are adoptive parents or who were themselves adopted are probably likely supporters. It should be noted, however, that sometimes loyalty to political parties or campaign donors may supersede personal consideration. In addition, friendships; family relationships; and business, religious, or professional affiliations may also influence a lawmaker's support for an issue (Haynes & Mickelson, 2010). Therefore, it is important to know as much about legislators' positions as possible on issues before approaching them about supporting or opposing a specific bill (DeVance Taliaferro & Ruggiano, 2010).

When considering the degree to which lawmakers are likely to be influenced by lobbyists and the degree of power they possess in the legislative process, critical information includes the elected official's political party affiliation and the degree to which members of that party can control the legislative process (by virtue of a majority of votes or chairmanship of committees), the elected official's voting record on the issue, and the names and professional or industry affiliations of campaign donors (Hardina, 2005). Voting record information is generally available online from websites maintained by the legislative body of interest and by various advocacy organizations that trace voting histories and issue legislative "report cards" that rank legislators in terms of how they have voted on issues important to them.

The composition of the electoral district that the official represents is also important (Haynes & Mickelson, 2010). Members of some demographic groups may have similar voting patterns. Hence, the question of whether the district has a large number of Black/African American or Latinx voters or the number of people in the district who are wealthy may affect such factors as party affiliation, voter turnout, and those individuals who are likely to be elected in that district. In addition to potential votes and campaign donations, politicians often base support for an issue on what they perceive their constituents to need or want (Hoefer, 2019).

It is also important to know about citizens and interest groups who are likely to support or oppose legislation and to identify those people and organizations that could be persuaded to join the lobbying coalition. Linkages among interest groups and other organizations can be critical in determining whether a bill has enough public support to pass. Therefore, as with other types of organizing work, part of the background research process should focus on determining the power resources held by members of the interest group, their positions on the issue or bill, and their likely allies or opponents in the process (Jansson, 2017). As noted in Chapter 6, one of the best sources of information for documenting political power and identifying the vested interests of lobbying groups and individual politicians are campaign donations (Hardina, 2005). Information about federal donations can be found in the online database constructed by the Center for Responsive Politics (www.opensecrets.org). State and local governments in the United States also require that candidates for public office file regular reports on campaign donations. Much of this information can also be obtained online.

THE ROLE OF INTERPERSONAL SOCIAL WORK SKILLS IN LOBBYING FOR LEGISLATION

There are a number of specific components involved in lobbying specific legislators and other public officials. Lobbying activities include disseminating written or electronic materials containing information about an issue, establishing relationships with politicians and other government decision makers, making lobbying visits or meeting with officials, and providing public testimony at hearings. Each of these tasks requires a specific set of skills similar to those used by social workers to engage with individuals in clinical practice settings, community members, and professional colleagues.

Written, Phone, and Electronic Communication

Typical methods of written and electronic communications with public officials include typed or handwritten letters, postcards, or electronic messages transmitted via social media, email, or web pages. In addition, many organizations encourage their constituents to phone legislative offices, especially in instances in which there is a short time frame prior to the scheduling of a vote on an issue. Although legislative staff are expected to both track and respond to all correspondence, letters, emails, and phone calls are considered the most effective means of soliciting attention for an issue (Gelack, 2008). Phone calls should be short, accurate, and quickly reference the issue under consideration and the bill number if the call is in reference to pending legislation (Hoefer, 2019). The staff member likely will ask for the caller's contact information in order to assess constituent support or opposition to specific legislation (Haynes & Mickelson, 2010).

In addition to phone calls, elected officials and their staff prefer to receive personal letters and emails clearly written by the constituent rather than preprinted or generic form letters, postcards, or petitions that simply require the respondents name, signature, and contact information. Letters and emails require an actual time commitment from the writer and often contain personal stories about how a person is affected by an issue. Consequently, anyone who has taken the time to complete a letter is viewed as genuinely concerned about the issue and likely to take additional action (e.g., voting, making donations, or participating in an election campaign) in relation to the issue (Gelack, 2008; Haynes & Mickelson, 2010).

Lobbying communications, whether written, electronic, or via phone, should be short and accurate and contain the following information:

- the elected official's name and address—rather than a form letter in which this information is not specified;
- identification of the issue of concern;
- a specific request from the writer (e.g., support or opposition for a piece of legislation or an amendment); if the communication is in reference to a pending bill, the number and title of the bill should be included;
- a description of why the writer is concerned about the issue, including facts, personal connections to the issue, personal experiences, stories about how others are affected by the issue, and references to common values and beliefs that should be considered in reference to the bill or issue at hand (e.g., fairness, equity, or efficiency);
- a clear statement about the writer's opinion on the issue; and
- contact information for the writer (e.g., name, address, phone number or email address); in many instances, it is not uncommon for the writer to receive a follow-up communication from the legislative office, acknowledging receipt of the communication and describing the lawmaker's position on the issue (Haynes & Mickelson, 2010; Hoefer, 2019; Box 11.1).

Box 11.1

LETTER—LOBBYING FOR AN ISSUE

City Council Member
Roberto Gonzalez
City Hall
123 Main Street
Milltown, California 12345
Dear Council Member Gonzalez:

I'm writing to ask for your support for a bill to shut down the local meat-rendering plant. As you know, people in your district are adversely affected by the poor air quality and the smell from the plant. My children cannot play outside on days in which the plant is in operation. My youngest daughter, Caroline, age 9, has just been diagnosed with asthma. In addition, my son David's high-school baseball team has been adversely affected by the poor air quality as well. Due to warnings from the district about local air quality and ozone levels, the school district has been forced to cancel baseball practice at least six times this year and games have been cancelled twice. This is a problem because the opportunity to play sports is extremely important for a growing adolescent's health and well-being.

In addition, I'm concerned about how the unregulated meat-rendering plant and other sources of pollution in my neighborhood adversely affect the health and quality of life for members of our community. The U.S. Department of Environmental Protection reports that one of the key triggers of asthma for most children is air pollution. In addition, Black/African American communities are more likely to be adversely affected by asthma. According to the Environmental Protection Agency, 13% of all Black/African American children have asthma compared to 8% of White children, 8% of Latinx children, and 12% of American Indian children. They are also more likely to be hospitalized or die from asthma than other children. In our community, based on hospital records and a state health survey, asthma rates among children are estimated at 10%, with the rate for Black/African American children at 14%, higher than the national average.

I urge you to support our efforts to introduce legislation in the Mytown City Council to rescind the condition-use permit for the meat-rendering plant and shut it down as a first step in improving the health of children in the Westside Community.

Sincerely, Elizabeth Andrew, Westside Neighborhood Organization

NOTE: The source of asthma statistics cited in the letter is the United States Environmental Protection Agency. (n.d.). *Children's environmental health disparities: Black and African American children and asthma.* https://www.epa.gov/sites/default/files/2014-05/documents/hd_aa_asthma.pdf.

Building Relationships With Public Officials

Building relationships with legislators and members of their staff is often the key to successful lobbying (Jackson-Elmore, 2005). Wise (2007) conducted a qualitative study with professional lobbyists working at the federal level to represent the healthcare industry in order to examine the importance of relationship building in their work. Respondents felt building business and personal relationships with members of Congress was critical for successful lobbying. Elements of good relationships described in the interviews included honesty, presenting both sides of an issue when lobbying, developing trust, and exchanging information with the elected officials and staff members. These actions were viewed as key to increasing the lobbyists' access to decision makers and information they needed about the legislative process in order to do their jobs. Although these lobbyists viewed all forms of communication, emails, letters, phone calls, and faxes as important tools, emails were viewed as the most efficient way to lobby and exchange information, whereas face-to-face interaction was considered to be the most effective method. DeVance Taliaferro and Ruggiano (2010) conducted a similar study with employees of nonprofit organizations. Their respondents also emphasized the importance of building personal relationships with public officials, describing the process as "developing goodwill through communications or activities" or "just talking to one another" (p. 5).

It should be noted that developing a relationship with lawmakers themselves may not be as critical as "getting to know" their legislative aides. These gatekeepers control access to public officials and their appointment calendars. In addition, staff members are often the people who will directly interact with constituents and other lobbyists to obtain information, schedule public testimony, or look for media opportunities to disseminate the lawmaker's position on the legislation. In many circumstances, the lawmaker will not be available to meet with lobbyists; instead, meetings will be arranged with senior staff members.

One of the first things to assess when developing a lobbying team with constituency group and coalition members is whether any team members have an existing relationship with legislative staff or even with the family members of elected officials (DeVance Taliaferro & Ruggiano, 2010). These individuals can relay the information and the requests they receive from constituents and, in some cases, assist them in trying to persuade the lawmaker. They may also have positions of their own that differ from that of the lawmaker or can actively be looking for additional information to provide the decision maker.

Components of Successful Lobbying Visits

Lobbying often occurs during individual or group visits to the office of elected officials or government bureaucrats. Successful lobbying visits require scheduling an appointment in advance and careful research on the issue involved, the status of the legislation, and the decision maker's position on the issue (Richan, 2006). Making appointments is easier if a member of the lobbying team has a previous relationship with the public official or legislative aide. Once an appointment is scheduled, a letter or email should be sent by a team member to the official's office conveying a note of thanks for the opportunity to schedule the appointment (Richan, 2006). This also has the advantage of confirming the time and date of the lobbying visit.

Another preparatory measure is to plan for the meeting in advance and prepare an informal presentation to be given during the meeting (Hoefer, 2019). The presentation should include the same type of information given in a lobbying letter: factual information about the issue and the potential impact of the legislation, bill number and status of any pending legislation, and personal stories about how individuals will be impacted by the legislation. The group should also be prepared to make a specific request in reference to the legislation. The Autism Research Institute (2007) advises their members to prepare carefully for lobbying visits:

- Make sure that you have a least one request per lobbying visit and be able to communicate why it is important, using three key points. Limiting the message to three key points helps ensure that the members of the lobbying team stay focused on the issue.
- Decide in advance which member of the lobbying team will share a personal story about the issue. The story is important to make a persuasive case for the lobbying team's position on the issue, but should not dominate the time allotted for the visit.
- Practice the presentation, including the personal story and the request, prior to the visit.
- Bring printed material with information about the issue or proposed legislation with you to the visit.
- Document the visit. Delegate at least one member of the team to take notes that can be shared with other members of the organization or coalition. Also take pictures of the visit. Documentation can be shared with the press and the public. This also serves as a recruiting tool to inform prospective members or volunteers about the activities of the organization or coalition group.

Richan (2006) recommends two additional steps to take after the visit. The first involves group reflection. As with other types of reflection, points to consider are whether members of the lobbying team feel that the visit was successful, if the official actually made a commitment to the group or indicated how they would vote on the issue, and what aspects of the presentation and the overall visit were particularly effective (Avner, 2013). The second step should be to send a thank-you letter to the official. Such a letter should be sent regardless of the success of the visit; it opens up a pathway for establishing an ongoing relationship with the decision maker.

One other thing to be aware of in advance of the meetings includes the fact that lobbying visits are intended to be reciprocal. Lobbying visits are most successful when they provide public officials with information about an issue, particularly facts and figures that they can present and share during committee hearings, media interviews, and floor debates (Richan, 2006). However, as with public speaking and media relations, facts are only one component of building a persuasive argument. Respondents in the DeVance Taliaferro and Ruggiano (2010) study emphasized the importance of including agency clientele or people directly affected by an issue in lobbying visits. In addition to the presentation of factual information, in order to make a "persuasive case" to the lawmaker, it is critical that people directly affected by an issue be able to describe their experiences and how the proposed legislation may help or harm them. These personal stories can also be shared by the lawmaker when justifying support or opposition to a particular issue; by combining facts with emotion in order to frame issues, the public is more readily able to connect with the importance and real-life implications of the issue. In addition to providing information during the visit, contact information should be provided for follow-up and the lobbying organization should be responsive to further requests for information, public testimony, meetings, or other reasonable legislation-related requests from the lawmaker. Even when the outcome of the visit does not result in influencing the official's position on the issue, it may provide an opportunity to develop a relationship that can be used in the future for lobbying or in facilitating legislative compromises.

Public Testimony

Providing public testimony on a piece of legislation or a policy offers an important opportunity to engage in lobbying. Generally, in state legislatures and the U.S. Congress, opportunities to provide testimony take place during legislative committee hearings. Invitations to present testimony are most often extended by committee chairs, committee members, or legislative staff (Avner, 2013). As noted by Richan (2006), committee chairs and staff often have an agenda of their own when setting up a hearing. They may want to hear from people with a variety of viewpoints or simply want testimony that validates their own viewpoints. In addition, hearings may be held on controversial issues simply to give opponents the opportunity to state their views even though it may be unlikely that the final decision on the issue or legislation can be changed. Consequently, previous lobbying relationships often play a role in determining the individuals and groups that will be permitted to testify. Therefore, providing public testimony is not only an opportunity to give input on an issue; it also is one of the primary techniques used to establish "exchange" relationships with public officials.

The provision of testimony, as in other forms of lobbying, requires careful preparation. As described earlier in this chapter, background research on the issue, the decision-making process, and vested interests, values, voting records, and backgrounds of the decision makers should be examined prior to the hearing (Avner, 2013). A written copy of the testimony should be prepared in advance as well as any fact sheets that can be distributed to the decision makers and members of the audience. There also may be an opportunity to present the committee with a more detailed policy brief that describes policy alternatives, states the facts, and makes recommendations for action (Jansson, 2017). Visual presentations may also be used if permitted by the legislative body (Hoefer, 2019). The oral presentation should be practiced in advance. Testimony length is generally short, 10 minutes or less, unless otherwise specified (Jansson, 2017).

The lobbying team should choose an individual in advance to give the testimony, a constituency group member, an expert allied with the group, or the organizer may be called on to give the testimony. However, the most persuasive type of testimony is presented by people who have actually experienced the social issue, who are negatively affected by the previous policy, or who will benefit from new legislation (Haynes & Mickelson, 2010).

CASE VIGNETTE: PUBLIC TESTIMONY TO ADVOCATE FOR HOUSING EQUITY

A public housing resident and 2019 graduate of the Thrive in the 05 L.E.A.D. Academy (i.e., **l**ead, **e**mpower, **a**dvocate, and **d**ecide; the leadership training academy for neighborhood residents) was invited to testify before the U.S. House of Representative's Committee on Financial Services in the fall of 2021. The following excerpt is from the hearing transcript:

"My name is Michael Edmonds. I am a resident of public housing in Tucson, Arizona and I currently serve as the secretary of the Tucson House Resident Council where I live. I am begging on my behalf, and for those who are in similar situations as myself and my neighbors, that you provide all of the funding that is necessary towards housing in the Build Back Better Act. Housing is key to a better America. [...] After couch-surfing among bouts of homelessness for over a decade, I was offered the privilege to live in Tucson House in 2019. After moving in, I immediately began to investigate my options to get a job, return to college, begin a business, and get involved in my new community. After attending some meetings in my building, I was invited to more and other meetings throughout the community. I became actively involved in the "Thrive in the 05" initiative in my neighborhood, which is a community-driven collaboration that involves crime reduction, neighborhood improvements, and workforce and economic development, including a Choice Neighborhoods Planning and Action Grant from HUD focused on Tucson House. I was appointed Secretary of the Tucson House Resident Council, became a member of the Thrive in the 05 Steering Committee, volunteered as a Street Ambassador for the City's transportation department, and was appointed by Tucson's Mayor and Council to their Commission on Equitable Housing and Development, of which I am now the Vice Chair. When the COVID-19 pandemic began, my role in the Tucson House Resident Council changed because the primarily older and disabled residents were in need of daily assistance and attention, including food, personal care items, and other requests that were communicated to me.

My neighbors were suddenly isolated, scared, and extremely vulnerable to the disease. These requests from residents—varied and sometimes unique—have been ongoing. Myself and the rest of the Tucson House Resident Council began to coordinate weekly door-to-door food deliveries to residents. We helped pass out care packages of hygiene and personal care items and gave out books and puzzles to keep residents occupied in their apartments. We created a free thrift store in the building and helped new formerly homeless residents who arrived with nothing to furnish their apartments. I also provide tech support to many residents throughout the building who need help with their phones or computers so they can access services remotely and connect with loved ones. I host a monthly virtual Zoom show where residents can hear directly from City staff or other providers while we are still limiting in-person meetings. […] The stable housing that Tucson House provides has been life-changing for many residents during the pandemic, especially those who were formerly homeless like myself. However, the physical needs of our 70-year-old building have created additional stress and uncertainty for residents during this time. […] I urge you to fully fund the housing component of the Build Back Better Act so that myself and my neighbors can live in safe, high-quality housing that meets their needs. Thank you for this opportunity to testify today."

—M. Edmonds (October 21, 2021)

Testimony provided at hearing: A Strong Foundation: How Housing is the Key to Building Back a Better America. The transcript can be read in its entirety at the following link: https://docs.house.gov/meetings/BA/BA00/20211021/114160/HHRG-117-BA00-Wstate-EdmondsM-20211021.pdf

Public testimony generally includes the type of information provided in a written lobbying communication (such as a letter) or office visit: a brief analysis of the content and impact of the legislation that includes facts, figures, and a story about how the speaker or people one represents will be affected by the legislation. The Community Tool Box offers the following suggestions for the content of personal testimony at a public hearing:

- Open the presentation by giving your name and background information (such as your job, where you live, or why you should be considered to have expert knowledge or important information about the issue).
- Describe how the situation under discussion or the issue affects you or people you know or represent.
- Describe how the policy or legislation under discussion will positively or negatively affect you as well as the people whose interests you represent. Give examples.
- Ask a value question about the impact of the policy or legislation. Is it good or bad? Who will be positively or negatively affected by it? Who benefits? Who loses?
- Close by thanking the decision makers for the opportunity to speak to them (Work Group for Community Health and Development, 2022).

Most important, the testimony should contain a specific "ask" or request for the legislative body to take specific action on the legislation (Avner, 2013). The testimony should also be focused on making a persuasive case or argument that supports your request. If you cannot actively persuade the decision makers, good testimony can also result in positive media coverage and additional public support (Baumgartner et al., 2009; Richan, 2006).

In addition, the person providing the testimony should be prepared to answer questions from elected officials. In some cases, the testimony can be expected to be friendly (from lawmakers who are allies or prospective allies) or adversarial (from opponents). To some extent, potential questions can be identified in advance and responses prepared (Richan, 2006). Often it is helpful to have additional facts and figures ready that support your position.

Other Communication Techniques for Wrapping Up Support for Legislation

Getting successful votes to move legislation out of committee is only one stage of the process. Typically, bills are debated on the floor of the legislative house or other public decision-making body and there is a predefined process for voting. The final vote often requires a final push by the lobbying team. Avner (2013) recommends the following actions:

- Send a final reminder to legislators about your group's position on the issue. Emails or other communications with factual information are important. Last-minute phone calls can also be made.
- Try to obtain media support for the issue, with publication or broadcast just before the vote.
- Have members of your lobbying team with "expert" or personal knowledge of the issue on hand to advise legislative supporters during negotiations or prior to the vote.
- Mobilize supporters to be present in the legislative body on the day of the vote with matching t-shirts, buttons, or other forms of group identification and membership so that the legislators know you have strength in numbers.
- Consider sending emails or tweets to supporters or potential supporters just before the vote—you can simply ask for support or set up a brief, last-minute meeting.

THE RELATIONSHIP BETWEEN LEGISLATIVE AND POLITICAL CAMPAIGNS

Both legislative advocacy and political campaigning have been defined as components of political social work (Rocha et al., 2010). In actual practice, both of these activities are interrelated. In order to obtain legislation that meets certain needs or goals, office holders who will support specific legislative priorities must be elected. Involvement in political campaigns is one of the many ways to build a relationship with elected officials. Hence, relationship building is one of the primary ways in which these two types of social action, lobbying and political campaigns, are linked (Hoefer, 2001). However, there are a number of barriers that limit the involvement of organizers and social workers who are paid employees of public and nonprofit organizations in political campaigns.

Using Political Campaigns to Build Relationships With Legislators

Many of the techniques used in community organizing are similar to those used in political campaigns. Candidates and their campaign staff must "get to know" the community, build relationships with individuals and organizations, recruit volunteers and donors, often through tapping into existing social networks, and identify community challenges and solutions for alleviating them (Lane, 2011). However, political campaigns differ from other forms of organizing in terms of the almost exclusive emphasis on outcomes rather than process. Also, timelines for task accomplishment are shorter. There also is a greater need to develop resources, especially money and a reliance on recruiting and retaining volunteers for many of the basic tasks associated with campaigns: raising funds, contacting and scheduling volunteers, canvassing neighborhoods to identify potential voters and confirmed supporters, and monitoring electoral processes. Consequently, relationship building is central to successful campaign work. Often candidates and people seeking to influence the legislative process build up relationships over time that are used to recruit volunteers, voters, and donors for political campaigns (Kraft & Furlong, 2021; Schultz, 2003).

Building relationships is also a pragmatic approach for counteracting the often negative influence of campaign donations (DeVance Taliaferro & Ruggiano, 2010). Professional lobbyists often work for employers who make substantial campaign donations to candidates who can be expected to support their legislative priorities. Without monetary resources, organizers look for other opportunities to influence elected officials. Votes or the expectations that organization or community members will support one candidate over another are often influential in efforts to persuade public officials to take a stand on an issue. Sometimes it takes more than the expectation of votes to gain access to decision makers—it may require actual fundraising or donations to the candidate or engagement in campaign activities on the part of community members and organizers. Some organizers engage in both community and election work to achieve social change, serving as volunteers on election campaigns or moving between paid positions as community workers or campaign staff. Organizers may also seek election to political office. In addition to President Barack Obama, prominent former community organizers who moved on to election work include U.S. Senator Barbara Mikulski (D-MD); former civil rights movement leader, the late U.S. Representative John Lewis (D-GA); and the late U.S. Senator Paul Wellstone (Dreier, 2008; Wellstone, 2001).

Barriers to Legislative Advocacy and Political Involvement

Social workers are often encouraged to become involved in the political process. The NASW (2021) *Code of Ethics* is very explicit about a social worker's responsibility to engage in politics:

> *Social workers should engage in social and political action that seeks to ensure that all people have equal access to the resources, employment, services, and opportunities they require to meet their basic human needs and to develop fully. Social workers should be aware of the impact of the political arena on practice and should advocate for changes in policy and legislation to improve social conditions in order to meet basic human needs and promote social justice. (NASW, 2021, Section 6.04a)*

Despite this mandate, there are a number of impediments to the involvement of social workers and community organizers in campaigns as volunteers. Social workers may not receive sufficient education on legislative advocacy or knowledge of potential roles for social workers in political campaigns. In addition, there are legal restrictions on these activities for employees of public and nonprofit organizations (Rocha et al., 2010).

In terms of legislative advocacy, nonprofit organizations incorporated under 501(c)(3) of the Internal Revenue Code may only spend 20% of the first $500,000 of their annual budgets on all lobbying activities and smaller percentages of additional amounts of their annual budgets (up to $1,000,000 per year) for direct lobbying (Internal Revenue Service, 2021). Within these restrictions are some exempt activities such as lobbying to protect the funding that the agency receives from government sources, providing nonpartisan information about policy issues, responding to a legislative request for information, or providing public testimony. Other nonprofit organizations incorporated as advocacy organizations under 501(c)(4) of the IRS Code face no such restrictions (Kerlin & Reid, 2010). It should be noted that the difference between these two types of nonprofits is that contributors to 501(c)(3) organizations can receive tax deductions. Most 501(c)(3) organizations provide services although some may combine service delivery with advocacy activities consistent with the federal expenditure limits. However, donations to nonprofits incorporated as advocacy organizations are not tax deductible. In some cases, nonprofits may set up companion organizations that operate under the two different IRS designations, allowing them to undertake both types of activities (Rocha et al., 2010).

There are similar IRS restrictions on political activities. Nonprofit organizations incorporated under 501(c)(3) of the tax code may not be directly involved in political campaigns nor can employees of such organizations participate in election activities as part of their paid employment. In general, these organizations may not make campaign contributions (Internal Revenue Service, 2006). In addition to restrictions on organizations, the Federal Hatch Act prohibits government employees from engaging in political activities on the job, interfering with political campaigns, or soliciting donations from other government employees (United States Office of Special Council, 2011). This federal legislation also covers state and local government employees whose positions are paid using federal grants. State and local governments also have similar laws prohibiting political activities by their employees (Knapp & Diehm, 2009).

Opportunities for Legislative Work and Political Involvement

In addition to conducting legislative campaigns or lobbying on individual issues, social workers and community organizers may work for advocacy organizations or interest groups in which work responsibilities can include both lobbying and policy analysis. Social workers with organizing skills may also find employment as legislative aides, working directly with politicians in the development of legislation, and serving as staff members in local constituency offices. This type of employment involves casework on behalf of individuals seeking help in obtaining government services (Ortiz et al., 2004).

There are a number of opportunities for organizers and other social workers to be involved in political campaigns "off the job." In the United States, nonprofit organizations may conduct nonpartisan voter registration drives, provide voter information and education, or sponsor community forums (Internal Revenue Service, 2006; Jansson, 2017). In addition, social workers and organizers can make campaign donations or volunteer several hours per week on a campaign. Volunteer work on campaigns can range from stuffing envelopes and conducting one-on-one interviews, organizing house parties, or making phone calls; to recruiting volunteers, voters, or donors; to coordinating media opportunities and developing policy briefs or serving on the campaign's steering committee (Hardina, 2004; Haynes &

Mickelson, 2010). Volunteers can also serve as poll watchers (monitoring the election process) or election judges. Often, involvement of social workers in electoral politics is essential for obtaining policies and services for underserved, under-resourced, underrepresented, and minoritized groups of people. When people from a particular demographic group are considered likely to vote, they have a better chance of influencing legislation. However, there are numerous reasons why minoritized people or people living in poverty may not vote to the same degree as other citizens, including voter ID requirements and restrictive legislation making it difficult for former felons to register to vote. Consequently, ongoing advocacy efforts are needed to preserve and strengthen voting rights for the people typically served by members of the social work profession (Siegel, 2011).

Federal law permits interest groups to set up separate organizations called *political action committees* (*PACs*) to make donations (Kerlin & Reid, 2010). PACs solicit donations from their members and give these donations to candidates (Haynes & Mickelson, 2010). Multiple donations from individuals give the PACs that transfer these funds to candidates a certain degree of influence and increases the likelihood that they will have access to these decision makers if they are elected to office. The NASW has a PAC, the Political Action for Candidate Election (PACE). It raises money from social workers and endorses candidates who are assessed to be likely to support the profession of social work and issues of interest to social workers and the people they serve (NASW, n.d.).

In addition to campaign donations and endorsements, social workers can also manage political campaigns or run for political office (Jansson, 2017). According to the NASW, in 2021, five members of Congress were social workers: Senators Kyrsten Sinema (D-Arizona) and Debbie Stabenow (D-Michigan), and Representatives Karen Bass (D-California), Barbara Lee (D-California), and Sylvia Garcia (D-Texas). Social workers also hold state and local offices (Lane, 2011).

PUTTING VALUES INTO ACTION: CHANGING LAWS AND POLICIES TO PROMOTE SOCIAL JUSTICE

As noted in Chapter 1, all social workers, including community practitioners and community organizers, have an ethical obligation to fight for social justice (Reisch, 2011). Although the primary goal of community organizing is assisting minoritized and marginalized communities to obtain resources, respect, and basic human rights, community work in itself is often insufficient or inadequate to achieve social change goals. Consequently, changes in laws and policy must be made to address systemically entrenched biases, disparities, and injustices. In fact, much of community-organizing practice involves asking government decision makers to enforce existing laws or develop new ones in response to documentation of need or harm to individuals and families. For example, tenants' rights organizers often put pressure on city governments to enforce building codes when they find that people are living in rented dwellings that are unheated, without water, or otherwise unsafe. Organizers who document that little in the way of affordable housing is available for people in poverty may seek a legislative solution when they find out that state governments can pass legislation and take action to make sure that federal funds for affordable housing can be allocated for use in their community.

Such conditions require both legislative advocacy and political skills for effective community practice. As in other types of organizing, action plans must be developed and community members included in designing the plan and carrying it out (Avner, 2013). Chu and colleagues (2009) emphasize that more than simply a commitment on the part of social workers is necessary to achieve social change:

> *Important as social justice is to the core purposes of social work, its pursuit would be incomplete without a concomitant commitment to the enhancement of people's well-being and problem-solving capacities. The quest for social justice must be undertaken hand in hand with the quest for individual well-being, societal harmony and mutual respect. (p. 288)*

Consequently, community members must be fully involved in the preparation of legislative campaigns. Steps in campaign-related action plans that integrate group dialogue and reflection techniques can be summarized in the following way:

- Organize a lobbying team consisting of community members, people with experiential or expert knowledge about the issue, and individuals and groups who have contacts or relationships with lawmakers or their staff members.
- Join or form a coalition to increase the lobbying group's strength in numbers.
- Find a "window of opportunity" to introduce legislation, connecting your goal to an issue in the news or proposal from another organization or group.
- Establish policy goals. If drafting a policy proposal, incorporate both policy goals and values into the title of the proposed legislation. Make sure that you understand alternative options for addressing the issue and know the pros and cons of these approaches.
- Specify a legislative proposal's content and find legislative sponsors.
- Conduct an assessment of your coalition's power resources and sources of influence possessed by likely allies and opponents. Be ready to counter the power and influence of opposition groups.
- Use group processes to engage constituency group members in the development of a strategy for the campaign and tactical methods.
- Assign tasks to constituency group members. Identify people who can provide public testimony or who can recruit others for participation in grassroots lobbying. Provide training or coaching sessions as needed.
- Implement the campaign, using tactics in a logical order consistent with the timing and requirements of the legislative process.
- Provide information to the media and use press contacts to disseminate your message and relevant facts about the legislation that you propose.
- Urge the public to take action (call, write, or meet with legislators).
- Set up a mechanism for group dialogue and reflection in order to make situational adjustments in the campaign and evaluate the outcome.
- Work for goal attainment, but be ready to compromise on the final version of the legislation. Always have a fallback position or a "plan B."
- Be ready to try again if the desired outcome does not work. Consider using the political process to influence legislative decision-making, endorsing a candidate, making donations, conducting voter registration drives, or working on an election campaign (Hardina, 2002; Haynes & Mickelson, 2010; Jansson, 2017; Richan, 2006; Schultz, 2003; Box 11.2).

> **Box 11.2**
>
> **LEGISLATIVE CAMPAIGN: THE CASE OF THE MEAT-RENDERING PLANT**
>
> *Alicia Martinez and members of the Westside Organization plan their legislative campaign to shut down the meat-rendering plant. They identified a number of components of their campaign:*
>
> **Goal:** Shut down the meat-rendering plant.
>
> **Background Research:** Alicia describes the process for decision-making in the city council. To submit legislation, a city council person must agree to sponsor it. It also helps if the sponsor can solicit support among the other six members of the council. Currently, only three members seem to be concerned about environmental issues, three consider themselves to be pro-development, and at least one member is considered to be a swing voter. It is also important to have the city council member from the district most affected by the legislation be the sponsor. In this case, it is Council Member Gonzalez. Two members of the constituency group know Council Member Gonzalez personally. Mx. Brown worked on their campaign and Mx. Andrew's son is on the same high school baseball team as Council Member Gonzalez's son, Mateo. Other key information about council members is that at least one member of the council, Council Member Thomas, is a business associate of the owner of the meat-rendering plant. For additional information about their legal rights, the group meets with a local attorney who suggests contacting the Environmental Protection Agency (EPA) to report pollution if city council action fails or suing the city. Alicia also informs the group that they have received calls from other local and statewide coalition groups that are willing to lend support to the cause.
>
> **Strategy:** Social Action
>
> **Tactics:** Establish a coalition of organizations to lobby city hall. Solicit support from Council Member Gonzalez; schedule lobbying visits with other city council members (both potential allies and opponents); ask coalition members to send letters and make calls to members of the city council; take local reporters on a pollution "tour" of the neighborhood near the meat-rendering plant; prepare fact sheets about environmental racism and the effects of asthma on children; and stage a press conference and rally on the day of the city council vote. Group members also plan to "pack" the council chamber with supporters in matching "Shut it Down" t-shirts on the day of the city council vote.
>
> **Plan B:** Take legal action or make a formal complaint to the EPA.

An example of a national campaign that applied most of these techniques involved efforts, sponsored by a variety of immigration, student, community, and religious groups, was the Dream Act campaign of 2010. The Dream Act offers a path to citizenship for undocumented children of immigrants if they complete military service or college (United States Student Association, 2009). Supporters formed a broad-based coalition and recruited supporters via the news media, YouTube, and the internet. They further publicized the issue through rallies, media interviews, marches, and acts of civil disobedience such as hunger strikes and sit-ins (Brumback, 2011; Hoggard, 2010). Media attention was also brought to the issue when numerous participants in the campaign came out or were exposed by others as undocumented (Marcum, 2010). The campaign also involved a broad-based grassroots lobbying effort and visits to members of Congress. A *Dream Act Lobbying Kit* that included sample letters to elected officials and flyers were made available to supporters via the internet (United States Student Association, 2009). Although the 2010 Dream Act campaign was not successful, supporters and their allies continue to work diligently to pass the Dream Act.

END-OF-CHAPTER RESOURCES

KEY TAKEAWAYS AND SUMMARY

Legislative campaigns are similar to other types of action campaigns, but they focus on lobbying government officials to take specific types of action. Lobbying may be carried out as part of a larger campaign to achieve a goal for which there must be a change in legislation. As an alternative, a legislative campaign can simply focus on the passage of a bill, amend proposed legislation, or block a bill. In order to effectively carry out a legislative campaign, advocates must be knowledgeable about the content of legislation, the structure of the legislative decision-making process, and the vested interests and backgrounds of the government officials who must be influenced to make the decisions. In addition to research, members of the lobbying team must use a variety of interpersonal skills to influence lawmakers. Lobbyists send letters, make phone calls, and use electronic communications to influence decision makers. They also meet with public officials and provide testimony at public hearings. The community organizer's role in the process includes the provision of information and training to constituency group members and relationship building with public officials and their staff that can be used to facilitate the lobbying process. In some cases, both constituents and organizers may participate in election campaigns in order to elect potential allies to office and build working relationships with them. In both legislative and political campaign work, building strong relationships with participants and decision makers is essential. In Chapter 12, another intervention method that requires strong social work skills, community development, is described.

RESOURCES

- Our stories have power: A storybanking guide by Community Catalyst: https://www.communitycatalyst.org/resources/tools/storybanking-toolkit
- University at Buffalo School of Social Work (Host). (2021, October 20). "Voting Is Social Work" featuring Madeline Pérez De Jesús and Cindy Dubuque-Gallo [Audio podcast episode]. In *inSocialWork*. https://www.insocialwork.org/voting-is-social-work

ACTIVITIES

1. With your classmates, debate the following questions about the legislative action plan presented in Box 11.2:
   a. Is a lobbying campaign an appropriate mechanism for addressing this social problem?
   b. Should other methods be used prior to using this method? What are they? What factors should determine the use of a specific strategic approach?
   c. What power resources are held by the members of the lobbying team?
   d. What power resources are likely to be held by opponents?

e. Should background research be primarily focused on Council Member Gonzalez? What other information is needed about power resources and vested interests of likely opponents? Is information that indicates that Council Member Thomas is a business associate of the owner of the meat-rendering plant sufficient to identify a possible conflict of interest? Why or why not?

f. In what circumstances, if any, is it appropriate to use the threat of legal remedies in the lobbying process?

ASSIGNMENTS

1. Engage in at least two of the following activities and present an oral report to your classmates on your experiences.
   a. Write a letter or send an email to a legislator about an issue of concern to you.
   b. Participate in a lobbying visit with a group. Observe the process and participate in the presentation or dialogue with the legislator or legislative staff.
   c. Attend a legislative hearing and observe the process: the role of the chair, the roles of additional committee members, the types of questions asked of the people providing testimony, the content of and the values expressed in the testimony, and the positions or groups represented in the presentation of oral testimony.
   d. Observe a strategy session of a political campaign, attend a poll worker training session, or volunteer for a campaign activity such as precinct walking or making phone calls to prospective voters.
2. Write and present testimony on an issue of concern to you in class. The testimony should contain facts, a personal story, and an "ask." Make sure that the content of the testimony is accessible to your audience (your classmates). Make sure your argument is persuasive.
3. Interview an elected official or a legislative staff member. Focus the interview on the official's perception of the effectiveness of various lobbying methods and the degree to which decision makers can be influenced by these various approaches.
4. With constituency group members, design a legislative campaign that focuses on a specific issue, contains a goal, identifies specific values that should be incorporated into the legislation, and outlines a specific strategic approach and tactical options. Use the action plan chart in Chapter 8 to plan your campaign.
5. Conduct background research on a legislator to identify their vested interest in and likely position on a specific issue. Use public records, internet databases, and personal interviews to document this information.

A robust set of instructor resources designed to supplement this text is located at http://connect.springerpub.com/content/book/978-0-8261-5835-2. Qualifying instructors may request access by emailing textbook@springerpub.com.

KEY REFERENCES

Only key references appear in the print edition. The full reference list appears in the digital product on Springer Publishing Connect: connect.springerpub.com/content/book/978-0-8261-5835-2/part/part04/chapter/ch11

Brown, M. E., Livermore, M., & Ball, A. (2015). Social work advocacy: Professional self-interest and social justice. *Journal of Sociology and Social Welfare, 42*, 45–63.

Chu, W., Tsui, M., & Yan, M. (2009). Social work as a moral and political practice. *International Social Work, 52*, 287–298. https://doi.org/10.1177/0020872808102064

Hardina, D. (2004). What social workers need to know about the right to vote. *Social Policy Journal, 2*(4), 53–70. https://doi.org/10.1300/J185v02n04_05

Hardina, D. (2005). Using the web to teach power analysis: Identifying campaign donors and elites. *Social Policy Journal, 4*(2), 51–68. https://doi.org/10.1300/J185v04n02_05

Hoefer, R. (2001). Highly effective human services interest groups: Seven key practices. *Journal of Community Practice, 9*(2), 1–14. https://doi.org/10.1300/J125v09n02_01

Jackson-Elmore, C. (2005). Informing state policymakers: Opportunities for social workers. *Social Work, 50*, 251–261. https://doi.org/10.1093/sw/50.3.251

Lane, S. (2011). Political content in social work education as reported by elected social workers. *Journal of Social Work Education, 47*, 53–72. https://doi.org/10.2307/23044434

National Association of Social Workers. (n.d.). *PACE: Building political power for social workers.* https://www.socialworkers.org/advocacy/pace

Rocha, C., Poe, B., & Thomas, V. (2010). Political activities of social workers: Addressing perceived barriers to political participation. *Social Work, 55*(4), 317–325. https://doi.org/10.1093/sw/55.4.317

Wise, K. (2007). Lobbying and relationship management: The K Street connection. *Journal of Public Relations Research, 19*(4), 357–376. https://doi.org/10.1080/10627260701402457

SOCIAL WORK SKILLS FOR COMMUNITY BUILDING

LEARNING OBJECTIVES

After reading this chapter, students will be able to:

- Contrast the concepts of community building, asset building, capacity development, and social capital development.
- Recognize the major social work skills required for a community practitioner to be effective in community-building efforts.
- Discuss the role of social networks in community building.
- Describe the consensus-organizing approach.

INTRODUCTION

One of the traditional goals of community-organizing work has been to build a sense of community or belonging among people living in the same location or among individuals experiencing similar social problems or issues. *Community building* involves efforts to increase social capital, civic engagement, and improve neighborhood capacity to foster and strengthen healthy communities. In this chapter, theoretical perspectives on community building, social capital development, and capacity building are examined. Although some of these concepts have been previously discussed in this textbook, this chapter defines community and economic development and examines models that can be used to increase community connections: community building, asset development, social capital approaches, capacity building, and consensus organizing. Specific types of social work skills used for the community-building process are also described: building strong relationships, strengthening social networks, strengthening relationships between people and organizations, and strengthening participant or stakeholder engagement and commitment to community-building efforts. In the last section of this chapter, the application of these techniques to principles associated with the strengths perspective in social work practice is examined.

THEORETICAL PERSPECTIVES ON COMMUNITY DEVELOPMENT: COMMUNITY BUILDING, SOCIAL CAPITAL DEVELOPMENT, ASSET BUILDING, AND CAPACITY DEVELOPMENT

Biddle and Biddle (1979) describe *community development* as a process of social change that is based on the premise that all people have good intentions and will act collectively to make their communities better, acting not merely based on self-interest but also for the common good. As with other types of community practice, this method contains a combination of process and task goals. Vidal and Keating (2004) describe community development as "a place-based approach; it concentrates on creating assets that benefit people in poor neighborhoods, largely by building and tapping links to external resources" (p. 126). Essentially, community development is viewed as using collaboration and consensus-oriented methods to improve the collective well-being of community residents. However, what is often debated is the best process to use to accomplish these goals (Stoecker, 2004).

In addition to asset development, the concept of building community is often explicitly used as a rationale for community development practice. It is based on an assumption, articulated in the social capital literature, that in many neighborhoods, people (particularly in urban areas) have few connections with one another and, as a result, are limited in their ability to address neighborhood conditions such as crime, substance abuse, substandard housing quality, and lack of access to nutritious food (Fraser & Kick, 2005; James et al., 2001; Theall et al., 2009). Consequently, neighborhood residents without sufficient social support may also experience poor health, hunger, houselessness, lack skills and training for jobs that pay more than the minimum wage, and be less likely to have completed high school (Fertig & Reingold, 2008; Ohmer, 2010; Petersen, 2002; Small & Newman, 2001). This lack of personal relationships is also viewed as interrelated with the concept of *sense of community* and experiences of personal and political empowerment (Hughey et al., 2008; Peterson et al., 2008). As noted earlier in this book, in addition to identification with a specific community, other aspects of sense of community include perceptions of emotional safety or security, feeling as if one has a personal stake in what happens within the community, and the recognition by community members of markers or indicators that tell others who belongs in the community—such as common traditions or values, the use of formal or informal language, clothing, and geographic boundaries (Cnaan & Rothman, 2008). Sharing an emotional connection to one's community with others and believing that the individual can influence what happens in the community, that collective action is possible, and that individual needs can be met are also indicators of a sense of community (Nowell & Boyd, 2010). The degree of individual participation in community decision-making is often used to determine whether people feel a sense of belonging, commitment, or responsibility to one's community or their neighbors. As noted previously in this textbook, strong empirical evidence suggests that sense of community and citizen participation increase experiences of personal and collective self-efficacy (Itzhaky & York, 2002; Ohmer, 2010).

Given Putnam's (2000) research on civic engagement and other empirical literature (Figueira-McDonough, 1991; Sampson et al., 2002; Small, 2007; Wilson, 1996), which seems to indicate that under-resourced, marginalized, and minoritized communities are characterized by experiences of isolation and low levels of participation in social networks, community development has focused on community building and increasing the capacity of community residents to improve conditions in their own neighborhoods (Kay, 2006). Chaskin (2001) defines *community capacity* as the:

> *Interaction of human, organizational, and social capital existing within a given community that can be leveraged to solve collective problems and improve or maintain the well-being of a given community. It may operate through informal social processes and/ or organized effort. (p. 295)*

Cnaan and Rothman (2008) describe *capacity building* as a method of community development that encourages neighborhood self-help efforts, responsible leadership, and a commitment to civic engagement. Other goals they identify include promoting social change with minimal conflict and stimulating economic growth. Including local residents in the development process through consensus-oriented decision-making is also an important goal of this process. According to Saegert (2006), other activities associated with this approach include increasing the organizing skills of participants, assisting residents in identifying common goals and taking action on those goals, sustaining resident involvement in change efforts, and increasing the ability of local organizations to engage in social change. Often these activities are facilitated through intermediary organizations that provide resources, training, and technical assistance and serve as connectors—linking community groups to institutions and government organizations outside of the neighborhood (Vidal & Keating, 2004).

Delgado (2000) developed a neighborhood-initiated approach to capacity building that focuses on the resources and talents of neighborhood residents. They call this approach *capacity enhancement* rather than capacity development because:

> *It fundamentally implies that there is a resource-asset in place and that all one needs to do is foster its growth. To use the metaphor of a seed, after a seed is planted, all it needs is water and sunshine. With development, the assumption is that there is no resource and, as a consequence, the practitioner must create it through some form of active intervention. (pp. 9–10)*

Delgado argues that a focus on capacity enhancement is critical because little in the way of community practice models address community building from a strengths perspective rather than a deficit model, especially when applied to communities of color.

A focus on building on existing neighborhood strengths is also evident in Kretzmann and McKnight's (1993) asset-based approach. Asset building as a community-organizing model was developed in part due to John McKnight's strong assertion, as expressed in their book, *The Careless Society* (1995), that the provision of social services can foster the dependence on service provision of people experiencing poverty and may actually harm individuals rather than help them. They argue that instead of services, community change should focus on the rights of individuals to have jobs, live in healthy neighborhoods, and be free of racism and other oppressive practices. Community development should "increase interdependence in community life through a focus on the gifts and capabilities of people who have been excluded" (McKnight, 1995, p. 132).

According to Oliver (2001), asset and social capital approaches are preferable to deficit-based approaches that view people in poverty as captive to social and economic forces and incapable of taking action to improve their communities. They argue that communities already possess numerous assets that can be used for community improvements, and define an *asset* as:

> *A special kind of resource that an individual, organization or entire community can use to reduce or prevent poverty and injustice. An asset is usually a "stock" that can be drawn upon, built upon, or developed, as well as a resource that can be shared or transferred across generations. (p. xii)*

Asset building has an explicit link to the philosophy associated with social capital development. As noted in Chapter 6, Putnam (2000) described two types of social capital. *Bonding social capital* consists of relationships among individuals that originate within social networks and are characterized by reciprocity and trust. Members of these networks have similar values. Consequently, a strong network may facilitate social control by bringing order and stability to a community. *Bridging social capital* consists of relationships that are developed among members of different networks and demographic groups. To this typology, Woolcock (1998) added a third type, *linking social capital*, which involves relationships between local networks and institutions, including organizations located outside the community. Social capital theory in community development is based on the assumption that local networks can use these linkages to effectively leverage assets from outside the community to achieve community-building goals.

The community development perspective on social capital often draws on the sociology literature on this topic that predates Putnam's *Bowling Alone* (Aguilar & Sen, 2009; Frisch & Servon, 2006; Kay, 2006; Saegert, 2006; Theall et al., 2009). Bourdieu (1986) and Coleman (1990) both used the term *social capital* to describe how communities function. Bourdieu (1986) described social capital as consisting of actual or potential resources held collectively by groups or social networks that are generated through exchange-related relationships that could be material or symbolic, such as feelings of obligation. Such networks can be used to develop connections with others to advance an individual's or a group's interests and political power. They viewed social capital as something that could be exchanged with or used to generate other forms of capital, including cultural, physical, and economic resources. By cultural resources, they meant expectations about how people should act in society rather than the values associated with specific subcultures or ethnic groups. Coleman (1990) focused on the individual's role in developing resources that can be used for individual and community improvements. They argued that social capital is produced when individuals use their skills and capabilities to exchange resources with others. Both social capital and building trust among social networks or community members are essential for accomplishing collective goals, disseminating information, and obtaining external resources for the community.

Warren and colleagues (2001) define *assets* as a type of social capital found in collaborative relationships and nurtured through trust-building among individuals and groups. Drawing on Kretzmann and McKnight's (1993) definition of *asset building*, they assert that the purpose of social capital development in under-resourced communities is to obtain investments from sources outside the community, such as education and training, in order to improve the financial condition of families. As noted by Putnam (2000), social capital is only one form of capital available to community residents. Other types of community capital include *human capital* (jobs and job training), *built* or *physical capital* (housing and infrastructure), *financial capital* (money and the availability of loans and credit), *natural* or *environmental capital* (land use), *political capital* (decision-making and political power), and *cultural capital* (Flora & Flora, 2008; J. Green & Haines, 2016; Light, 2004; Silverman, 2004). *Cultural capital* is often broadly defined, especially when applied to communities of color, focusing on the strengths, values, and traditions of ethnic or other historically excluded demographic groups (Delgado, 2000). According to the community capitals framework, healthy, vibrant communities possess strengths of resources in all seven types of community capital (Emery & Flora, 2006).

In all of these approaches—community building, capacity building, asset development, and social capital formation—common threads include three primary approaches for bringing people together: increasing the strength of community networks, especially in terms of resource exchange and interpersonal relationship development; forming or increasing membership in local community organizations and associations; and increasing linkages between local groups and external organizations (Kay, 2006; McKnight, 1995; Schneider, 2007). Such linkages are used to increase neighborhood access to community capitals and technical assistance that can be used for community improvements. These assumptions are based on a belief that neighborhood residents in under-resourced communities are not only isolated from one another, but are also relatively isolated from the greater society and therefore have difficulty obtaining financial capital.

The literature on these interrelated theories that guides community development also identifies both advantages and disadvantages of each approach. Warren and colleagues (2001) argue that although political oppression and social exclusion are legitimate concerns that contribute to the lack of social connection in many communities, the difference between this approach and deficit-based models is that it is based on the belief that through the collective action of community residents, partnerships can be forged with government agencies and other investors that can be used effectively for community improvement. However, Fraser and Kick (2005) identify a dilemma in the use of this approach; this model places responsibility for community improvements on individuals and families who historically have been excluded from the political process and the market system. Their review of case studies related to community building indicates that often such efforts are either initiated or dominated by government agencies and private enterprises, but can be successful if governance systems are established that do not engage in a top-down or "prescriptive" approach, ensuring a balance of power as well as shared responsibility among participants, including residents.

According to James and colleagues (2001), viewing communities purely in terms of their social capital can be problematic. Communities may contain strong networks that lack some characteristics other than bonds among members such as political power. In addition, some groups of people in these communities may be, due to social stigma or other reasons (e.g., people who are houseless or engaged in sex work), excluded from these networks. We also know very little about how people view their participation in networks and what membership actual means to them. For example, DeFilippis (2001) argues that although people in poverty lack economic capital, they are not necessarily lacking in social capital as defined by Putnam (2000; i.e., interpersonal relationships, social networks, and trust); they merely lack the ability, in some circumstances, to leverage social capital to obtain financial rewards.

Stoecker (2004) expresses concern that aspects of asset-based and social capital approaches focus on self-reliance and place the blame squarely on the backs of disadvantaged groups if they fail to generate the assets needed to improve their communities or find jobs.

TRAUMA-INFORMED AND RESILIENCY-FOCUSED COMMUNITY AND ECONOMIC DEVELOPMENT APPROACHES

Community and economic development efforts often focus on a few specific activities designed to improve community relations: the financial well-being of community residents; improvements in housing stocks and affordable housing; job creation and training; strengthening community business and industries; and increasing the availability of credit, mortgages, and investment opportunities (Gittell & Thompson, 2001; Krumholz et al., 2006; Littrell & Brooks, 2010). Development and reinvestment programs may be state or federally funded, with funds distributed by state and local governments and operated through local governments or community organizations. Intermediary organizations, such the Local Initiative Support Corporation and the National Reinvestment Corporation, are often established in some cities and regions to link local community development organizations with a variety of partner organizations, potential funding sources, and private investors (Garkovich, 2011; Gittell & Vidal, 1998). These nonprofit organizations also provide technical and administrative assistance to local development projects. As noted in Chapter 10, inspired by the research literature that links poor health outcomes to specific neighborhoods, there are also specific foundation or government-funded community change initiatives (CCIs) that focus on improving the quality of life of families and communities in specific "place-based" areas (Coulton et al., 2011; Petersen, 2002).

Community development efforts may also focus on smaller scale changes such as initiating health-promotion and prevention activities, improving neighborhood safety, engaging residents in physical activity, improving recreational facilities, increasing access to nutritious food, encouraging families to accumulate savings; building worker cooperatives, providing financial counseling to families, increasing educational attainment or opportunities, or negotiating community benefit agreements with developers in return for tangible benefits such as jobs or housing (Birkenmaier & Curley, 2009; Majee & Hoyt, 2009; Ohmer et al., 2009; Parks & Warren, 2009; Shobe & Boyd, 2005; Subban, 2007).

Recently, community development efforts have also included initiatives designed to include principles related to *sustainability* in development efforts (Portney, 2005). *Sustainability* is a concept that incorporates a set of principles about how communities should utilize available resources in planning and development efforts. These principles are based on the recognition that many natural resources such as oil, coal, or clean air and water, may soon be depleted and that concrete steps should be taken to limit their use or to develop new technologies as alternatives to their use. According to Hembd and Silberstein (2011), sustainability practice focuses on what communities explicitly need rather than want. Current needs are to be met in a manner that does not compromise the use of these resources by future generations. Sustainability practice places priority on distributing scarce resources to members of under-resourced, minoritized, and marginalized communities. It also recognizes the interconnections among the health, well-being, skills, and capabilities of individuals and the natural environment, physical capital such as housing, roads, public transportation, buildings, and the global economy. Sustainable development practices often incorporate environmental concerns, green technology, and characteristics designed to promote healthy living such as bicycle paths and programs intended to decrease the use of pesticides and other pollutants (Portney, 2005).

Although much community development work is facilitated through government agencies, resident-controlled community development corporations (CDCs) also play a role. Many of these organizations coordinate their efforts with federal programs, state and local redevelopment agencies, and other community-based organizations (Frisch & Servon, 2006). However, researchers such as Silverman (2003, 2009) have examined decision-making in CDCs and found that legal, jurisdictional, and cooperative relationships with local and state governments often limit the power of local residents to make decisions for their own communities. In addition, the composition of CDC boards often is not representative of community residents in terms of race and ethnicity, gender identity, and socioeconomic status. Research indicates that participants in community development efforts often have difficulty agreeing on goals due to different perceptions of self-interest influenced by racial identity, ethnicity, and socioeconomic status; LGBTQIA+, women, people of color, and members of other minoritized and marginalized groups may also encounter barriers to asset acquisition related to sexism, racism, and classism, when trying to acquire resources from government agencies, banks, and other private investors and foundations (Gittell & Thompson, 2001; Moore, 2005).

Consequently, concerns about the degree to which CDC and other community development organization boards represent the interests of community members have resulted in increased effort by organization directors and funders to increase community participation (Dorius, 2009). According to Midgley (2005):

Effective community development involves the creation of an authentic partnership between government and local people and the judicious use of the market to promote sustainable growth. Too often, traditional community development has involved a prescriptive, bureaucratic "top down" process that has stifled local initiative. Community development must institutionalize pluralism and recognize the right of local people to manage their own affairs. (p. 164)

Several specific models of community development practice have been developed to facilitate equitable partnerships among community members, government agencies, business interests, and private investors. These models include practice modules consistent with consensus organizing, asset building, social capital maximization, capacity development or enhancement, and community-building approaches. Saegert (2006) argues that these approaches and traditional types of social action organizing have similar goals: problem resolution, developing common social change objectives, leadership development, and fostering participant commitment to the change effort. However, Saegert differentiates between both types of community-organization models. Although social action organizing focuses on power and resource differentials, community builders "seek to nurture a broad range of overlapping social networks within which different combinations of individuals and organizations can reach a consensus about the achievement of particular goals" (Saegert, 2006, p. 279).

More recently, social workers and other community practitioners are embracing trauma-informed and resilience-building frameworks for community-building initiatives. *Trauma-informed community development* focused on promoting resilience in communities as a means for achieving positive, sustainable social change (Neighborhood Resilience Project, 2022). Trauma-informed community development recognizes that members of communities living in places where there is concentrated poverty often experience toxic stress from exposure to violence, structural racism, and other daily stressors rooted in living in poverty, as well as isolation and disenfranchisement (Falkenburger et al., 2018). Members of these communities have often experienced historical trauma, such as negative experiences with local government or other outsiders making promises for community improvements and positive changes that never materialize, and these false promises and the lasting effects of oppression and disinvestment in what were most often once-vibrant communities leave residents feeling hopeless that change is ever going to happen.

Community organizers and practitioners cannot expect a community-building initiative to be successful, sustainable, or meaningful to a community without acknowledging this collective "community trauma" and supporting the healing of the community. According to Falkenburger and colleagues (2018, p. 2), "outlets for community members to express their collective trauma, efforts to reframe community narratives, peer support networks, and investment in community health and well-being are opportunities for healing from trauma." Cultivating community supports; promoting healing, resilience, and well-being; and providing avenues for leadership development and training to foster or bolster the development of residents as their own agents of community change are all strategies of trauma-informed community development models (Neighborhood Resilience Project, 2022). The trauma-informed community development model embraces the idea that community leadership is essential in planning, designing, and implementing community-building change strategies, that power by those traditionally holding power (e.g., local government, developers, researchers) must be shared with community members, and that community members need to be supported in leadership and decision-making roles (Falkenburger et al., 2018). The trauma-informed community development model is closely aligned with participatory action research in that they both value the principle of shared expertise, recognizing residents as experts with the ability to accomplish their goals through community change strategies, and view the social work community practitioner, organizer, or researcher role as one to provide connections, coaching, training, and support as needed to co-create positive community change.

Falkenburger and colleagues (2018) lay out the principles, strategies, and practices of the Trauma-Informed Community Building and Engagement Model (Table 12.1). This model acknowledges community-level trauma and provides a guide for trauma-informed approaches for working with residents of marginalized communities.

COMMUNITY DEVELOPMENT PRACTICE AND ENVIRONMENTAL JUSTICE FOR SOCIAL WORK

An important consideration for community practitioners in community-building initiatives is the connection between community development and environmental justice. Many minoritized and marginalized communities that have a high concentration of people living in poverty, when compared to the general population, disproportionately experience the detrimental impacts on health and well-being of exposure to environmental hazards

TABLE 12.1 Principles, Strategies, and Practices of the Trauma-Informed Community Building and Engagement Model

PRINCIPLES	STRATEGIES	PRACTICES
• Structural frame/social justice • Do no harm • Acceptance • Community power • Sustainability	• Community-driven research toward community organizing and policy change • Peer-to-peer approaches • Creative/personal expression and placemaking • Grief work, emotional support and restorative justice	• Acknowledge harm done and promote consciousness. • Honor history and celebrate culture. • Never overpromise. • Make community growth and accomplishments visible. • Ensure consistency. • Support meaningful community engagement structures. • Promote safety. • Remove participation barriers. • Provide compensation. • Foster social cohesion. • Engage in reflective process.

SOURCE: Adapted from Falkenburger, E., Arena, O., & Wolin, J. (2018). *Trauma-informed community building and engagement.* Urban Institute. https://www.urban.org/sites/default/files/publication/98296/trauma-informed_community_building_and_engagement_0.pdf.

(e.g., air pollution, exposure to toxic waste, brownfields, urban heat islands, occupational environmental hazards; Gochfeld & Burger, 2011). For example, *brownfields* were the result of industrialization; they refer to areas where factories, landfills, or refineries operated near poorer, urban neighborhoods and caused a great deal of pollution. Environmental justice involves advocating for improved conditions to protect minoritized communities and community members from environmental hazards (Dewane, 2017).

In recent decades there has been a rising movement in social work to "green social work." The Council on Social Work Education (CSWE) Committee on Environmental Justice defines *environmental justice* as:

> *Environmental justice occurs when all people equally experience high levels of environmental protection and no group or community is excluded from the environmental policy decision-making process, nor is affected by a disproportionate impact from environmental hazards. Environmental justice affirms the ecological unity and the interdependence of all species, respect for cultural and biological diversity, and the right to be free from ecological destruction. This includes responsible use of ecological resources, including the land, water, air, and food.* (CSWE, 2019, para. 3)

Community organizers and practitioners play an important role in advocating for and facilitating efforts to promote environmental justice for vulnerable communities (Jackson, 2017; Kirshenbaum, 2018). Environmental justice should be a fundamental consideration in place-based community development initiatives. Using a trauma-informed community development lens, community organizers and practitioners can serve as advocates for environmental justice while working in partnership with vulnerable communities to address the detrimental, historical impacts of environmental injustices. Community practitioners are especially well suited to advocate for environmental justice by convening cross-sector partners and members of communities harmed by environmental hazards to pursue sustainable development practices.

CASE VIGNETTE: SOCIAL WORK AND ENVIRONMENTAL JUSTICE

In the spring of 2018, a partnership was established between a school of social work and a school of planning and landscape architecture in the Southwestern United States. The social work faculty members were working on a broader community development effort to holistically address resident health and well-being and sought additional expertise on the environmental justice work via the school of planning and landscape architecture. Together, faculty, students, and community partners embarked on a community development initiative focused on environmental justice in an under-resourced neighborhood that was at risk of becoming an "urban heat island" (i.e., an area within a city that is substantially warmer than nearby rural areas due to population density, a lack of natural groundcover and vegetation, and city surfaces that trap and retain heat; U.S. Environmental Protection Agency, 2019). The collaboration resulted in community listening sessions, windshield surveys, and environmental assessments to research the environmental issues and develop solutions. A noteworthy outcome of the collaboration was a student-led project that secured grant funding to redevelop a local park and green space by the local elementary school. The project goals were to preserve and improve the environment, to conserve energy and natural resources, to promote recreation and walkability, to enhance quality of life and neighborhood sense of place, and to mitigate the effects of the urban heat island. Environmental improvements across the two locations included stormwater harvesting basins to preserve rainwater, the creation of a bird habitat, tree planting to increase the shade canopy, the installation of an improved walking path, and a community art mural (Figure 12.1).

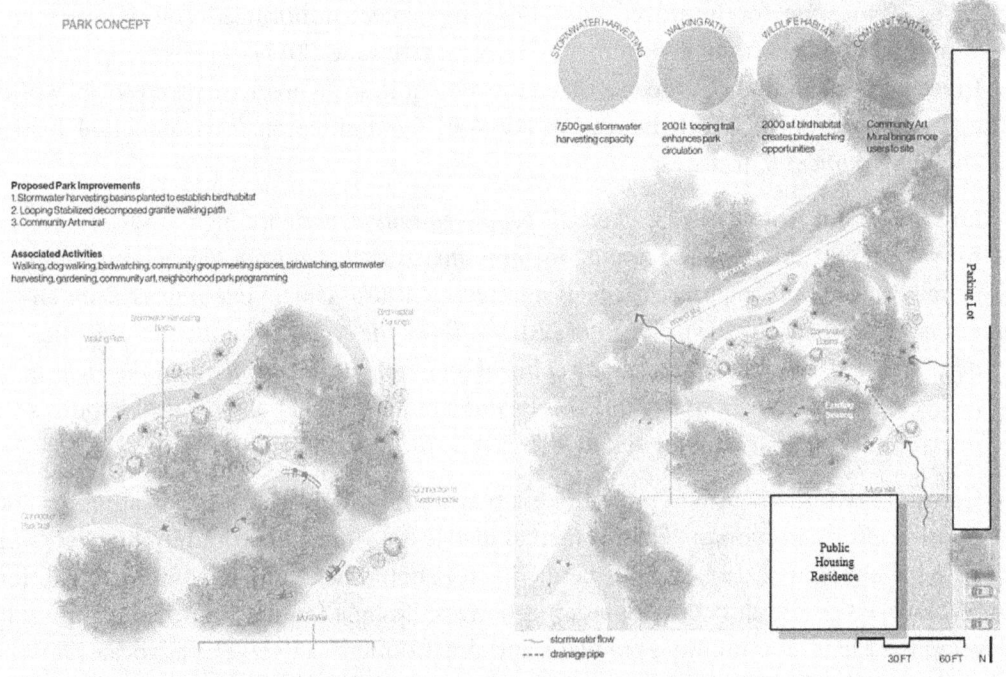

FIGURE 12.1 Park concept showing environmental improvements.
SOURCE: Reproduced with permission from Jonathan Choi.

COMMUNITY DEVELOPMENT MODELS THAT STRENGTHEN CONNECTIONS AMONG PEOPLE

Community development approaches focus on bringing together people in communities often from diverse ethnic, cultural, and income groups, and, as such, with a variety of interests and needs. Each of these models requires practitioners to identify community issues and needs as well as existing assets and resources. Community groups set goals, develop action plans, implement interventions, and evaluate what they have done (J. Green & Haines, 2016; Ohmer & DeMasi, 2009). Although some community developers may not exclusively use one model or another, there are a number of distinct approaches identified in the research, training, and practice literature. These approaches roughly correspond to the major concepts identified earlier in this chapter, community-building approaches, the asset-building approach, social capital development, capacity development, and consensus organizing.

Community Building

The term community building is often used generically to refer to efforts to improve relationships among diverse groups that can be used to facilitate community improvements through consensus and cooperation. Community building may be oriented exclusively toward developing a sense of commitment to a community or collective efficacy with a focus on individuals, families, and groups that are typically minoritized, marginalized, or isolated by society such as youth, people with disabilities, or members of the LGBTQIA+ communities (Walter, 2009). Communities can also be established online in chat rooms or social media groups as people exchange ideas and resources (Leung et al., 2010). However, building a sense of community is often a necessary first step in efforts to engage in other activities to improve neighborhood life. Community-building approaches can be used for a wide variety of efforts, including neighborhood improvements, economic development, increasing affordable housing or improving existing homes or apartment buildings, health promotion or prevention activities, safety initiatives, or improving access to healthy foods (Messinger, 2004; Petersen, 2002; Singh, 2003). One of the main goals of this approach is to increase connections among community members and decrease experiences of isolation among individuals and families as a means of increasing the health and well-being of community members. In many conceptualizations of the word *community building*, the term *self-help* is used. It can be applied to grassroots improvement projects or well-funded initiatives promoted by government agencies or foundations to "help the community help itself." According to Labonte (2009), external funding often is needed for neighborhood development in under-resourced communities. Hence the purpose of such efforts should be not to foster self-help, but community self-reliance, the ability of local residents to negotiate development initiatives, goals, and implementation procedures with external funders and organizations and have a significant amount of decision-making control with each project.

There are more extensive, broad-based approaches to community building as well. Community building as a form of community development practice is often associated with comprehensive community initiative (CCI) approaches. CCIs focus on asset enhancement and social capital development and often combine the provision of social services; economic development; and individual, organizational, and capacity-enhancement activities to improve social and economic conditions for children and families in under-resourced communities (Brisson & Roll, 2008; Mulroy & Lauber, 2002). Schorr (1997) describes the rationale for this approach:

> *It endorses the idea that the multiple and interrelated problems of poor neighborhoods require multiple and interrelated solutions. The new synthesizers are determined to reverse "the economic, social, and political marginalization that has turned the urban poor into an "underclass" and their neighborhoods into "battle zones." They insist on combining physical and economic development with service and education reform, and all of these with a commitment to building community institutions and networks. (p. 318)*

CCIs typically operate through national intermediary organizations, such as the Annie E. Casey Foundation, the Ford Foundation, and the Local Initiative Support Corporation, and partner with CDCs, other local development agencies, and community groups (Brisson & Roll, 2008; Chaskin, 2001; Gittell & Vidal, 1998). They typically receive funding from national foundations as well as local, state, and federally funded redevelopment programs. Both funding and development activities are concentrated on a single neighborhood (Coulton et al., 2011) reducing fragmentation of services and the design of programs to meet local needs. Citizen participation in development using a consensus-oriented, collaborative decision-making process is an essential part of community building and helps reduce the likelihood that development planning and implementation will solely be conducted by outside organizations or funders (Brisson & Roll, 2008; Messinger, 2004), which is important to ensuring the effort is culturally appropriate and responsive to community priorities. Increasing resident sense of belonging and commitment to the community, strengthening social networks, forming new community organizations, and enhancing the capacity of individuals and local organizations to engage in development activities are also important components of this approach (Gittell & Vidal, 1998; Good Neighborhoods Initiative, 2007).

Asset Building

Most community-building efforts are designed to put the principles associated with the Kretzmann and McKnight (1993) asset-building approach into action (Lafferty & Mahoney, 2003). As described in Chapter 6, the assets approach incorporates the principles of self-determination and empowerment as well as the strengths perspective—including the assumption that everyone has a special skill, resource, or support network, or is resilient in the face of adversity—and can take proactive steps to make their own lives and their communities better. Hence, this is an approach that focuses on tapping into and strengthening the existing capacities of community members to take collective action to improve their own neighborhoods (McKnight & Kretzmann, 2009).

Instead of depending on funds provided by outside agencies and private investors, community members take action to leverage the external resources they feel are needed for neighborhood improvements. In such circumstances, these partnerships are characterized by mutuality and reciprocity rather than dependency on the donor. For example, if the community lacks a full-service grocery, community members can choose a location, find local investors and entrepreneurs, and conduct research to document the potential market value of an untapped customer base. These resources can be used to persuade a national chain to establish a store in the community. In addition to improving the assets of individual residents, McKnight and Block (2010) describe the formation of new organizations or "neighborhood associations" as one of the most important building blocks that should be used to bring people together for community change. It is through these associations of neighbors that residents come together to plan community development activities, obtain funds from outside the community, and take control of neighborhood improvement efforts.

One asset-building approach, not associated with the Kretzmann and McKnight (1993) model, focuses on increasing resident access to credit and financial institutions. Research indicates that people living in poverty have difficulty obtaining home loans, obtaining credit to start businesses, or even using basic banking services due to check cashing or bank fees or limited information about how such services work (Sherraden et al., 2003). One type of financial asset-building program, the Individual Development Account (IDA), focuses on helping people accumulate personal assets or wealth that can be used to purchase homes, enroll their children in college, or start small businesses. IDA programs are designed to increase access to banking services and the amount of money saved by families living in poverty as a mechanism for increasing human and economic capital, thereby providing a mechanism that may assist families to move out of poverty (Grinstein-Weiss et al., 2007). Participants receive financial education and matching funds through government programs when they make a deposit in a savings account. In some IDA programs, access to banking services is increased by locating them in community agencies.

Community development can also include working with banks, and even starting new banks or credit unions, to ensure they make home loans to community residents or help families complete credit or loan applications (J. Green & Haines, 2016). In addition, some programs focus on microenterprise projects, which are oriented toward giving small start-up loans to people with limited economic means who wish to start their own businesses (Schreiner & Woller, 2003). This approach has an obvious link to other forms of asset-based community development in terms of its emphasis on encouraging individuals to identify and develop their own hidden talents and skills, which can be applied toward both personal and community transformation.

Social Capital Approaches

The social capital development model is oriented toward increasing the size and strength of social networks and establishing or strengthening nonprofit organizations and associations that can be used to leverage external resources, develop the capacity to deliver social services, or stimulate community and economic development efforts (Kay, 2006). Therefore, it is often an integral part of community-building and asset-development endeavors (Mathie & Cunningham, 2003). According to Kubisch and colleagues (2010):

Community change efforts seek to build social capital in distressed communities for affective reasons—to ameliorate the corrosive effect that extreme poverty can have on interpersonal bonds and supports—and for instrumental reasons—to build the civic, economic, and political power of residents for collective action and community improvement. (p. 36)

Generally, social capital approaches can be categorized in terms of whether efforts focus on bonding, bridging, or linking social capital. According to Petersen (2002), bonding social capital among neighborhood residents can be categorized as consisting of two types of concrete behaviors as well as a set of attitudes that make it likely that they will engage in these activities:

- *Informal.* This refers to the extent to which people talk to or communicate with or provide social support and other types of help to one another.
- *Formal.* This refers to people attending meetings or rallies, participating in neighborhood watches, or organizing other types of activities in response to neighborhood needs.

People will not engage in these types of activities unless they have a sense of belonging or commitment to the neighborhood and are able to trust their neighbors (P. Green, 2011). Indeed, communities "move at the speed of trust." Therefore, development efforts may be oriented toward activities that encourage communication, resource exchanges, and trust among local residents; strengthening local networks of people and helping them to exchange resources such as information, support, material goods, or skills (such as car repair or child care) increases neighborhood resources and enhances personal feelings of self-worth (Kirst-Ashman & Hull, 2018; Stack, 1974). In addition, local governments can encourage the production of social capital by designing new housing or commercial developments that contain features, such as parks, playgrounds, walking paths, community gardens, cul-de-sacs, and other forms of open or semi-public space, that encourage social interaction (Kay, 2006).

Bridging social capital efforts often entails some of the community dialogue activities described in Chapter 6. According to P. Green (2011), one role for community developers or organizations facilitating local planning efforts is to ensure that a diverse cross-section of community members is recruited to participate in the process and that meetings are structured and facilitated in a manner that unites people across common interests and concerns. Bridging social capital can also be created when existing social networks are expanded to include diverse members or people who typically may be excluded in their communities (Gilchrist, 2019). Lopez and Stack (2001) argue that one important task for social network approaches is to provide opportunities for cultural bridging, a process designed to assist "members of a marginalized community [to] overcome social-cultural obstacles" (p. 47).

Individuals who have multiple affiliations with voluntary associations in their communities also help establish bridging relationships that increase the likelihood that these organizations will engage in collaborative efforts (Wollebaek & Selle, 2002). In some instances, social capital formation efforts may involve the provision of resources such as stimulating the growth of new organizations by providing technical assistance with funding proposals, the process of formalizing (called *incorporation*) nonprofit organizations for tax purposes, or recruitment and training of new board members.

Linking social capital efforts can involve establishing new intervening organizations or strengthening institutions that focus on linking community residents and existing networks to external organizations, government agencies, or the political process. In addition, intervening or intermediary organizations can act to create collaborative networks that can be used for social service or healthcare delivery or community development efforts (Cohen, 2001).

Capacity Building

This approach to development focuses on increasing the skills, capabilities, and assets at a number of different systems levels: individuals, families, social networks, local organizations, communities, and intermediary organizations, as well as policies and institutional structures that limit the ability of under-resourced neighborhoods to provide support, care, jobs, education, income, and other opportunities and services for their residents (Kubisch et al., 2002; Saegert, 2006). According to Chaskin (2001), both a sense of community and commitment to change must be present for communities to engage in capacity building. Social networks and organizational structures are also necessary if people and resources are to be engaged in the process. They identify four basic strategic approaches associated with increasing community capacity:

- the development of relationships and social networks;
- leadership development;
- a process in which citizen participation is facilitated; and
- resources that help increase the skills of individuals, the strength of organizations, and the amount of financial capital that can be used for community or economic development.

Specific capacity-development activities identified in the community development literature include job training for community residents; leadership training and development for neighborhood volunteers and other constituents; and technical assistance for local organizations related to board development, fundraising, evaluation, and staff development and training (Kubisch et al., 2002; Sobeck, 2008). Eisinger (2002) defines *organizational capacity* as characteristics related to whether organizations are able to meet their goals, use external resources and networks effectively, provide services in response to community demand, hire staff with specialized skills, and respond to changes in the external environment such as new technology or funder requirements. Capacity-building efforts may also be designed to increase the skills of organization managers and establish program accountability (Austin et al., 2011).

According to Kubisch and colleagues (2010), local organizations must also be able to collect community indicators and engage in social planning if these organizations are to effectively engage in the development process. In addition, Saegert (2006) argues that capacity development should also include increasing the capacity of community residents to engage in community organizing and lobbying public officials in order to increase political power and their ability to obtain funding and make improvements in their communities.

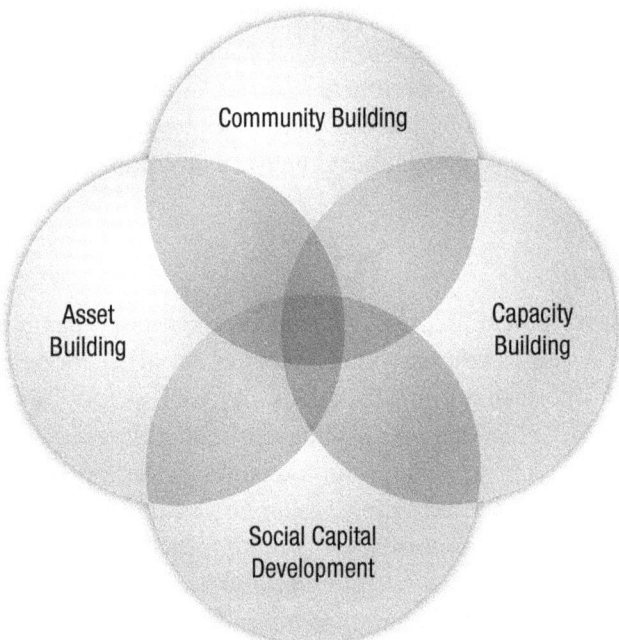

FIGURE 12.2 Interrelationships among community development concepts and theories.

Goals associated with successful capacity-building efforts include stronger community networks and organizations, an increase in the ability of neighborhood residents and organizations to problem solve, an increase in the jobs-related and leadership skills of community residents, and the achievement of specific community improvement-related outcomes. The achievement of capacity-building goals might be demonstrated by concrete actions taken and outcomes achieved in the pursuit of making community improvements, for example, the number of new affordable housing units available, a reduction in crime, or improvements in the health outcomes of neighborhood residents (Chaskin, 2001; Lafferty & Mahoney, 2003; Petersen, 2002; Figure 12.2).

Consensus Organizing

The consensus-organizing model is a framework for community building that promotes linking the self-interests of the community with the self-interests of outsiders in order to work toward a shared or common goal (Eichler, 2007). In 1967, Murray Ross and Ben Lappin explained consensus organizing as the process of strengthening and integrating community participation for social action, and defined the role of the community practitioner or organizer as one primarily concerned with building consensus (Perlman & Gurin, 1972).

Consensus organizing has roots in the settlement house movement, and assumes that a common ground can be reached among those with shared interests on any particular issue or problem (Cox et al., 1974). Consensus organizing unites interests within a neighborhood and aligns those interests with political, economic, and social structures

(Eichler, 2007), and is a blend of empowerment practice and the building of consensual relationships (Beck & Eichler, 2000). Tenets of consensus organizing include the assumption that power can be created through mutual self-interest, community members and people in power structures can work collaboratively to plan and carry out a change strategy, and relationship and partnership building is key to achieving sustainable, impactful change (Ohmer & DeMasi, 2009). The consensus-organizing model views power structures as potential partners and a support system for a common cause (Eichler, 2007). Consensus organizing as an approach to community building is appropriate when power does not have to be redistributed, and asserts that power can be developed and grown. Further, mutual self-interest is a motivator for change, not only self-interest (Beck & Eichler, 2000).

The consensus-organizing approach to community development has strong links to theories about how social capital is produced, focusing on methods to build both bonding and bridging capital (Beck & Eichler, 2000; Ohmer & DeMasi, 2009). It emphasizes collaborative approaches to community change, including instances in which participants have strong views about community improvements, and status, income, and ethnic differences that influence their preferences among development options. Consensus organizing first gained prominence when it was used to facilitate resident participation in a national community development demonstration project in the 1990s coordinated by an intermediary organization, the Local Initiatives Support Corporation (Gittell & Vidal, 1998). According to Beck and Eichler (2000), there are four basic assumptions inherent in this model:

1. When given reasonable choices, people can act rationally.
2. It is not necessary for power to be redistributed among people with different interests or social status. Instead it can be developed, shared, and grown.
3. People can make collective decisions based on mutual self-interest.
4. Coalitions and alliances can be developed that consist of people of diverse backgrounds and interests.

According to Ohmer and DeMasi (2009), consensus organizers use collaboration and dialogue to build strong relationships among community residents, business owners, and members of the external power structure that influence what happens in the community. They describe the role of the community developer as a bridge between residents and external resources. Ohmer and DeMasi (2009) describe the consensus-organizing approach as follows:

Consensus organizers believe that power can be created, shared, and harnessed for the mutual gain of communities and the external power structure. The goal of consensus organizing is the development of deep, authentic relationships and partnerships among and between community residents and stakeholders, and members of the external power structure to facilitate positive and tangible community change. (p. 13)

Many of the skills used in consensus organizing are similar to or the same as those used in other types of community practice: conducting assessments, engaging participants through one-on-one interviews, building relationships with potential community partners, facilitating group dialogues that bring people with different interests together, planning and conducting interventions, and evaluating outcomes (Ohmer & DeMasi, 2009). Community members work collectively to complete small projects, building skills and confidence. The central difference between this approach and social action lies in its central premise that power-holders should be regarded as potential allies of members of minoritized and marginalized groups, and that all the parties involved should be able to identify mutual interests and engage in cooperative strategies for community improvements.

"EARLY WINS": COMMUNITY EVENTS, ARTS, CULTURE, BEAUTIFICATION, AND GREENING INITIATIVES TO CELEBRATE AND REIMAGINE COMMUNITY

Delgado's (2000) model of capacity enhancement focuses on fostering the growth of culturally appropriate assets in urban areas and increases in the skills, self-confidence, and empowerment of community residents. Examples of the type of assets produced include community gardens, playgrounds, and art installations, such as community sculptures and murals, created by community members in response to the preferences and cultural values of residents. They link this model to ecological theory, which they describe as the process of identifying interconnected factors that affect human interaction. Specific components of the capacity-enhancement model include:

1. Conduct an asset assessment to identify local resources. The assessment must incorporate local norms and traditions. Residents must be involved in both the assessment and project-design phases of the process. However, external resources must also be used to develop the project.

2. Assessment and planning should take place within the context of extensive face-to-face engagement, meetings, and negotiation between the project beneficiaries and the community practitioner.

3. The intervention must correspond to the interests and common needs of project beneficiaries. The people who will benefit from the project must be involved in providing technical advice and access to many of the resources needed to develop the project. They must also be responsible for carrying it out. For example, if the group is developing a new playground, members could clean the land used, design the playground, contract with local government for the land and equipment, construct the playground, and develop a work plan for maintaining it. The organization that facilitates the project would also play a role, providing supervision, advice, and other resources needed to develop the project.

4. Participants should use a combination of internal (participant) and external (outside evaluator) methods to assess the project. The evaluator should facilitate dialogue among the residents and other participants in order to develop appropriate research questions and methods. However, it is essential that a formal evaluation process be used to examine program impact, process, and outcomes. Data from the project can be used to make decisions about future development efforts and disseminated to other community groups.

Although the capacity enhancement model can be used in many aspects of community building, it is particularly useful for bringing groups of people together to take action, mobilize resources, build capacity and social cohesion, and facilitate experiences of individual and collective empowerment. Community events, art and cultural installations and celebrations, and beautification and greening initiatives can make use of or create new public spaces that foster community building. Hosting a community event, such as a resource fair, block party, or neighborhood celebration, is a tried-and-true method for building relationships among community members. Building a community garden, hosting a community cleanup, installing a mural led by local artists with participation from the community in the installation, planting trees and other beautification projects are what community developers often call *early wins* or *action activities*. These activities bring people together in community and help keep participants motivating to engage for the long term. Neighborhoods that have suffered from decades of neglect or disinvestment do not change overnight, and significant community improvements take time; the community organizer or practitioner can use early wins as opportunities to celebrate community and small victories to help bring people together and keep people connected and working toward a common goal, even when the larger goals are yet to be achieved.

When determining an early-win project, the capacity enhancement framework can be used to identify local assets and resources and to engage in a project planning process that is inclusive, allows the community to hold or share the power in designing and decision-making about the project, and is responsive to community culture, traditions, and norms. Through this process, community members may form new bridging capital and create new partnerships with organizations and resources outside the community that can contribute assets to support project implementation. And the shared community assessment process of the project builds the skills and capacity of community members to evaluate the success of their own future projects, and to tell the story of the community-building initiative. Some examples of possible early-win projects include creative placemaking through community arts projects and greening (e.g., murals or tree planting), and relationship activation (through events such as block parties and other social activities, resource fairs and community celebrations).

INTERPERSONAL SOCIAL WORK SKILLS FOR BUILDING BRIDGES AND STRENGTHENING COMMUNITY CONNECTIONS

Interpersonal social work skills are critical for creating strong bonds among community residents and bridges between local groups and external organizations. Although some of these methods have been described in Chapters 3 through 6, such as community dialogue, coalition building, conflict resolution techniques, participatory action research, and Photovoice projects, community development practitioners and organizers employ additional techniques for building social capital in community development projects. These activities include skills for fostering strong relationships among neighborhood residents, strengthening social networks and community participation in decision-making, and building bridges and linkages between individuals and organizations.

Building Strong Relationship Bonds Among Individuals

One of the basic premises of community development work is that in some communities people simply do not know one another; do not have opportunities to meet one another or to act collectively; are not aware of services, policies, or their rights under the law; or do not have hope for or believe that social and economic conditions can be changed for the better. In many cases, community members are distrusting of one another or people they do not know (Pyles & Cross, 2008). Rubin (2000) describes the purpose of community development as fostering community empowerment, creating a sense that individuals who experience hardship are not alone, and that with collective action there is hope that things can change for the better. Therefore, at a basic level, community development work can be oriented toward creating opportunities for people to get to know one another. This can include introducing people to others with similar interests, providing or developing free "space" such as a room in a recreation center or a church that can be used for neighborhood activities, sponsoring events such as street fairs or cultural nights, or making efforts to develop neighborhood parks and playgrounds (Delgado, 2000; Gilchrist, 2019). Another technique that can be used to facilitate resident-controlled community development is by sponsoring or providing support to neighborhood self-help or mutual aid groups; providing a time, location, supportive resources (such as food or child care), and information about a specific issue that makes it feasible for community members to engage in group organization and self-help advocacy to address a local issue that affects them all (P. Green, 2011; Gutierrez et al., 1998; Miley et al., 2017).

McKnight and Block (2010) describe an approach to facilitate connections among individuals that relies on community volunteers that have a gift for bringing people together and identifying individual capabilities that can be used for the organizing process. Characteristics of "connectors" include:

- They are not leaders, but rather function as hosts, issuing invitations to others to participate.
- They are trusted members of the community.
- They have numerous connections to other people and organizations in the community.
- They are able to identify gifts and skills possessed by others and link people to specific activities or roles in which they can use these skills.
- They are capable of reaching out to people or groups that are often isolated or excluded from community life.

The social work profession often refers to these connectors as *natural helpers*, individuals who assist people in their communities who need information and support (Miley et al., 2017).

Strengthening Social Networks and Community Participation in Decision-Making

According to Brisson and Roll (2008), community development practice is based on the assumption that resident participation in neighborhood development can be used to increase community capacity for change and to develop additional activities to bring people together. This in turn leads to improved outcomes for individuals and the neighborhoods in which they live. Consequently, both strengthening social networks and facilitating participation in decision-making are essential components of the development process.

Gilchrist (2019) describes professional community development practice as a process that involves assisting individuals "in making strategic and opportune connections that create and maintain collective forms of organisation" (p. 167). People can be encouraged to participate in ongoing activities in which their time, resources, and talents can be used for community improvement work such as community-wide cleanup days, neighborhood watches, or participation in childcare cooperatives. Often these efforts recruit from or build on existing networks. In addition, community leadership structures, especially in minoritized communities, may contain opportunities for community developers to reach out to people who are already tied in to numerous networks such as clan leaders in Southeast Asian communities or church leaders in Black/African American neighborhoods (Grigg-Saito et al., 2008; Wallace, 2004). Generally, as in other types of organizing, participation in successful efforts—especially in situations that require hard work over time or that encounter many obstacles—develops or strengthens group solidarity, collective identity, and commitment. People are also able to form trusting relationships. Dialogue as well as resource and information sharing occur in the context of network building, establishing common bonds and trust (Gilchrist, 2019).

In addition to developing networks, a high level of participation is critical for ensuring that residents have a voice in development efforts and that resident voices are not subservient to prescriptive agendas set by funders, government agencies, or private investors who are also likely to benefit and profit from the development effort (Rubin, 2000). As in other types of participatory efforts, there are a variety of decision-making structures that facilitate participation ranging from local meetings of development groups, planning workshops, and formal positions on the boards of local organizations, local development oversight committees, or intermediary institutions. In addition, many development efforts are more grassroots efforts and facilitated locally, such as by local business councils, churches, or neighbors who come together to clean up their block or organize to improve local educational opportunities for their children. J. Green and Haines (2016) suggest that initiating resident input in development efforts can be as simple as facilitating a visioning workshop in which participants are asked to consider what they want to preserve, what they want to create, and what they want to change in their community.

However, beyond general guidelines about how to facilitate participant engagement in development, the practice literature on "facilitating community building" or "strengthening community networks" remains very limited. A number of research studies have documented the observations of community development specialists about what they do. For example, Dorius (2009) interviewed directors of CDCs to find out how they approached their work. A number of common themes related to activities carried out in these organizations were identified:

- The directors perceived their primary role as bringing people together.
- The approach they used to do this was communicating with constituents and facilitating decision-making processes in a manner that conveyed dignity and respect.

- They used educational approaches to help individuals to overcome self-perceptions of failure and institutional barriers to success and develop self-confidence and skills.
- They helped constituency group members to develop common goals and create a vision for community change.
- They engaged in activities that helped individuals, families, and the community as a whole gain economic self-sufficiency.

A similar study conducted by Carr (2009) included interviews with administrators of seven organizations involved in community development work in a small city. None of these organizations were CDCs; five were faith based. These respondents viewed community development efforts undertaken by their organizations as oriented toward strengthening relationships among community residents and organizations, creating a sense of community among participants, and developing working partnerships with other organizations that increased their ability to provide concrete services to individuals and families. They assisted residents in the development of leadership and other skills and educated both local residents and the general public about social conditions and their impact on the community. These administrators also engaged in efforts to inform the public and organizations about the effects of poverty and solicited their assistance in developing interventions for improving the neighborhoods served by the community development organization.

Strengthening Relationships Between People and Organizations

Most community development efforts rely on decision-making processes that are collaborative and consensus oriented. However, as noted by Chaskin (2001):

> *Communities, however, are not uniform collectivities. They contain people, organizations, relationships, and interests that may or may not converge around a given issue at a given time. [. . .] The problem of creating and acting on community consensus is often made more difficult by the breadth of the agenda, the ambiguity of roles and expectations among various actors, and the tension that arises from the conflict between the cost and the incentives for participating in the proposed action. (p. 316)*

This analysis suggests a number of consensus-building strategies, including (a) limiting the initial scope of community development efforts, (b) building on small successes over time (e.g., "early wins"), (c) negotiating specific roles and responsibilities within the group context, and (d) allowing for flexibility and change as the process and community priorities evolve. As with other types of organizing and planning efforts, residents living in poverty need supportive services to sustain participation, including meals, transportation, and childcare.

The number and length of meetings should be regulated to permit involvement by people with busy and complicated lives. Meetings, events, and other practices and policies associated with the development effort should respect and incorporate cultural practices and provide mechanisms for translation during meetings or issuing documents in languages other than English. In addition, resident concerns about which individuals and groups should represent the community can be addressed by making the process as inclusive as possible and setting up resident councils or other participatory structures (Gittell & Vidal, 1998; Hunt, 2007).

In addition, community residents should have roles that move beyond passive participation in meetings. According to Gilchrist (2019), community volunteers who serve as "connectors" or who excel at linking people across systems can also function in this capacity to link community residents to organizations both inside and outside the community. Such connections create a community that is resilient enough to engage in community improvement activities and to adapt to changes in the external environment, including economic downturns, resident mobility, and changes in laws and social policies. Community control over the process of development and, at minimum, a place at the bargaining table for community members in talks with government agencies or private developers is generally regarded by most community development specialists as essential. This ensures that community revitalization projects reflect community interests and prevent negative impacts such as the displacement of residents living with limited economic means and minoritized communities and gentrification that can occur with neighborhood improvements due to higher housing prices (Kubisch et al., 2002; Saegert, 2006; Silverman, 2004; Stoecker, 2004; Wyly & Hammel, 2004).

Labonte (2009) offers some guidelines for creating equitable partnerships between community residents and outside development groups:

- All groups that participate in the development process should have their own sources of community legitimacy and power.
- Each community group should have constituents in the neighborhood to which they are accountable. Constituency group members should be able to provide a source of power and support that can be used to advocate for neighborhood preferences.
- All partner groups should have clearly defined mission statements and goals.
- All partner groups should commit to at least one primary goal that they all share. This may require a commitment to a long process for developing a shared agenda.
- External partners should be committed to working cooperatively with community groups.
- The various organizations and groups involved should identify common objectives and roles for the members of the partnership and community workers. Community development workers should not be expected to simply push the agendas of external organizations.
- There should be a written partnership agreement and an evaluation mechanism.
- All partners should be committed to the principles of diversity and respect for all participants.

In addition to these principles, capacity, asset, and social capital-building approaches should integrate cultural values and traditions into community-building efforts (Satterwhite & Teng, 2007). According to Chino and DeBruyn (2006), culturally competent practice models "work from the 'ground up,' reversing the top-down application of Western science to classic [community development] that too often results in programs that are 'outside-in' and 'community placed' rather than community based" (p. 12).

PUTTING VALUES INTO ACTION: BUILDING ON STRENGTHS AND ASSETS

One small-scale approach to community development has gained a great deal of attention for its potential to create strong bonds among community members and to contribute to improved nutrition and health among community residents (Delgado, 2000). Community gardens are suitable for multisystem interventions, and considered an early win that increase the residents' sense of community and community capacity, assets, and social capital (Draper & Freedman, 2010). In this section of the chapter, the use of community gardens for community development is examined using the community capacity framework illlustrated in Figure 12.3. This intervention model is also consistent with the strengths perspective, an approach to social work and community practice that is intended to increase an individual's sense of competence, future orientation, and motivation for change (Miley et al., 2017).

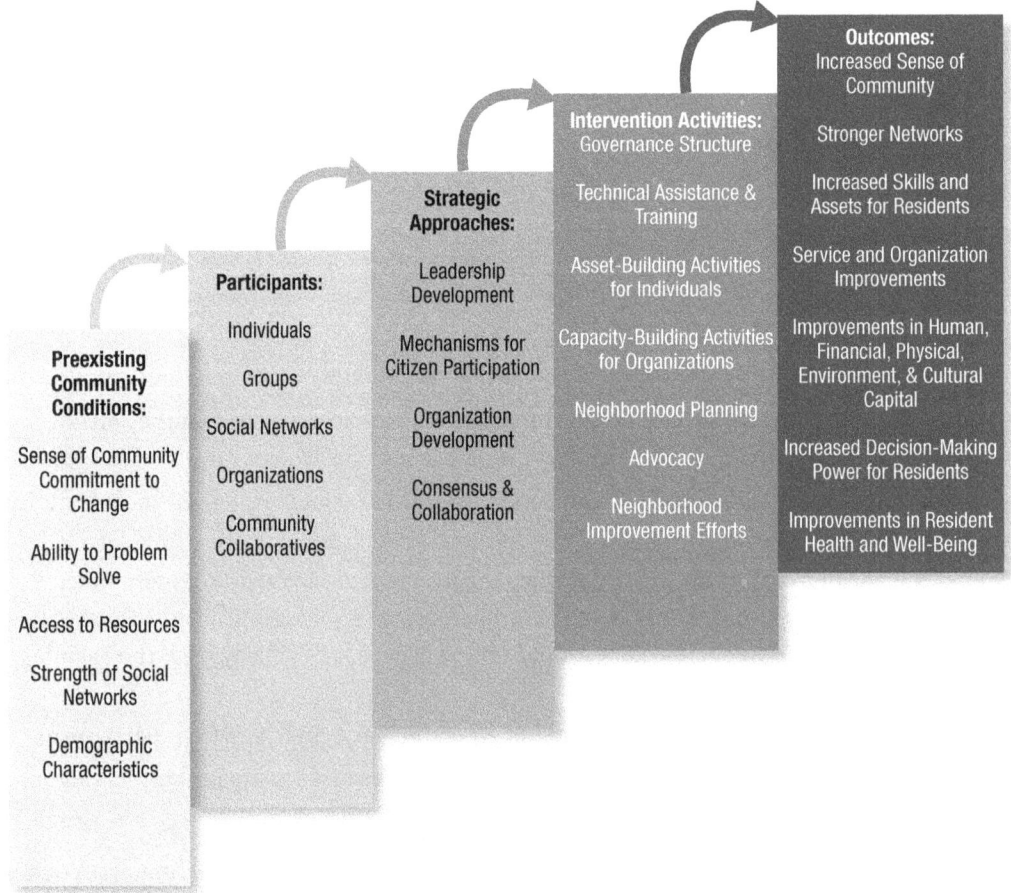

FIGURE 12.3 Theoretical assumptions about capacity-building approaches.

In the community context, experiences of self-competency and empowerment are essential for the development of collective self-efficacy, the belief that adverse situations can be reversed if people, bonding and working together, take action (Rubin & Rubin, 2008).

Preexisting Community Conditions

Community gardens are primarily publicly owned and operated, provide access to community residents, and involve some type of democratic decision-making process that is inclusive of neighborhood residents (Draper & Freedman, 2010). They have been identified in the public health and community-organizing literature as an appropriate intervention for dealing with four primary issues:

- They improve poor health outcomes among community members, including high rates of obesity and diabetes among children and families living in poverty.
- They benefit communities with limited resources, access, or capacity and can be used to provide healthy and nutritious food for families living in poverty. Many neighborhoods in under-resourced communities do not have full-service grocery stores. Fruits and vegetables are often expensive. For some minoritized populations, food resources may be available. However, these choices may not be culturally appropriate (e.g., local food pantries may not be able to distribute such products as rice or corn meal to Southeast Asian and Latinx families; Armstrong, 2000; Saldivar-Tanaka & Krasny, 2004; Twiss et al., 2003).
- They can help communities that lack bonding social capital, including social networks, local clubs or associations, or nonprofit organizations that can be counted on to bring people together to address social problems. The use of small-scale projects to bring neighbors together has traditionally been used as a community intervention to reduce experiences of isolation and improve psychological well-being (Armstrong, 2000).
- Community gardens provide a vehicle for applying the principle of sustainability, minimizing resident use of assets (such as pesticides or food purchased from national chains and originating in factory farms) that may harm the environment. The use of sustainable methods may be useful as a recruiting tool to foster participation among young people or others outside the community committed to environmental activism and consequently create bridging of social capital (Holland, 2004; Twiss et al., 2003).

Participants

The community garden approach is a method that can be implemented by a group of neighbors, facilitated by neighborhood organizations and churches, or coordinated with assistance from local government, foundation grants, or regional or national technical assistance organizations. Often community gardens are established as collaborative partnerships among a number of public agencies, nonprofit organizations, and local groups (Ohmer et al., 2009; Twiss et al., 2003). The intervention can be developed with minimal resources beyond land, water, equipment and seeds; small grants and in-kind donations from individuals and businesses may be solicited in order to obtain these resources. However, obtaining a source of water or conducting an analysis of soil quality may require negotiations with city agencies or working with an intermediary organization. External organizations may provide staff members to coordinate the project or offer technical assistance workshops (Armstrong, 2000).

Strategic Approaches

The primary goals of most community gardens are to improve the health and well-being of community residents by providing a source of healthy, nutritious food and to increase experiences of empowerment with community residents through self-help activities. Gardens incorporate basic community development principles such as leadership development, citizen participation, and consensus and collaboration within the group and external agency partners (Draper & Freedman, 2010; Ohmer et al., 2009; Saldivar-Tanaka & Krasny, 2004). Although "outside" resources may be used, community gardens are essentially a "bottom up" approach to community development in which local residents act together to utilize available resources (such as land or professional gardeners) to improve their lives and the community (Holland, 2004). Gardens can also provide an opportunity to turn a community problem (such as vacant lots in which garbage and other debris are dumped or in which drug dealing takes place) into a community asset (Holland, 2004; Saldivar-Tanaka & Krasny, 2004). According to Schukoske (2000), up to 20% of all land in urban areas is vacant, posing a serious threat to the health and safety of residents, and reducing social capital by limiting interaction of local residents in open, public spaces in their communities.

Another reason that a community garden may be an appropriate intervention method in minoritized communities is that it provides an opportunity for immigrants who formerly made a living from agriculture to carry out family and cultural traditions and obtain food that is familiar, healthy, and culturally appropriate (Twiss et al., 2003).

Intervention Activities

In addition to planting a community garden, other actions are required to conduct the intervention, which in turn lead to outcomes other than simply starting a garden or harvesting healthy food. For example, planning the garden, soliciting volunteers and resources, and performing basic gardening activities (planting, maintaining, and harvesting) require forming an organization, assigning roles and responsibilities, and motivating volunteers to complete their work. Therefore, it also increases individual capacity, including the acquisition of leadership skills, the ability to train and mentor volunteers, and the development of culturally appropriate communication and dissemination tools such as newsletters and web pages. Participants also engage in other basic community-organizing tasks such as group dialogue, project implementation, media and public relations, and evaluation (Twiss et al., 2003).

Community gardens face several types of obstacles or outright barriers to success, including vandalism or difficulties obtaining access to land (such as vacant lots), or city zoning requirements that require members of the group to take collective action to preserve the garden (Armstrong, 2000; Draper & Freedman, 2010). In some cases, land used without authorization or for a minimal city fee may be subject to confiscation by the city for redevelopment purposes (Schukoske, 2000). The need for a group response to such outside threats can serve as a mechanism to increase the capacity of communities to advocate for themselves (such as the use of group advocacy or organizing techniques, lobbying, research, and media relations), and the development of solidarity and stronger bonds among volunteers and their supporters.

Outcomes

Community gardens have the potential to produce numerous outcomes on multiple system levels. In addition to supplying residents with healthy food at no or low cost, and increasing physical activity, they help to create or strengthen community networks, improve individual skills, and improve organization and community capacity (Draper & Freedman, 2010). Gardens can also improve the appearance of the community, increase the likelihood that neighbors will maintain the surrounding area and engage in other beautification efforts, and provide residents with a place to meet and visit with one another. The garden is also a setting in which cultural events can occur, creating bridging social capital. Consequently, they also provide an open space in which social networks and resource or information exchanges can be facilitated and future organizing efforts can occur (Armstrong, 2000; Saldivar-Tanaka & Krasny, 2004). Some research studies on community gardens report that residents perceive the gardens to have reduced crime in the neighborhood and contributed to improvements in their sense of personal safety (Draper & Freedman, 2010). In addition, gardens have been found to contribute to the development of individual and collective perceptions of a sense of community, trust among participants, and experiences of personal empowerment (Holland, 2004; Ohmer et al., 2009).

END-OF-CHAPTER RESOURCES

KEY TAKEAWAYS AND SUMMARY

Community development efforts focus on building a sense of community, connectedness, and trust among community members. Although these priorities for community practice are considered essential in every aspect of community work, building a sense of community, connectedness, and trust are also necessary if explicit efforts are to be made to make material improvements in community conditions. Since the 1990s, community development practice has been guided by theories about sense of community, capacity building, and asset and social capital development. Practice models that are derived from these theories incorporate strategies and tactical methods that require consensus building and collaboration among different groups of community stakeholders that hold varying degrees of power. In addition to the consensus-organizing approach, community development practice is oriented toward building strong relationships among individuals and groups and improving individual, network, and organizational capacity to develop assets, skills, and acquire financial capital. It also focuses on improving the community's access to jobs as well as human, physical, environmental, and cultural capital. Social workers and community organizations can use collaborative methods to link people, networks, groups, and organizations via group dialogue in order to facilitate community-building initiatives. As in other types of social work and community practice, organizers often need the support of supervisors in carrying out assessments, interventions, and evaluations. In Chapter 13, supervision processes for community practitioners and organizers are described.

RESOURCES

- *Investing in What Works for America's Communities: Essays on People, Place, and Purpose* (E-book published by Federal Reserve Bank of San Francisco and Low Income Investment Fund): http://whatworksforamerica.org/pdf/whatworks_fullbook.pdf
- TedxExeter. (2016). *Cormac Russell, Sustainable Community Development: From What's Wrong to What's Strong*: https://youtu.be/a5xR4QB1ADw

ACTIVITIES

1. Divide the class into two teams in order to debate a community development-related issue. Conduct research on this topic prior to the day the debate is scheduled. The debate question is: Should community or economic development efforts originate inside or outside of the community? What are the pros and cons of each approach?

ASSIGNMENTS

1. Observe and participate in a local community volunteer effort oriented toward neighborhood improvement, for example, a neighborhood cleanup, park maintenance, planting or maintaining a community garden, setting up a fundraising event, painting a mural, or neighborhood beautification. If you have the opportunity to do so, interview two or three volunteers and at least one of the project coordinators. Write a three-page paper that describes the project in terms of the issue to be addressed, goals, project activities, volunteer roles, and accomplishments. Were goals obtained? What motivated

people to participate? How effective was the effort in terms of volunteer recruitment, volunteer engagement in activities necessary for goal achievement, and the sense of community or commitment displayed by the volunteers?

2. Recruit at least five to 10 volunteers for a specific community project and conduct the activity. Make sure that volunteers have a primary role in planning and conducting the event. Write a five-page paper that evaluates the process and outcome of this activity using the concepts presented in this chapter such as sense of community, capacity building, asset development, and social capital enhancement.

3. Conduct informal interviews to identify members of at least one community network. The network should either link community residents, connect residents to organizations, or foster connections and joint projects in the community. Determine network membership, the number of people or organizations in the network, the type of help or assets exchanged, and the capacity of the network to encourage specific community improvements or resource attainment.

4. Conduct research on at least one community or economic development project in your neighborhood funded with grants or contracts from community agencies, institutions, private investors, or external grants and contracts. Use a combination of sources to write a historical account of the project: observation, interviews, newspaper and other media accounts, reports, and any other publicly accessible documents that you can obtain. Describe the issue addressed, goals, participants, intervention activities, and how the project was evaluated. In your judgment, was the project a success? What groups benefited from the project? Did some groups benefit more than others? Why? How did the various groups perceive the outcome?

A robust set of instructor resources designed to supplement this text is located at http://connect.springerpub.com/content/book/978-0-8261-5835-2. Qualifying instructors may request access by emailing textbook@springerpub.com.

KEY REFERENCES

Only key references appear in the print edition. The full reference list appears in the digital product on Springer Publishing Connect: connect.springerpub.com/content/book/978-0-8261-5835-2/part/part04/chapter/ch12

Beck, E. L., & Eichler, M. (2000). Consensus organizing: A practice model for community building. *Journal of Community Practice, 8*(1), 87–102. https://doi.org/10.1300/J125v08n01_05

Brisson, D., & Roll, S. (2008). An adult education model of resident participation: Building community capacity and strengthening neighborhood-based activities in a comprehensive community initiative. *Advances in Social Work, 9*, 157–175. https://doi.org/10.18060/175

Coulton, C., Chan, T., & Mikelbank, K. (2011). Finding place in community change initiatives: Using GIS to uncover resident perceptions of their neighborhoods. *Journal of Community Practice, 19*, 10–28. https://doi.org/10.1080/10705422.2011.550258

Emery, M., & Flora, C. (2006). Spiraling up: Mapping community transformation with community capitals framework. *Community Development, 37*(1), 19–35. https://doi.org/10.1080/15575330609490152

Mathie, A., & Cunningham, G. (2003). From clients to citizens: Asset-based community development as a strategy for community-driven development. *Development in Practice, 13*, 474–486. https://doi.org/10.1080/0961452032000125857

Moore, K. (2005). What's class got to do with it? Community development and racial identity. *Journal of Urban Affairs, 27*, 437–451. https://doi.org/10.1111/j.0735-2166.2005.00245.x

Ohmer, M. (2010). How theory and research inform citizen participation in poor communities: The ecological perspective and theories on self- and collective efficacy and sense of community. *Journal of Human Behavior in the Social Environment, 20*, 1–19. https://doi.org/10.1080/10911350903126999

Pyles, L., & Cross, T. (2008). Community revitalization in post-Katrina New Orleans: A critical analysis of social capital in an African American community. *Journal of Community Practice, 16*, 383–401. https://doi.org/10.1080/10705420802475050

Sampson, R., Morenoff, J., & Gannon-Rowley, T. (2002). Assessing "neighborhood effects": Social processes and new directions in research. *Annual Review of Sociology, 28*, 443–478. https://doi.org/10.1146/annurev.soc.28.110601.141114

Small, M. (2007). Racial differences in networks: Do neighborhood conditions matter. *Social Science Quarterly, 88*, 320–343. https://www.jstor.org/stable/42956298

LEADERSHIP, TEAMWORK, AND SUPERVISION IN MACRO SOCIAL WORK PRACTICE

LEARNING OBJECTIVES

After reading this chapter, students will be able to:

- Describe the importance of supervision in social work community practice.
- Discuss the purpose and major components of work plans.
- Recognize how empowerment theory applies to supervision and teamwork in community practice settings.
- Recognize supervisory tasks that guide supervisors who work with students or new community practitioners in community practice settings.

INTRODUCTION

In this chapter, leadership, teamwork, and organizational culture for macro social work practice are introduced. *Staff supervision* is defined and models of supervision for community practice in social work field internships, organizations, and campaigns are examined. This includes the development of work plans for organizing staff and the use of the supervisory process to analyze team and individual performance as well as organizational and community dynamics. Specific supervisory skills for community practice are described, including the development of self-awareness and cultural humility, verbal and written communication, engagement and dialogue skills, and the ability to encourage self-determination and self-empowerment in others. In addition, supervisory skills for helping social work interns or staff members develop effective group-work skills for issue identification and assessment, making ethical decisions, planning projects, campaigns, and taking action, and evaluating community change efforts are described. In the final section of this chapter, supervision as a parallel process in which supervisors serve as role models and help social work community practitioners (e.g., organizers, program managers, coordinators, advocates) develop the skills needed to encourage empowerment in others and, in turn, discover empowerment for themselves, is discussed.

LEADERSHIP, TEAMWORK, ORGANIZATIONAL AND TEAM CULTURE

In recent years, social work leadership has increasingly received attention as an area within the field that needs greater opportunities for professional development. Social work scholars have emphasized that—despite the recognized need for social work leadership and managerial skills in community practice and clinical social work settings—there is a dearth in leadership and management training in most social work educational programs (Knee & Folsom, 2012; Peters, 2017). S. Colby Peters (2018) proposes the following definition of *social work leadership*:

> *A collection of organisational, relational, and individual behaviors that effect positive change in order to address client and societal changes through emotional competence and the full acceptance, validation, and trust of all individuals as capable human beings. (p. 40)*

Although there are numerous leadership models for social work practice that are useful for their utility in promoting resilient organizations and team cultures, and facilitating effective teamwork, the resilient leadership model and facilitative leadership are discussed here.

The three characteristics of resilient leaders and organizations include (a) a firm grasp on reality; (b) a belief in the mission and the work to be done; and (c) the ability to be flexible and adaptive, and to improvise when necessary (Coutu, 2002). Resilient leaders and organizations are able to face professional and organizational challenges, recognizing the reality of the situation and distinguishing between what can and cannot be changed. This leads to organizational and leadership accountability, and ownership of the situation and challenges an organization faces is critical for effective leadership—without it, we may not believe that change is possible, but when we recognize challenges for what they are and face them, we can think creatively about how they can be addressed or resolved. Finding meaning in one's work is an important characteristic of resilient leadership, and by accepting reality in the face of challenges and deciphering the meaning therein, this leads to the ability to experience self- and organizational empowerment that is helpful in keeping us on track to achieving our goals. And when a leader is able to face reality and find meaning and purpose in their work they are better prepared to adapt, be flexible, and respond creatively, using solution-focused problem-solving methods to maximize the capacity and resources of their organization, and to inspire others and their team in the process.

According to Folkman (2017), resilient leaders communicate powerfully, are bold risk takers, are coachable, build meaningful and trusting relationships, develop others, are decisive, and are champions for change. Resilient leadership is important for community practitioners and community organizations because in this work they constantly encounter new challenges, have to make difficult decisions, and function in ever-changes circumstances as community needs and priorities shift, and resiliency allows leadership to successfully navigate those challenges.

Cultivating resilience is an important task for leaders, as it prepares leaders to stay on track to achieve goals, be flexible and prepared to make adjustments when necessary, think creatively and be innovative, inspire their teams, and navigate professional and organizational challenges with courage and conviction. Resilient leadership can be cultivated by the practice of reflection and assessment (e.g., understanding one's motivations, strengths, and areas for improvement), the commitment to continuous learning and growth (e.g., challenging oneself to continually learning and practicing new ideas, engaging in professional learning opportunities, taking risks and learning from what works and what does not), the practice of being purpose driven (e.g., pursuing a goal with intention and meaning), and the cultivation of networks of supporting relationships (e.g., developing a robust professional network to gain different perspectives and support for strength and guidance; Gavin, 2019).

Resilient leaders and organizations can engage in facilitative leadership practices to promote effective, high-functioning teams and develop resilient leadership within team cultures. Facilitative leadership is an especially useful approach to facilitating teamwork and establishing group culture, as it maximizes the strengths and contributions of group members and prioritizes the use of active listening skills, encouraging participative team discussions, fostering creative thinking, promoting creative problem-solving and informed decision-making, managing conflicting perspectives and intervening without taking over control of the group process, being objective and nonjudgmental, supporting teams at the stage of development where they are, encouraging group reflection and learning, and honoring and including differing learning styles in team processes. Cufaude (2018) describes the characteristics of facilitative leaders in leading organizations and teamwork as

- accepting and valuing silence, staying in a reflective mode beyond the normal comfort zone;
- moving from advocacy to inquiry in an effort to enhance dialogue;
- clarifying group inferences by returning to the observations that led to them;
- believing that everyone holds a piece of the truth;
- viewing conflict between ideas as normal and healthy;
- honoring individual perspectives and exploring the value of minority viewpoints;
- clarifying the team's mental models and the assumptions that are influencing their thinking; and
- expanding the team's sense of possibilities through creative thinking before jumping into action with critical and constructive thinking.

For leadership and teamwork to thrive, it is important to cultivate an organizational and team culture that is supportive, empowering, relevant for members of the organization and members of the communities they serve. *Organizational culture* has been defined as the "shared assumptions, beliefs, values and behavioral expectations of organizational members" (Chenot et al., 2009, p. 132). Social work organizational cultures should include a focus on cultural competency, anti-racism, and equity. Constructive organizational cultures are characterized with proficiency in operations and responsiveness to the community, and foster high levels of achievement and motivation with its members (Chenot et al., 2009; Cooke & Szumal, 1993; Glisson & James, 2002). Empowerment organizational cultures intentionally establish decision-making structures and processes that create and foster spaces and activities for team members and people served by the organization to ensure inclusivity, equity, and representation. These practices are designed to foster experiences of self-empowerment for team members, community members, and leaders of the organization.

Social work organizational leaders set the tone for organizational culture, and everyone participating in the organization has a responsibility to contribute to the culture. Organizational culture is evident in everything from the methods and tone of intra- and interorganizational messages and communications (e.g., messages within the organization, and messages to the community and to partner organizations); the mission (i.e., overall goal and purpose of the organization) and vision (i.e., what the organization aims to achieve) statements of the organization; onboarding practices; and guiding policies and procedures, behaviors, and interactions among leadership, staff, and students; within teams; and with the community members the organization serves; to the actual physical appearance of the organization (e.g., websites, entryway to the organization's offices and building, pictures on display in hallways). The cultural competence, cultural responsiveness, and relevancy of an organization can be understood, to a degree, based on whether messages are communicated in an accessible way, pictures on walls reflect the families that are served, and written materials are available in appropriate languages and for the intended audiences.

Bowen (2008) developed a structure for organizational culture assessments consisting of eight domains that can be used to review organizational statements, plans and documents such as mission and vision statements, strategic plan, human resource policies, program curricula, and other general organizational policies and procedures in conducting an organizational culture assessment. Bowen's (2008) eight domains of organizational culture include an assessment of practices, policies, and priorities involving

- cultural responsiveness within the organization;
- human resources;
- cultural training;
- language accessibility;
- organizational framework and integration;
- information and messaging for people served by the organization and the larger community;
- data collection, evaluation, and research; and
- partnership with the community.

Social work leaders and team members can conduct self-assessments to understand their organizational culture and map out their ideal cultural practices, identify gaps and opportunities for growth, and make adjustments when necessary to build a stronger, more inclusive, more productive, empowering and healthy organizational culture for their teams and the people they serve. Social work supervisors can foster organizational culture and promote accountability to the culture for team members through their approach to supervision.

DEFINING STAFF SUPERVISION, ROLES, AND TEAM PROCESSES

Supervision for community practitioners is an often-neglected component of social work training. More common, when social workers discuss supervision, the context involves the provision of micro social work, direct practice, or clinical interventions in which the social worker and supervisor discuss the social worker's options for engagement, assessment, intervention, and evaluation of practice with individuals, a family, or a group of clients, as well as psychological factors (either the client's or the worker's) that may enhance or block change or affect the social worker's ability to engage with the client (McTighe, 2011). However, in organizational settings, supervision involves providing supervisees with instrumental tools to promote and enhance work performance (e.g., knowledge and skills) and affective (e.g., emotional) support for motivation, well-being, and fulfillment in their work (Chenot et al., 2009). *Supervision* also refers to monitoring, controlling, and evaluating the team and employee's work performance and taking appropriate actions to recruit, hire, train, sanction, reward, or terminate individual staff members (Hardina et al., 2006; Kadushin & Harkness, 2014; Kirst-Ashman & Hull, 2018). It also refers to the process of professional development in which the social worker and community practitioner's strengths, skills, and knowledge, are enhanced in order to strengthen not only the organization's resources and capacity, but also the worker's own interpersonal social work skills, capabilities, and career trajectory (Tsui, 2005). Kramer Tebes and colleagues (2011) provide a definition of *social work supervision* that incorporates activities associated with clinical supervision and the more generic set of skills necessary to ensure accountability to the organization. Supervision is: "a supportive professional relationship in which one individual has responsibility for and authority over the work and work life of another" (p. 190). However, this description of supervision as a manifestation of responsibility for and authority over others can be challenging for many community practitioners and social work leaders, as it seems to be at odds with basic social work and community-organization principles that focus on establishing mutual, equitable partnerships and respectful relationships among organization participants and teams (English, 2005; Kadushin & Harkness, 2014).

In traditional community organizations, there are typically several roles, including administrative leadership (e.g., president, chief executive officer, chief operating officer, chief financial officer), administrative support (e.g., office manager, administrative specialist, grants manager), other leadership and supervisors (e.g., program director, manager, program coordinator, supervisor), program staff (e.g., community practitioner, community organizer), team members receiving training or providing additional capacity or service (e.g., social work interns, service members, volunteers), and a board of directors, community action board, or other type of governing body that oversees the strategic direction of the organization, makes organizational decisions, and supervises the administrative leadership. Any of these roles can be filled by social workers, and social workers trained in macro practice are particularly well suited for roles in administration, management and leadership, supervisory roles, or community practice direct-service roles (e.g., community practitioner or organizer), and learner roles. Social workers with specialized training may have titles such as *grant writer*, *policy analyst*, or *community development specialist*. Social workers also serve in board positions. Regardless of the title or official role, most social workers in community practice participate in team processes, meaning they are one member or part of a larger team, holding unique responsibilities and assigned tasks in their position that contribute to carrying out an action campaign, change strategy, or program. Because of the dynamic nature of community work, social workers in community practice are often called on to step up and help out in team processes in response to the ever-changing demands and needs of the communities with which they work, and as such may be required to temporarily or permanently shift positions or take on new responsibilities at any given time in order to provide additional capacity to fulfilling the mission of the organization. Many times, this involves providing supervision for program staff or learners within the organization (such as social work interns and volunteers).

Not much is known about how community practitioners qualify for and obtain supervisory positions (Bobo et al., 2010). Some social work graduate programs offer advanced training in social work leadership and organizational management. Oftentimes, when looking to fill a leadership gap, community organizations may opt to assign their most experienced staff member to a supervisory position and hope that the individual they appoint has the practice wisdom, patience, and background to provide supportive supervision and guidance to others. In these cases, the social work practitioner appointed to a leadership role can request resources and training in management and supervision if they feel they need more preparation for this new role. According to Traynor (2002), organization investment in staff supervision and training for community practitioners is critical for two reasons: (a) turnover among community practitioners is often high due to burnout and feelings of isolation within the organization, and (b) organizing tasks completed improperly (such as constituent recruitment or forming alliances with other organizations) may require hours of valuable staff time to repair. Consequently, money spent on cultivating a strong, supportive, and structured organizational culture; creating staff supervisory structures; and training staff in supervision is money well spent.

New community practitioners or organizers may have the good fortune of obtaining appropriate support from their peers and colleagues or benefit from structured training and workshops available through training academies or other educational groups. However, such resources are not always available, and some may be cost prohibitive, making skill acquisition from peer networks or outside entities inconsistent or not always a viable option. This is why having skilled leadership and supervisors for community practitioners and organizers is essential, in order that the organization has the internal capacity to adequately support and guide practitioners; reduce job-related stressors; and correct, redirect, and manage staff when needed. According to Bobo and colleagues (2010), effective supervision is essential because:

It is the best kind of training that is available to organizers, helping them be strategic and thoughtful about their work on a regular basis, forcing them to prioritize, to evaluate and learn from their mistakes, to see how their work fits into the bigger picture of the organization. (p. 308)

MODELS OF SUPERVISION AND TEAM BUILDING FOR COMMUNITY PRACTICE

For supervision to be effective, it should be incorporated into an organization's strategic plan, policies, and administrative decision-making structure, as part of an ongoing plan to develop staff capacity and resources (Kadushin & Harkness, 2014). Although social work supervision in general focuses on the integration of skills, values, and knowledge, supervision of community practice employees also focuses on accountability to the organization, donors, and constituents. Although there are some similarities in how social work interns and employees are trained, there are also differences in terms of how work performance is monitored and assessed. Although social work education examines student acquisition and application of skills and competencies, community organizations often create explicit work plans for employees that identify specific day-to-day activities that must be accomplished. In both approaches, regular, consistent dialogue takes place between the supervisor and staff member to help community practitioners analyze work performance, examine community and organizational processes, and engage in self-reflection.

Differences in Supervision by Settings: Comparing and Contrasting Field Instruction, Organization Settings, and Campaigns

Supervision and social work instruction in schools of social work for community practice can range from structured learning experiences in the classroom, service-learning opportunities that are connected to course or curriculum requirements, and social work field internships that either incorporate specific macro skill-building assignments or that focus on the students' acquisition of advanced skills required for a specific practice concentration (Gamble, 2011; A. Johnson, 2000; Plitt Donaldson & Daughtery, 2011; Salcido et al., 2002). In some cases, the acquisition of community practice knowledge involves explicit research or advocacy assignments that provide opportunities for experiential learning (Danis, 2007; Heidemann et al., 2011; Timm et al., 2011). Although much of the literature on the use of applied or experiential methods of learning indicates that they are often successful in helping students acquire macro skills, not much is known about the consistent implementation of these methods, the skills students typically develop, or how they actually acquire these skills (Wilson, 2011).

Changes in Council on Social Work Education (CSWE) curriculum policies, first implemented in 2008, require that accredited social work programs regularly assess whether students have developed specific social work-related skills or competencies. CSWE defines social work practice competencies as specific outcomes that should be produced as a consequence of students gaining knowledge and skills, and demonstrating ethical principles and practice values in social work field internships as well as in the classroom (Wayne et al., 2010). However, as field placements offer direct applied learning experiences within a variety of human service organizations, the CSWE Education Policy and Education Standards (2008) designated the field practicum as the ideal setting in which this integration should occur. CSWE describes competency-based field instruction as the *signature pedagogy* for social work programs, a unique method through which members of the profession gain instruction about practice norms and roles (Wayne et al., 2010). As part of the accreditation process, schools of social work collect evaluation data that verify whether students have actually acquired these competencies. Typically, the student's performance in field practicum is evaluated using a standard list of skills or competencies in the form of a learning contract that the student is expected to acquire in the social work internship. Field instructors (sometimes called field supervisors) are responsible for assigning these competency ratings and, in some circumstances, ratings may be developed through ongoing dialogue with the social work intern and representatives (field liaisons) from the social work program.

In contrast to social work field instruction, although supervisory procedures for organizational staff and new community practitioners should include the provision of ongoing professional development and training, they also focus on ensuring that employees perform daily tasks that are essential to the organization's mission, ongoing campaigns, or projects in a manner that is efficient, effective, and reflective of the organization's culture, mission, vision, and goals. Many people who engage in community practice or organizing careers are not social workers; community practitioners may be graduates of other types of professional programs that include some content on community organizing, planning, or development (e.g., public health or urban planning), or they may be self-taught activists who will benefit from formalized training when they enter the community practice field (Staples, 2009). Consequently, some community organizations and training or certification programs have developed explicit standards and expectations for core skills and competencies that they expect to see demonstrated in the practice skills and behaviors of new community practitioners (Bobo et al., 2010). The types of skills often taught in these programs include interviewing, relationship building, recruitment, coalition building, and working with groups to identify common issues, assessing what is happening in the community, examining power dynamics, planning campaigns, taking action, and evaluation (Alliance for Justice, 2010; Schutz & Sandy, 2011; Sen, 2003; Whitcher et al., 2010).

The Midwest Academy is a community-organizing training academy in the United States that offers curriculum and training manuals on supervision. They offer guidance on supervising staff that is fairly consistent with other types of nonprofit sector employment, but note that organizing work has some distinct differences from other types of employment (Bobo et al., 2010). For example, ideology and values are often equally or more important in motivating staff in community-organizing practice than money and other employment-related benefits. In addition, the work environment in community practice changes constantly; indeed, the one thing organizers can consistently expect in community practice is change, and to expect the unexpected. This requires that community practitioners are flexible, creative, adaptable, and able to respond to ever-changing situational demands (Schutz & Sandy, 2011).

Three primary supervisory priorities for leadership in community practice include (adapted from Bobo et al., 2010):

- Supervising campaigns, events, programs, or activities; managing the development, planning, implementation, and evaluation of theories of change in the delivery of change strategies.
- Supervising the professional development, leadership development, and daily task management of staff; identifying, prioritizing, delivering, and securing resources for individual and team professional development training opportunities.
- Building the organization, including the organizational culture, teamwork and guiding principles for intraorganizational team processes; management tasks such as recruiting and onboarding new team members, staff, and interns; leading strategic visioning and keeping the organization mission driven and accomplishing goals; gaining public legitimacy, credibility, and trustworthiness for the organization; soliciting community-buy in and partnership support; raising funds and securing resources; and training volunteers and board members for leadership roles.

Regarding the above supervisory tasks for building the organization, the community practice supervisor may hold sole responsibility, share responsibility, or delegate responsibility and supervise its delivery by other leadership in the organization. In order to facilitate skill development and team collaboration and accountability, community organizations provide orientations for new employees, may make arrangements for new hires to be mentored by more experienced colleagues, and seek out external opportunities for workers to be explicitly trained in skill development and specialized knowledge (such as laws and social policies) through workshops and conferences sponsored by training institutes or advocacy organizations.

The other context in which community practitioners may work is in political or legislative campaigns. Legislative campaigns are likely to be housed within a coalition or organization and unless the organization structure is temporary and transitory, supervision is likely to resemble that of a typical community organization with specific expectations and work plans for community practitioners and documentation of accomplishments. For example, staff hired to obtain signatures on petitions, register voters, or advocacy campaigns will be organized into teams and be required to achieve specific objectives (Kerns, n.d.).

The management structure of political campaigns differs from other types of community-based or advocacy organizations, typically characterized by shorter timelines and other situational demands that also require flexibility on the part of staff and managers. They are also likely to have centralized decision-making structures that involve limited direct input into goals or strategies on the part of staff members who are not managers. The reliance on campaign volunteers often requires that a high degree of the staff member's time commitment will involve ensuring that volunteer constituents receive the proper training and support and participate in the right activities, at the right time, and the right place. Consequently, complex types of activities requiring volunteers are often difficult to control, manage, or supervise (Delany, 2009; Stirland, 2008). In legislative campaigns, technology is useful in providing centralized management with uniform procedures and scripts for community practitioners and volunteers to use when contacting voters. However, the use of cell phones and online data repositories permit much of the campaign work to be conducted outside of the campaign office, making some types of direct oversight of volunteers and staff impossible, but also allowing for micro-targeting of various types of voters and rapid responses to situational demands (Schlough et al., 2011). However, as with other types of organizing work, paid staff (as well as teams of volunteers) will likely be asked to comply with specific expectations for tracking task completion (e.g., number of phone calls, number of one-on-one interviews, number of volunteers recruited, or the amount of money raised).

Fulfilling Funder Expectations and Meeting Organizational Demands: Designing Work Plans

Employer expectations are only one set of criteria that are used to develop job descriptions. As noted in Chapter 10, most foundations, individual donors, and the government agencies that fund community projects will require documentation of what the organization has accomplished in terms of the goals, objectives, activities, and timelines to keep track of the impact of their investment. In most instances, the organization will need to provide this information at regular intervals during the course of an action campaign or change strategy. One way for a social work manager to ensure that this can be accomplished and that the organization is accountable to donors is to provide individual staff and teams with an explicit work plan, derived from the list of objectives and activities submitted to donors, that specifies exactly what they are expected to accomplish (Bobo et al., 2010).

For most organizations, the overall work plan should have its origins in the strategic plans and strategy charts developed by constituency group members. The work plan for an individual staff member should represent a percentage of the overall work to be conducted to reach specific goals and objectives for the organization, or a larger percentage of the overall work if the staff member is managing a team for the project. For example, if the organization has indicated that it expects to recruit 100 new members and form 20 block clubs during the next 6 months for an organizing campaign, then the individual organizer's work plan will specify how much of this plan is their responsibility (Table 13.1). It is

TABLE 13.1 Sample Work Plan for an Organizing Campaign: Community Practitioner's Work Plan for an Environmental Organizing Campaign

CAMPAIGN GOALS	OVERALL CAMPAIGN OBJECTIVES	COMMUNITY PRACTITIONER'S OBJECTIVES	COMMUNITY PRACTITIONER'S ACTIVITIES	COMPLETION DATE
Increase public support for antipollution efforts.	Recruit 100 local volunteers for outreach and publicity efforts to raise awareness about the harmful effects of pollution.	Recruit a minimum of 25 local volunteers for an antipollution campaign.	Conduct a minimum of 50 one-on-one interviews with local residents. Conduct at least five focus group meetings to determine how local residents perceive the effects of pollution on their lives. Conduct a minimum of two press conferences to publicize the impact of pollution on the lives of local residents.	June 30
Reduce local sources of pollution.	Obtain commitments from at least 15 local officials to increase city and state regulation of pollution.	Obtain commitments from at least eight public officials to work toward increased regulation of pollution.	Coordinate at least 20 lobbying visits to public officials with local volunteers. Develop a policy brief that can be distributed to local officials and other lobbying material. Testify at five public hearings on the negative effects of pollution.	September 30

important that the work plan specifies timelines and target milestones for task accomplishment; this provides benchmarks for accountability that can be used to reflect on progress and troubleshoot challenges during supervision sessions. It is also critical that work plans take shape in the context of dialogue between the supervisor and the worker (to ensure that expectations are understood and that there is worker buy-in) and that planned activities are specified and will lead toward the completion of each task (Indianapolis Neighborhood Resource Center, n.d.). For example, does the worker have a specific skill that can be used to accomplish a task (e.g., knowledge of website development, or graphic design abilities) or have preexisting relationships with constituents or community leaders that can be used for recruiting purposes?

It is also essential for social work managers and supervisors to follow up on task accomplishment with staff and team members to provide feedback, support, and assessing strengths or gaps in skills used in the field. Although some of the skills used are similar to those used in leadership development with volunteers (such as motivation techniques and praise for work well done), it is important for community organizations to have an explicit system for monitoring work performance (Larson et al., 2003; Perlmutter et al., 2001). Specific methods that can be used to structure supervision for community practitioners include:

- Require community practitioners to report to the supervisor on a regular basis.
- Require both individual and written reports.
- Request that additional documentation be provided to illustrate worker activities and skills such as meeting agendas, minutes, or notes from one-on-one interviews.
- Schedule staff meetings and retreats that permit analysis of organizing efforts, help motivate staff, and create an atmosphere in which teamwork is fostered and encouraged.
- Set clear performance standards for the community practitioner and periodic, regularly scheduled performance evaluations (Bobo et al., 2010).

Supervision as Praxis

Supervisory sessions in social work internships as well as for employees in community-based organizations should also include ongoing dialogue between the community practitioner or intern and social work supervisor in terms of how task accomplishment could be improved and what interpersonal social work and professional skills are necessary to do the job (Burghardt, 2011). As noted in Chapter 9, supervision often requires engagement in *reflective practice*. Reflective practice is an essential skill for social worker professionals, as regular self-reflection on beliefs, values, assumptions, biases, and attitudes provides clarity and understanding about the ways in which the community practitioner is approaching their work tasks; problem-solving and other challenges; how their work is influenced by their positionality, judgments, and worldviews; and what they can do to improve their performance with this knowledge (i.e., reflexivity). The supervisor must assist the staff member in developing an understanding of appropriate methods and a structure for conducting their own internal analysis of their practice skills, knowledge, and values. ben Asher (2010) identifies four basic skills that are essential for this process. The supervisor must be able to build a strong, trusting relationship with the staff member, provide direct support consisting of both psychological and material resources to aid in task accomplishment, accurately assess the worker's strengths and weaknesses, challenge the worker to take risks, and follow up appropriately in response to whether or not the task has been accomplished successfully. This may mean working with the staff member to find ways of improving task accomplishment in the future or to build on successful completion of the task by tackling another challenge. Generally, supervision in this context may bear some passing similarities to social work supervision in that the supervisor poses a series of questions that require the community practitioner to engage in critical self-reflection and analysis (Tsui, 2005). Reflective practice and reflexivity are especially important practices for new community practitioners and social work interns to learn.

While the supervisor ensures new staff members and interns engage in reflective practice, it is a practice that social workers use throughout their careers, much like the practice toward cultural humility. As such, the supervisor must also engage in their own personal self-reflection of supervisory practices in order to examine difficulties in motivating staff or managing their work effort. The following has been adapted from Bobo and colleagues (2010), and includes several questions that supervisors should regularly ask themselves to reflect on their performance as supervisors.

- Do I hold official supervisory responsibilities for this person (i.e., can I hire, fire, issue performance improvement plans, or otherwise hold them accountable)? If not, what options do I have in terms of motivating them to do specific tasks? What options do I have with regard to correcting them if they veer off course or have difficulty meeting deadlines?
- Do I assign tasks in an appropriate manner and provide reasonable deadlines that are enforced? Are assigned tasks clear (e.g., do the interns/staff understand what is expected regarding their performance and how to carry out the task?)? Are interns/staff provided with the appropriate resources, knowledge, and support to carry out the task? Are interns/staff prepared for critical thinking and independent problem-solving, and can they distinguish between when it is important to problem-solve and when they should seek support?
- Do I communicate clearly about how specific tasks fit within long-term program, campaign, or organizational goals? Do I communicate in a way that the intern/staff understands how this task fits in the "bigger picture?"
- Do I encourage intern/staff creativity, cultivate their strengths, position groups for effective teamwork experiences, and provide professional development opportunities?
- Do I provide clear directions in terms of what decisions can be made at the discretion of the intern, staff, or team level, and what decisions must be approved by me as the supervisor or made by other organizational leadership?
- Do I affirm interns/staff/teams and give them recognition or praise when it is warranted? Do I provide constructive and honest criticism and recommendations for areas of professional growth when it is needed?

- Do I approach all workers with respect? Do I treat team members equitably and fairly? Do I approach supervision with cultural humility and from an anti-racist lens? Do I avoid dealing with my own privilege or biases in supervisory situations?
- Do I make decisions in a timely manner when required or requested? Do I meet with interns, staff, and teams regularly and consistently?
- Am I reluctant or do I refuse to delegate work to interns, staff, or teams? Do I delegate too much? Do I provide space for creativity and autonomy for interns, staff, and team members as appropriate? Do I not provide enough structure? Or do I micro-manage how the work is completed?
- Do I seek out training and professional development for myself when I identify areas in which I can improve my supervisory practices? Do I acknowledge and take ownership when I make mistakes? Do I seek support, mentorship, and coaching from leadership and my supervisors, peers, or other professionals when I need it?

Several difficulties that social workers in supervisory positions often face in relation to staff management include:

- Setting appropriate boundaries with interns, staff, and teams. As social workers engaged in supportive supervision, it can be difficult to differentiate between the supervisor role and the social work role. Although social workers can and should use our skills, values, and ethical code in supervision, most social workers are also trained in case management and sometimes even psychotherapy. It is a slippery slope that can be harmful for individuals, organizations, and teams when clear boundaries are not established and maintained that differentiate between the social work practitioner and the social work supervisor. For example, an intern or staff may need clinical support to address mental health needs, and it would be inappropriate for a supervisor, even one licensed in clinical social work, to treat the situation as if they were treating a client. Instead, the supervisor can ascertain what resources are available through health insurance or other networks for the student or employee, and provide this information to their supervisee so that the worker may seek out and receive services in an appropriate clinical setting.
- Motivating employees can be a challenge in any work setting, inside and outside of social work. When an intern or employee does not respond to efforts by the supervisor to motivate the worker toward task completion, sometimes the social work supervisor may take on the task themselves just to get it completed. This can be problematic because it stifles the opportunity for professional growth for the intern or employee, creates a more intensive workload for the supervisor, and can leave all involved feeling disempowered, dissatisfied, and undervalued. Sometimes this may seem to be the only solution to getting the task completed if there is an impending deadline and there is not enough time to troubleshoot or provide additional training for the team member. If that is the case, and the supervisor does take over responsibility for the task and complete it on their own, care should be taken after the experience to problem-solve and critically reflect

about where things went wrong. Did the team member not ask for help when help was needed? Was the team member not prepared for the task, or did they not have the skills or knowledge necessary to take ownership of the task? Was the supervisor preemptive in taking over the task, and, if so, what led to that decision—did the supervisor lack confidence or trust in the team member that the task would be completed effectively without their involvement? Was the worker experiencing burnout or some other mental health or life experience that interfered with their ability to complete the task? Critical reflection and problem-solving can help the supervisor and supervisee identify what went wrong in the process of task completion, what barriers were present, find common ground, and make a joint plan for the future about how to avoid or overcome similar challenges.

- There are many reasons a team member might fail to complete a task or fall short of meeting expectations in following through with their responsibilities. Reasons may include a lack of motivation, enthusiasm, or interest in the work at hand, distractions in other aspects of their professional or personal lives (e.g., tense relationships with coworkers, family or health problems), lack of confidence or fear of failure, a gap in skills or knowledge needed to perform the task; and work exhaustion, burnout fatigue, or secondary trauma. A supervisor may be reluctant to criticize, correct, or sanction the intern, employee, or team member for their inability to meet their performance objectives. Recourses for supervisory sanctions or corrections should be included in organizational policies, and may include establishing a performance improvement plan, issuing a warning for underperformance, or otherwise officially documenting the incident in the employee record. In the case of underperformance or unethical conduct by a social work intern, the supervisor may set up a meeting with the field liaison or director of the student's social work program to mediate the situation and to help problem-solve. Although the supervisor may be reluctant to address the issue by sanctioning or providing negative feedback and criticism of the team member, perhaps because they do not want to hurt the team member's feelings, facilitate a disempowering experience, or focus on negative aspects of the work, it is ultimately a disservice to the supervisee and the entire team and organization to let performance issues go unaddressed. Ignoring performance issues stifles the opportunity for professional and personal growth for the supervisee, may lead to low morale for other team members, and will likely continue the pattern of unacceptable behaviors or performance, lead to a repeat of the same situation at a later date, or possibly worse—an even greater issue down the line that is harder to address. For these reasons, it is important for the supervisor to set a standard for addressing performance issues as they arise, speaking honestly and transparently with the team member to understand what went wrong and to assess whether the situation can be rectified, and to create a plan of action as a result of the performance issue, whether it is new or re-articulated work expectations and responsibilities, some form of restoration, or termination.

SPECIFIC SUPERVISORY SKILLS FOR COMMUNITY PRACTICE IN SOCIAL WORK

Although there are similarities in the types of interpersonal and analytical social work skills that community practitioners, developers, and planners use, regardless of model of practice, preparing social work students for these types of positions also involves the incorporation of basic social work knowledge, skills, and values into the supervision process (Tsui, 2005). As described in Chapter 1, there are a number of interrelated skill areas in which social work instruction and supervision should be provided in both field settings and paid employment. The set include self-awareness and reflexivity; cultural competence and humility; effective verbal and written communication, engagement, facilitation, and dialogue skills; the ability to encourage community self-determination and self-empowerment; practicing in teams and group work for issue identification, problem-solving, and assessment; weighing ethical options for the use of strategies, activities, and tactics; planning processes and taking action; and conducting evaluations (Hardina & Obel-Jorgensen, 2009).

Supervision for Developing Self-Awareness, Reflexivity, and Cultural Competence and Humility

As noted earlier, self-awareness, reflexivity, and cultural competence and humility require that the community practitioner become familiar with the community, the history and values of community members, understand power relations and how community residents are affected by them, and the power resources and strengths that can be used to address community challenges and concerns. Community practitioners must also become self-aware and engage in reflexive practices to understand how their own positionality—histories, social status, biases, values, and privilege—shapes their ability to identify with and establish meaningful and productive relationships with colleagues, community members, and other partners (Burghardt, 2011). The supervisor is obligated to assist the new community practitioner in the development of *cultural competence* and *cultural humility*, the willingness to abandon self-conceptions about possessing expert knowledge or power over others; to learn about the traditions and values of members of other cultures, diverse demographic groups, and communities; to understand the sources and impact of institutional and systemic oppression; and to become an active and effective ally in fighting with the community against oppression and discrimination (Abrams & Moio, 2009; Ross, 2010).

The supervisor's role in this process is to help the community practitioner or intern examine their experiences and reactions to the community and provide information and referrals that facilitate opportunities to learn from community members (Y. Johnson & Munch, 2009). For example, the supervisor can provide contact information for or facilitate introductions with community leaders and cultural groups, including potential gatekeepers and community guides, and attend cultural events with the new practitioner, organizer, or intern. Task assignments such as ethnographic interviews, oral histories, or observing and eventually providing staff support for meetings, events, or activities intended to honor, serve, or address the interests of specific demographic or cultural groups can assist the new social worker in learning cultural competency-related skills. In addition, social work values and ethics can be enhanced through dialogue with the new community practitioner about the various cultural competency standards used by social workers, including both the National Association of Social Workers (NASW; 2021) *Code of Ethics* and the NASW (2016) *Standards on Cultural Competence*, with special emphasis on strategies for meeting these requirements in community settings. Social work students and new community practitioners should always remember that cultural competence is a lifelong process; and everyone can and should continue to learn from others (Gutierrez et al., 2005; Y. Johnson & Munch, 2009). Developing cultural self-awareness, gaining cultural knowledge, understanding and addressing power imbalances, and holding systems accountable in the pursuit of equity are all components of cultural humility. Cultural humility requires being comfortable in the role of lifelong learner, being curious and open to learning about other cultures, and considering the impact that cultural differences might have on your interactions with different communities and community members of different cultures. The supervisor provides opportunities for interns, staff, and teams to discuss cultural humility in supervision and to create strategies for team members to continuously learn, practice, and grow their cultural competency skill set. Cultural competence is the foundation for cultural humility (Figure 13.1).

Supervising Effective Verbal and Written Communication

Communication is the key to effective relationship building and engagement as well as the ability to influence others. These skills include making presentations and public speaking in order to provide information to others, building a case for a particular course of action, or establishing collaborative partnerships or coalitions. Communication also includes the ability to create promotional materials (such as flyers and brochures), press releases, and research or policy reports. Increasingly, communication also involves the use of e-blasts and social media to spread the word about a social issue, frame messages, recruit participants, disseminate information, network with others, and rally people to a cause. As noted earlier in this text, community practitioners should not only develop these skills for themselves, but also assist constituents and community members in the development of these types of skills (Sen, 2003).

There are a number of supervisory tools that can be used to facilitate the development of community practitioners with strong communication skills. For example, work tasks can include the expectation that the community practitioner design flyers or write press releases in preparation for organization sponsored events. Technical skills can be developed or strengthened by asking the community practitioner to maintain field notes, a newsletter, a website, or a social media presence in promotional campaigns for the organization or a specific initiative. The organizer's ability to frame messages and to communicate them to others should be assessed by the supervisor on a regular basis, and the supervisor should provide notes for improvement. New community practitioners should also be assigned to conduct outreach on other constituency groups and organizations and participate in presentations, make speeches, or provide testimony at public hearings (Hoefer, 2019; Richan,

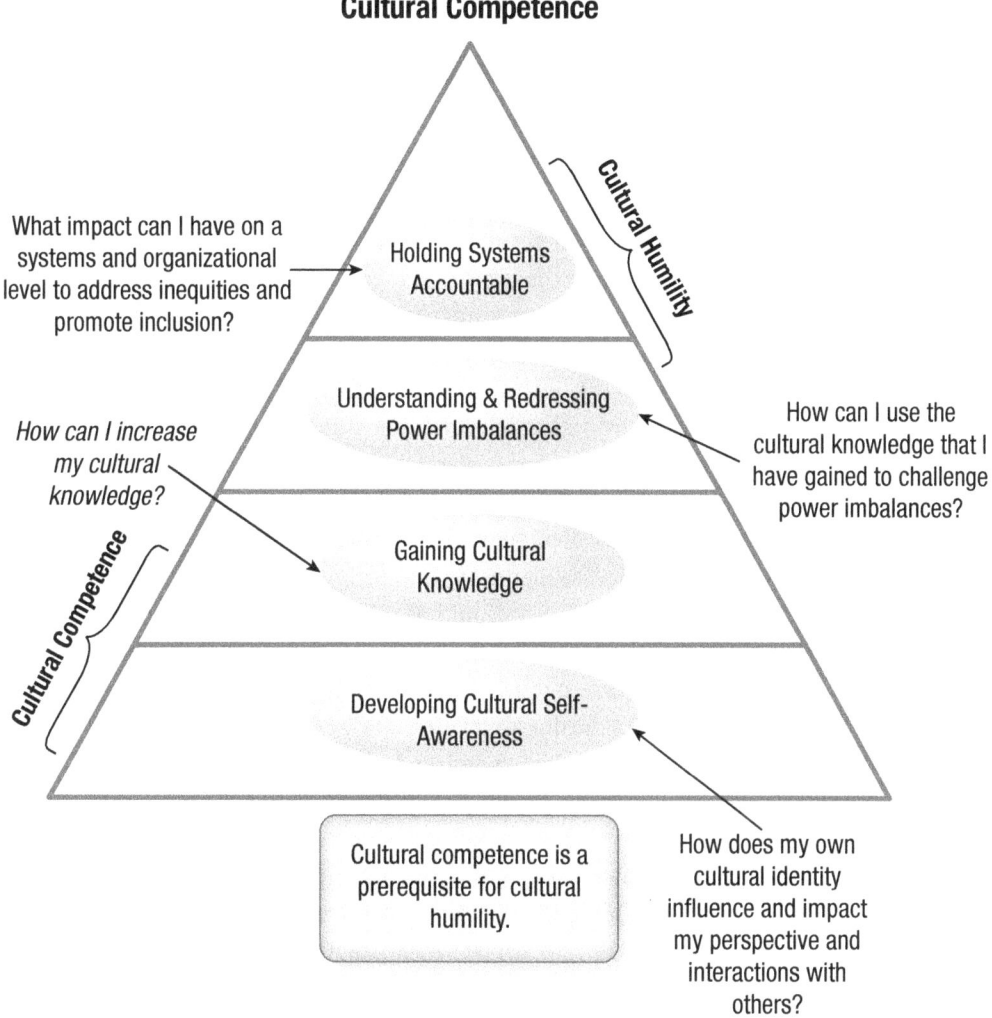

FIGURE 13.1 Cultural competence and cultural humility.

SOURCE: Adapted from Project READY (Reimagining Equity and Access for Diverse Youth). (2022). *Project READY: A free online professional development curriculum.* https://ready.web.unc.edu/about-us.

2006). Supervisors should be prepared to assist the new community practitioner in writing and practicing presentations and assessing their ability to effectively deliver information in public settings.

One potential area of dialogue between the supervisor and worker may involve examination of the degree to which attempts to use news or social media have been successful (Pyles, 2013). Did the organizer's communication result in actual press coverage? Was it the type of coverage expected? If not, how could this campaign be strengthened? Did the message reach the right audience? Was there a better way to reach the target group? Once the community practitioner has acquired basic skills, the next step should be using those skills to help or train constituents to work with the media. Participation in such efforts should help the staff member or social work intern strengthen these communication skills; dialogue can be initiated in terms of best training methods, how to facilitate the development of individual volunteers, and how to motivate constituents to engage in these types of tasks independently.

Supervising Engagement, Facilitation, and Dialogue Skills

Engagement, facilitation, and dialogue skills include the ability to conduct one-on-one interviews for relationship-building, recruitment, and information-gathering purposes as well as the ability to facilitate intergroup dialogue and meetings, and to plan, structure, and carry out larger events, such as community forums, in which community consultation and decision-making can occur. As noted previously in this text, effective dialogue skills include the ability to guide the group process, ensure that all participants have the opportunity to participate, establish common ground across member differences, and manage conflict (VeneKlasen et al., 2007). Effective engagement also requires that community practitioners gain a particular degree of comfort in talking to strangers and using those conversations to achieve specific types of outcomes that make it possible to hold an event, lobby for a cause, or achieve specific goals related to planning, development, or organizing campaigns. The goal of these engagement opportunities should also be to establish long-term effective relationships with constituents, key informants, and decision makers that can be used in the future and can help the organization establish strong network linkages to other potential volunteers and influential contacts (Hardcastle et al., 2004).

Supervisory tasks include role plays and exercises to help the community practitioner use basic social work interviewing and relationship-building skills to reach out to constituents and representatives of partner organizations. Clear expectations should be set for the number and quality of interviews to be conducted and the degree to which documentation is required. Also helpful is dialogue to help the community practitioner understand that although these skills are intrinsic to social work practice with other systems, their application in community practice differs substantially from agency practice in that the individual is not a client seeking service, but a potential partner with expertise, skills, and strengths that could be of benefit to the community practitioner or the campaign or project in which the community practitioner or social work intern is assigned. Conducting interviews on doorsteps or at community events can also be more challenging in terms of time constraints, unexpected occurrences, and the difficulties inherent in record keeping. It should also be emphasized that some people whom the community practitioner will approach will not want to participate and in those cases their privacy and self-determination should be respected.

Role plays and exercises should also focus on the new organizer's ability to facilitate and manage teams and groups, recruit members, set agendas, and work with team and group members to achieve goals (Wint & Sewpaul, 2000). Learning to facilitate often requires a developmental process in which the staff member observes groups, co-facilitates with an experienced organizer, and eventually leads the group. In terms of larger events, new community practitioners should have a variety of opportunities to assist in the setup and coordination of workshops, meetings, and community forums. Supervision can focus on the examination of how effective such events have been in achieving organization goals and the various options that should be explored in planning future events.

Supervision That Encourages Community Self-Determination and Self-Empowerment

Once participants in community practice-related activities have been recruited, community practitioners need to find ways to ensure their meaningful inclusion in decision-making. In some cases, organizations have established decision-making structures and long-standing relationships with community leaders and volunteers. However, authentic inclusion is often difficult to achieve; new participants may not feel comfortable stating their views and organizational decision-making structures (e.g., board and committee membership and governance rules), organizational ideology, power differentials between leaders and constituents, and the ego or personalities of staff members and participants may limit the degree to which input from other participants is solicited and decision-making is shared (Hardina et al., 2006; Toomey, 2009). Such impediments can severely restrict the development of true partnerships between community-organization staff and community members.

The supervisor can assist the new community practitioner or social work intern by analyzing existing decision-making patterns, suggesting strategies for restructuring meetings or supporting new leaders, and identifying methods that could be used to help all participants be included in the decision-making process (Bess et al., 2009; Hunt, 2007). Basic social work methods, such as using positive affirmations, identifying individual strengths, and encouraging these individuals to use their expertise to help the organization, can be used to encourage participation and identification with the group (Miley et al., 2017). Essentially, empowering practices foster experiences of personal self-efficacy in group members (Itzhaky & York, 2002). Consequently, encouraging group members to volunteer for tasks needed for group maintenance and action, following up when these tasks have been accomplished, and recognizing and acknowledging group members are all essential to facilitating the empowerment process; the supervisor should assist the new community practitioner in the development of these skills (Haski-Leventhal & Cnaan, 2009; Zastrow, 2015). In addition, the new community practitioners or social work interns should be encouraged to strengthen their own group-work skills, using exercises and posing questions to group members that foster active participation (VeneKlasen et al., 2007). Conflict-management skills are also important, particularly in situations in which some individuals dominate the discussion or disputes arise among members (Zastrow, 2015). Establishing ground rules early in the formation of groups can help prevent individuals from dominating, debating, or disputing during discussions.

Supervision When Using Group Methods for Issue Identification, Problem-Solving, and Assessment

Skill development for issue identification, problem-solving, and assessment takes place on two levels: the new community practitioner must develop the capacity to enter a community and learn about issues, social problems, and the strengths of community members and use both informal and formal methods to conduct assessments. However, the social work intern or new community practitioner must also be prepared to work with constituents, partner organizations, and external consultants to conduct focus groups, use storytelling processes, conduct community forums, visioning and listening sessions, and other types of group dialogue sessions to identify issues of concern to constituents and to conduct assessments (Pippard, 2004). Social work interns and new community practitioners need adequate training in research skills, the ability to recommend and apply research methods that are feasible and realistic (both in terms of time commitment, resource requirements, cultural appropriateness, and community interests, with consideration for the potential burden for participants), and the interpersonal and professional skills necessary to work cooperatively with constituents and partner organizations to develop research plans (Stoecker, 2013). Community practitioners will also need to work with constituents to identify power resources held by group members, community decision makers, allies, and opponents of the desired change strategy (Homan, 2016).

In addition to skills related to engagement with constituents and facilitating community self-determination and self-empowerment, supervisors can help social work interns and new community practitioners choose appropriate research techniques, develop group dialogue skills suitable for issue identification, and provide information on workshops and training sessions that will assist social work interns, community practitioners, and constituent leaders to learn about innovative techniques such as asset mapping, social network analysis, Photovoice, the development of neighborhood-specific social indicators, geographic information system mapping tools, and power analysis (J. Johnson et al., 2010; Plitt Donaldson & Daughtery, 2011). The new community practitioner may have unrealistic expectations about using these techniques and their appropriateness and accessibility for community members. Consequently, supervision may focus on examining the various options and helping the new community practitioner make appropriate recommendations to constituent leaders about the use of potential research methods. In many circumstances, the community practitioner will be called on to actually coordinate research studies, follow up with volunteers, negotiate access to research settings, provide training for interviewers or survey administration, maintain data files, and participate in data analysis and report writing. The supervisor will need to provide oversight and help the new community practitioner design appropriate strategies for making sure that each stage of the process is completed appropriately and in a timely manner.

Supervising Teamwork and Group Methods to Assess the Ethical Implications of Strategies, Activities, and Tactics

Every type of action taken in the context of community practice has ethical implications, ranging from the people who should be included in group decisions, the selection of partner organizations, the choice of assessment and evaluation techniques, and strategic activities and tactical options available for organizing development and planning. Social work interns and new community practitioners must develop the knowledge, skills, and values that allow them to examine both their own ethical options and work with group members to identify ethical issues that may occur during the implementation of community interventions (Hardina, 2004; Mondros & Wilson, 1994).

Although social action or conflict-related tactics pose some of the most serious challenges for community groups in terms of potential harm to participants or opponents, other types of decisions may have ethical implications as well. Some of the ethical issues that may be encountered in community practice include questions about who should benefit from community development efforts, whether the organization or coalition should work with people or organizations known to engage in unethical practices or with questionable motives, or whether funds should be accepted from donors who may impose restrictions on the organization or alter the course of its advocacy efforts (Minkler & Pies, 2009; Reisch & Lowe, 2000).

Supervisory tasks to help the social work intern or new community practitioner include weighing the ethical implications of various options and engaging in dialogue about how social work ethical codes can be applied in community settings, and whether other ethical frameworks or the social worker's personal values can be used to examine ethical options (Kirst-Ashman & Hull, 2018). Although many of these decisions will be made by organization board members, administrators, and constituency group members, there will be some ethical choices that must be made by the community practitioner alone. For example, does the community practitioner have any conflict of interest or a personal stake in the outcome of any decision made by the organization or constituency group (Reisch & Lowe, 2000)? Has the community practitioner done enough to ensure that constituency group members are fully informed about potential strategies, activities, and tactical options, and the potential negative effects about any course of action (Kahn, 2010)?

Social work interns and new community practitioners will also need to examine the ethical implications of decisions made by constituency group members and help them assess the possible consequences of a number of tactical choices. To some extent, becoming knowledgeable about what can occur in various situations is a matter of practical experience. However, the supervisor can help prepare the community practitioner by assigning reading material (case studies or narrative accounts of organizing campaigns) or requiring that the community practitioner interview experienced community practitioners and community leaders about what they have learned from prior organizing efforts (Clemens & Minkoff, 2007; Somma, 2006). The supervisor can also provide assistance by helping the community practitioner examine available tactical choices and proposals and giving advice about how to facilitate consensus-building sessions with constituency group members and partner organizations to discuss the options available to them, what is likely to happen under different scenarios, and engage in contingency planning (Hardina & Obel-Jorgensen, 2011). It is also essential that new community practitioners develop the ability to state their own views, particularly in situations that have ethical implications (such as harming individuals or groups), or that can affect the organization's legitimacy and credibility in the community (Piat, 2000). This is particularly critical for social workers in that members of the profession are bound by the mandates in the NASW (2021) *Code of Ethics* and the International Federation of Social Workers (2018) *Global Social Work Statement of Ethical Principles* to engage in ethical practice.

Supervising Teamwork and Group Methods for Planning Processes, Action Campaigns, and Taking Action

As described in Chapters 7 and 8, planning action campaigns, responding to unexpected occurrences and situational demands, and taking action are commonly the most complex aspects of the organizing process. Successful campaigns require that the community practitioner have multiple relationships with any number of colleagues, constituents, group leaders, board members, supervisory staff, media reporters, external consultants and advisors, partner organizations, elected officials, and other decision makers (Staples, 2016). New community practitioners will need to develop skills related to handling requests for assistance and logistical support, following up with volunteers who have task assignments to complete, and filling in any gaps in participation with new recruits, while managing their own tasks.

New community practitioners will need assistance from their supervisor in determining what needs to be done and in what order (e.g., priority setting), in keeping track of the actions taken using appropriate methods of documentation and in responding to situational demands (ben Asher, 2002; Schutz & Sandy, 2011). In addition, group-work skills are also essential since not only will the staff member or organization sometimes need to change the direction of a planned approach, but also group members facilitated by the practitioner from the community will also need to do so; in most situations they will either need to be consulted about or have control over any response to an unexpected occurrence. The group dialogue process will often involve complex discussions about activities and tactics and the likely outcome of each (Burghardt, 2011). Such discussions may also involve whether or not negotiations should take place with partner organizations or opponents and what should and should not be offered in the bargaining process.

In this phase of the organizing process, the supervisor should be available for consultation about how to best handle emerging challenges, changes in circumstances, and negotiations and who should be included in the decision-making process. The supervisor may also be a participant in these decision-making sessions. The community practitioner or social work intern may need guidance about the implications of various activities and tactics, including group member experiences and perceptions about the effectiveness of these methods. The supervisor may be able to suggest alternative plans of action and how group members should be advised about the choices available to them. In such cases, it may be helpful for the supervisor to engage the community practitioner in some role plays or exercises that illustrate how choices should be made in a group process or how bargaining between two parties can occur (VeneKlasen et al., 2007). The supervisor should also be a good resource for the new community practitioner or social work intern in terms of developing appropriate "plan Bs" or safety plans in response to situational demands (Timm et al., 2011).

Supervision That Facilitates Participatory Evaluations

As described in Chapter 10, evaluation-related skills are those that pertain to informal assessments of one's own practice, informal consultative team and group processes in which the implementation of projects or campaigns are examined, and formal evaluations of intervention processes and outcomes. The community practitioner will need to apply research skills, values, and knowledge in the evaluation process and, in some situations, provide training in research methodology and data analysis to others (Bowers Andrews, 2004).

The role of the supervisor in this process has to do with providing assistance on two levels: the application of and strengthening of formal research skills by the new community practitioner and ensuring that community members have ample opportunity to participate in, and, in many circumstances, have control over the evaluation process. The new community practitioner needs to steer a course between relying on personal or other sources of expert knowledge and recognizing that experiential knowledge (and in some cases formal research skills) held by community members are also essential in ensuring that all voices are heard and that full assessments of what works and what does not work in the organizing process are made (Craig, 2011; Schmuck, 2006). The supervisor should also help the community practitioner recognize that two other sources of information are often integrated into the evaluation process: practice knowledge held by organizing staff (in terms of organization experience with evaluation methods) and donor requirements for documentations and evaluation of grant- or contract-funded activities.

As noted earlier in this chapter, other supervisory tasks related to evaluation are to assist the community practitioner in self-evaluation of practice experiences, and to identify any additional skills the community practitioner needs to ensure that the work is completed as expected and in a timely manner. In most situations, supervisors will likely be active participants in informal group or organizational assessments about programs and organizing campaigns and can further discuss the issues raised in these assessment sessions during one-on-one supervisory meetings with the new community practitioner. In terms of formal evaluations, the supervisor can help community practitioners understand the organization's procedures for evaluation, the relationship between funding and evaluation requirements, and work with the community practitioner in producing formal research-related documents such as funding proposals, logic models, formal research agreements (with partner organizations or external consultants), evaluation plans, and research dissemination reports (Netting et al., 2017). However, the most important skills the new practitioner will need for participatory research are the interpersonal social work skills necessary to facilitate group evaluation methods (Stringer & Aragon, 2021). Supervisory strategies can include exercises and role plays related to research options or working through difficult decisions with constituents and critiques about how research studies or reports are progressing (Schmuck, 2006).

USING TECHNOLOGY FOR TEAM PLANNING AND PROCESSES

There are a number of web-based platforms that are useful for supervisory relationships with community practitioners. Project management platforms can help the community practitioner, intern, and other team members stay organized, communicate, and share documents and calendars all in a single place (e.g., Microsoft Teams, Basecamp). The supervisor can have access to these platforms to check in periodically on project progress and identify areas that may need attention or time dedicated to problem-solving in supervision sessions. Teams can also use document-sharing platforms to collaborate on documents simultaneously (e.g., Google Docs), and a supervisor and supervisee can use these types of platforms to share plans for supervision or a tasks table that indicates a timeline and specific activities, and real-time updates on progress for project completion.

Other scheduling platforms allow teams to easily schedule meetings both within and outside of the organization (e.g., Calendly, Doodle Poll), and shared internal electronic team or individual calendars can be used to schedule regular supervision sessions and also for the supervisee to keep their supervisor informed of their whereabouts when they are out in the community. Video-conferencing platforms (Zoom, Google Hangout) allow team members to connect conveniently and supervision sessions can be facilitated even when team members are traveling to conferences or other work-related events across long distances, or through use of these platforms on smartphones while out in the community. Platforms such as Slack allow supervisors and their team members to communicate quickly and while on the go and can also be used via apps on smartphones.

There are countless options for technology-based tools to enhance the supervisory relationship and work of community within and across teams and organizations. When considering which tools work best for a particular team or a particular project, it is important to take the time to test out different options via demos and then make selections as a team. Ultimately, those team members who will be using the tools most frequently will want to have a say in which platforms would work best for them. Other considerations to consider include whether the platforms are compatible with smartphones, whether they can be used offline (if that is important for the work), as well as privacy and security features.

PUTTING VALUES INTO ACTION: PARALLEL PROCESSES AND ENCOURAGING COMMUNITY PRACTITIONER AND COMMUNITY MEMBER SELF-DETERMINATION AND EMPOWERMENT

Bobo and colleagues (2010), in describing how supervision should be structured in community-organizing initiatives and community organizations, caution that despite practice principles that involve fairness, equitability, and inclusive decision-making styles, someone must be in charge of following up with staff to make sure that work has been accomplished in the manner and time frame intended. Consequently, the model they describe involves certain constraints. Community practitioners must work in a manner consistent with the organization's mission and philosophy, while also being responsive to the needs and preferences of the communities with which they work. Therefore, one dilemma for community organizations is establishing a hierarchical management structure that facilitates staff training, task completion, and accountability while also encouraging staff member experiences of self-competency and self-empowerment, creativity, innovation, the ability to problem-solve, engage in reflective practice and critical thinking, and work both independently and within teams. Another consideration on the part of the organization is facilitating the new staff member's or social work intern's ability to work within the confines of the organization's structure, mission, policies, and governing rules. Supervisors are often responsible for providing orientation sessions to new hires, informing them of specific policies and procedures, advising them about any implicit or unstated expectations about how workers should behave or perform specific tasks, and mentoring them about how to best advocate for change in the organization when change is warranted (Hardina et al., 2006; Kaminski et al., 2000). Supervisors must be prepared to both supervise new staff members and work with them collaboratively as colleagues, peers, and team members. In most instances, supervision is a parallel process in which the supervisor offers general guidance and serves as a role model in the transmission of organization-related goals, skills, knowledge, and values to the new community practitioner (Hardina et al., 2006). In turn, it is expected that the community practitioner not only acquires these skills, but transmits some of them to other new team members in need of coaching, community leaders and partners, and students, service members, and other volunteers who contribute to the work of the organization (Boehm & Staples, 2002).

One theoretical perspective essential to social work that can be used to examine how transformation within one system can be used to affect changes in others is empowerment theory. Empowerment theory is especially relevant for community practitioners because it contains strategies for making changes within systems and organizations and also provides guidance as to how organizations should be structured to enhance the capabilities and experiences of self-competency and self-empowerment of staff members as well as the people served by the organization (Gutierrez et al., 1998; Hardina et al., 2006; Wallach & Mueller, 2006). It is not possible to "empower" others, as that implies the organizer is the one holding the power and it is a gift they are then giving to or sharing with someone else; instead, every person holds and cultivates their own power and empowerment originates from within, and supervisors and organizational leaders can foster an empowering organizational and team culture within which staff, interns, volunteers, and community members are encouraged to and provided opportunities to activate their own power. Organizations that establish an empowerment culture design decision-making structures that include people served by the organization and also engage in activities that create space for fostering self-empowerment in organizational team members. In community organizations, community members hold space on decision-making bodies, such as advisory councils, community action boards, boards of directors, and other committees, and are provided opportunities to take leadership and decision-making positions in the organization. This ensures that community members, including—and perhaps most important—those served by the organization, have a voice in guiding strategic planning, directing the provision of services, organizational priorities, and activities, and are advocates for improvements in organization procedures and policies.

In a typical nonprofit organization, staff members do not serve on boards of directors and therefore may have limited input into organizational decision-making. One of the dilemmas faced by community organizations is how to set up a management structure in which staff are encouraged to provide input into management decisions and advocate for policy changes and improvements in workplace conditions (Devine, 2010; Turner & Shera, 2005). Particularly for community-based organizations in which mutual learning and partnership among staff and constituents is valued, decision-making structures need to be fluid and flexible, allowing staff some discretion over their work, the ability to bargain for improvements in work conditions, and some degree of participation in program, campaign, and event planning (English, 2005; Wallach & Mueller, 2006). Community practitioners need to feel supported and valued, that they have opportunities for professional development and career advancement, and that decisions about workplace conditions and work assignments are made in a fair manner (Bobo et al., 2010; Turner & Shera, 2005).

Another way to view organization leader and supervisor responsibilities for establishing an empowerment culture and promoting staff self-empowerment is to direct activities undertaken by the organization in a way that enhances experiences of staff self-efficacy, perceptions of one's own ability to handle assigned tasks, and provides opportunities for team members to assume greater responsibility in support of organization goals (Gutierrez et al., 1995). Professional development activities that can be used to foster self-empowerment include sending workers to training and workshops; identifying worker strengths, interests, and aptitudes; finding opportunities for workers to apply specialized knowledge or skills in challenging work situations; and promoting workers through the ranks (Kaminski et al., 2000; Shera & Page, 1995). In addition, community practitioners, given the complexity of organizing in ever-changing circumstances in a variety of community settings and venues, benefit from having some degree of autonomy in their work, discretion over some types of decisions, the ability to think on their feet, and respond creatively to situational demands. These types of characteristics are often encouraged by organizations with empowerment cultures (Petter et al., 2002).

The use of workplace teams has also been found to enhance experiences of empowerment among organization staff, requiring that they learn to work together cooperatively and develop a sense of collective identity and solidarity (Brownstein, 2003; Daily & Bishop, 2003; D. Johnson & Johnson, 2017). Additional benefits associated with workplace teams include reductions in worker turnover and burnout; increases in job satisfaction, work performance, commitment to the organization; and experiences of personal empowerment and self-competency among staff members (Siebert et al., 2011).

Another method often used to facilitate cooperation and sense of community among staff members is group supervision (Kadushin & Harkness, 2014; Wayne et al., 2010). One of the advantages of this method is that the group facilitation skills employed by the supervisor can serve as a guide to organizing staff who are assigned to facilitate workplace teams, committees, or groups of constituents. Group supervision also serves as a source of peer support and provides an opportunity for staff members to learn from their peers. A social work supervisor can alternate group supervision with one-on-one supervision as needed in order to both promote peer support and provide individualized coaching and supervision.

Organizations may be structured as a set of interconnected teams in which a formal structure is established that allows for effective communication among all organization members (D. Johnson & Johnson, 2017). Small community organizations may minimize or eliminate management hierarchies, using consensus-oriented decision-making models such as worker cooperatives or collectives in which all members have equitable status and power to manage the work of the organization (Majee & Hoyt, 2009; Morrison & Branigan, 2007). It should be noted, however, that in organizations that encourage the development of strong personal bonds among staff people with the intent of minimizing the social distance between administrators and other employees, it may be difficult to implement accountability standards or make decisions about how performance problems should be handled (Morgen, 1994). Also, in larger, more dispersed organizations that operate in a number of locations, such informal or partnership models may not be feasible, requiring that the organization maintain a centralized decision-making structure with designated leaders (Swarts, 2008).

Supervisors must be ready to allocate responsibilities and power appropriately, encourage the development of staff skills and competencies, and focus on the well-being of staff members and constituents in addition to the maintenance and capacity of the organization (Turner & Shera, 2005). They must be able to provide support and inspire staff to do their best, work as members of a team, and use their skills to develop flexibility and creativity in response to situational demands (Hardina et al., 2006; Jaskyte, 2004).

END-OF-CHAPTER RESOURCES

KEY TAKEAWAYS AND SUMMARY

Becoming a skilled community practitioner is often a matter of professional experience, values, knowledge, and strong interpersonal and analytical social work skills. Community practitioners are expected to engage in reflective and critical thinking and to be flexible, innovative, and creative; provide support and guidance to individuals, groups, and organizations; and interact productively with partner organizations, elected officials, and powerful decision makers to influence legislation and policies and change community conditions (Lietz, 2010). However, community practitioners must also be accountable to the communities they serve, their constituents, and the organizations in which they work. Social workers employed as community practitioners or completing social work internships are also expected to follow the social work *Code of Ethics* (NASW, 2021). Although some community practitioners do not receive formal training, social work students and program graduates do have access to training in interpersonal social work skills and analytical methods that can be applied in community-organization settings. Supervisory structures established in community organizations are designed to provide training and support to new community practitioners and student interns and ensure accountability to the organization and its mission. Social work supervisors in community organizations and other macro-related settings (such as government agencies or legislative settings) have a responsibility to help students integrate social work skills and the experiential knowledge necessary to work with constituents and other decision makers. Supervision should be a parallel process in which students and employees gain the self-confidence and experiences of self-efficacy and personal empowerment necessary to promote community empowerment and community self-determination.

RESOURCES

- Training for Change has a number of trainings, workshops, and resources available to support the work of community practitioners: https://www.trainingforchange.org
- inSocialWork podcast series—Episode 9: Dr. Hilary Weaver, "Culturally Competent Supervision": This episode features Dr. Hilary Weaver speaking at the Fourth International Interdisciplinary Conference on Clinical Supervision, convened in Buffalo, New York, spring 2008. Dr. Weaver discusses diversity issues in the context of

supervision, highlighting the transactional model of identity and the critical role supervisors have in promoting, modeling, and developing cultural competence within human service organizations.

- Audio: https://www.insocialwork.org/episode-9-dr-hilary-weaver-culturally-competent-supervision/
- Transcript: https://www.insocialwork.org/wp-content/uploads/2021/06/insocialwork-episode-9.pdf

ACTIVITIES

1. **Small-group discussion questions:** What attributes would you associate with effective supervision for community practitioners? What types of personality traits and skills should supervisors have? How does this differ from some of the supervisors that you have had in past employment or internships? What type of supervision complements your personality? What should a supervisor know about you to assist you with completing your work objectives?
2. **With a classmate, role-play a supervisory session using the following scenario:** A social work intern at a community organization has been asked to conduct at least three one-on-one interviews with community leaders who have cultural backgrounds that are different from that of the intern, but has not been able to do so. A supervisory meeting has been set up so that the field instructor can explore why the intern has been unable to meet this objective. In this role play, items to be discussed should include the intern's comfort with the assignment; past experience conducting interviews; how one-on-one interviews may be similar to or different from in-agency interviews with clients; and whether the intern has received enough information, guidance, and training from the supervisor or organization in carrying out this assignment. Methods that can be used to obtain entry to culturally different communities should also be discussed.

ASSIGNMENTS

1. Write a three- to four-page analysis of the supervisory structure of your field agency and attach a chart that illustrates how you perceive the organization to be structured in terms of supervision of staff. (See example ideas for organizational charts here: www.orgcharting.com/org-chart-of-social-service-organization) The paper should examine lines of authority (who is responsible for decision-making and to whom supervisors and administrative staff report), procedures for holding staff accountable, and policies that staff are required to follow. Also describe procedures that a staff member can use to advocate for changes in organization policies and procedures and to what degree such advocacy is encouraged by the organization.

2. Conduct an informal organizational assessment of your field placement based on your experiences and by using a document review approach (e.g., review the website, mission, and vision statements as well as policies and procedures). Write a five- to eight-page paper that answers the following questions: (a) Provide a brief overview of the organization—what type of organization is it? What is the mission and vision statement? Who does the organization serve and how does it serve those people (e.g., what programs or services are provided?)? (b) How would you describe the organization's culture—is it an empowering culture? If so, how? If not, why not? Does the organization value cultural competency and cultural responsiveness? Describe how this is evident or where the organization could strengthen its approach to culturally responsive practices. In your review of documents and based on your experiences, does the culture appear to be empowering, anti-racist, equitable, and/or inclusive? Is there diversity represented in leadership, including on the board of directors, community action board, or other committees? Are people the organization serves represented in leadership and decision-making structures? How could this be improved? (c) Describe leadership practices and approaches within the organization. Are leaders demonstrating characteristics of resilient leadership? Facilitative leadership? In what ways? How could this be strengthened? What types of training and supervision are offered to staff, interns, and other team members? Does this promote cultural competency? Does this promote effective team and leadership processes? Finally, conclude your paper by recommending at least three areas and strategies for strengthening the organization's culture. Consider sharing these recommendations with your field supervisor or field instructor.

A robust set of instructor resources designed to supplement this text is located at http://connect.springerpub.com/content/book/978-0-8261-5835-2. Qualifying instructors may request access by emailing textbook@springerpub.com.

KEY REFERENCES

Only key references appear in the print edition. The full reference list appears in the digital product on Springer Publishing Connect: connect.springerpub.com/content/book/978-0-8261-5835-2/part/part04/chapter/ch13

Gamble, D. (2011). Advanced concentration macro competencies for social work practitioners: Identifying knowledge, values, judgment and skills to promote human well-being. *Journal of Community Practice, 19*, 369–402. https://doi.org/10.1080/10705422.2011.625914

Hardina, D., & Obel-Jorgensen, R. (2009). Increasing social action competency: A framework for supervision. *Journal of Policy Practice, 8*(2), 89–109. https://doi.org/10.1080/15588740902740074

Jaskyte, K. (2004). Transformational leadership, organization culture, and innovativeness in nonprofit organizations. *Nonprofit Leadership and Management, 15*, 153–168. https://doi.org/10.1002/nml.59

Knee, R. T., & Folsom, J. (2012). Bridging the crevasse between direct practice social work and management by increasing the transferability of core skills. *Administration in Social Work, 36*, 390–408. https://doi.org/10.1080/03643107.2011.604402

Lietz, C. (2010). Critical thinking in child welfare supervision. *Administration in Social Work, 34,* 68–78. https://doi.org/10.1080/03643100903432966

Peters, S. C. (2017). Social work leadership: An analysis of historical and contemporary challenges. *Human Service Organizations: Management, Leadership, & Governance, 41,* 336–345. https://doi.org/10.1080/23303131.2017.1302375

Peters, S. C. (2018). Defining social work leadership: A theoretical and conceptual review and analysis. *Journal of Social Work Practice, 32,* 31–44. https://doi.org/10.1080/02650533.2017.1300877

Ross, L. (2010). Notes from the field: Learning cultural humility through critical incidents and central challenges in community-based participatory research. *Journal of Community Practice, 18,* 315–335. https://doi.org/10.1080/10705422.2010.490161

Turner, L., & Shera, W. (2005). Empowerment of human service workers: Beyond intra-organizational strategies. *Administration in Social Work, 29*(3), 79–94. https://doi.org/10.1300/J147v29n03_06

Wint, E., & Sewpaul, V. (2000). Product and process dialectic: Developing an Indigenous approach to community development training. *Journal of Community Practice, 7*(1), 57–70. https://doi.org/10.1300/J125v07n01_05

SOCIAL WORK SKILLS IN A GLOBAL CONTEXT: ADVOCATING FOR HUMAN RIGHTS

LEARNING OBJECTIVES

After reading this chapter, students will be able to:

- Recognize the responsibility of social workers to uphold the International Federation of Social Workers' *Global Social Work Statement of Ethical Principles.*
- Describe the impact of globalization on the Global South.
- Summarize the antiglobalization and environmental justice movements.
- Define *first-generation*, *second-generation*, and *third-generation rights*.

INTRODUCTION

The human rights perspective is often used to examine the process of globalization and its effects on people served by the social work professions. In this chapter, the human rights perspective, introduced in Chapter 1, provides a framework of values for an examination of community organizing and social work practice internationally. One of the rationales for international human rights standards, including the process of globalization and its negative impacts on health, well-being, wage standards, and migration, is described. The responsibility of social workers, as identified in the International Federation of Social Workers' (IFSW's; 2018) *Global Social Work Statement of Ethical Principles*, to advocate on behalf of human rights is also examined. In addition, an overview of the practice of community organizing in the international context is provided with a focus on the practice of social planning, and community development for enhancing social and economic development in the Global South is presented. The use of social action and transformative organizing approaches in the struggle for human rights worldwide is also discussed. In the last section of this chapter, the implications of a global perspective for social work and community practice are examined.

PUTTING VALUES INTO ACTION: HUMAN RIGHTS

Philosopher Amartya Sen (2004) asserts that the recognition of human rights implies that individuals who are in a position to do so are ethically obligated to take action to make sure that human rights are achieved. Often, the human rights perspective is equated with social and economic justice. However, Lundy and van Wormer (2007) distinguish between the two terms. The principle of *social justice* pertains to whether people are treated equitably, how resources are distributed, and whether people have basic political or civil rights. Groups that experience political, social, or economic marginalization and oppression seldom have access to all the goods and services that they need; consequently, they experience economic injustice and are unable to maintain a basic standard of living. The term *human rights,* on the other hand, explicitly pertains to universal standards established to measure individual and collective political, social, and economic rights and whether these standards have been met (Healy & Thomas, 2021).

According to Murdach (2011), the origin of the human rights perspective occurred in the 18th century in the United States' *Declaration of Independence* (1776) and the *Declaration of the Rights of Man and of Citizens* (1789). However, Wronka (2017) and Ife (2001) place the origins of the concept of human rights in the 17th century. John Locke and other philosophers developed the concept of *natural rights,* the belief that all men have natural rights as a consequence of simply being human and consequently should be treated in a manner that is equal to everyone else. Although these philosophical assumptions influenced independence movements in the United States and France, the notion of equality was limited to certain segments of the population. Women and people without property were not given the right to vote or serve on juries; slaves and non-White people were not deemed worthy to share these natural rights (Ife, 2001). In addition, Locke, Hume, Rousseau, and Voltaire and other philosophers emphasized property rights and freedom from arbitrary rule or government regulation (Wronka, 2017). Locke's writings also attributed poverty to moral failure on the part of individuals. These ideas are now associated with the contemporary philosophy of individualism, the idea that individuals are solely responsible for their status in society and their ability to acquire the income, goods, and services that they need (Segal & Kilty, 2003).

As noted by Murdach (2011), individualism and its association with the human rights perspective is actually at odds with other philosophies about how wealth and resources should be distributed such as egalitarianism (equal treatment for everyone) or utilitarianism (the greatest good for the greatest number). Another criticism of this approach is that the concept is Eurocentric and inconsistent with conceptualizations associated with other cultures that focus on group or collective rights and shared responsibility for community well-being (Donnelly, 2007; Ife, 2001). The original *Universal Declaration of Human Rights* (United Nations, 1948) also did not provide an exhaustive list of rights for members of all minoritized and marginalized groups. (Bakker, 2007; Wetzel, 2001).

However, what we currently think of as human rights, as described in the *Universal Declaration of Human Rights* (United Nations, 1948), has evolved over time and has been strengthened to include additional categories of rights beyond those identified as natural rights by 18th-century thinkers. Ife (2001) identifies three waves or generations of rights:

- *First-generation rights* are those initially identified during the Enlightenment, which have evolved over time. They include political and civil rights such as freedom of speech and assembly, the right to vote, citizenship rights, freedom of religion, and equal treatment under the law. Also included in these categories are rights that have been interpreted as accruing from others such as freedom from discrimination, the right to privacy, and freedom from torture. Most of these rights are specified in legal codes and government constitutions, but, of course, vary by country and may not always be enforced.

- *Second-generation rights* include individual and group-related social, political, and cultural rights. They pertain to the right to obtain certain social benefits, including jobs, good wages, education, healthcare, and food. Although recognized in the *Universal Declaration of Rights* (United Nations, 1948), there is little international consensus that all people are entitled to these benefits or that governments are required to provide them.
- *Third-generation rights* are those that belong to communities, demographic groups, or countries and include the right to benefit from world trade and economic growth, the right to engage in economic development or advancement, the right to live in a stable society, and environmental rights. Environmental rights include the right to clean air and water. This set of rights is a purely a 20th-century phenomenon and is not fully recognized, except in some of the various international conventions and treaties. Obtaining international agreements on these rights is often difficult as such efforts are often viewed as limiting the economic rights of some individuals or restraining economic activity (Bakker, 2007).

The human rights framework has been highly influential in guiding international development efforts and social movements to acquire social, economic, and political rights among members of minoritized and marginalized groups. Human rights work is most often conducted by the United Nations and regional organizations such as the African Union, the Organization of American States, and the European Union (Healy & Thomas, 2021; Wronka, 2017). It is also undertaken by numerous international organizations such as Doctors Without Borders, Amnesty International, and Human Rights Watch (Ife, 2001). Although these organizations have name recognition and resources, thousands of national, regional, and local organizations conduct human rights work, or make appeals to the United Nations or government bodies to address human rights violations. As noted in Chapter 1, human rights have been formally recognized as a component of social work practice through the work of the IFSW (Dominelli, 2010; Healy & Thomas, 2021; Murdach, 2011). Values associated with the human rights perspective have also been incorporated into criticisms of recent economic trends, such as globalization, as well as responses to economic hardship by government agencies and nonprofit organizations engaged in community development and social planning or engaging in social action to fight injustice (Midgley, 2007).

THE PROCESS OF GLOBALIZATION: IMPACT ON HEALTH, WELL-BEING, WAGE RATES, AND MIGRATION

One of the rationales for adopting a standard or universal human rights perspective has to do with the process of globalization and its effects on individual and group well-being, health, and economic status. *Globalization* is a term given to recent trends related to economic production and consumption (B. Edwards, 2011). It is premised on the assumption that economic activity and its impact in a variety of contexts (economic behavior, government policies, poverty, personal health and well-being, and immigration) are interconnected. As such, what happens in individual countries as a result of government action and economic activity has an impact on other nations (Healy & Thomas, 2021; Lundy, 2004). Technology also plays a role in globalization, creating better opportunities for people to stay interconnected using the internet, cell phones, and other communication devices (Midgley, 2007).

The process of globalization is also enhanced through decisions made by international organizations such as the World Trade Organization (WTO), the World Bank, and the International Monetary Fund (IMF), which have a role in setting global economic policies, and also by large transnational corporations that engage in economic activity, sell products, and employ workers in numerous countries (Lundy, 2004). Consequently, economic activities in some nations contribute to reductions in wages, poverty, poor health, pollution, and other social conditions in others (Fox & Meier, 2009; Rispel et al., 2009). Poor living conditions also contribute to the migration of people from one country to the next who seek better employment, economic opportunities, and an improved quality of life (Xu, 2007). Therefore, globalization does not simply foster economic connections among countries; it also has a profound influence on policies, practices, and social systems in most countries and the lives of most individuals and families (Dominelli, 2010).

According to Ife (2001), the basic critique associated with the process of globalization is that rather than improve economic well-being, it creates both "networks of power" and "networks of inequality" that transcend national boundaries. Aided by the internet and other communications technology, wealth and power are accumulated by people with assets while others are isolated and excluded. Western industrialized nations tend to benefit from globalization, whereas other countries, primarily located in the Global South, often experience economic deprivation (Midgley, 2007).

Another consistent critique of the globalization movement is that organizations, such as the IMF and the World Bank, are responsible for contributing to economic hardship by emphasizing policies characterized as "neo-liberal" and originating in the 1980s in the economic policies of Margaret Thatcher in the United Kingdom and Ronald Regan in the United States. These policies were designed to promote lower taxation and reductions in funding for public programs (Ayers, 2004; Lundy, 2004; Midgley, 2007). Transnational organizations, such as the World Bank, the IMF, and the WTO, have a large influence on the economic systems of member nations, especially countries in the Global South that apply for loans or credit from these institutions. Originally established after World War II to fund development projects and controlled by Western industrial nations, the IMF in partnership with the World Bank can demand that countries adjust their economies in order to qualify for loans (Prigoff, 2000). The Structural Adjustment Program often requires cuts to public services for the people in poverty, healthcare, and education funding; the deregulation of public services such as transportation or energy, a switch from subsistence agriculture to crops that are exported resulting in increases in food prices, suppression of unions and wage rates, and the provision of favorable regulations or other benefits to encourage relocation of transnational corporations rather than encouraging local investments (Lundy, 2004). It may also result in the depletion of natural resources (such as rain forests or water) and resources held by Indigenous or culturally diverse communities, increasing poverty and further marginalizing members of these communities (Prigoff, 2000; Reed, 2002). Such environmental damage can also contribute to the migration of these populations to other countries.

Although such conditions may be necessary to qualify for loans or credits from transnational institutions, often these economic policies have a negative impact on most residents of the countries that adopt them; many of these nations are so impoverished that what they really need to do is spend money on roads, education, and other improvements that will aid economic development (Delonis, 2004; Lundy, 2004; Prigoff, 2000). For example, the country of Haiti has historically suffered from a huge debt crisis that negatively affected its ability to develop a functioning economy or provide for its citizens. The debt originated in part from financial arrangements that secured Haitian independence from France in 1804; in 2010, a devastating earthquake occurred, killing many residents, destroying housing and infrastructure, and placing many people at risk of deadly diseases such as cholera; one relief measure taken by wealthy countries and transnational banking organizations was to "forgive" Haitian debts ("G7 Nations," 2010). As noted by Lundy (2004), countries in the developing world are not alone in facing economic troubles and cuts in public programs due to the demands of IMF and the World Bank. In 2011, some of the western industrialized nations with large public debts due to heavy borrowing from other nations and the worldwide economic downturn also were required to pare down welfare programs and other public benefits to qualify for credit and loans, leading to public protests in European countries such as Greece and Portugal (Associated Press, 2011; Donadio & Kitsantonis, 2011).

Often, trade agreements, such as the 1994 North American Free Trade Agreement (NAFTA), permitted industrialized countries to operate unregulated (in terms of worker safety and environmental protection) industries in countries such as Mexico (Delgado-Wise & Marquez Covarrubias, 2007). This allowed international corporations to pay people less in these countries than they would in Western industrialized nations. Consequently, there were fewer jobs for manufacturing and service industry workers in countries, such as Australia, Canada, the United States, and the European Union, because these jobs have been relocated to Africa, Asia, and Latin America, where wage rates are substantially lower (Prigoff, 2000). Advocacy organizations have documented the adverse effects of these arrangements. Transnational corporations often purchase products made in places such as China and El Salvador or operate plants in these countries and then look the other way when workers are mistreated or abused (Kernaghan, 2011).

Large corporations may flood foreign markets with products or agricultural goods that drive prices in those countries down and limit economic opportunities, negatively impacting income, wage rates, and citizen health. However, corporations in industrialized countries hire immigrants to work in jobs that require few skills and pay low wages (Castle, 2004). Therefore, the economy in these countries is often dependent on a supply of labor from this source. Often people migrate from the Global South, where there are few employment opportunities, to industrialized nations in search of a better life. Some of these immigrants are undocumented, meaning that they were unable to obtain visas or other documents that permit them to live and work legally in their new countries. Workers without legal papers and working permits often have low levels of education and skills, making it less likely that they can legalize their immigration status, and ensuring that they will be locked into low-paying jobs (Nawyn, 2010).

In addition, industrialized countries differ in terms of policies on legal immigration and access to benefits such as welfare and healthcare (Xu, 2007). Legal immigrants (such as skilled workers and refugees) are treated differently than people with few job skills or undocumented immigrants. Armed conflict, natural disasters, and climate change increase economic hardship and force many people to flee from their homes for safe haven in other countries (Dominelli, 2010; Frederico et al., 2007). If refugees cannot be fully integrated into the economies of their new countries, they may remain indefinitely in "refugee camps" until they can be resettled elsewhere or return to their countries of origin (De La Puente, 2011). Often, immigration controls are implemented when people become fearful of others who are different from them, or questions are raised about possible competition for low-wage work from refugees, undocumented workers, or other immigrants (Boateng, 2009; Xu, 2007). Another international issue involves human trafficking, with people being moved from their countries of origin against their will and often involving threats of violence for uncompensated labor or the sex trade; in some cases, they may be kidnapped and ransomed back to their families when they try to negotiate with traffickers for safe passage into industrialized countries (Androff, 2011; Castle, 2004; Healy & Thomas, 2021).

Despite these issues, economists often view the impact of globalization positively, citing the growth in transnational business transactions and markets, and the growth of low-wage employment opportunities in the Global South (Midgley, 2007). Economic processes related to globalization have also promoted increased privatization of previously provided government- or nonprofit-provided goods and services, such as energy, water, and education, as well as welfare, child protection, mental healthcare, and other services provided by social workers, thereby increasing the profits of the businesses and corporations that provide them (Dominelli, 2010; Lundy, 2004). Some social workers have argued that privatization of social services limits their autonomy over their work and their ability to adequately serve people in need (Healy & Thomas, 2021; Ife, 2001). Dominelli (2010) summarizes the criticism of the process of globalization from a social work perspective:

The poorest people on the planet have been adversely affected, through loss of jobs, low-paid work that is insufficient to provide a decent standard of living, health hazards, rising food and energy prices, environmental degradation, armed conflict and resource depletion. (p. 600)

INTERNATIONAL SOCIAL WORK AND COMMUNITY PRACTICE: APPLYING INTERNATIONAL FEDERATION OF SOCIAL WORKERS PRINCIPLES AND TAKING ACTION

Healy and Thomas (2021) define *international social work* as "international professional action and the capacity for international action by the social work profession and its members to promote human dignity and human rights and enhance human well-being" (pp. 7–8). They identify four specific components of international social work practice: everyday practice methods that take place in the social worker's country of origin but that have a relationship to international issues, actual international practice, international professional social work exchanges, and international advocacy and policy development. The IFSW (2005), in partnership with the International Association of Schools of Social Work, has developed global standards for social work education that mandate that practice should be guided by the IFSW's (2018) *Global Social Work Statement of Ethical Principles* and the *Universal Declaration of Human Rights* (United Nations, 1948) as well as other U.N. charters or covenants of rights (see Chapter 1 for a list of some of these documents). However, it should also be noted that standardization of professional practice methods, including advocacy for a universal set of human rights, requires an understanding of cultural and human interaction patterns that may be specific to cultures or societies that are non-Western in orientation. In such situations, social workers, especially those working cross-culturally or transnationally, must work to adopt social work methods that are appropriate for the political, social, and economic environment as well as the population served (Jonsson, 2010). Rankopo and Osei-Hwedie (2011) argue that the use of culturally appropriate or Indigenous practice methods is critical for effective practice. The IFSW also issued a policy statement on the rights of Indigenous Peoples (IFSW, 2017). According to Weaver (2019), the IFSW statement on Indigenous Peoples "affirm the fundamental nature of human rights for individuals and collectives. Recognition of collective rights places these documents far ahead of other international human rights documents and scholarship" (p. 81). Indeed, the conceptualization of human rights as something belonging to individuals rather than collectives is based on Western societal values; the IFSW document moves beyond this problematic conceptualization.

In addition to cultural relevance, human rights advocacy demands practice strategies that are generally outside the scope of traditional practice methods. Although the international origins of many social problems should be obvious to most social work practitioners, not all social workers engage in human rights-related practice, nor are they mandated to do so. Lundy and van Wormer (2007) note that in contrast to the social work codes of ethics adopted in many countries and the IFSW (2018) *Global Social Work Statement of Ethical Principles,* the National Association of Social Workers (2021) *Code of Ethics* does not include a provision for social workers in the United States to uphold human rights principles. This omission is problematic because:

> *Social workers have a responsibility to advocate for human rights and social justice and to question exploitative structures. We can begin by addressing the urgent need for economic security, social equality and better social services and programs. In holding the state accountable for the social protection of the population and the human rights standards, as codified in international law, the effectiveness of the social work mission will be enhanced. (Lundy & van Wormer, 2007, p. 733)*

Sen (2004) identifies four types of actions associated with ethical practice from a human rights perspective: (a) securing formal recognition (such as in a charter of rights) that people actually have these rights, (b) organized advocacy to urge governments to comply with these rights, (c) monitoring to make sure that governments actually comply and to pressure them to do so, and (d) legislation to make sure that compliance is required under a country's legal code. In addition, advocacy groups may also file formal complaints with various U.N. bodies and other international organizations (Healy & Thomas, 2021). Although such efforts cannot force compliance, they can draw public, governmental, and media attention to the issue and help pressure authorities to take action. All these activities are consistent with the various codes associated with social work practice worldwide. Ife (2001) explicitly links social work practice on behalf of human rights to the three generations of rights identified earlier in this chapter:

- *First-generation rights.* Social workers should advocate for constitutional protections for civil and political rights as well as the enforcement of these rights. Although citizens of countries in the developing world do not necessarily have these rights (such as freedom of speech, the right to vote, equal protection of the law, and freedom from arbitrary imprisonment), it is also probable that in some industrialized nations human rights violations can occur. For example, discrimination and high levels of unemployment are issues that occur in every country despite provisions in the

United Nations' (1948) *Universal Declaration of Human Rights* related to freedom from discrimination and a right to employment. Same-sex marriage and banning the death penalty are also considered basic human rights in some countries, but not others, providing an opportunity for human rights advocacy on the part of social workers. However, Ife (2001) notes that although advocacy should be undertaken by social workers, it should not be on behalf of communities or community members; rather, it should be in partnership with them.

- *Second-generation rights.* Social workers should act to preserve cultural and social rights through direct practice and practice in organizations. Services should be provided in a manner that respects the cultural values of participants and that is adequate to meet the needs of the people served. Social workers can also engage in social action to facilitate policies that reduce poverty and provide access to education and healthcare.
- *Third-generation rights.* These rights pertain to collective rights related to economic development, a clean environment, and a stable society. Therefore, the practice methods that should be used are community development and planning as well as social action-oriented community organizing.

SOCIAL PLANNING AND COMMUNITY DEVELOPMENT: APPLYING STANDARDS FROM THE UNITED NATIONS' UNIVERSAL DECLARATION OF HUMAN RIGHTS

Often community development and social planning practice are similar in purpose and designed to lift communities and demographic groups out of poverty or increase access to jobs, healthcare, or education. These activities may be coordinated by government agencies or nonprofit organizations. Often the only distinction between the two processes is that in social planning, recommendations are made and decisions are finalized as to how development is to occur. In community and/or economic development public and private agencies establish programs or build roads, factories, or other types of facilities to improve financial or social well-being. International development work is described in the literature as pertaining to one of two types of countries: nations (primarily in the Global North) that are highly industrialized, and countries (many of them former colonies of European countries or the United States) that are not highly industrialized with large numbers of people who live in poverty. Most of these countries are located in the Global South and have agricultural crops or natural resources, such as oil or timber, that are sold to or consumed by the industrialized nations (Healy & Thomas, 2021; Midgley, 2007). Midgley (2005) describes the origin of the term *community development* in terms of efforts of the colonial powers to modernize or "develop" the Global South. Although the stated intent was to improve economic and social conditions for people in many Asian, African, and Latin American countries, often such development efforts actually benefited industrialized nations rather than the citizens who were intended to benefit (Dominelli, 2005; Fox & Mason Meier, 2009). Although economic development efforts have had more success in some countries than others, governments, nonprofit organizations, and citizen advocacy groups have adopted approaches similar to those used in the Western industrialized nations to stimulate economic development and improve social conditions for their residents.

Commonalities and Differences in Local Participatory Planning Efforts: Cross-Country Comparisons

Social planning and community development activities often take place in the Global South as government-mandated efforts to increase industrialization, jobs, and access to technology and financial capital for their citizens (Alasah, 2009; Midgley, 2010). Often, these programs are funded in part by the World Bank or IMF and focus on building roads and industrial capacity (Oladipo et al., 2007). In some situations, these processes are conducted by and coordinated through central governments and rely on rational planning methods (Widianingsih & Morrell, 2007). In some cases, these efforts may be perceived by residents to benefit some population groups (often the political or economic elite) more often than others, creating additional hardships for citizens (Rajgopal, 2002). Often preexisting ethnic, racial, or class-based disputes (in some cases dating back to colonial governments), actual warfare, or new migration patterns may limit inclusion in financial or political decision-making and acquisition of benefits as a result of economic growth to a handful of demographic groups in diverse societies (Grodofsky, 2007; Ravensbergen & Van der Platt, 2009; Schmid & Salman, 2005).

In part, competing claims and demands from different segments of the population may precede efforts on the part of governments in the Global South to implement policies and procedures designed to increase citizen participation in planning and governance. Sometimes these approaches are used in conjunction with other social capital-related techniques to improve civic engagement, individual capacity, and skill building (Grodofsky, 2007). Gaventa and Valderrama (1999) differentiate between two different types of citizen participation efforts: indirect participation in the political process (i.e., electing representatives) and direct participation in local planning efforts. Consequently, participation in government planning efforts serves as a vehicle for building democratic institutions, linking citizens to government agencies ensuring that government services are accountable to the public, and building social integration and solidarity.

In addition, citizen planning councils are prevalent in the Western industrialized countries and the Global South in both capitalist and socialist countries. They are typically viewed as a means to reduce the harmful effects of social marginalization and to provide opportunities for under-resourced, minoritized, and other marginalized communities to have input as to what services they should receive (Bowen, 2007). They also provide an opportunity for people to participate in local decision-making, thus strengthening citizenship rights (Moffat et al., 1999; Schmid & Salman, 2005). According to Lestrelin and colleagues (2011), participatory approaches are believed to lead to better planning processes and more meaningful outcomes, making it more likely that development efforts will be sustainable over time.

Research indicates that there are strengths and limitations of participatory planning approaches in international contexts. For example, Yen and Luong (2008) describe the adoption of a participatory approach to planning at the village and communal levels in Vietnam. The strengths of this method are that when a variety of groups become involved in the process, both equity and transparency are improved. The limitations of the process include the time and resource commitments required and the lack of skilled facilitators to effectively engage residents in planning.

Effective involvement of citizens in planning also requires sufficient resources, leadership, and people willing to volunteer for participation (Buccus et al., 2008; Moffat et al.,

1999). However, many projects are not sufficiently funded and often emphasize outside expertise rather than provide adequate opportunities for the participation of community residents, especially those people who are considered of lower socioeconomic status. In addition, decision-making processes are often dominated by local elites and tend to exclude people who traditionally have been minoritized or marginalized within the culture, including women and people in poverty (Hicks, 2011; Ravensbergen & Van der Platt, 2009; Widianingsih & Morrell, 2007).

Gaventa (2004) identifies a number of steps that can and should be taken by governments to strengthen citizen involvement in planning:

- Ensure that participation in planning is one of the legal rights granted to citizens.
- Make a clear delineation of the rights and roles of all participants.
- Provide citizen opportunities for direct representation of individuals and community organizations on government planning councils.
- Provide leadership training and financial incentives to citizens serving on the councils.
- Decentralize decision-making processes so that opportunities to participate are available on a local level.
- Ensure "seats at the table" for women, racial and ethnic minoritized group members, people of limited economic means, and members of other politically marginalized groups.
- Provide skilled facilitators and other resources to make sure that effective dialogue and deliberations take place among diverse participants. Skills for facilitators should include conflict resolution, negotiation, and active listening.
- Make sure that participants and other leaders have support from, and are accountable to, strong community organizations.
- Encourage a culture of information sharing, transparency, and accountability on the part of government participants.

Establishing Economic and Social Development Standards: The Role of Transnational Organizations

Social rights, the right to maintain an adequate standard of living, including access to jobs, education, and healthcare, are among the most controversial of the rights listed in the *Universal Declaration of Human Rights* (United Nations, 1948) and in subsequent U.N. covenants and charters. As noted earlier in this chapter, direct provisions of some of these services and resources and, in some instances, even taking action to ensure that people have equitable access to jobs, education, and healthcare are often viewed as at odds with principles related to individualism, the idea that people should be responsible for obtaining their own resources, goods, services, and social status (Segal & Kilty, 2003). According to Mishra (2005), it has been difficult for the United Nations to enforce these standards for a number of reasons: they require voluntary compliance by countries, the various U.N. charters and covenants are somewhat vague about how countries are to meet these standards, and some countries simply do not have the economic resources with which to comply, especially in the

Global South. It is also difficult to monitor the impact of government policies and actions in the attainment of these rights and even to agree how some of the outcomes specified in the standards are to be measured (e.g., poverty or access to healthcare).

In order to compare the degree to which various countries are "developed" or are able to address the economic needs of their residents, standardized measures of well-being have been developed by the World Bank, the Organization for Economic Cooperation and Development, and the United Nations (Healy & Thomas, 2021). These indicators are intended to measure social progress and make comparisons on a number of factors related to health, income, education levels, gender equity, infant mortality, economic development, and other measures of well-being (Estes, 2005). Although it is tempting to argue that achievement of these standards is based purely on a nation's wealth or individual responsibility for taking care of one's health and well-being (e.g., eating nutritious food, having one's children vaccinated, or seeing a doctor regularly), some nations in the Global North may have lower rates of health and well-being than other countries in the Global South. Given different measurement tools and standards, rankings may not be consistent among countries. For example, the United States was ranked 17th on the 2019 Human Development Index report issued by the United Nations (World Population Review, 2022a). The index includes indicators of life expectancy at birth, average number of years of schooling, the expected number of years of schooling, gross national income (GNI), and the average GNI per person (United Nations, 2010). In contrast, UNICEF (United Nations Children's Fund) data indicate that in 2020, the United States was ranked 50th in mortality rates for children under 5, a key human development indicator (World Population Review, 2022b). Income distribution or inequities, the provision of public services, the availability of clean water and sanitation, the status of women in terms of educational achievement and reproductive rights, and healthcare access may have an equal or greater impact than GNI on social indicators such as poverty and infant mortality (Collison et al., 2007; Fox & Mason Meier, 2009).

International Social Development and Aid Organizations

Many of the industrialized nations provide development assistance to nations in the Global South as well as technical assistance and other forms of foreign aid. Some of this assistance is used to attain political and economic goals (such as a strategic ally in a time of war, influence government policies, or access to raw materials) and in some situations it is provided primarily in responses to a natural disaster such as a flood, famine, or displacement due to an armed conflict (Healy & Thomas, 2021). This type of assistance is usually described as *relief* and typically includes food and health services along with other types of assistance (Keough & Samuels, 2004). These organizations often send staff members, employ local workers, or recruit volunteers with specialized skills (including social workers) to provide assistance (Lough et al., 2011). Development assistance and disaster relief may be delivered by international aid agencies established by the donor countries, or nonprofit organizations (called *nongovernment organizations*, or *NGOs*, in the international development literature).

Although these organizations provide valuable assistance, particularly material goods and services to people in poverty—especially after disasters—they have been critiqued on a number of levels. Some organizations offer services or development assistance that may be exclusively reflective of North American or Eurocentric values, and in the case of faith-based organizations, religious viewpoints (Berger, 2003; Jonsson, 2010). In addition, some of these organizations contract with Western governments to distribute foreign aid funds, raising questions about their motives and whether assistance serves some type of political agenda (M. Edwards, 1999). A related issue is that some development agencies focus only on material assistance (such as food) and do nothing to change economic, political, or social systems that have contributed to poverty, minoritization, and marginalization, and, worse, may simply sustain existing regimes and perpetuate harmful conditions (Offenheiser & Holcombe, 2003). Other concerns have to do with how assistance is transferred, and the possibility that food and other material goods or funds provided may actually benefit members of the country's elite residents or corrupt government officials rather than the intended beneficiaries (Alasah, 2009; Hicks, 2011).

Although NGOs and donor countries have taken steps to counter such issues, some of these concerns persist. At the beneficiary level, some international organizations have sought to ensure that community planning and implementation have decision-making mechanisms that include local residents (Kang, 2010). Offenheiser and Holcombe (2003) describe the human rights-oriented approach used by one of these organizations, Oxfam, as:

Assisting poor communities to overcome obstacles rather than about never-ending pursuit of grants for social goods. It assumes that people [living in poverty] have dignity, aspirations, and ambition and their initiative is being blocked and frustrated by persistent systemic challenges such as apartheid, biased lending policies, and nonfunctioning state service delivery systems. (p. 271)

Some international agencies focus primarily on economic development work. Such assistance includes environmental protection and types of assistance similar to that provided within the Western industrialized countries: human capital development (job training and education) as well as economic development and finance. Such assistance may also include the provision of technical assistance to upgrade agricultural practices or to improve infrastructure or making basic services (such as water filtration or clean energy) available in remote areas (Oladipo et al., 2007).

According to Healy and Thomas (2021), although some development agencies see their efforts as quite distinct from temporary provision of food and other direct services, the work of international aid organizations tends to fall on a continuum, with many agencies providing a mixture of programs and services in the regions in which they work that can include material assistance, efforts to engage residents in organizing and development activities, partnering with other agencies to improve service delivery, and policy advocacy. Methods used to facilitate international community development efforts that do not simply focus on direct relief resemble aspects of both classic community organizing and social capital approaches, including developing individual capacity, leadership skills, and civic engagement, and stimulating the development of citizens' organizations that can interact with and challenge government, at global, national, and local levels.

Strengthening Social Capital in Europe and the Developing World

Social capital development has been used extensively worldwide as a tool for economic and social development. Often, approaches to increasing social capital focus on strengthening bonding (i.e., within a group or community) and bridging (i.e., across groups or communities) capital in communities, or linking social capital by forming new associations and community groups that potentially will have the capacity to deliver social services or initiate new businesses and other economic endeavors (Kay, 2006; Lough et al., 2011). As with social capital approaches in the United States, this type of community development effort examines how interpersonal relationships and social networks can be used for economic survival and to improve individual well-being (Boateng, 2009; Oladipo et al., 2007). However, some researchers have noted that approaches designed to promote social capital formation differ by cultural context, gender identity, and geographic location (De Silva et al., 2005; Vaiou & Lykogianni, 2006).

The social capital approach has been used extensively for community development purposes in the European Union, Russia and other countries in the former Soviet bloc, and in the Global South. Social capital efforts within the European Union are oriented toward decreasing "social exclusion." Barata (2000) defines *social exclusion* as a "progressive process of marginalization leading to economic deprivation and various forms of cultural disadvantage" (p. 4). Individuals and groups can be excluded politically, economically, socially, and culturally; exclusion is associated with limited political power, lack of access to basic services, poverty, and poor health (Rispel et al., 2009). Social exclusion is related in part to social isolation and a lack of integration within economic systems; consequently, one of the strategies used to combat social exclusion involves increasing civic engagement and strengthening social networks using bonding and bridging social capital (Daly & Silver, 2008).

The European Union explicitly promotes social capital development as a mechanism that is intended to increase social cohesion and trust. Social capital programs focus on creating cooperative agreements among government agencies to deliver social welfare and employment services, fostering collaboration between governments and NGOs in policy development, increasing NGO capacity to participate in policy formulation and economic development, and promoting civic engagement.

Similar efforts to promote social capital formation have been undertaken in Russia and other former Soviet bloc nations. Prior to the 1980s, before the collapse of Soviet control, most social issues were addressed by communist-controlled central governments rather than through civic engagement (Despotovic et al., 2007). Efforts initiated in the 1990s to increase social capital were intended to increase local self-help and development efforts (Babajaian, 2008). Projects operating from the "bottom-up" were also designed to stimulate community participation, social integration, experiences of empowerment, and collective action.

In some of the impoverished communities in these counties, social capital approaches to community development are intended to increase economic activity and well-being. In addition, the absence of nonprofit organizations in these nations has been viewed as an impediment to the development of an alternative to government delivery of services, or the establishment of a tradition of civic engagement (Despotovic et al., 2007; Ersing et al., 2007; Keough & Samuels, 2004). Consequently, community development efforts have focused on the provision of assistance to set up nonprofit organizations, develop organization and service delivery capacity, and stimulate the growth of civic participation and volunteerism.

In the Global South, much of the theoretical and community development work on social capital has been funded through the World Bank (Woolcock, 1998). Such efforts primarily focus on economic development. Social capital and civic engagement approaches are also used extensively as a response to displacement, economic deprivation, and psychological distress due to armed conflicts; these types of interventions are also used to develop solidarity and end divisiveness among members of different ethnic groups; to increase community capacity to develop potable water and other infrastructure projects; and to help residents obtain jobs, start new businesses, and accumulate land, money, and other assets (Alasah, 2009; Asian NGO Coalition for Agrarian Reform and Rural Development, n.d.; De La Puente, 2011; Oladipo et al., 2007). For example, Frederico and colleagues (2007) describe a project funded by an NGO in the Philippines to assist survivors of an armed conflict. Displaced by warfare, residents were allowed to return to their homes, but had lost housing, employment, farms, sanitation, and education. A social capital-related development project was initiated to assist community members living in refugee camps. In order to build community solidarity and trust, community information centers were established as meeting spaces, training was provided to community members for providing psychological treatment to others for trauma, money was distributed to residents to start cooperative business enterprises, and community leaders were trained to facilitate peace-building and reconciliation efforts to bring people together who had been on different sides of the conflict.

Small-Scale Economic Development: Microcredit Programs, Cooperatives, and Social Enterprise Efforts

Many social capital and economic development projects conducted by the Global South or emerging democracies focus on small-scale financing projects designed to foster individual businesses, social enterprise efforts, and worker cooperatives. Schreiner and Woller (2003) define *microcredit* or *microenterprise* programs as "tiny businesses, most have one employee the owner. Microenterprise development programs make loans and/or give classes to people [living in poverty] to help them start or strengthen their businesses" (p. 1567). The prototype microcredit loan program was developed by and implemented by the Grameen Bank. These loans initially were intended primarily to assist women, both individuals and small groups, in Bangladesh to develop craft, agricultural, and service-related businesses, offering these new business owners the opportunity to improve their economic status, provide adequate food and clothing for their children, and obtain a degree of financial independence from their husbands (Midgley, 2005; Young Larance, 2008). Recipients are required to repay the loans and also receive technical assistance. These programs are also intended to reduce women's isolation in patriarchal societies, providing them the opportunity to network with other women, and identify other resources that they can use to develop their businesses. The Grameen Bank and similar microcredit programs have been implemented worldwide and are among the economic development projects supported by the World Bank and available to both women and men for small-business development.

Microcredit programs have been critiqued on a number of levels. For example, Midgley (2005) argues that such efforts, used in isolation from other strategies, are not effective in reducing poverty. In addition, microcredit and other financial and human capital development approaches may very well put more money in the hands of women, but without changes in a wife's status in her household, these funds may simply be transferred to her husband and out of her control, or may increase the likelihood that a woman will experience domestic violence (Pardasani, 2005).

Another approach used for strengthening bonding and bridging social capital, making economic improvements and financing the growth of a social service sector involves the development of a "social economy" or networks of NGOs that produce goods and services (Quarter et al., 2001). These organizations are referred to as *social enterprises* and are intended to be primarily self-financing. However, they differ from other nonprofit organizations or businesses in that although they are oriented toward making money, all funds benefit the individuals or the community served in a manner that enhances the public good (Kay, 2006). These organizations can be initiated or encouraged by governments or international aid organizations, or developed through the initiative of community residents seeking to improve their communities. Most social enterprises function as cooperatives in which all members have equal status and can participate in organizational decision-making. For example, Ersing and colleagues (2007) describe a social enterprise in Romania, the Pentru Voi Bakery, which was established by local parents to provide employment opportunities for young adults with intellectual disabilities. Financing for the bakery was obtained through selling products, assistance from the city in which it is located, and international aid organizations.

Another strategy for promoting business formation has been the development of worker cooperatives to support craft work, agricultural endeavors, the fishing industry, or small-scale use of natural resources such as forests (Starr & Adams, 2003). Some of these projects may simply be intended to help people make a living; others also incorporate principles related to sustainability, emphasizing locally grown and environmentally friendly practices. In some cases, international linkages are established to market products internationally in order to expand local economies. These projects differ from microcredit programs in that they are collectively owned and operated by participants, often with specific governance structure and well-defined roles for members (Asian NGO Coalition for Agrarian Reform and Rural Development, n.d.). Although many of these efforts are initiated by local residents, international development organizations may provide technical assistance and start-up capital, or facilitate international marketing campaigns (Debbink & Ornelas, 1997).

SOCIAL ACTION AND TRANSFORMATIVE ORGANIZING: THE ANTIGLOBALIZATION AND ENVIRONMENTAL MOVEMENTS AND THE STRUGGLE FOR DEMOCRACY AND HUMAN RIGHTS IN THE DEVELOPING WORLD

In addition to community development and social planning, regardless of country, community work almost always includes some type of social action organizing to achieve social justice and obtain human rights for people who are minoritized or marginalized politically, economically, socially, and culturally. Sometimes this organizing takes place on a global basis as people identify common struggles, often those that have their origins in the process of globalization. In many cases, social workers and organizers are involved in assisting local groups to improve their standard of living by contesting the institutional practices that oppress them (Andharia, 2007). Organizing work also takes place in the context of regional and national struggles for political and economic rights and democracy.

The Antiglobalization and Environmental Justice Movements

Globalization has also increased the prevalence and size of social action organizing efforts. Efforts to consolidate power in the hands of international corporations and transnational organizations that regulate economies have engendered protests and civil resistance by international coalitions and social movements. According to Ayers (2004), the coming together of numerous organizations to oppose government policies and economic practices associated with the process of globalization has resulted in a large increase in policy advocacy by nongovernment organizations, unions, and other nonprofit or nongovernment organizations. These international coalitions are made possible by the use of the internet and other technology for communication, information provision, and recruitment purposes.

According to Routledge (2003), these broad-based coalitions create many challenges for member organizations, including the lack of actual face-to-face communication among activists, language barriers, and the fact that Western activists are more likely than their counterparts in the developing world to have the resources to travel to protests, meetings, and conferences or engage in international exchanges with other groups. These barriers also make it less likely that the organizations involved in antiglobalization work can agree on joint activities or tactics. Consequently, often decision-making processes in these international advocacy networks are characterized by a lack of trust and cultural class, gender identity, and other issues related to personal and collective identity (Conway, 2007). One of the primary tactical differences among participants in the antiglobalization movement has to do with the use of civil disobedience and tactics such as vandalism and direct confrontation that are often used by members of anarchist groups. This is in contrast to the nonviolent actions of other protestors (Laffey & Weldes, 2010). Although the various protests and street violence have brought attention to the movement (e.g., the Battle for Seattle at the WTO summit in Seattle in 1999), they have also contributed to police surveillance and suppression of participants (Ayers, 2004; Conway, 2003; DeFilippis, 2001).

Antiglobalization protests often take place in conjunction with international conferences facilitated by transnational organizations designed to advance consensus about economic policies, development aid, the use of natural resources, and the environment. In addition to WTO, IMF, and the World Bank, these organizations include the G-8 Industrial Nations, the Organization for Economic and Cooperative Development (OECD), and regional trade organizations in the Global South (Prigoff, 2000). One particular target for these protests at international summits is multinational corporations with a worldwide presence, such as Starbucks, Kentucky Fried Chicken, and Nike, which in addition to symbolizing corporate control are also viewed as interfering with traditional business and cultural practices in some countries (Laffey & Weldes, 2010; Rajgopal, 2002).

Linked to the antiglobalization movement are local and global environmental movements designed to preserve resident control of natural resources and prevent pollution, oil spills, and other threats to the health and well-being of local residents. Often, residents taking part in protests or civil disobedience against government or corporate entities are collaborating with global advocacy organizations to fight government or corporate practices and policies that harm the environment and limit their ability to earn income from agriculture, fishing, or other activities that are dependent upon access and control of natural resources (Ayers, 2004; Bakker, 2007; Reed, 2002). Examples of these types of protest activities include efforts to preserve the rainforests in the Amazon jungle in South America and efforts by Indian activists to prevent the flooding of agricultural areas by hydroelectric dam projects designed to promote energy creation and work to oppose corporate efforts to replace traditional farming methods with genetically modified seeds (Rajgopal, 2002; Starr & Adams, 2003). Often this work is described in conjunction with international efforts to promote sustainable development and protect environmental resources for future generations. One area of concern involves the right to water. Water supplies have been increasingly brought under the control of corporate owners and rather than being readily accessible or purchased through public agencies, residents may be charged high fees for its use, creating economic hardship and displacement of families and small farms (Bakker, 2007; Russell, 2010).

In addition to street protests directed against transnational organizations that engage in economic regulation and corporate control and efforts to stop the privatization or misuse of natural resources, some members of the antiglobalization, environmental protection, or sustainability movements have employed consensus and collaboration tactics to seek better strategies for using the world's resources. This "alter-globalization" movement has focused on setting up decision-making structures, most often referred to as *forums* as a means of countering the WTO and other trade organizations that are viewed as promoting harmful policies (Bakker, 2007). The most visible citizens group is the World Social Forum (WSF). Founded in Brazil in 2001 and convening annually, the WSF provides an open space or common ground for social activists worldwide to come together in one place to address common problems associated with the process of globalization. Conway (2007) describes the organization as "a world-wide, movement-based, multiscale, and multi-sited cultural process . . . a space of spaces, a network of networks" (p. 51).

The WSF provides an opportunity to engage in democratic processes outside established practices in order to identify common values and social identifies and develop social movement strategies (Porta, 2005). Although organized through an international council, members do not engage in political advocacy nor does the organization seek to represent the viewpoints of participants. Policy proposals brought to the council are debated by members and decisions are made by consensus. In addition to the WSF, a number of regional forums have been initiated and numerous other organizations and decision-making structures have adopted similar approaches such as the World Water Forum and the World March of Women and representatives of many of these smaller gatherings participate in the WSF (Bakker, 2007; Conway, 2007; Porta, 2005).

Struggles for Democracy and Human Rights in the Developing World

DeFilippis (2001) argues that for the antiglobalization movement to be successful it must focus on how globalization affects people at the local level, and how local economies impact the international economy. This is particularly important in terms of organizing efforts in the Global South, particularly those that focus on improving the economic, political, and social status of under-resourced populations and communities in poverty. Some of this work is facilitated with funding and staff from international development organizations that work from the top-down in implementing U.N. standards, whereas local efforts are locally initiated from the "bottom-up" (Pardasani, 2005). According to Ife and Fiske (2006), this approach is preferable because "people are involved in constructing ideas of human rights for themselves and . . . human rights emerge from everyday lived experience" (p. 305). Consequently, such efforts are also culturally competent and move away from definitions that may be most relevant in a Western context.

Human rights struggles and organizing work often focus on changing traditional attitudes and power relationships. For example, many community-organizing efforts in the Global South focus on women's empowerment (Boateng, 2009; Hicks, 2011; Jonsson, 2010). Pardasani (2005) describes the efforts of women attending a literacy program to develop an antialcohol campaign in a small village in India that focused on the negative impact of drinking on families and in which participants initially put pressure on local shops that sold alcohol to close. The campaign was so successful that it was supported by the mayor and the state government and spread to other small communities. The success of the effort helped the participants obtain a grant from the state government to establish a cooperative credit union that provided funding to women for small business start-ups. De La Puente (2011), in describing efforts to encourage women's leadership in a refugee camp in Dafur, argues that it is essential that international development agencies challenge gender inequities that may not be solely based on cultural patterns, but are encouraged and enforced by relief organizations themselves. Instead, development efforts should provide opportunities for participation in planning as well as leadership roles for women.

In addition to local organizing projects that focus on changing power relationships, organizers and activists in the developing world often risk their physical safety and lives to challenge repressive regimes. In 2011, residents of a number of Middle Eastern countries fought for access to economic resources and democratic governments in countries such as Tunisia, Egypt, Syria, and Yemen. Press reports indicated that high rates of youth unemployment and disparities in wealth among members of different social classes were among the reasons that protests occurred; similar conditions are also prevalent in other countries in the Global South (Githongo, 2011).

Some of the positive aspects associated with globalization were viewed by the media as critical to the success of these movements, including increased access to information about other countries and how to engage in activism, the use the internet and social media for organizing purposes, and the ability to use cell phones and text messaging to communicate and coordinate protests (Moore, 2011). The internet was also credited for improving the dissemination of information about the protests to the rest of the world and making it possible for women, who are often isolated, but had access to computers, to plan and participate in the protests (Shalhoub-Kervorkian, 2011).

THE IMPLICATIONS OF A GLOBAL PERSPECTIVE FOR SOCIAL WORK AND COMMUNITY PRACTICE

As described in the previous section, much of the literature on international social work and approaches through which community organizers and practitioners should respond to globalization have examined the role of practitioners in international development organizations, social capital development, or economic development. However, there are a number of critiques of traditional international development and social work approaches to work in the Global South that have implications for community practice. For example,

Jonsson (2010) argues that, "if empowerment strategies seek to have an emancipatory effect on people who are marginalized and discriminated against, they must go beyond developmental goals, such as higher productivity, higher consumption and higher formal education" (p. 404). Guo and Tsui (2010) have called on social workers to extend their use of the strengths perspective to move beyond a focus on individual strengths, assets, resilience, and protective versus risk factors to one that recognizes that people are in poverty, socially minoritized, or politically marginalized due to social and political structures and their lack of access to political power. This framework suggests that strategies that involve individual or collective rebellion and resistance to oppressive policies or structures are also strengths that should be factored into social work assessments. For example, simple noncompliance with service requirements or agency policies could be viewed as strengths in some situations. However, rebellion and resistance can also be interpreted to include a full range of social action-related activities that include challenges to existing government structures as well as personal transformation and empowerment. Guo and Tsui suggest that the following questions be added to strength-based assessments for international social work and community development:

1. How does the behavior of social service users differ from the behavior of the dominant classes?
2. What is the relationship between the behavior or customs of social service users and their social positions? Do they have other options available to them?
3. What social capital resources do members of minoritized and marginalized groups have that will help them improve the quality of their lives?
4. What type of strategies do they typically use to improve their lives and counteract oppression?

Dominelli (2005) also argues that most classic community development models are paternalistic, conducted *on behalf of* people in poverty, or in a manner that exploits under-resourced or less developed communities or their limited resources. They advocate instead for a "holistic interactional approach" that builds on the transformative model of community organization, which emphasizes self-help and capacity building, but also mobilizes people to take action at all system levels and that incorporates values such as sustainability, interdependence, reciprocity, and mutuality and focuses on strengthening relationships and building solidarity. Consequently, in Dominelli's model, an assessment should include the following systems:

- individual, family, groups, organization, and community;
- the country or countries in which the individual, family, or group resides or has previously resided or in which the organization or community is located;
- the amount of power possessed by the individual, family, group, organization, or group and how they are affected by the power possessed by others;
- the actual physical resources possessed by the individual, family, group, organization, or community;
- the cultural, social, psychological, political, or spiritual/religious resources available to the individual, family, group, organization, or community;

- how the individual, family, group, organization, or the community are affected by social, psychological, political, or spiritual/religious forces operating nationally or transnationally; and
- the community's capacity to mobilize to take action to address issues that are negatively impacting its members.

This type of systems analysis can also lead to the identification of specific effects of globalization that have local implications in Western industrialized nations and suggest action strategies to address these issues. For example, there may be a link between family hardship and loss of income due to a local garment factory shutting down, government policies that make it economically more feasible for corporations to open plants oversees, and working conditions and wages in factories in Guatemala, operated by the same corporation (Lightman et al., 2005). In addition, social workers, including community organizers and practitioners, should possess knowledge about the impact of globalization on new immigrants, the reasons for their relocation, the impact of immigration policies on their entry into a new country, their status under the law and the benefits or sanctions that accrue from this classification, and the hardships and experiences they have before and after entry into the new country (Nawyn, 2010; Xu, 2007). A systems analysis also allows for an examination of how family systems operate within a global context in situations in which family members are located in two or more countries, the effects of relocation, and how they remain connected to loved ones across national boundaries (Healy & Thomas, 2021).

END-OF-CHAPTER RESOURCES

KEY TAKEAWAYS AND SUMMARY

The process of globalization affects almost every aspect of modern social life, including health and well-being, the ability to earn an adequate wage, transnational migration, poverty rates, the provision of social welfare services, houselessness, hunger, and maintaining a sustainable environment. As described in the IFSW statement of ethical principles, a response to these issues provides a variety of opportunities for social workers to work locally or across borders to address globalization problems. Traditional and innovative methods used by community practitioners and organizers can include aspects of social planning, community development, social action, and transformative approaches to developing human capacity and promoting human rights. However, a response to social exclusion requires not only advocacy and monitoring of social conditions; it also requires recognition of the inherent strength and dignity of all people and explicit efforts on the part of practitioners to partner with local groups and international coalitions in the struggle for social justice.

RESOURCES

- International Federation of Social Workers: https://www.ifsw.org
  Note: The IFSW website also has specific resources and information by region (IFSW Africa, IFSW Asia and Pacific, IFSW Europe, IFSW Latin America and Caribbean, IFSW North America). See https://ifsw.org/regions
- National Association of Social Workers Foundation: Resources for International Social Work: https://www.naswfoundation.org/Our-Work/International/International-Resources

ACTIVITIES

1. Identify a local issue or community problem linked to globalization. Describe the problem, assess the origins of the problem, and describe how the problem is affected by the process of globalization. Identify all the systems (family, community, economic, political, social, international) affected by the problem and in which changes can be made to alleviate the impact on the individual and family. You may use an eco-map, social network map, genogram, or another type of graphic to analyze and illustrate the issue.

2. Conduct an ethnographic interview with a recent immigrant. Focus on the respondent's immigration experiences, the reason for immigration, culture, positive aspects of the immigration process or the transition between different countries, hardships (if any) experienced in both countries, and the respondent's perceptions of how the two cultures differ in terms of available resources, government policies, and values. Prepare a 10-minute presentation for class. Focus on what you learned from the interview.

3. Using the following link (www.ifsw.org/social-work-action/world-social-work-day), read about the history of World Social Work Day. Conduct some research on the annual themes of World Social Work Day. How do these themes map onto the IFSW *Global Social Work Statement of Ethical Principles* described in the chapter? How has this day been celebrated across the world? What stands out to you? Discuss in small groups.

ASSIGNMENTS

1. Review at least one article about international social work or community-organizing practice. Possible sources for your article review include the following journals, which focus on international issues: *International Social Work,* the *Community Development Journal, Social Development Issues,* and *Urban Studies.* United States-oriented journals, such as the *Journal of Community Practice,* the *Social Service Review,* and the *Journal of Sociology and Social Welfare,* also publish articles about international issues. Write a three- to five-page paper that describes the topic of the article and the application of

the contents of the article to social work or organizing practice. Compare the article to a similar study or description of practice about social work in the United States or another country with which you are familiar. What aspects of practice seem to be similar in both countries? How do the practice methods described uphold the principles in the IFSW *Global Social Work Statement of Ethical Principles* or United Nations' *Universal Declaration of Human Rights*?

A robust set of instructor resources designed to supplement this text is located at http://connect.springerpub.com/content/book/978-0-8261-5835-2. Qualifying instructors may request access by emailing textbook@springerpub.com.

KEY REFERENCES

Only key references appear in the print edition. The full reference list appears in the digital product on Springer Publishing Connect: connect.springerpub.com/content/book/978-0-8261-5835-2/part/part04/chapter/ch14

Androff, D. (2011). The problem of international slavery: An international human rights challenge for social work. *International Social Work, 54*, 209–222. https://doi.org/10.1177/0020872810368395

Dominelli, L. (2005). Community development across borders: Avoiding dangerous practices in a globalizing world. *International Social Work, 48*, 702–713. https://doi.org/10.1177/0020872805056988

Edwards, B. (2011). Social work education and global issues: Implications for social work practice. *Education, 131*, 580–586.

Ife, J., & Fiske, L. (2006). Human rights and community work: Complementary theories and practices. *International Social Work, 49*, 297–308. https://doi.org/10.1177/0020872806063403

Midgley, J. (2007). Perspectives on globalization, social justice, and welfare. *Journal of Sociology and Social Welfare, 34*(2), 17–34.

Murdach, A. (2011). Is social work a human rights profession? *Social Work, 56*, 281–283. https://doi.org/10.1093/sw/56.3.281

Rankopo, M., & Osei-Hwedie, K. (2011). Globalization and culturally relevant social work: African perspectives on indigenization. *International Social Work, 54*, 137–147. https://doi.org/10.1177/0020872810372367

Segal, E., & Kilty, K. (2003). Political promises for welfare reform. *Journal of Poverty, 7*(1/2), 51–57. https://doi.org/10.1300/J134v07n01_04

Sen, A. (2004). Elements of a theory of human rights. *Philosophy & Public Affairs, 32*, 315–356. https://doi.org/10.4324/9781315251240-6

INDEX

AASWSW. *See* American Academy of Social Work and Social Welfare
ACLU. *See* American Civil Liberties Union
ACORN. *See* Association for Community Organizations for Reform Now
ACOSA. *See* Association for Community Organization and Social Action
action campaign
    bargaining and negotiation, 197–198
    barriers for action, 182–183
    change management, 173–176
    closing, 199
    field notes, keeping, 196–197
    formal meeting, 192–193
    funding and resources, 179–181
    group work, 188–189
    interpersonal skills, 190
    local media, 193–194
    logic models, 174, 177–178
    logistics, 190–191
    public speaking, 195–196
    risk assessment, 186–188
    situational and contextual demands, 183–184
    SMART objectives, 179
    social media, use in, 189–190
    success tips, 181–182
    tactical considerations, 185–186
    theories, 174
    values into action, 199–202
active listening, 39
American Academy of Social Work and Social Welfare (AASWSW), 13
American Civil Liberties Union (ACLU), 66
antiglobalization, 347, 361–363
anti-racism, 10–11
Association for Community Organization and Social Action (ACOSA), 153
Association for Community Organizations for Reform Now (ACORN), 78

background research, 267, 270, 276, 283
bargaining and negotiation
    action campaign, 197–198
    organizational partnerships, 83–84
barriers
    for action, 182–183
    institutional, 308
    language, 362
BIPOC. *See* Black, Indigenous, people of color
Black, Indigenous, people of color (BIPOC), 7
bonding social capital, 290, 300, 358–359, 361
bonds, 291, 310
bridging social capital, 290, 300, 358–359, 361

case vignettes
    collaborative responsibility, 81
    digital communication in community engagement, 43–44
    Helping Hands, care bags, 195
    interview style survey, example, 33
    leadership development, 153
    Photovoice, 127
    public testimony, 276–277
    storytelling, 99
    Thrive in the 05 community-based initiative, 231
    volunteer recruitment, 63
CBPR. *See* community-based participatory research
CHWs. *See* community health workers
CIT. *See* critical incident technique
CMSM. *See* Community Mobilization through Social Media
community
    definition, 29–30
    gaining entry, 31–33
    interview style survey, example, 33
community assessment
    asset mapping, 124–125

community assessment (*continued*)
   assets and capital identification, 115–118, 125–127
   change initiatives, 137–138
   community-based participatory research (CBPR), 119–120
   engagement phase, 113–114
   group methods, 121–122
   participatory action research, 118–124
   power analysis, 131–137
   purpose, 114–115
   social indicators, 129–131
   traditional methods, 128–129
   values into action, 138–141
   youth-led participatory action research, 120–121
community-based participatory research (CBPR), 119, 146, 245
community development, 2
community groups
   application of principles, 209–210
   praxis process, 210–211
   problem-solving approaches, 209
community health workers (CHWs), 47
community members
   cross-cultural organizing, 48–49
   mutual learning and partnership, 9–10
   need for social change, 30–31
   one-on-one key informant interviews, 34–37
   volunteer leaders, 47
Community Mobilization through Social Media (CMSM), 42–43, 190
community organizers, 29–31, 33, 37, 40–42, 45, 47–48
   participant recruitment, 53
   volunteer recruitment, 53–54
community-organizing models
   diverse contexts, 1–2
   practice areas, 1–2
   primary method, 2–6
   process and task-related skills, 2–4
community planning
   action plans, 156–160
   advocacy organizations, 148
   agreement or consensus, 164–167
   citizen participation, 149–150
   civic engagement, 148–149
   decision-making and leadership, 146–147
   government-mandated citizen involvement, 154–155
   group methods, 161–164
   informing and consultation, 146
   institutional structures, 147–148
   interpersonal skills, 156
   leadership training, 149–153
   manipulation and therapy, 146
   member engagement, 156
   organizational structures, 154–155
   participation on boards, 154
   peer and professional networks, 153
   values into action, 167–169
community practice
   participant's role, 215–216
   self-reflection, 213–215
constructivist evaluation. *See* emergent or constructivist evaluation
Council on Social Work Education (CSWE), 323
critical incident technique (CIT), 242
critical race theory (CRT), 211
CRT. *See* critical race theory
CSWE. *See* Council on Social Work Education
cultural competency
   ethnographic interviews, 45–46
   self-awareness, 45
   social workers, 10–11, 16
   transparency, partnership, and inclusion, 49–50
   values into action, 44, 49
cultural humility
   social workers, 1, 10, 16
   values into action, 44

decision makers, 270–271
decision-making process, 269, 276
   and leadership, 146–147
   power analysis, 270–271
DMI. *See* Drug Market Intervention
Dream Act campaign of 2010, 283
Drug Market Intervention (DMI), 231

EBP. *See* evidence-based practice
emergent or constructivist evaluation, 243
environmental justice movements, 362–363
Environmental Protection Agency (EPA), 273, 283
EPA. *See* Environmental Protection Agency
Europe, social capital approach, 358–359
evidence-based practice (EBP), 230–231

Faith in Action network, 73, 76, 77, 80. *See also* Pacific Institute for Community Organizing (PICO)
feminist organizing approaches, 4–5

geographic information systems (GIS), 124
GIS. *See* geographic information system
globalization, 347, 349–350, 352, 361–364
Global South
    economic improvement programs, 361
    microcredit programs, 360–361
    small-scale economic development, 360
    social capital, 360
    social planning in, 355–356
GNI. *See* gross national income
gross national income (GNI), 357
group dialogue
    authority legitimization, 216–217
    capacity building, 216
    collaboration, 217
    community conversations, 99–101
    focus groups interviews, 103–105
    intergroup dialogue, 107–108
    nominal technique, 102–103
    outcomes, 107–108
    ownership, 217
    planning, 95, 100–102
    priorities, 101–103
    problem-solving model, 94–96
    purpose, 93–94
    storytelling, 97–99
    study circles, 106–107
    values into action, 108–109
    volunteers, 97, 99, 102

human rights perspective
    in developing world, 361, 363–364
    first-generation rights, 353
    globalization effects, 347
    group well-being, 349–350
    neoliberal policies, 350–352
    second-generation rights, 354
    third-generation rights, 354
    Universal Declaration of Human Rights, 354
    values into action, 347–349

IAF. *See* Industrial Areas Foundation
IFSW. *See* International Federation of Social Workers
IMF. *See* International Monetary Fund
Industrial Areas Foundation (IAF), 76
International Federation of Social Workers (IFSW), 11–12
    IFSW *Code of Ethics,* 11–12
    IFSW *Global Social Work Statement of Ethical Principles,* 347, 352–353
International Monetary Fund (IMF), 350–351, 355, 362
interpersonal skills
    action campaign, 190
    community planning, 156
    core competencies, 17–20
    legislative campaigns, 271
    organizational partnerships, 80
    participatory evaluation, 249–251
    praxis, 217–218
    social work, 14–17
interviews
    community assessment, 33
    micro practice skills, 37–40
    one-on-one key informant, 34–37
    preengagement process, 39–40
    types of probes, 39

jobs, 349, 351–352, 354–356, 360

key decision makers, 269
knowledge, 366

leadership
    control, of group process, 319
    powerful communication, 318–319
    primary priorities, 324
    resiliency, 318–319
    three characteristics, 318
legislative campaigns
    background research, 267
    components, 265–267
        meat-rendering plant, example, 283
    content, 267–269
    goals, 265
    interpersonal skills, 271
    letter, example, 272–273
    lobbying tips, 274–275
    political involvement, 278–281
    processes, 269–270
    public testimony, 275–278

legislative campaigns (*continued*)
   relationship with public officials, 273–274
   tips for voting, 278
   values into action, 281–282
   written and electronic communications, 271–272
LGBTQIA+ groups, 7
linking social capital, 290, 300, 301, 359
lobbying team, 266–267, 274–276, 278, 282

macro social work practice, 1–2
   Grand Challenges, 13–14
   leadership, 317–319
   organizational culture, 319–320
   roles and team processes, 320–321
   self-care, social work practitioners, 22
   supervision, 320–321, 322, 323–325, 327–330
      parallel processes, 340–342
      skills, 331–339
   technology, 42
      for team planning and processes, 339–340
mezzo social work practice, 1–2
micro social work practice, 1–2
   interview skills, 37–40, 40–41
   technology, 42
minoritization, 7
minority communities
   discrimination, 2, 7–8, 10–12
   promoting empowerment, 48
multicultural approaches, 4–5

NAFTA. *See* North American Free Trade Agreement
NASW. *See* National Association of Social Workers
National Association of Social Workers (NASW)
   on action plans, 153, 187
   Code of Ethics, 6–8, 10–12
   on community practice, 279, 281, 289
   on macro social work, 1, 6–8, 10–11, 332, 337, 350–351
National Neighborhood Indicators Partnership (NNIP), 130–131
neoliberal policies, 350–352
Network for Social Work Management (NSWM), 153
NGT. *See* nominal group technique
NNIP. *See* National Neighborhood Indicators Partnership

nominal group technique (NGT), 93, 96, 102–103, 109
North American Free Trade Agreement (NAFTA), 351
NSWM. *See* Network for Social Work Management

OECD. *See* Organization for Economic and Cooperative Development
organizational culture
   eight domains, 320
   employer expectations, 325–326
   strategic plans and chart, 326–327
organizational partnerships
   bargaining and negotiation, 83–84
   building alliances, 71
   coalition, 75–76
   collaborative, 74–75
   community practice, 72
   consensus development, 84
   interfaith alliances, 76–77
   interpersonal skills, 80
   mutual learning, 85–86
   national organizations' role, 77–79
   power and resource sharing, 82–83
   relationship building, 80
   social movements, 79
   task forces, 73–74
   theories and perspectives, 73
   trust building, 81–82
   use of technology, 85
   values into action, 86–87
Organization for Economic and Cooperative Development (OECD), 362

PACE. *See* Political Action for Candidate Election
Pacific Institute for Community Organizing (PICO), 238. *See also* Faith in Action network
PAR. *See* participatory action research
Parent Leadership Project (PLP), 169
participant recruitment
   collective identity development, 66
   community organizer's role, 53
   flyers and tabling, 57–58
   framing, 64–66
   group and network membership, 66–67
   house meetings and living-room conversations, 59–60

media coverage, 61–62
motivation and engagement, 54–57
phone calls and texting, 58–59
street outreach methods, 60–61
success perceptions, 68
techniques and technologies, 57
values into action, 64
webpages, use in, 62–63
word of mouth, 62
participatory action research (PAR), 245–246
  advantages and limitations, 122–124
  community assessment, 118–124
  data collection methods, 124–125
  documentation, 129–131
  group methods, 121–122
  Photovoice, use in, 125–127
  practice activities, 140–141
  research instruments, 128–129
  strategic compatibility, 137–140
  strengths perspectives, 138–141
participatory evaluation
  case studies, 241–242
  challenges, 230
  community practice methods, 236
  critical incident analysis, 241–242
  empowerment, 246–248
  evidence-based practice, 230–231
  goal attainment, 236–237
  interpersonal skills, 249–251
  logic models, 232–234
  methods, 243–245
  participatory action research, 245–246
  process and implementation analysis, 240–241
  qualitative approaches, 242–243
  quantitative research, 238–240
  self-assessments, 248–249
  social indicator analysis, 237–238
  survey data, 237–238
  types, 235–236
  values into action, 251–255
Participatory Geographical Information Systems (PGIS), 124
People for the Ethical Treatment of Animals (PETA), 65
PETA. *See* People for the Ethical Treatment of Animals
PGIS. *See* Participatory Geographical Information Systems
Photovoice, 125, 126
  case vignette, 127

documenting community assessment, 125–127
limitations, 127
PICO. *See* Pacific Institute for Community Organizing
PLP. *See* Parent Leadership Project
Political Action for Candidate Election (PACE), 281
power analysis
  campaign donations, 133
  decision makers, 270–271
  force field and SWOT, 132–133
  group methods, 134–137
  interest groups, 133, 270–271
  mapping, 135–137
  newspaper and media, 134
  personal knowledge about members, 134
  social network, 131–133
  sources of power, 131–132
  website posting, 134
praxis, 209–210
  group dialogue, 216
  interpersonal skills, 217–218
  knowledge production, 212–213
  organizing process, 218–219
  theoretical framework, 210–212
problem-solving model, 16, 94–96

racism, 289, 293
rallies, 283
reflective empathy, 39
reflective responding, 39
reflexivity, 331–332
relationships, 290, 297, 301–303, 306, 308–310
resilience, 294
retrospective case studies, 242

SCRA. *See* Society for Community Research and Action
self-reflection, community practice, 213–215
social action, 2–3
social justice, 3, 7
  values into action, 64–65
social media
  action campaigns, 189–190
  use in community engagement, 42–43
  volunteer recruitment, 63
social planning, 2–4, 6
  citizen involvement, 356

social planning (*continued*)
  in Global South, 355–356
  in industrialized nations, 357–358
  international agencies' role, 358
  nongovernment organizations and donor countries, 357
  role of transnational organizations, 356–357
social problems, 93–94, 96–97
social work
  development approaches, 2–3
  global perspectives, 364–366
  international policies, 352–353
  interpersonal skills, 14–17
  macro social work practice, 2, 6–14, 21
  mezzo social work practice, 1–2
  micro social work practice, 1–2
social workers
  critical consciousness development, 9
  cultural competency, 10–11, 16
  cultural humility, 1, 10, 16
  empowerment, 5, 7–8, 10, 12, 17–18
  ethics, 6–8, 10–12, 14, 16
  gaining trust and conveying respect, 46–47
  Grand Challenges, 13–14, 21
  interviewing techniques, 39
  leadership positions, 21–23
  self-determination and empowerment, 8
  strengths perspective, 9
Society for Community Research and Action (SCRA), 153
storytelling, 97–99
structured group-work, 95–105
study circles, 106–107
supervision
  advanced training, 322
  challenges, 329–330
  Council on Social Work Education on, 323
  cultural competence and humility, 331–332
  curriculum and training manuals (Midwest Academy), 324
  definition, 320–321
  effective communication, 332–334
  engagement and facilitation, 334
  ethical implications, 336–337
  identification and problem-solving issues, 335–336
  meaningful inclusion, 335
  models, 322–323
  participatory evaluation, 338–339
  peers and colleagues support, 322
  planning action campaigns, 338
  as praxis, 327–328
  primary priorities, 324
  professional development and training, 323–324
  reflexivity, 331–332
  responsibility, 325
  self-assessment on performance, 328–329
  self-awareness, 331–332
  specific skills, 331
  structured learning experiences, 323
  task accomplishment, 327
  traditional roles, 321
  values into action, 339–342

task accomplishment, 327
teamwork
  in social work, 317–318, 319
  technology, use in, 339–340
technology, 57, 85, 339–340
third-generation rights, 354
T-PE. *See* transformative participatory evaluation
transformative model, 4
transformative participatory evaluation (T-PE), 245–246
transnational organizations, 356–357
transparency, 49–50
trust building, 81–82

UFW. *See* United Farm Workers
United Farm Workers (UFW), 217
United Nations
  human rights framework, 12–13
  on standard of living, 356–357
Universal Declaration of Human Rights, 12, 356–357
  human rights perspective, 354
  on social planning practice, 354

value assumptions
  creation of equal partnerships, 9–10
  macro social work skills, 6–7
value assumptions, 6–7
values into action
  action campaign, 199–202
  community assessment, 138–141
  community planning, 167–169
  cultural competence, 44, 49
  cultural humility, 44
  group dialogue, 108–109
  human rights perspective, 347–349

legislative campaigns, 281–282
macro social work, 6–7
organizational partnerships, 86–87
participant recruitment, 64
staff supervision, 339–342

World Social Forum (WSF), 363
World Trade Organization (WTO), 350, 362–363
WSF. *See* World Social Forum
WTO. *See* World Trade Organization

www.ingramcontent.com/pod-product-compliance
Lightning Source LLC
Chambersburg PA
CBHW081502050825
30652CB00026B/554